Critical Issues in Peace and Conflict Studies

Critical Issues in Peace and Conflict Studies

Theory, Practice, and Pedagogy

Edited by
Thomas Matyók
Jessica Senehi
Sean Byrne

LEXINGTON BOOKS

A division of

ROWMAN & LITTLEFIELD PUBLISHERS, INC.
Lanham • Boulder • New York • Toronto • Plymouth, UK

Published by Lexington Books
A wholly owned subsidiary of The Rowman & Littlefield Publishing Group, Inc.
4501 Forbes Boulevard, Suite 200, Lanham, Maryland 20706
www.rowman.com

Estover Road, Plymouth PL6 7PY, United Kingdom

Copyright © 2011 by Lexington Books
First paperback edition 2012

All rights reserved. No part of this book may be reproduced in any form or by any electronic or mechanical means, including information storage and retrieval systems, without written permission from the publisher, except by a reviewer who may quote passages in a review.

British Library Cataloguing in Publication Information Available

Library of Congress Cataloging-in-Publication Data

The hardback edition of this book was previously cataloged by the Library of Congress as follows:

Critical issues in peace and conflict studies : theory, practice, and pedagogy / edited by Thomas Matyók, Jessica Senehi, and Sean Byrne.
p. cm.
Includes index.
1. Peace—Research. 2. War—Research. 3. Peace. 4. Peace-building. 5. Peace—Study and teaching. 6. Peace-building—Study and teaching. I. Matyók, Thomas, 1953– II. Senehi, Jessica, 1959– III. Byrne, Sean, 1962–
JZ5534.C745 2011
303.6'6—dc22 2011008115

ISBN: 978-0-7391-4960-7 (cloth : alk. paper)
ISBN: 978-0-7391-7714-3 (pbk. : alk. paper)
ISBN: 978-0-7391-4962-1 (electronic)

™ The paper used in this publication meets the minimum requirements of American National Standard for Information Sciences—Permanence of Paper for Printed Library Materials, ANSI/NISO Z39.48-1992.

Printed in the United States of America

We dedicate this book to our friend and colleague, Dr. Karen Jenkins. Karen was a professor of conflict analysis and resolution at Metro Community College in South Omaha, Nebraska. On October 17, 2010, Dr. Jenkins was abducted and brutally murdered. We remember Karen as a loving, bright and caring person whose smile would always light up a room. We miss you.

Acknowledgments

We would like to thank Lenore Lautigar and Lexington Books for their confidence and willingness to put this work forward. Their ongoing support of this project ensures that voices not always connected with the field of peace and conflict studies are heard and advanced. Thanks are extended to Abigail Byle for her editing work and constructive comments. Cathryne Schmitz was instrumental in getting this book to press through her constant support.

Tom Matyók, Jessica Senehi, and Sean Byrne gratefully acknowledge the contributors to this volume for their support and willingness to engage in extending the academic horizon of the peace and conflict studies field. We also recognize the Arthur V. Mauro Centre for Peace and Justice, St. Paul's College, University of Manitoba, home to the PhD and joint MA program in peace and conflict studies, and the Program in Conflict and Peace Studies at the University of North Carolina at Greensboro. Special thanks also go to Renee Matyók for her belief in the significance of this project.

Contents

Biographies of Contributors

Ousmane Bakary Bâ is assistant professor in the School of Social Work at Université de Moncton. In addition, he is an affiliated professor at the Mauro Centre for Peace and Social Justice, University of Manitoba. He has conducted ethnographic research in diverse areas. He is the author of two books: *Exil et culture: Génocide ethnique, fractures, deuil et reconstructions identitaire* and *La créolisation dans les contexts coloniaux*. He is originally from Senegal.

Thomas E. Boudreau graduated with his PhD in social science from the Maxwell School at Syracuse University in 1985. He is the author of two books, *Sheathing the Sword* (1991) and *Universitas* (1998), over a dozen articles, and is currently working on a third book, *The Law of Nations: A Pluralistic Legal Order in a Violent World*. He has taught peace studies, international relations, and conflict analysis at Syracuse and American Universities, as well as the University of Pennsylvania. Currently, he is professor and chair of conflict analysis and dispute resolution at Salisbury University in Salisbury, Maryland.

Sean Byrne is professor of peace and conflict studies, and head of the PhD and joint MA programs in peace and conflict studies at the University of Manitoba, and director of the Arthur V. Mauro Centre for Peace and Justice at St. Paul's College at the University of Manitoba. He is author of *Economic Assistance and the Northern Ireland Conflict: Building the Peace Dividend* (2009) and *Growing Up in a Divided Society: The Influence of Conflict on Belfast Schoolchildren* (1997). He is a co-editor of *Reconciliable Differences: Turning Points in Ethnopolitical Conflicts* (2000) and the *Handbook* *of Conflict Analysis and Resolution* (2009). His research has been supported by the Social Sciences and Humanities Research Council Canada. He is a native of Ireland.

Jason J. Campbell is assistant professor of conflict resolution and philosophy at Nova Southeastern University's Graduate School of Humanities and Social Science. Dr. Campbell is the founder and executive director for the Institute for Genocide Awareness and Applied Research (IGAAR). His research interests focus on international conflict resolution and genocide prevention.

Paul Cormier is a member of Lake Helen First Nations Red Rock Indian Band in Northern Ontario, Canada. He is a member of the Wolf Clan and his traditional spirit name is Ma'iingan, or "Wolf" in Ojibway. He has a master's degree in conflict analysis and management. Currently, he is a doctoral student in peace and conflict studies at the University of Manitoba. His research interests are in traditional indigenous peacebuilding, land disputes relating to indigenous peoples and identity-based conflicts, and indigenous land rights, with the long-term objective of bringing peace to the indigenous peoples of the world by a reconnection to traditional lands.

Nathan C. Funk is associate professor of peace and conflict studies at the University of Waterloo's Conrad Grebel University College, with previous appointments at American University and George Washington University. He obtained a doctorate in international relations from American University in 2000. His writings on international affairs, the Middle East, track-two diplomacy, and the cultural as well as religious dimensions of peacebuilding include *Ameen Rihani: Bridging East and West* (2004) and *Islam and Peacemaking in the Middle East* (2009).

Johan Galtung, professor of peace studies and founder of TRANSCEND international, a peace development environment network, was born 1930 in Oslo, is the author of 151 books, and has been a mediator in well over one hundred conflicts (see www.transcend.org). One of his most recent books is *The Fall of the US Empire—And Then What?* (see www.transcend.org/tup).

Nancy Hansen, associate professor, is director of the Interdisciplinary Master's Program in Disability Studies at the University of Manitoba. She is researching in the areas of literacy, culture history, health care, ethics, and human geography as they relate to disability issues in daily life.

Sherrill Hayes is assistant professor of conflict studies and dispute resolution at the University of North Carolina at Greensboro (UNCG). He holds a PhD in social policy from the University of Newcastle upon Tyne and both a BS and MS from UNCG in human development and family studies. He has worked as a child custody and family mediator in both court and non-profit settings in the U.S. and the UK and continues to practice different forms of family dispute resolution, including mediation, education, and parenting coordination.

Myrtle Hill is senior lecturer in the School of Sociology, Social Policy and Social Work at Queen's University Belfast, where she teaches on disability studies and on the Northern Ireland conflict. She has published widely on Irish religions and women's and social history, and, in addition to ongoing disability research, is currently leading a research project on widening participation in higher education in Northern Ireland.

Peter Karari is a doctoral student in peace and conflict studies at the Mauro Centre, University of Manitoba. His doctorate research focuses on ethno-political violence and peacebuilding in Kenya. He has worked as a programme coordinator with Compassion International–Kenya and as the chief executive officer with Oxfam GB–Kenya. He holds a BA in social work from the University of Nairobi in Kenya and an MA in peace and conflict research from Otto von Guericke University in Germany.

Neil Katz has been professor and director or co-director of five conflict resolution programs in the Maxwell School of Syracuse University. Neil is currently the chair of the Department of Conflict Analysis and Resolution at Nova Southeastern University. Along with his emeriti faculty status, Neil continues to teach conflict resolution, negotiation, mediation, and leadership classes at Syracuse University as an adjunct faculty member of the Maxwell School's renowned Public Administration Program, and as a teaching associate with the Program on the Analysis and Resolution of Conflicts (PARC).

Peter Kellett is associate professor and head of communication studies at the University of North Carolina at Greensboro. His teaching and research focus on the use of narrative methodology and dialogue theory and practice in the analysis and transformation of conflict. His most recent publications include, with Peter Kellett, Thomas Matyók, Sarah Blizzard, Cherie Avent, and Elizabeth Jeter, "Interracial Conflict and Campus Hate Speech: The Case for Dialogic Engagement in College Settings," in Deborah Brunson, Linda Lampl, and Felicia Jordan-Jackson, *Interracial Communication: Contexts, Communities, and Choices*.

Alka Kumar is associate professor of English at the University of Delhi, India. She now lives in Winnipeg and is currently a doctoral student in peace and conflict studies at the University of Manitoba. Her interests lie in the fields of development, religious conflict, and human rights.

Brenda A. LeFrançois is associate professor in the School of Social Work at Memorial University. Broadly her research interests include ethnographic and participatory research within the field of mental health. She has published several journal articles on the topic of mental health in relation to children's rights, parent/child relationships, power relations, and resistance to psychiatric oppression.

Andrea Levy has a PhD in history from Concordia University and completed post-doctoral studies in sociology at the Université de Montréal. She currently works as an independent scholar, editor, and journalist. Her research areas include the intellectual history of the New Left, peace and ecology as social movements, the nature of work and precarious labor, and municipal politics; among other interests she has contributed to various scholarly journals and written chapters for a number of edited volumes. She is also a regular contributor to and longstanding member of the editorial committee of *Canadian Dimension* magazine.

Marie Olson Lounsbery is assistant professor of political science at East Carolina University. Her current research interests include the causes, processes and resolution of intrastate conflict, particularly intrastate rivalry. Her most recent book is *Civil Wars: Internal Struggles, Global Consequences* (2009) with Frederic Pearson.

Thomas Matyók is assistant professor in the Program in Conflict and Peace Studies at the University of North Carolina at Greensboro. His research interests include the education and training of conflict workers, the changing nature of war, violence, and institutions of peace. Currently, Tom is a research scholar at the Center for New North Carolinians investigating the impact of violence on refugees and immigrants. He is the convener of TRANSCEND-USA, a global peace and development network. Tom possesses substantial knowledge of international, organizational, and cross-cultural conflict resolution processes. He has negotiated significant international agreements and has been recognized for his abilities by the United States Coast Guard and United States Army, as well as national and international human rights organizations.

Siobhan McEvoy-Levy is associate professor of political science and director of the Peace Studies Program at Butler University, Indianapolis. Born and raised in Northern Ireland, McEvoy-Levy received her master's and PhD degrees from the University of Cambridge (UK) in 1999, a first-class BA honors degree from The Queen's University, Belfast in 1991, and a diploma in journalism from the College of Business Studies, Belfast, in 1987. McEvoy-Levy has over a decade of experience conducting international research on youth and conflict, including field research in the U.S., Europe, and the Middle East.

Amos Nadan is in the Department of Islamic and Middle Eastern Studies, Hebrew University of Jerusalem, Israel. He is senior research fellow at the Moshe Dayan Centre for Middle Eastern and African Studies at Tel Aviv University, and a former research fellow of the Truman Institute for Peace, Hebrew University. In 2004 he published *The Palestinian Peasant Economy Under the Mandate: A Story of Colonial Bungling* with Harvard University Press. In 2007 he coedited *Islam in Africa and the Middle East: Studies on Conversion and Renewal, Variorum,* with Michel Abitbol and Nehemia Levtzion. He lives in Jerusalem with his wife and three children.

Robin Neustaeter is a peace activist, educator, and mother. She has been teaching courses and conducting workshops in the areas of education and conflict resolution for ten years. Currently, she is a doctoral student in peace and conflict studies at the University of Manitoba.

Frederic S. Pearson is director of the Center for Peace and Conflict Studies, professor of political science, and Gershenson Distinguished Faculty Fellow at Wayne State University. He was previously professor and research fellow at the University of Missouri–St. Louis and twice a Fulbright scholar in the Netherlands and UK. An authority on international military intervention, arms transfers and conflict resolution, Dr. Pearson was editor of the 2001 special issue of the *Journal of Peace Research* on identity-based disputes and conflict management, and in 2000 he was a governmental consultant on U.S. National Security, Twenty-first Century, in Washington, DC.

Jean Poitras is associate professor of conflict management at HEC Montréal. He developed a comprehensive knowledge of conflict management through his experience as a consultant and from the results of his research projects.

For more than fifteen years now, Dr. Poitras has been helping professionals develop their negotiation and mediation skills. His research program focuses on the intervention strategies used in mediation and negotiation, as well as on the development of diagnostic tools to measure the levels of conflict in organizations.

Jodi Read is a doctoral student in peace and conflict studies at the University of Manitoba. She was a designer of the Mennonite Central Committee U.S. Immigration Listening Project. She has facilitated focus groups in ten churches on the West Coast of the U.S. At Eastern Mennonite University, she conducted interviews with documented and undocumented immigrant Mexican workers in the region. For seven years, she served with Mennonite Central Committee in Bolivia and Chile. She worked toward diverse project goals such as income generation, peacebuilding, and domestic violence.

Brian Rice teaches courses on aboriginal history and culture in the Department of Education at the University of Winnipeg. He wrote the Aboriginal history series for the National Library of Canada called the *Kid's-Site of Canadian Settlement*. More recently, he co-authored an article featured in the book *From Truth to Reconciliation,* which was handed to the prime minister of Canada during his apology to residential school survivors, as well as being an advisor to the Truth and Reconciliation Commission. He is also the main researcher on Aboriginal content for the History Game Canada.

Jessica Senehi is associate professor in peace and conflict studies at the University of Manitoba, and associate director of the Arthur V. Mauro Centre for Peace and Justice at St. Paul's College. At the University of Manitoba, in 2007, she established the award-winning graduate-level Summer Institute for Peace and Renewing Community. In 2006, she established the Winnipeg International Storytelling Festival: Storytelling on the Path to Peace, presented by the Mauro Centre for Peace and Justice. Her research focuses on the role of storytelling in peacebuilding, cultural conflict, and gender.

Anna Snyder is associate professor in the conflict resolution program at Menno Simons College, an institution affiliated with the University of Winnipeg, Canada. Her research interests include women's peace organizations, Aboriginal/non-Aboriginal reconciliation, and transnational nongovernmental network conflict. She has published articles in journals such as *Globalizations, Conflict Resolution Quarterly*, and *Canadian Woman Studies*. Her conflict resolution practice is focused primarily on healing and reconciliation efforts between Aboriginal and non-Aboriginal peoples on the issue of residential schools, including Canada's Truth and Reconciliation Commission.

Arnaud Stimec is associate professor at the University of Nantes, where he teaches negotiation, conflict management and organizational behavior. His research is related to negotiation, mediation, conflict management, and occupational health. He is editor of the academic journal *Négociations* and the author of two books. Arnaud Stimec is also an experienced mediator in different fields (workplace mediation, industrial relations, community and family justice) and acts frequently in an action research setting linking conflict management and occupational health.

Charles Thiessen is a PhD candidate in peace and conflict studies at the Arthur Mauro Centre for Peace and Justice at St. Paul's College, University of Manitoba. He has spent two years employed as an aid and development worker in Afghanistan and Uzbekistan. His research on peacebuilding in Afghanistan is published in *Exploring NGO Educational Project Work: Working Towards the Healing of Afghanistan And Other Conflict-Affected Nations* (2008). He has also co-authored numerous articles on peacebuilding processes in Northern Ireland in *International Politics*, *Humanity and Society*, *Peace and Conflict Studies*, *Civil Wars*, and *Peace Research*.

Hamdesa Tuso is associate professor of conflict resolution and sociology at the Department of Conflict Analysis and Resolution of Nova Southeastern University. Prior to that, he taught at the conflict resolution programs at Antioch University and George Mason University. His areas of interest include indigenous processes of conflict resolution, nationalism, ethnicity and conflict, organizational conflicts, and theories of social conflict. During 2006–2007, he was selected as the Distinguished Visiting Esau Professor of Conflict Resolution Studies, Menno Simons College, the University of Winnipeg, Canada. He is the founder and director of the African Working Group (AWG).

Jean-Guy Vaillancourt is professor emeritus of environmental sociology, sociological theory, and sociology of religion in the Department of Sociology, University of Montreal, Quebec. He received the prestigious 2009 Michel-Jurdant prize for the environmental sciences in Quebec from the Association of *Francophone pour le Savoir*, previously known as the French Canadian Association for the Advancement of Science. Professor Vaillancourt was the first social scientist to receive this award. He has published thirty-five books or special journals, as well as hundreds of articles, chapters, and book reviews in sociology and has been a visiting professor in Viet Nam and Brazil.

Christina J. Woolner recently completed an MA in international peace studies at the University of Notre Dame, and holds a BA in global studies and religion and culture from Wilfrid Laurier University. Her research interests include the role of culture and religion in conflict transformation, and peacebuilding in refugee and diaspora communities. Christina is currently a project officer at Project Ploughshares in Waterloo, Ontario, and is working on a program that seeks to strengthen cooperation among Caribbean countries to reduce gun crime.

Preface

This book started as a conversation regarding the absence of diverse critical voices outside the field of peace and conflict studies (PACS) comprising conflict analysis and resolution and peace studies whose many relationships weave together to create the web of life on the planet. The usual suspects write many of the books we regularly use in our classes. Clearly, we do not deny the contributions to theory and practice made by classical and founding readings in the field. Our concern is that the plethora of voices from outside the emerging PACS discipline is not being heard. We see the field beginning to travel along a narrow path.

For example, the voices of indigenous people and citizens from the global South are missing from the field. Their absence contributes to a strong Western-centered approach in much of the field's scholarship, practice, and pedagogy. This edited volume is our contribution to addressing some of the limitations that come with a privileged Western approach to the study and resolution of conflict.

This volume provides a useful framework for the study and critical analysis of the field. Students and faculty are provided essays divided into three areas of analysis: theory, practice, and pedagogy. The contributions of Johan Galtung, a recognized founder of the PACS field, and Neil Katz, a significant actor in the field's growth through his advancement of conflict analysis and resolution studies at Syracuse University, serve as bookends.

Our unique backgrounds and experiences informed our selection of individual contributors. We are committed to the field's definition and growth as a field of study, and feel it necessary to bring forward those at the creative edge of peace and conflict studies. We believe there is room at the PACS table for individuals from throughout the academy. Our experience in developing, leading, and teaching in PACS programs at the Mauro Centre for Peace and Justice at St. Paul's College in the University of Manitoba; the Program in Conflict and Peace Studies at the University of North Carolina at Greensboro; and the Department of Conflict Analysis and Resolution at Nova Southeastern University influence our approach to the study and practice of the field. We advocate for the removal of barriers that can keep cutting-edge ideas out of the field. PACS is too complex an interdisciplinary field to be compartmentalized and restricted by bureaucratic definitions of where knowledge is housed.

Peace and conflict studies work is a serious activity requiring the very best of all of our global community. Good intentions are not good enough. Scholarship and informed practice across many fields of study is required. We advance this book as a step forward, inviting everyone genuinely interested in nonviolently transforming conflict to walk the path of peace.

Designing a Way Forward

Why This Book? Why Now?

Thomas Matyók

The world community is in desperate need of an expanding peace narrative. Throughout the world, targets of unrestrained violence cry out for just peace. War narratives are plentiful, while peace-centered narratives are routinely marginalized. In a post-9/11 world, peace advocates are sometimes portrayed as unpatriotic, naive, or sympathetic to terrorist claims. National and international structures prove unable to construct a global, positive peace culture. We live in interesting times.

Passionate peace voices are needed to counter the ongoing din created by war narratives. But, an holistic peace narrative constructed of diverse voices remains absent. Scholars of peace and conflict studies often espouse the rhetoric of inclusion, but the reality of practice often falls short of expressed ideals. Peace narratives need to transcend narrow disciplinary boundaries. Working to achieve positive peace is everyone's job. What is called for is a critical analysis of where we are and where we are going. In this book, scholars from diverse fields step forward to contribute to that critical analysis. The contributors discuss critical issues in the emerging field of peace and conflict studies, and suggest a framework for the future development of the field and the education of its practitioner-academics.

Peace and conflict studies scholars routinely claim that the field is multi/trans/poly/post-disciplinary. If that is truly the case, where are the diverse voices? Why does the rhetoric differ from the reality? Why is the field dominated by a select few? The introduction of diverse peace voices in this work is a conscious step toward correcting some of these shortcomings.

Within these pages, ideas from a diverse group of scholars across academic fields, all of whom are engaged in some form of peace work, are shared.

Whether practicing in education, health care, business, policing, military, social work, community development, or any number of other areas, we are all performing peace work. Peace and conflict studies cannot be owned by an anointed elite and held unavailable for others. The field resists control by the few.

An expanded view of peace and conflict studies allows a broad academic horizon that easily accommodates multiple voices. The multiple and diverse contributing voices are necessary in a *design-oriented* field of study that strives to bring academics and practice together in the collaborative, forward creation of a positive peace culture. Peace scholarship and practice does not need to define and own a specific parcel of academic space and knowing; rather, it is actually advanced through expanded dispersal.

RELEVANCE OR IRRELEVANCE

Without broad-based acceptance, in and outside the academy, as a legitimate field of study and practice, peace and conflict studies risks slipping into the void. The worst condition possible for any academic discipline is one of irrelevance. However, advanced here is acceptance of the field as moving in new directions, away from what was toward what can be.

Often, peace scholars seem to be missing in action during crises. Scholars and practitioners in the field need to step forward and establish their presence in conflict resolution. One factor that contributes to the perceived absence of peace scholars in times of crisis is the confusion between the peace movement and peace science or peace scholarship. The peace movement is a temporary grouping of people opposed to war for any number of reasons. Peace science and peace scholarship is on-going peace development.

PEACE SCHOLARSHIP

Peace and conflict studies includes scholars and practitioners throughout the world working in peace studies, conflict analysis and resolution, conflict management, alternative dispute resolution, and peace and justice studies. They come to the peace and conflict studies field with a diversity of ideas, approaches, disciplinary roots, and topic areas. This type of variation speaks to the complexity, breadth, and depth of knowledges needed to apply and take account of conflict dynamics and the goals of positive peace.

There are a number of key concerns and dilemmas that continue to challenge the field. Studying critical issues facing the field of peace and conflict studies provides a means by which academics, students, and practitioners can develop theory, practice, pedagogy, and research methodology to confront the complexity of contemporary conflicts. Every discipline must continually engage in actions of critical reflection and assessment in order to build upon and realize the field's development.[1]

What distinguishes the field of peace and conflict studies from other academic disciplines? The field's unique character is an outcome of its designer-like approach to the study; resolution, and nonviolent, peaceful *transformation* of conflict creating a path to the way it could be. Yet the preparation of peace and conflict studies practitioners is often disjointed and unfocused. Academic programs are a little of this, and a little of that.

PEACE AND CONFLICT STUDIES AS DESIGN DISCIPLINE

The contributors to this book provide an expanded view of the field and argue for a leading-edge definition of the discipline of peace and conflict studies. Defining peace and conflict studies using medieval approaches to knowledge development is not good enough. What is called for is an entirely new way of defining knowledge development within the field. Currently, peace and conflict studies is often found at the academy's margins. It is not uncommon to find programs in schools of interdisciplinary studies using faculty from throughout the university to teach the field. The field seeks acceptance into the established canon of academic subjects. But we suggest it is not about gaining acceptance to academia's center; rather, it is about creating a new center. We are about nonviolent, social change in pursuit of positive peace. The field is an activist oriented discipline inviting all to participate.

Peace and conflict studies introduce a new disciplinary definition. Presently, the academy pushes two ways of knowing: scientific and humanistic. Scientific knowing can tell us "what *it* is," and humanistic knowing can tell us "why *it* is," but that is not good enough in a liquid reality, which moves beyond and breaks down disciplinary boundaries.[2] Design disciplines, such as peace studies, introduce "what *it* can be."[3] This difference takes knowing out of the academy and places it in the world. It becomes real practice and academics engage in a dialectical relationship.

Present in the here-and-now, peace and conflict studies is essentially a future-centered discipline. Not content with the what and why of conflict, the field orients on what the future can be, it designs a path forward. In designing a just future, a new disciplinary approach is required; one that transcends narrow, disciplinary boundaries, one that deconstructs in-order-to construct. This approach moves beyond multi/trans/poly/post disciplinary thinking that results in fractured approaches to complex conflict problems. It also moves the field to accept and integrate all disciplines as they become components of peace and conflict studies. Terms such as multi/trans/poly/post can serve, simply, as expressions of tolerance, not acceptance. Design points the way forward in a collaborative way. A design approach to disciplinary thought invites partners to engage in an open epistemological space.

Peace development is a process of becoming, not a state of being. Design does not seek ownership of knowledge terrain. Rather, design is modern-day utopian thinking bringing all knowledge to address the complex social issues of our time. It is a wickedly complex process. But, we are not alone. Creativity occurs at the interchange of widely divergent fields of knowledge within and outside of the social sciences. Fields of study such as interior architecture can point the way toward a new approach to learning and knowledge construction that we can participate in developing. Rather than viewing peace as a static condition, we see it as a condition in eternal flux, always becoming. Peace and conflict scholars and practitioners design a future condition. The design is the act. A knowledge commodity culture is not able to address peace development's constant changing condition. Peace as design is recognized in action.[4]

LIQUID MODERNITY

Rapidly changing political, social, and economic conditions require peace scholars and practitioners to create theory and pedagogical approaches that support practice. Suggested is the notion that peace and conflict studies will increasingly function in a liquid modernity,[5] transcending disciplinary boundaries as it engages the development of future centered knowledge. Globalization's unbounded, fluid nature requires approaches to peace development that are at the creative edge. To paraphrase Albert Einstein, we cannot get out of today's social problems with yesterday's thinking. Needed, then, is a new center that recognizes the interconnectedness of disciplines unrestricted by artificial boundaries that partition knowledge. Modern, complex problems require an interdisciplinary approach to resolution and transformation. And, just as theory informs practice, practice needs to inform theory and pedagogy in a never-ending feedback loop.

IT IS ALL INTERNATIONAL

May I offer a brief word about the national, international divide? I suggest it is all international. Globalization and transnational corporations are making the national a quaint fiction. Peace and conflict scholars and practitioners are increasingly of the mind that interconnectedness is the global condition. It is no longer possible to speak of solely local or national conflicts. All conflicts include micro, mesa, macro, and mega elements. Peace and conflict work occurs at all levels of analysis, often simultaneously.

International is becoming a term that poorly describes our current condition. In our hyper-globalized social space, our political, social, and economic problems are too complex and too wide ranging to be limited by geographic boundaries, a key requirement of an international paradigm. Problems, and resolutions, transcend nation-state boundaries disrespectful of physical boundaries. To meet this complexity, we need to include the voices of scholar practitioners from indigenous cultures to bring diverse knowledge systems and approaches into the peace and conflict studies field.[6]

The contributors in this book provide a step forward along the path leading to a global culture defined by positive peace. Diverse peace voices focus on presenting the full range of the field of peace and conflict studies. And they contribute to the needed critical analysis of where the field is and where it is going.

BIBLIOGRAPHY

Abbott, A. *Chaos of Disciplines*. Chicago: University of Chicago Press, 2001.

Baumann, Z. *Liquid Modernity*. Malden, MA: Polity, 2000.

Galtung, Johan. "Towards a Conflictology: A Quest for Trans-Disciplinarity," in *Handbook of Conflict Analysis and Resolution,* Dennis Sandole, Sean Byrne, Ingrid Sandole-Staroste, and Jessica Senehi, eds. London: Routledge, 2009.

Mac Ginty, Roger, and Andrew Williams. *Conflict and Development*. London: Routledge, 2009.

Mendoza, H.R., and T. Matyók. "We Are Not Alone: When the Number of Exceptions to a Rule Exceeds its Usefulness as a Construct, it is Time for a Change," in *Meanings of Design: Social, Cultural and Philosophical Essays about People, Spaces and Interior Environments*, Tiiu Poldma, ed. New York: Fairchild, in press.

NOTES

1. Andrew Abbott, *Chaos of Disciplines* (Chicago: University of Chicago Press, 2001).

2. Zygmunt Bauman, *Liquid Modernity* (London: Polity Press, 2000).

3. H.R. Mendoza and Tom Matyók, "We Are Not Alone: When the Number of Exceptions to a Rule Exceeds its Usefulness as a Construct, It Is Time for a Change," in *Meanings of Design: Social, Cultural and Philosophical Essays about People, Spaces and Interior Environments*, Tiiu Poldma, ed. (New York: Fairchild, in press).

4. Mendoza and Matyók, "We Are Not Alone."

5. Bauman, *Liquid Modernity*.

6. Johan Galtung, "Towards a Conflictology: A Quest for Trans-Disciplinarity," in *Handbook of Conflict Analysis and Resolution,* Dennis Sandole, Sean Byrne, Ingrid Sandole-Staroste, and Jessica Senehi, eds. (London: Routledge, 2009); Roger Mac Ginty and Andrew Williams, *Conflict and Development* (London: Routledge, 2009), 175–181.

Part One

Theory

Chapter 1

Peace and Conflict Studies as Political Activity[1]

Johan Galtung

A culture of peace is a culture that promotes peace and peace can be understood in a number of ways, as it impacts so many aspects of life. First, peace is to violence what health is to disease, it can exist within a person or group. A person can be healthy in the same way that a person, a group, a state, a nation, a region, a civilization can be peaceful. Peace also exists between persons, groups and so on, so peace is a form of love.

Love is the union of body, mind and spirit, or, to be more precise, the union of those unions. It is the miracle of sex and physical tenderness; the miracle of two minds sharing joy and suffering, *sukha* and *dukkha* as Buddhists say, resonating in harmony; the miracle of two persons having a joint project beyond themselves including reflecting constructively on the union of body, mind, and spirit. The body is the economy, the mind is the polity, and the spirit is the culture, particularly the deep, collectively shared, subconscious culture. The fourth source of power in this union, the military, is not addressed, as my concern is peace by peaceful means.

Unfortunately, many institutes and universities doing peace studies are actually doing war studies, counting violent conflicts meticulously, analyzing them, and sometimes looking into how they ended, the cease-fire. In a cease-fire process, a third party may step in, punishing them if they break the cease-fire and rewarding them if they do not, making the cease-fire pay for itself. This process may or may not be a good approach to peace, but it is not the same as a peace process. Peace, as pointed out using the love metaphor, is a positive relation between parties, of union, togetherness. The condition for peace is mutual respect, dignity, equality, and reciprocity; in all three areas, spirit, or culture, mind, or polity, and body, or economy.

CULTURE

Each culture, in my experience, has some kind of gift to a world culture of peace, such as the Western equality for the law, the Polynesian *ho'o pono pono*, the Somali *shir*, the Cheyenne *calumet*. The idea of a big world parade of contributions to world culture is excellent, although it would be difficult to engage in mutual learning on such a global scale. To demonstrate the importance of spiritual richness, I would like to highlight some concepts from a brief sampling of world religions:

- From Judaism: truth is not a declaration of faith but an on-going process through dialogue with no end, like in the Talmud.
- From Protestant Christianity: the Lutheran *hier stehe ich, ich kann nicht anders*, here I am, I have no alternative; the significance of individual conscience and responsibility; and equality in the face of the Creator.
- From Catholic Christianity: the distinction between *peccato* and *peccatore*, between sin and sinners, of a stand against the sin but at the same time pardoning and forgiving the sinner.
- From Orthodox Christianity: the optimism of Sunday Christianity as opposed to the necrophilic Friday Christianities of the other two: Christ has arisen and is among us.
- From Islam: the truth of Sura 8:61, when the Other shows an inclination toward peace, then so do you; peace breeds peace; the truth of *zakat*, of sharing with the poor.
- From Hinduism: the Trinitarian construction of the world, as Creation, Preservation and Destruction. Applied to conflict, this concept means: pursuing creation by seeing conflict as a challenge to be creative, preserving the parties, avoiding destruction.
- From Buddhism/Jainism: nonviolence, *ahimsa* of course, but also to all life, bringing in the whole earth, not only the human part, and the earth-human interface. Part of this, what is known in Japanese Buddhism as *engi*, that everything hangs together, causation is co-dependent, with no beginning, and no end; nobody is totally guilty or totally innocent. We all share responsibility in reducing *dukkha*, or suffering, and increasing *sukha*, or fulfillment, and liberation for all, including ourselves.
- From Confucianism: the principle of isomorphic harmony, harmony inside ourselves, inner peace, in the family, school, at work, in society, in the country and the nation, in the region and the civilization, with all levels inspiring each other.

- From Daoism: the principle of yin-yang, the good in the bad, and the bad in the good, and the bad in the good in the bad, and good in the bad in the good, and so on—a complexity far beyond Western dualism.
- From Humanism: the idea of basic human needs, to some extent reflected in basic human rights as a guideline for human action in general and politics and economics in particular.

I recommend that we pick the best from all and not waste time wrestling with strange, obscure, even anti-peace messages.

The major sociopolitical obstacle to a culture of peace is the culture of war and violence, as portrayed in the media. Violence on television has several aspects, both explicit and implicit. The minor, explicit factor is the display of unbridled violence with the victim lying in his or her own blood and the perpetrator escaping. The first major implicit factor is the lack of display of the invisible effects of violence, the sorrow suffered by the bereaved, the trauma, the hatred, the urge for revenge and revanche, and the sense of glory in the perpetrator who got away with it. The second major missing factor is the lack of display of alternative ways of handling conflict, through conflict transformation, empathy, nonviolence, creativity. No TV violence study has covered all three adequately and they deserve attention.

There is a direct link from interpersonal violence to interstate wars. War journalism systematically focuses on violence and on who wins, like a soccer game, leaving out the invisible effects and the alternatives to war. Peace journalism starts with two questions: "What is the conflict about?" and "What are the possible solutions?" A president who has nothing better to offer than "the conflict is between good and evil" and "the solution is to crush evil" will not survive sustained questioning and can only create war propaganda in a war culture.

But the war culture is also based on what is said, such as being a Chosen People by the Almighty, accountable only to Him. This world order has their God on top, then the Chosen People under God (leaving no space for international law and human rights), then chosen allies, then the rest, including the United Nations (UN). They see themselves as exceptional, with the right, even the duty to be in breach of human rights and UN resolutions, whether the Almighty is Yahweh, God, or Alla'h. War culture is based on chosenness, glory, and trauma, backed up by dualism, Manichaeism and the promise of a violent encounter, and Armageddon. These days we hear it from fundamentalist terrorists and fundamentalist state terrorists. Moderates ought to unite to create a peace culture of empathy, creativity, and nonviolence.

Peace can only be based on equality and equity. A structure without these basic rights is not giving to others what they demand for themselves. Equality before the law is a Western contribution to a culture of peace; exceptionalism is the opposite—anti-peace. This concept exists for genders, generations, and groups in society, for states and nations, for regions and civilizations. The human spirit is capable of accommodating cultures of war and cultures of peace; like the human body, it is capable of hosting both pathogens, which are dangerous to self and others, and sanogens, which are beneficial. The culture of a society must have its members open their hearts to the immense significance of the human spirit for a more peaceful civilization, driving out anti-peace. But peace is made neither by culture alone nor by politics and economics alone. It is made by all three, synergistically. The formula for peace is always equality, equity, and mutual respect. We have to learn to celebrate not only the peace elements in our own culture but also those in others, by celebrating each person's gift to humanity.

A nonviolent boycott, as modeled by Gandhi, is a way to stand against aggression. There is talk of boycotts of U.S. products, building on successful action against the apartheid regime in South Africa, against Deutsche Shell in the North Sea, and against the French nuclear testing in Polynesia. The purpose of the boycott is to turn U.S. corporations against U.S. belligerence and disrespect for treaties and world cooperation. The boycott would cover consumer goods such as movies, Coca Cola and MacDonald's, American cars and gasoline, U.S. capital goods and currencies, and U.S. bonds and stocks. Supporters demand that governments do not buy these goods and would start with the most reprehensible corporations. The average profit of a U.S. corporation is around 6 percent, meaning that even modest participation will have a major impact. Even a 3 percent decline in sales will place the trustees and executives of major corporations in a dilemma between loyalty to Washington and their own profits.

Likely corporate counter-measures against a boycott will include:

- pressure on governments to outlaw the boycott, which is problematic because market freedom is a major part of neoliberal ideology;
- corporations asking Washington for compensation, which is problematic given the U.S. economy in general and the federal budget;
- decreasing expenditure by laying off more workers, which is problematic because collective protests are now increasing very quickly; and
- U.S. boycotting of products from boycotting countries, which is problematic given U.S. consumer dependence on foreign products, and solidarity, buying from U.S.-boycotted countries.

The boycott should be informed by Gandhian nonviolence. The purpose is to reduce and eliminate the U.S. military and economic grip on the world, not to kill U.S. children. An emergency relief program for those who suffer in the United States should be considered. There is nothing in conflict and peace theory saying that we shall build compromises to everything and treat everybody equally. The conflict between slave and slave-owner, between colonialist and colony, was not solved by compromise, but by resisting evil.

ECONOMICS

In the guidelines for the economics of peace, the first goal is the satisfaction of basic needs, which can be done locally or nationally. The second goal is equity, with equal exchange guiding trade relations globally. The most important goals for economic activity are to give people a life in dignity and to build relations between countries that are equitable. An economy that kills 100,000 people a day, a quarter of whom are starving, and three quarters of whom are suffering a deficit in affordable health services is not acceptable. Neither are trade relations that consist of grabbing the natural resources of other peoples and protecting the robbery by military means.

The cultural aspect of peace addresses the surface and the deeper, both individually and collectively held, cognitions and emotions that relate to peace and violence by legitimizing volitions and action in favor of one or the other. Emotionally the task is to break down positive evaluations of violence and negative evaluations of peace and to build up the negative evaluations of violence and positive evaluations of peace. A major shortcoming of peace studies so far is the single-minded focus on the former, and the lack of focus on making peace more attractive (excepting opportunity cost analyses of arms races). Non-economic factors also have to be brought in, including what happens to people who are positively inspired, not filled with fear. Without abandoning emotive approaches there is a good case for trying cognitive approaches. Cognitions are seen less in terms of negative or positive (critical approach, very linked to emotions) and more in terms of true/false (empiricist approach) and narrow/broad (constructivist approach).

One approach to the understanding of violence studies is frustration, or blocked goal attainment, and more particularly that the goal is blocked by other goal pursuits (by Self or Other), that is, conflict. The more the goal has needs character (for survival, well-being, freedom, identity) the more likely the violence; and the more the contradiction has conflict character, the more likely is violence against Other. If Self and Other are collectivities, then the violence is called war.

Left out completely in this kind of theory is the role of culture, assuming that structure is implicit in needs satisfaction. And yet (deep) culture steers the cognitions. An empiricist, narrow cognition, like *si vis pacem, para bellum*, limits the cognitive space; a constructivist, searching approach expanding the cognitive space is often much more promising. My own work over forty years on and in forty conflicts would point to the liberating function of transcending the space of possible conflict outcomes seen by the actors. By disembedding the conflict from where it has been embedded and re-embedding it at a more promising place, violence no longer looks inevitable.

To arrive at this dialogue with the actors, not about them, is the tool. This process presupposes empathy with the actors and among them, a belief in nonviolent possibilities and a creative, constructivist attitude to the incompatibilities/contradictions.

A basic question, then, is to what extent these three traits are located and/or can be developed in existing cultures. My own experience would point to participation in conflict and training in conflict participation as more promising than perusing/scanning cultures for peace nuggets. Gandhi was fighting the UK empire, meaning UK invasion and occupation, which was an evil empire, judging by the reaction to the Sepoy mutiny 150 years ago or to the 1919 Amritsar massacre. Churchill not only referred to Gandhi as a semi-naked fakir, but also sincerely hoped he would fast himself to death. But in 1947, Gandhi's nonviolence prevailed and India became independent, followed by the rest of the empire. Both India and England are blossoming—India with a brilliant linguistic federalism and phenomenal economic growth, and England heading the same way, but still with some residual imperialism.

The U.S. global empire was the successor to the UK global empire, Israel was the successor in the Middle East, and Australia in the Pacific. All three countries pursue settler colonialism, invasion and occupation, as seen today by the United States in Iraq, Afghanistan, and partly Saudi Arabia, and by Israel in Palestine. There is massive resistance in all four areas, because people hate being invaded and occupied, regardless of invader-occupier creativity in legitimizing the exercise.

How did Gandhi resist? By brilliantly transcending the conflict between the *kshatriyah varnadharma* of violent heroic struggle, and his own *swadharma* of nonviolence into a nonviolent, heroic struggle known as *satyagraha*. To many people, *satyagraha*, above all, means nonviolent struggle resisting direct and/or structural violence, but there is much more to *satyagraha*, particularly five points that go beyond such terms as "struggle," "resistance," "heroic," and "sacrifice" into deeper and wiser politics than victorious invasions.

All five points apply to the four current anti-imperial struggles. The struggles spell an end to fundamentalist Christian U.S. and hard Zionist Israeli imperialism, but the Gandhian points would raise United States and Israel to conviviality with others. The Gandhian messages are not only to the invaders—occupiers in Washington-Jerusalem—but also to the invaded—occupied peoples in Iraq, Afghanistan, Palestine, and Saudi Arabia.

POINT 1: NEVER FEAR DIALOGUE

Gandhi had dialogue with everybody during his many struggles, including with the viceroy of an empire he had come to loathe, and it was fruitful. It is frustrating to watch a U.S. secretary of state travel in and out of Israel, assuring Israelis that she will meet with neither Hamas nor Hezbollah, nor Damascus, nor Tehran, when that is exactly what she has to do to make her points and maybe learn some new ones. This approach also applies to a Mullah Omar and a Hektamayar, representing the religious and the national resistance, on top of which comes the resistance from the overwhelming majority of Afghans, who simply want neither invasion nor occupation. The conditionality approach, first NATO out, then talks, is highly understandable, but that point can be much better communicated in a dialogue covering all issues.

POINT 2: NEVER FEAR CONFLICT: MORE OPPORTUNITY THAN DANGER

For Gandhi, conflict was a challenge to know each other, to have something in common and not be irrelevant to each other. He preferred violence to cowardice and conflict, disharmony to no relation at all, and the nonviolence of the brave and relations of harmony. Conflict can be understood the Anglo-American way as violent clashes of actors-parties or as an incompatibility of the goals of those actors-parties. The former perspective leads to control of one or more party, usually of the Other, even to incapacitation-expulsion-extermination. The latter may lead to problem-solving.

A conflict can be seen by the less mature and very self-righteous as a chance to impose oneself, to prevail, to "win." By the more mature, conflict can be seen as an occasion for Self-examination rather than Other-censure, a search for that possibly new reality where legitimate goals of all parties can be accommodated, such as the Muslim world's goals of respect for Islam and the Western world's goals of democracy and free markets. The West could learn deep respect for economic transactions as human transactions from Islamic economics and Islam could learn deep respect for more diversity of views and opinions from the West.

The major medium in which all conflicts unfold is time, which leads to the third and fourth points. Diplomats negotiate ratifiable agreements in the game of goals, values, interests as they present themselves synchronically, in the present. But in real life, the past throws long shadows into the present. Conflicts are often asynchronous, as the parties live in different time zones—years, decades, centuries apart, all with their own Greenwich Mean Time. As the advisor to Serbian president Cosic, Professor Stojanovic, said of the U.S. approach before the 1999 NATO attack on Serbia, the United States suffers from excessive presentism, aware neither of history nor of what the future may hold in store of good, bad, and worse.

POINT 3: KNOW HISTORY OR YOU ARE DOOMED TO REPEAT IT (BURKE)

Gandhi knew the history of the English and their empire often better than they themselves while he was also at home in his own, with the facts and the equally important fiction (like the Mahabharata). He realized that the UK imperial inclination to glory and ruling the waves (with some land thrown in) had to be fought at its root, by spinning chains of nonviolence into the very heart of England, and he did.

But history sediments layers of trauma, not only glory, in the collective memory. How can we ever understand the resistance of the four without understanding the traumas suffered in the countries involved, such as by Iraq, including the Baghdad massacre by the ilkhan and the pope in 1258 and the United Kingdom carving out Iraq in 1916. In order for the victims and perpetrators to be reconciled, acknowledgment of the traumas and conciliation are much overdue.

POINT 4: IMAGE THE FUTURE OR YOU WILL NEVER GET THERE

"Be today the future you want to see tomorrow" was Gandhi's way of translating this point into positive non-cooperation and civil disobedience, emptying the oppressive structures while at the same time shedding light on the future and training the *satyagrahi* for positive peace and conviviality. Gandhi's vision went beyond independence, *swaraj*, to a world that included the occupier.

Maybe there is a message here for all six parties to think, speak and act in terms of a future together? Is a Middle East Community—modeled on the

European Community that accommodated former Nazi Germany—of Israel's five border countries (Lebanon, Syria, Jordan, a fully recognized Palestine, and Egypt), with a formerly hard Zionist Israel, possible?

POINT 5: WHILE FIGHTING OCCUPATION CLEAN UP YOUR OWN HOUSE!

Gandhi was certainly resisting the English empire and fighting for *swaraj*. But that did not prevent him from attending to such ills of his own Mother India as untouchability, discrimination against women, misery, and the increasing gap between Hindus and Muslims. The latter ultimately led to the partition, which, with the disastrous change of the proposed borderline by the last viceroy, Lord Mountbatten, led to a bloodbath and a trauma, exacerbating for generations the protracted Kashmir conflict.

That the colonizers also critiqued untouchability and discrimination against women, outlawing its extreme expression in the *suttee,* did not prevent Gandhi from attacking these social ills. He did not simply deny any truth also held by the chief antagonist, as some who become victims of polarization. Nor did he attack caste because the colonizers often used it as one of their levers in their "divide et impera" tactic to dominate India. He fought it as evil in its own right.

What could the occupiers and occupied learn from Gandhi in addition to turning from violence to nonviolence? The United States could learn to struggle energetically to lift the bottom 50 percent of society, where basic needs are concerned; to decrease the gap between rich and poor; to restore the dignity of the First Nations, the Inuits, and the Hawaiians; to end discrimination; and to reduce the alienation and fear underlying the violence and drug abuse in society. Israel could learn to lift Arab Israelis into first-class citizenship, to reduce the increasing gap between rich and poor and between Ashkenazim and Sephardim and other groups, and to reduce the corruption and normless hedonism tearing at the society.

In Iraq, the Sunnis could learn to give up their goal of running Iraq from Baghdad, Kurds and Shias could learn to fight nonviolently for their inalienable right to open borders with other Kurds and Shia Arabs, and they all could learn to find a unity in diversity somewhere between federation and confederation, and to preserve such gains as literacy, welfare state, and freedom of choice for women to wear the hijab or not. Afghanistan could be managed by Afghans, but would enter a contract with drug-consuming countries: we reduce the supply and you reduce the demand by creating more humane societies and we monitor each other. Palestine could learn to continue the

Hamas struggle against corruption, renew the society, lift non-Muslim Palestinians into first-class citizenship, and pursue energetically the struggle for more gender equality on the basis of the Qur'an. Saudi Arabia could learn to bridge the gap between *wahhabism* and Western materialism, to be up front searching for alternative non-polluting and non-depleting ways of converting energy, to pursue energetically the struggle for more gender equality on the basis of the Qur'an, and to explore non-Western forms of democracy.

The problem is how to channel the energies produced by a conflict so that the parties blossom. The three (and a half) occupations have to be lifted and the invaders have to go home and dismantle their imperial structures. Both sides must be liberated from the disastrous tie of imperialism. By fighting the Gandhian way, both sides can blossom, because these energies are used positively.

As Sonia Gandhi said in her concluding address of the first International Day of Nonviolence, "Let us embrace nonviolence, and become truly human." We live in a context of two major and related processes. The first is regionalization, based on high-speed transportation and communication, but coming up against cultural borders. Four exist—the EU, the AU, the SAARC and the ASEAN—and four are to come: Estados Unidos de America Latina y el Caribe (ALC); a Russian Union (RU), with autonomy for all non-Russians; an East Asian Community like the SCO, with 50 percent of humanity; and an Islamic Community (OIC), the ummah from Morocco to Mindanao.

The second is the decline of the U.S. empire, which, if handled well, may be a blessing for the U.S. republic, as it was for the eleven EU member colonial countries liberated from empires.

There are three components of an early warning:

1. direct violence: beyond throwing a first stone, capability and intention proven by a general tendency to participate in wars, among other reasons to create hierarchies, hegemonies;
2. structural violence: a position higher up or lower down in a hierarchy of exploitation-repression-alienation, to preserve the hierarchy or to destroy it; and
3. cultural violence: the cultural justification of 1 or 2.

A War Participation Index, based on the number of wars a state has participated in divided by the number of years of existence of the state, seems to confirm this trend. The top four countries are the United States of America: 3040; Israel (1947–1985): 1842; the Ottoman Empire and Turkey: 1552; and England and Great Britain: 1277. What do these four have in common? They all share structural violence, both in the sense of settler colonialism within and world and regional empire-building without. There is also cultural violence, based on hard readings of Abrahamic religions, hard Protestantism for the United States and the United Kingdom, hard Islam for the Ottoman Empire, and hard Zionism for Israel. In all three, we find dualism with Manichean overtones, seeing oneself as good and opponents as evil, and Armageddon as the final arbiter—the DMA syndrome. There is also the idea of being Chosen by the Eternal, a sense of past and future glory, and the significance of past trauma suffered on the road—the CGT syndrome. Both syndromes are important building blocks for deep violence. Of course, dialectically they also inspire the same syndromes in the other side. Today we witness that spiraling, cultural confrontation.

Hierarchies produce intractable conflicts. Peace assumes a high level of equity, an *equiarchy*, and the road to peace is paved with the acceptance of the Other as an equal partner in negotiation and dialogue. But if one or more of them are informed by a highly inequitable deep structure sustained by a deep culture, peace by peaceful means becomes more difficult. A cornerstone in the EU approach is to promote cultures of human rights and structures of democracy. These are excellent, bene per se. But the assumption that peace follows in their wake is based on a logical fallacy with serious consequences. Violence in general, and war in particular, is a relation between two or more states, and so is peace. But democracy/human rights may be properties of none, or one or more of them, and may be very good for inner peace. Make democracy a relation parliament, like in a regional, or even global, UN, based on free and fair elections, and we are in inter-state, inter-nation peace business. The first response is working on another relation between the parties, some unresolved conflict. "Conflict prevention" is meaningless, but "violence prevention" certainly is not. There is no "post-conflict," but hopefully there will be a "post-violence." The view of conflict must change from the Anglo-American view of conflict as clash of persons, groups, or parties into conflict as a clash of goals. Seeing conflict as a clash of goals makes it a problem to be solved, by creating a reality where legitimate goals can be accommodated and become compatible. When seeing conflict as a clash of parties, the inclination is to see one or more party as needing to be controlled, often violently; concepts matter.

Mediation means mapping conflicts, parties-goals-clashes, testing goals for legitimacy, and bridging legitimate goals and that calls for empathy, nonviolence, and creativity. Conciliation means acknowledging past wrongs, elaborating how and why, and then defining a future together. The goal is to enact in the present, imagine with the parties a vision of a compelling future, and be sensitive to traumas and glories of the past.

Let us explore five cases of mediation and five of conciliation, based on my own experiences in the process (see www.transcend-nordic.org and our UN manuals for Transcend and Sabona approaches). What does peace in the Middle East look like, between Israel and its neighbors? Much like the European Community imaged by two French statesmen, including the atrocious Nazi Germany, who painted a compelling future on the wall, a community of six, invoking the future to overcome the past and even the present. This community was an astounding success; inviting us all here and now to continue the good work.

A Middle East Community of six, including Lebanon, Syria, Jordan, Palestine (fully recognized), Egypt, and Israel, with the members willing to contract to something like 4 June 1967 in exchange for security through peace; the opposite is a non starter. Others may join, such as Turkey or Cyprus, maybe in an Eastern Mediterranean Community. Israel may develop very tight EU relations and Arab countries will join the Organization of the Islamic Community. Through all this, there could be a MEC with open borders, rights, and obligations.

Currently, there is a possibility of a major U.S.-Iran nuclear war, which is not a border problem but a conflict rooted in the past. Acknowledgment by the United States and the United Kingdom of the wrongs done by CIA and MI6 in 1953 in deposing a legitimate prime minister and initiating 25 years of dictatorship might trigger Sura 8:61 in the Qur'an: "When your enemy inclines toward peace you shall do the same." Iran did so in both 2001 and 2003 with no response, but nonetheless, this is the direction of peace. The possibilities for the future include the world's biggest oil consumer and potentially biggest oil producer joining to elaborate large scale non-fossil fuels projects together. This collaboration would take moral courage and some history/textbook revisionism, building on the masters, the Germans, some ten years after the conflict resolution built into the Treaty of Rome.

In Iraq, it is necessary to build on past successes. The EC was an internal inter-state success, as was German textbook revision creating good relations with the 25 invaded countries on today's map and the three nations exposed to genocide, Jews, Cinta-Roma, and Russians. The Helsinki Conference on Security and Cooperation in Europe was also a success, so make a Conference for Security and Cooperation in West Asia, financed by the EU. Kurdistan could also be on the agenda, as a confederation of four autonomies, without drawing new borders.

Over the years, there have been numerous instances of Western aggressions against Muslim countries, like France attacking Egypt, and England Mysore, in 1798, like Italy bombing oases in Libya in 1911, and Spain—Franco—Xauen in 1925. The perpetrator suffers from amnesia; the victim never forgets. This history leads to the U.S./West War on Terror, a complex conflict with acts of war like 9/11, 07/07 in London and 11 M(arch) in

Madrid, and massive killing and torture in Iraq and Afghanistan. Spain under Zapatero handled 11M masterfully. Morocco's ambassador was not expelled, nor was Rabat bombed as somebody might have done. He traveled to Rabat for top level dialogue, no doubt also about Ceuta-Melilla, legalized almost half a million illegal Moroccans in Spain, pulled Spanish troops out of Iraq and launched an Alliance of Civilizations in Madrid in October 2005.

There are also the actions of Sykes-Picot, the foreign ministers of United Kingdom-France, who in 1916 promised the Arabs independence to kill and overthrow the Ottoman Turks. They so did and were colonized, Iraq and Palestine for England and Syria and Lebanon for France. Rulers used rulers to define their artificial entities. An Anglo-French-Arab history book about 1916 may help to address the wrong, as Arab school children live that trauma, even if English-French do not.

Let us move from the West-Christian/Arab-Muslim conflict to the conflict in the Balkans. Kosovo/a, with Serbs (Kosovo) having clear historical legitimacy and the Albanians (Kosova) with clear self-determination, democratic legitimacy, as well as historical. Both status quo as part of Serbia and independence as a unitary state are clearly untenable and will lead to endless violence. Division is untenable for at least two reasons: viability and the right of all to consider Kosovo/a theirs with free travel and interaction. Instead, there should be an independent federal Kosovo/a, with autonomous Serbian cantons, in a confederation with Serbia and Albania. Of course, majority-based self-determination for Kosova sets a precedent for Bosnia-Herzegovina.

There is an Ottoman shadow over the region, which brings us to Turkey-Armenia and the question of conciliation. The conflict seems to be trilateral with Kurds being promised freedom if they would do the dirty job. They did and got no freedom. This act provides a context for the conflict today and the role of the Turks. Unconditional acknowledgment implies unconditional compensation and this example could stand in the way. One resolution is to build the joint future of neighbors around the contested mountain Ararat, making Ararat a Mountain of World Peace, not only for the three Abrahamic religions, but for humanity. It could be run under joint Turkish-Armenian administration, UN aegis, and paid by the EU. This coalition is one way to approach the past via the future and may also work for Myanmar. It is also important to open the EU for Turkey and Armenia and the Caucasian Community. There is conciliation work to be done for formerly colonial countries and for many EU charter members. But conciliation without conflict resolution is pacification. Like ceasefire or money for development, it simply buys time before violence erupts again. All roads to peace must pass through deep conflict resolution. And price stabilization in return for keeping EU-ACP division of labor is shallow, not deep. The East Asia formula was industrialization with tariff protection and welfare state and deeper transformation is needed.

The EU is facing a very important choice: the civilian peacekeeping favored by the Commission or the military version with rapid deployment favored by the Council? The latter might like to fill the gap left behind when the United States withdraws troops, like the British did East of Suez in 1965. The Third World, the chosen battlefield, like Orwell's Malabar Coast, might have some advice to offer about taming the forces favoring interventions and enhancing those favoring creative solutions. The Chinese could offer some advice from the many comments addressed to themselves at the seventeenth congress of the Chinese Communist party. India may have advice about high electoral participation in a country with well above a billion population to one with less than half of that. The world does not need a new empire but rather inter-regional structures for joint planning.

As the South African foreign minister expressed at a conference, with the United States and Israel tellingly absent, on the whole issue of colonialism, this is not about money/compensation, but about dignity. Dignity is promoted by perpetrators acknowledging, elaborating and designing new ways of entering the future together. Dignity is a relation with symmetry, reciprocity, equity. One approach, building on the UNESCO German-Polish experience and the German approach in general, would be to invite a major joint history project on colonialism, with slavery included. This project would also focus on the Arab-Muslim world, and others.

In order to contribute something to solving big problems you must think big thoughts. Check your thoughts and let them grow with the people concerned. That can be done better by NGOs in the field than by diplomats in sterile rooms with linear agendas. The Track 1 government versus Track 2 civil society—with NGOs, local authorities, the young, and the women—is problematic, as they become confused and Track 1 hopes for results from Track 2. The strength of civil society is direct contact, which is high on empathy and less inclined to violence. Creativity remains a crucial commodity. Its scarcity among diplomats geared toward correct process does not guarantee its presence in civil society, except for artists, engineers, architects, and so forth. Both tracks can be trained in, say, non-Western *ho'o ponopono*, *ga ca ca*, and *shir* conciliation approaches, and then work hand in hand. The civil society can do all three: peacemaking, peacebuilding, peacekeeping. The nongovernments can probably do it better than the governments. Thus, civil society can make ten thousand dialogues blossom within and among conflict parties, find out where the shoes pinch and what future society, region, world they want to live in—which Middle East or Kosovo/a. They can let all that information flow together and watch the GNIP, the Gross National Idea Product, grow. Something will emerge, peace may be made; governments may clinch the deal.

Peace must be built; webs of togetherness must be woven, humanizing where there has been dehumanization, and depolarizing where there has been polarization. Peace has to be kept by numerous and competent nonviolent peace forces inserting themselves so densely between violent parties that there is not enough space left for battle.

As to gender and generation, these are also important aspects. In general, men are more deductive, from grand principles, and women more compassionate, unless they permit PhDs in those grand principles to stand in the way. In general, the older generation has a more closed, and the younger a more open, discourse, more sensitive to new aspects and new ideas. Thus, in a conflict, women should meet the women on the other side(s), the young the young on the other side(s).

This fine conference has 4 tracks: Security and Development, Strengthening Cooperation, Lessons Learnt-Geography, Lessons Learnt-Thematic—with 4 sessions for each on specifics and 16 rapporteurs. The theme of this conference is "Strengthening Capacities to Respond to Crises and Security Threats." Crises only exist for the West, despite the permanent crisis of the majority of the world's peoples are still due to the colonialism of 11 of the EU members. Security easily becomes ours, the threats are to us. There is a paranoia in the West, seeing enemies everywhere, adding to Western manicheism and autism; them versus us, with crises generated by them, not by us.

The root cause of the violence of crises and threats is usually unresolved conflict, so the next conference should focus on "Resolving Conflicts and Building Peace." For example, the piracy crisis off the Somalian coast and beyond is an unacceptable crime. But so are 220 trawlers from EU countries like Denmark and Spain off the coast of a failed state depriving Somalia of seafood export products and food, in addition to dropping toxic, possibly nuclear, waste. Operation Atalanta will not solve this but will displace mutual aggression to worse places. *Audiatur et altera pars*, listen to the other side and find a solution accommodating both.

The tool of conflict resolution is mediation; there are five points involved in mediation:

1. Resolution Orientation: The root cause of violence is usually unresolved conflict(s). The conflict must be identified and then a solution must be found.
2. Incompatible Goals and Means: We tend to judge ourselves by our best intentions, that is, goals, and adversaries by their worst behavior, that is, means. Identify their best intentions or goals and look at your own behavior or means. These two indispensable jobs are often best done by an outside mediator.

3. Mapping the conflict: Identify the actors, their goals/means, and their clashes and incompatibilities with empathy.
4. Legitimizing: Test the goals/means for legitimacy, using Law, Human Rights and Basic Needs as standards, with impartiality.
5. Bridging: Explore new social realities under which legitimate goals of all parties may be reasonably satisfied with creativity.

For anything to work the day after tomorrow it has to be aired the day before yesterday so that somebody in due course of time can say, "It has always been my conviction."

In conclusion, our problems are located in the past, in the present and in the future, or in two of them, or in all three. There are the traumas of the past, and the method is conciliation. There are traumatic days, months, years, decades, centuries. These are festering wounds deep down in the social bodies, to be cleaned up through acknowledgment, preparing the ground for a cooperative future. There are the conflicts of the present, and the method is mediation, for conflict resolution. These conflicts are Gordian knots that are not to be cut by brutal violence, but to be unraveled. There are the challenges of the future, and the method is peacebuilding, cooperative, symbiotic-equitable projects producing harmony.

NOTES

1. This chapter is based upon four lectures presented by Johan Galtung given between 2007 and 2009. They are: (1) "Peace Research/Studies vs. Christian Zionism World Views," Eleventh World Congress for Center for Inquiry-International, Scientific Inquiry and Human Development, Beijing, 2007. (2) Keynote Address: "From Early Warning to Early Action: Developing the EU's Response to Crisis and Longer Term Threats," Palais Charlemagne, EU Commission, Brussels, 12 November 2007. (3) "Gandhi and the Struggle Against Imperialism: Five Points, International Day of Nonviolence," 2 February 2007, United Nations, New York. (4) Concluding Remarks: "Wrapping Up, The Road Ahead," European Commission, *Making the Difference: Strengthening the Capacities to Respond to Crises and Security Threats*, Brussels, 4 May 2009.

Chapter 2

When the Killing Begins

An Epistemic Inquiry into Violent Human Conflict, Contested Truths, and Multiplex Methodology

Thomas E. Boudreau

In the following pages, *violent* human conflict will be defined, in a preliminary way, as a human encounter in which one or both parties seek to achieve specific goals by physically coercing, harming, or killing, if possible, the other party.[1] "Party" or "parties" in this case refer to other groups of human beings, spanning from individuals to the ethnic group, to the nation-state. In violent conflict, one or more parties see another group or groups as an obstacle to the obtainment of their goals. Rather than forsake these goals, the group is willing to engage in violent behavior in order to convince, coerce or even destroy the other group or groups that are perceived, or actually do, stand in the way.

One of the characteristics of such lethal contests is often the presence of intensely competing epistemologies, dealing with each side's privileged knowledge claims and discourse on what constitutes valid knowledge and the "true" account of the conflict. Violent human conflict almost always involves an intense competition over which side's truth will endure and become the privileged discourse of description and analysis. For instance, epistemic pluralism, which can be defined as competing descriptions and narratives of the same factual conditions,[2] is almost always a characteristic result of such conflicts. In other words, unlike most social conflicts, in lethal contests there is often an absence of a shared epistemology among the contending sides; "truth" itself is contested and considered a great prize in violent human conflict. As we shall see, the complexity of the struggle is compounded by the presence of contested and competing geographies, human agencies, and intended outcomes. The problem then, from a methodological perspective, is how to capture and investigate the composite complexity of this phenomenon in which knowledge claims, and truth itself is almost always deeply contested.

This challenge presents a profound epistemic problem. Epistemology is the study of the origins, nature, methods and limits of knowledge. Ever since the Enlightenment, scholars and scientists have largely assumed that educated people looking at the same or similar factual situation would come to the same or similar conclusions. In violent human conflicts, this is patently not the case. Participants with the same or similar backgrounds and educations often make wildly different knowledge claims concerning the same supposedly factual conflict.

So, this essay attempts to answer the epistemic question: How do we know and study such violent human conflicts? In the following pages, we will explore the origins, nature, and limits of knowledge claims concerning such conflicts, and then attempt to provide a "multiplex" methodology for investigating these conflicts as they actually exist in their unique ontological site or local setting.[3] Such a complex and unique phenomenon, often characterized at its core by epistemic pluralism, can't be easily captured in a single theory or methodology; it requires a compound and sequential method of inquiry and investigation to match the compound realities occurring in a violent conflict.

As we shall see, Graham Allison's classic text *Essence of Decision* provides a prototypical case study of such a multiplex approach in conflict analysis. In this book, Allison uses three sequential conceptual frames of reference to analyze the 1962 Cuban missile crisis. By doing so, he demonstrates the methodological power of using multiple modeling to analyze a specific conflict in order to achieve a richer and more complete understanding of a unique event. In the following pages, Allison's path-breaking case study and methodological innovations will be developed one step further; specifically, the concept of a multiplex methodology will be introduced that incorporates a causal matrix consisting of multiple frames of reference using revelatory[4] and contingent[5] causality in order to discover new knowledge concerning a complex phenomenon such as human conflict. In particular, this essay will argue that multiplex methodology provides a preliminary means of insuring the construct validity of the *causes* as well as *effects*.[6] The essay will end by making an argument for using case studies as a preliminary, necessary but not sufficient method of understanding each unique, violent and complex human conflict.

BACKGROUND COMPLEXITY, CAUSALITY, AND VIOLENT CONFLICT

Violent human conflict is one of the most, if not the most, complex social phenomenon that human beings experience. In violent human conflict, especially those involving ethnic groups or entire nations, participants often have deep convictions that frequently have bloody consequences in organized action[7] concerning contested geographies, historical narratives, moral grievances, religious values, or sometimes even competing cosmologies and gods.[8] Such complex social organizations in collision create significant dilemmas for any researcher attempting to understand their full scope and significance. Linear thought, or what Max Weber describes as "operational rationality," with its emphasis on single-sourced cause and effect, simply doesn't reflect and can't capture the complex realities, epistemic pluralism, and contested causes of violent human conflict. From this perspective, to "single source" the cause of a deadly human conflict and attribute it solely to "interests," "needs," or "identity" is almost always oversimplified. To investigate deadly disputes using a single type or disciplinary system of methodology usually results in a reductionist and incomplete understanding of a complex phenomenon such as human conflict.

This does not mean that the pursuit of understanding into violent social conflicts is eclectic or improvised. On the contrary, this is an extremely complex phenomenon that we are trying to understand and no single method, no single approach can claim to have a monopoly on the truth, especially when the "truths" of the conflict are in such deadly competition. We will need multiple methods and multiple schools of thought even to begin the process of understanding and explaining violent conflict accurately.

In fact, Gandhi was among the first to note the existence of these contested truths in human conflict. During his illustrious career, he described his method of nonviolently campaigning against British colonialism as *satyagraha*—which literally means truth force—which required that the other sides' contested narratives be incorporated as well into a new "Gandhian synthesis" that reveals the truths for both sides of the conflict, a process that Joan Bondurant describes as the "Gandhian dialectic."[9] This reality is one of the reasons Gandhi's autobiography is entitled *Experiments with Truth*. He recognized that contested truths are often embedded in the very fabric of human struggle. Gandhi refused to take comfort in reducing the complexity of conflict to one main "cause" or "truth."

So, the first prerequisite of "true" knowledge claims is that they should accurately reflect in their origins the complexity of the actual phenomena that they purport to describe, understand or explain.[10] This is why the investigation of conflict necessarily involves, at first, the use of compound or multiple steps of inquiry in progressive sequence emphasizing different types of causality. In particular, using such causal constructs requires true *interdisciplinary studies and inquiry*, a branch of knowledge largely lost, in my judgment, since the ancient Greeks and Aristotle.

INTERDISCIPLINARY INQUIRY: A MISSING LINK

Interdisciplinary is the preliminary and often missing first stage of inquiry between philosophy, pure theory or "speculative reasoning"[11] and the subsequent, specific domain disciplines of the social sciences. Interdisciplinary inquiry seeks to *understand* a unique phenomenon in its embedded existence while subsequent disciplinary methods seek to explain a phenomenon in terms of the prevailing episteme of "identify and difference."[12] In particular, violent human conflict is always embedded in a unique and often local place and historical time.

Uniqueness is often lost in the frenzied rush among scholars to generalize and create theory, often out of very thin gruel; yet we should not sacrifice the uniqueness of time, place, person, or conflict so glibly. In short, uniqueness and generalization require different modes of rationality and inquiry. So, in the following essay, "understanding" will refer to the knowledge that results from studying a unique phenomenon, while "explanation" will refer to the knowledge claims made in attempting to generalize into a more comprehensive theory. In my judgment, the true test of rationality—based on the Latin word "ratio," meaning "reckoning" or "calculation"—is to decide what ratio or combination of uniqueness and generality "fits" or belongs in the analysis of any unique phenomenon. Such rationality is the "ultima ratio" of interdisciplinary inquiry.[13]

In our current study, the explicit assumption is that such interdisciplinary inquiry is necessary in order to capture accurately the *uniqueness* of a complex phenomenon such as violent human conflict in its original ontological site, or "local realism" (a term borrowed from quantum mechanics). Such uniqueness can't be uncritically and quickly reduced to often overgeneralized and theoretical assumptions concerning place and a unique historical moment existing as Cartesian coordinates in a presumed universal time and space continuum; making such generalizations is pure theoretical fiction, especially if the premises of such theoretical generalization have not been specifically confirmed or falsified in subsequent research. In short, interdisciplinary inquiry is a way to capture and understand *uniqueness*; only when the phenomenon is understood as it actually exists can attempts to generalize from it be made.

Such an interdisciplinary methodological approach is necessary to correct the most egregious omissions of current theories or research on human conflict. First and foremost is that theories about violent human conflict suffer from what Cook and Campbell describe as "construct under representation" which they define as "the operations failing to incorporate *all the dimensions* of the construct."[14] They see this as a serious threat to construct validity in general. In the following essay, I will attempt to address this threat to construct validity in the field of conflict analysis by developing interdisciplinary causal constructs of violent social conflict.

A vivid example of construct under-representation in the field of conflict analysis is the almost predictable lack of maps and geographical analysis in any publication dealing with violent human conflict, as though human conflicts happen in a topographical void. Fighting for contested geography is often the lifeblood of armies and insurgencies, yet is barely mentioned in the growing literature in conflict analysis. Military establishments throughout the world spend an inordinate amount of time preparing and reading maps in specific conflicts or wars while theoreticians of the same conflicts rarely, if ever, use maps in their analysis; this omission only highlights the poverty of current causal constructs in the field. Notable exceptions to this are the book *Contested Lands* by Professor Bose[15] and the parallel development in the field of geography of "contested geographies" as a developing field of sub-specialization.[16]

An added danger to the validity of research, besides the construct under representation, is that the construct validity of effects is often overgeneralized. Disembodied theory building is often given the pride of place in the production of new "knowledge" in conflicts. Hence, the unique people, place and historical moment of each violent conflict are largely lost and replaced by the overgeneralized construct validity of one or two effects such as identity formation or interest based outcomes that may be prevalent across many different, though certainly not all, mortal conflicts.

Finally, to make matters more complex, any single cause of the competing knowledge claims that originate from highly contested epistemic encounters between knowing subjects, such as claims to contested geography, can constantly *interact* with other causes and thus intensify the conflict's complexity. So, at first glance, the compound realities of lethal contests almost defy traditional definition and description; scholars have and will inevitably contest the sources, substance and significance of such conflicts almost as hotly as the combatants themselves. To decipher this complexity, the scholar as researcher and experimenter needs to combine different, compound, and parallel methods of interdisciplinary inquiry in order to understand the complex causalities and compound realities of violent human conflict. Thus, the immediate task is to reveal or disclose the full complexity of a unique phenomenon, such as violent social conflict through interdisciplinary research. This exploration is what the multiplex methodology seeks to accomplish. Simply stated, it provides a way to study an embedded and unique phenomenon while also providing a method for careful, calculated generalization, after all the causal constructs have been identified.

As we shall see in the next section, multiplex methodology uses a dual system, or causal matrix, consisting of revelatory and contingent causation in investigating conflicts. An accurate interdisciplinary understanding of dual nature of causation in insuring the construct validity of causes in violent human conflicts is a necessary, but not sufficient condition for their eventual understanding. When combined, each of these causal systems provide a *point d'appuie*, or departure point, for entering and deciphering the hermeneutical circles (like the descending circles of Dante's *Inferno*) that surround and suffuse violent conflicts between human beings.

MULTIPLEX METHODOLOGIES: A NEO-ARISTOTELIAN FRAMEWORK FOR CONFLICT ANALYSIS

A multiplex methodology is not so much a single "method" to collect data; instead, it is a compound, contingent and sequential structure of inquiry in case studies that utilizes parallel and multiple processes of data collection, using a variety of disciplinary methodologies to insure the "construct validity of causes" that incorporate all dimensions of the conflict. A multiplex methodology first seeks to provide *revelatory structures of inquiry into the conflict* consisting of rival hypotheses that involve contingent causal constructs and their interrelationships identified in a tentative causal constellation. Such contingent constellated causal structures[17] disclose possible relationships that can then be tested and corroborated in the conflict's unique ontological site using process tracing[18] and subsequent disciplinary methods of data collection, confirmation[19] or falsification.[20] Only once such a contingent process of revelation and subsequent confirmation or falsification of constellated causal representation is conducted can the radical uniqueness of a phenomenon be left behind and more general theories of a phenomenon or conflict be constructed, or implied. In this way, for instance, the epistemic pluralism found in almost all violent human conflicts can be identified or revealed and investigated.

To accomplish this discovery, the Aristotelian famous fourfold causal structure can be employed as the basic structure of multiplex methodology. "Cause" here will be used in its original Greek meaning—naming to "reveal or disclose" that which is. Specifically, the ancient Greek word *aitia*, which Aristotle uses in both his *Physics* and *Metaphysics*[21] to describe his fourfold causal structure, always meant to "reveal" or to "disclose." For Aristotle, this fourfold causal framework concerning the material, efficient, formal, and final "causes" of a specific phenomenon was a *revelatory structure of inquiry*.

Hence, the first use of "cause" in a multiplex methodology requires the researcher to reveal or disclose, if possible, the full range of contested truths concerning geography, ecology, history epistemology, needs, interests, and goals found in a violent human conflict. This process should be done *in parallel* for both or all groups involved in a deadly dispute by going to the participants themselves, rather than relying on "experts" or theory. After the construct validity of causes is assured, then the process of careful generalization from the particular can begin, if necessary, by using contingent causality consisting of confirmation and falsification techniques of verification.[22]

In view of this, I believe that a violent human contest can best be studied in a preliminary way by Aristotle's sequential fourfold causal structure consisting of the following interrelated concepts that are looking for contested truths in the following areas: (1) *The Material Cause*, which consists of the inevitable ecological and geographical embeddedness of the conflict; the purpose of this "cause" is to reveal or disclose the unique ecologies, contested geographies (localities), competing or contested maps and actual typologies (human perception of these localities) often involved in violent human conflict. Elsewhere, I describe the material cause as the ontological site unique in time and place that inevitably characterizes human life.[23] (2) *The Efficient Cause or Human Agency*, consisting of competing or contested human behavior, needs, emotions or agencies engaged in a violent human conflict; this cause also includes the contested histories of previous encounters where actual confrontations, attacks and battles occurred that often characterize the groups in actual conflict. Emotional analyses of violent human conflicts are one of those often missing causal constructs, yet obviously deeply felt hurt or anger can contribute significantly to a human conflict, so this factor is included here for possible investigation. (3) *The Epistemic Cause*, as the "formal cause" which Aristotle defines as the "ways in which we describe" the resulting structure. Following his lead, the formal cause can be characterized as how those who make knowledge claims *describe and justify* their verbal assertions. Hence, it will be described here as the epistemic cause or causes including the competing knowledge claims, contested histories, competing and socially defined identities, discourses and narratives by all the epistemic communities[24] involved in violent human conflict used to explain and justify their actions including, among other things, dehumanizing and legitimating the killing of another human being (Camus). (4) *The Final Cause* or goals of the participants in a lethal struggle can either be a win/lose Nietzschean "Will to Power" *or*, using the appropriate conflict resolution methods of intervention and transformation, the win/win "Will to Empower" benefitting potentially all the participants in a violent human conflict. This resolution is where third party intervention and efforts at conflict resolution can play the greatest role, especially by providing reframing or alternative frameworks of understanding to the participants themselves or seeking the common ground, if any, within the contested narratives of the competing groups. Ideally, each of these sequential "causes" of conflict must be confirmed or falsified for each unique conflict before subsequent theoretical generalization can proceed.

THE FIRST CAUSE: THE MATERIAL PRECONDITIONS OF LIFE

The specific *sequence* of these "causes" is deliberate and demonstrates the interdisciplinary nature of the subsequent inquiry. In particular, it is significant that Aristotle posts the efficient cause *second* in the sequence of his fourfold causal structure. For Aristotle, positing human agency *first* as the "efficient cause"—free from material conditions or constraints—would have been literally heresy, and considered an act of hubris in the classical Greek world in which he lived. For Aristotle, human life was always found and embedded in an ecological or *material* foundation. (Unfortunately, even reference to Aristotle's *Physics* is an impoverished translation of his original intent in this regard; the original title of his lectures was in Greek: "Φυσικῆς ἀκροάσεως" or *phusikes akroaseos*, meaning "Lectures on Nature.") In short, for Aristotle, human life is never found in abstraction from its material or "natural" preconditions for its biological existence; unlike the conception of human agency found in many modern social sciences such as economics,[25] human life was always inexplicably embedded in the natural world for Aristotle and the ancient Greeks. So, in Aristotle fourfold causal structure, revealing nature can be truly and accurately portrayed as the "first cause."

For instance, in Greek, *ikos* means "home." Thus, the original meaning of the word "ecology" in Greek literally means the study of one's true home. So in today's world, the basic level of neo-Aristotelian analysis in such an inevitably embedded existence is now the earth as a whole including its ecology upon which all human life exists and depends.

Unfortunately, the modern social sciences have apparently forgotten this key Aristotelian insight in their various definitions of human agency, which often contain no reference at all to our material or biological conditions as the "first cause" of existence.[26] For instance, according to economic theory, the human agent exists from the neck up and is often viewed as being solely concerned with maximizing his or her utilities or interests.[27] This single-mindedness is described as "rational" behavior, as though human life exists in a biological void. So, it is possible in today's university to educate economists who have little or no understanding of the earth's ecology or of the profound interrelationships between the environment and economic activity.

Furthermore, this basic definition of rational human behavior does not explain, within its own terms, the motivation or behavior of the millions of police, firemen, soldiers or even teachers throughout the world who work for something other than monetary reward. The environmental impact of economic decisions is rarely if ever studied or anticipated, as the BP oil spill in the Gulf in 2010 vividly illustrates. In fact, the earth's ecology is rarely listed in the index of most college or MBA text books, even though economic decisions are having a decisive and deleterious impact on the earth's ecology. In other words, Aristotle's *first cause* is largely looked over or even totally ignored by the so-called "rational" agents of economic theory, which have profound consequences for people's actual choices and human ecology in the modern world. This behavior is theoretical fiddle playing while the world burns. Thus we need to return to the wisdom of the ancient Greeks and to Aristotle, for whom human life was always embedded in a material and ecological foundation which is appropriately paced here as the first cause.

Finally, scholars such as Clifford Geetz or Anthony Giddens have critically noted that the modern social sciences, especially in the Anglo-American world, often implicitly assume the preeminent ascendancy of methodological individualism, often apparently free from any material and even social conditioning or constraints.[28] This methodological individualism has explicitly or implicitly become the dominant paradigm in grading, graduate schools, pedagogy and purposes of the modern disciplinary domains throughout the modern world, especially in the field of economics. We will not make the same mistake here.

This commitment does not meant that the researcher must slavishly follow his sequential causal constructs in investigating a specific and unique phenomenon; each researcher can posit different (though obviously related) causal constructs within each level of the fourfold structure. For instance, if we add Marxist materialism to the first level of analysis, the first cause can also reflect the various group's economies and economic interests in conflicts that inevitably interact with the material and biological basis of life. As we shall see, such causal constructs contained within this fourfold causal construct ultimately depend on the explicit choices of the researcher.

In his original and classic work *Essence of Decision*, Graham Allison offers a three-fold modeling of the Cuban missile crisis, which illustrates the potential versatility of scholars in choosing relevant frames of reference to investigate a conflict or crisis.[29] By using these separate frames of reference, Allison revealed very different processes of decision-making and the resultant policies that impacted upon the most dangerous nuclear crisis that the world has witnessed to date. In short, there is a certain latitude in choosing the various constellated causal constructs at each step as long as the choices are made explicit and justified by the circumstances of each unique conflict. Such flexibility in the construct of the methodology reflects the need for intensely focused interdisciplinary inquiry.

There should always be a first cause consisting of life's material and ecological preconditions. But other frameworks of analysis can be added here or to subsequent causal factors. For instance, in his essay on the *Question of Technology*, Heidegger posits the efficient cause as human agency *last* in his reconstruction of Aristotle's fourfold sequence of causes.[30] This potential for reformulation, addition and even rearrangement of the subsequent causal structures provides potentially greater revelatory power in any subsequent analysis. This restructuring is also why this fourfold causal structure is referred to as neo-Aristotelian, since it may usually involve a refinement, reinterpretation or elaboration of Aristotle's original fourfold structure. As the works of Haywood Alker and others attest, there has been a resurgence in neo-Aristotelian analysis in the social sciences in recent years.[31] As we shall see, such a preliminary neo-Aristotelian analysis is best done in a preliminary way by a case by using *case studies* to understand violent human conflict. We will come back to this critical point shortly.

THE EFFICIENT CAUSE AS HUMAN AGENCY

An assumption of multiplex methodology is that, in its actual existence, human life or agency is pre-theoretical and ontological; that, in its most basic form, human agency is already immersed, involved and "thrown" into the world; in short, human existence as "Being in the world"[32] is used here to describe this pre-theoretical and pristine.[33] The further presumption in this neo-Aristotelian framework is that human agency and especially contested human agencies are always situated in such a unique ontological site that can't be universalized, spatialized or temporalized into general theory about human behavior, unless the precise embeddedness of a particular conflict is specifically confirmed or falsified in subsequent research. In short, human agents, especially in violent conflicts, aren't theoretically interchangeable. When the killing begins, there is rarely, if ever, at first a "universal knower," enjoying full information, who can comprehensively scan the resulting carnage from the Mt. Olympus of scientific objectivity; this subjectivity is also true for the participants who are usually deeply engaged in their unique conflict. For instance, an Irishman may kill or die for a united Ireland, but might care less about Israel or India. An Israeli might kill or die for a greater Israel, but might care less about a united Ireland or India. An Indian soldier may kill or die in the Kashmir for a greater India, but may care less about a united Ireland, or for Israel. The point is that specific material conditions often "cause" or reveal specific subsequent human behavior or agency. Of course, we can abstract from each of the conflicts in Ireland, Israel or India and make wonderful Platonic generalizations about the "ideal" of human conflict in more abstract theory. Yet such rarified theory comes at the cost of the unique knowledge and understanding to be gained by looking at the specific geographies, contested typologies, cultures and epistemologies involved in violent human conflict. Such knowledge acquisition of the "ontological site" and local realism is one of the primary purposes of interdisciplinary inquiry. It should not be lost lightly in the rush to make theoretical generalizations about human conflicts.

THE THIRD CAUSE: "WHAT THE THING IS DEFINED AS BEING ESSENTIALLY"

The origins of Aristotle's third cause, the formal cause, need further clarification within the context of an interdisciplinary causal structure revealing and examining violent human conflict. Aristotle's understanding of the "formal" cause is partially in reaction to his teacher Plato, who believed that true knowledge consisted in the *recollection* of the ideal forms. Yet Aristotle—his most gifted pupil at the Academy—was not so sure; in particular, Aristotle was uncomfortable with Plato's notion of the transcendent "Ideal." Rather than look for *aitia* of a form in transcendence, Aristotle looked for a phenomenon's form in nature, which is consistent with his overall metaphysical view of a world in becoming, developing from a potentiality to the actual, like the famous Aristotelian acorn, driven by the phenomenon's unique telos, or purpose, as its becomes a "final" cause—in this case, the oak tree.

So, rather than describe a phenomenon's "ideal" cause, as Plato might, as in a revealing or disclosure of a phenomenon's form, Aristotle describes the "formal" cause, which is often roughly translated as the phenomenon's "essence"; but a more accurate understanding is, as he describes it, "the *form or characteristics* of the type, conformity to which brings it within the definition of the thing we say it is, whether specifically or generically."[34] In another translation of this passage Philip Wheelwright substitutes the word "pattern" for the word "characteristics," noting that the original word is *paradeigma*, "i.e. what the thing is defined as being essentially."[35] Thus, for Aristotle, there are two key characteristics of the formal cause: "the *definition* of the thing we say it is" and its *pattern* which is also often described as its "essence." The former aspect of language as the *revelatory power* is often overlooked in Aristotelian studies, yet it is critical to the act of "revealing or disclosing" the pattern or essence which, for Aristotle, is true knowledge.

In short, how we define the pattern or essence in nature is true knowledge, and consists, as Heidegger states in his essay on *The Question of Technology*, of a bringing forth or a revealing.[36] This latter neo-Aristotelian definition of the third cause as epistemic is, one should note, more consistent with the Aristotelian meaning of "cause" as *aitia*. This understanding gives birth to Aristotle's classical concept of causation as a revelation of the complex configuration of causal relationships that characterize any unique phenomenon, not as a Platonic *recollection of the Ideal.*

Given this, the "form" or "characteristics" found or revealed in human conflict is often the persistent pattern of "unity within differences"; this is because, as Coser and Simmel state, "people unite to fight!"[37] Following Foucault's lead, this "unity within differences" could be described as the basic *episteme* of conflict.[38] This basic episteme is also found, I believe, in complexity theory and with fractals in chaos theory (the latter subject studied by Lewis Fry Richardson, who also pioneered the mathematical analysis of arms races and fractals, but this is the subject of another essay). Suffice it to say here that this basic pattern or episteme of complexity, chaos (fractals), and conflict theory is a significant "embedded" rival that could possibly replace the prevailing episteme (defined here as a basic revelatory structure), according to Foucault, of "identity and difference" that characterizes the modern age up to now.

In turn, such a pattern or *paradeigma* found in conflict fundamentally results from the *epistemic encounter*, which can be defined as the basic social encounter or engagement between two or more human beings who are simultaneously active hermeneutical agents that are continually interpreting and reinterpreting, not only their surrounding material contest, but also each other in a constant process of social construction, cooperation, competition and conflict.[39] Whether it's across the boardroom or across the battlefield, people confront each as knowing, interpretive beings. When found in peacetime, such an epistemic encounter is often a variation of the "I-Thou" encounter so cogently and potently characterized by Martin Buber in his philosophical works.[40] For Buber, the "I-Thou" encounter represents the human encounter (of each other) in its greatest potential and promise.

As Buber notes, these "I-Thou" or epistemic encounters are factually distinct from encounters with oneself or one's self-consciousness, such as a Cartesian encounter consisting of *Cogito Ergo Sum*. Furthermore, the form or characteristic of this "cause" is qualitatively different than a human subject's encounter with an object—even though each participant in a deadly human conflict may wish to objectify and dehumanize the other as a "thing" or an "I-It."[41]

When contested, these encounters often result in very different interpretations, narratives and "explanations" of the same unique event. This difference gives rise to the resulting *epistemic pluralism*, mentioned above, that challenges the Enlightenment idea that the same or similar people with similar backgrounds or beliefs will view the same event in the same or similar way.

In a violent human conflict, due to the resulting epistemic pluralism, the Enlightenment idea of a universal knower rarely, if ever exists, especially at first. In fact, the results are often the reverse; the contested assertions and descriptions of such epistemic encounters and the resulting epistemic pluralism in violent conflicts often create "rhetorical" or even "Rorschach" realities that might tell us more what the participants want to see, or believe themselves, concerning volatile and traumatic events. They also may be trying to convince the world of the righteousness of their actions rather than impartially describing the "pure facts" on the ground, if such can be found. Instead, all too often, the participants' interpretation of contested events proves to be partial, perspectival[42] and prejudiced[43] in a violent human conflict.[44]

As an epistemic cause of the conflict, the researcher should first simply record and compare these contrasting assertions and narratives among the participants of the conflict, as well as possibly match them against the efficient cause to see if there is a consistency between talk, thought and action. The simple "fact" is that epistemic pluralism exists, consisting of often profoundly different narratives and accounts of the same or sequential encounters in a violent human conflict. Researchers should record this fact, if it is actually found to exist. Later, in the next section, we will see how such research may be useful in looking for common ground among the competing narratives and thus help move the contending parties in a conflict from a zero sum to a positive sum outcome.

So, as used here, the epistemic cause reveals how the participants describe their own involvement in the conflict, the conflict itself and the other side's possible dehumanization as the conflict proceeds. Thus the epistemic cause reveals the progressively wider hermeneutical circles of attributed causalities, contested histories, as well as competing narratives and justifications of a unique conflict. Such an analysis of the epistemic causation of human conflict is necessary, though not sufficient, to develop and define multiplex causal constructs that presents a robust and accurate representation of each unique conflict.

THE FINAL CAUSE: THE WILL TO POWER VERSUS A WILL TO EMPOWER

Most violent human conflicts, especially in their escalatory or protracted periods, are characterized by a "will to power" in that each side wants to win. Yet, as the continuing costs of the conflict become more fully apparent, there is often a rethinking by one, both or all parties to the conflict concerning how to settle or even resolve the bloody contest in which they are engaged. If the goal is "unconditional surrender," then the end result can only be the physical destruction of the opposing side's government and often a large proportion of its population and homeland. So, not surprisingly, the outcome for many violent conflicts, considering the extraordinary costs of "total victory," is often conditional and incomplete. This reality requires that each side begin to think about what the other side wants, as the conflict reaches an apparent stalemate.[45]

At this point, national diplomats and those trained in conflict resolution can have their greatest impact.[46] Diplomats and other nongovernmental or track II specialists[47] can help each side reformulate their positions and desired goals to find some common ground or include some of the needs and goals of the other side.[48] At this point, both or all sides are, in effect, trying to empower both themselves and the enemy other in order to live peacefully together in the future. This juncture is the critical transition point of the conflict from a zero/sum or "win/lose," to a positive sum or "win/win."[49] There are a variety of mechanisms that can help at this point, including third party intervention,[50] peace initiatives,[51] facilitated workshops,[52] and mediation.[53] A multiplex analysis of such a conflict should be able to identity the possible "salient points,"[54] common ground, or even transformational forces[55] that already may exist in the conflict's competing narratives and goals so that all sides can come together, settle, manage, or resolve their differences and let their children grow up in peace.

PARALLEL PROCESSES OF INQUIRY

To be accurate, a multiplex investigation into human conflict must strive to represent accurately the contest truths of both or all sides to the deadly dispute. This representation requires, first and foremost, going to the participants themselves for understanding of a unique conflict. It also requires, as an integral part of a multiplex methodology, that *parallel processes* of inquiries into the construct validity of causes be conducted in both or all epistemic communities engaged in violent conflict. The idea of simply interviewing an "expert" on the topic may be acceptable in journalism, but is simply not adequate in any scholarly analysis of conflict, or, for that matter, any other subject involving contested truths. There needs to be parallel inquiries in all of the affected and involved groups in order to represent accurately the exact issues and contest truths that divide the warring sides, in short, by going directly, if possible, to the participants themselves in parallel investigations of contested truths. As Professor Brian Polkinghorn[56] always admonishes concerning methodological issues, "Let the data do the talking!" This work can be done by creating parallel structures of inquiry as a basic standard of validity (not to mention integrity) in preliminary research. In this way, multiplex methodology seeks to create epistemic structures that enable, if not require, the researcher to reveal and disclose the sources as well as the significance of contested truths among the participants themselves.

These constellated causal constructs have to be developed *in parallel* for both or all sides to the conflict and include their possible interrelationships. This process requires, if applicable, conflict mapping[57] that begins with the actual contested geographies of the conflict's ontological site and the resulting epistemic pluralism.[58] The end result of this stage of multiplex methodology is a representational map or "conceptual constellation"[59] of the parallel contingent causalities and their complex configuration of interrelationships that reflects as accurately as possible the actual and unique violent conflict.

Such parallel and almost inevitably contested causal constructs is why this methodology is called multiplex. The original meaning of the word "multiplex" is to send out simultaneous, multiple messages often traveling in opposite directions on the same wire. The word has more modern connotations of manifold viewings, as in a multiplex cinema with multiple theaters. The multiplex methodology presented here incorporates all of these antecedent meanings in its effort to reveal manifold, parallel and often contradictory causal constructs concerning the same phenomenon. This result can best be achieved, in the first instance, in a case study.

CASE STUDIES: CAPTURING THE LIVING FIRE OF CONFLICTS

As Robert Yin states, a case study is most appropriate when the researcher "wants to cover contextual conditions—believing that they might be highly pertinent to [the] phenomenon of study,"[60] As argued above, human agency is inevitably embedded in "contextual conditions" within the ontological site, the location and often the source of human conflict. To understand these conflicts in their local realism, the case study is, in the first instance, the preferred methodology of research.

As we have seen, human conflict is, in its first instance, a uniquely local phenomenon, both in time and space. Furthermore, as argued above, the ontological site is in such conflicts often an extremely complex and contested location consisting of competing geographies, narratives, interests, identities and gods. Yin's argument for a case study seems to anticipate this complexity of human conflict:

> "The case study inquiry copes with the technically distinctive situation in which there will be many more variables of interest than data points, and as one result relies on multiple sources of evidence with data needing to converge in a triangulating fashion, and as another result benefits from the prior development of theoretical propositions to guide data collection and analysis."[61]

Yin is speaking to the central strength of a case study, namely its ability to capture a unique and embedded phenomenon in the inherent complexity of its ontological site.[62] First, he cites the need for multiple sources of evidence, a feature described above as multiplex modeling and methodologies, to best understand and differentiate the data between the parties engaged in a unique conflict.[63]

In view of this, when dealing with lethal contests between human beings, a good case study should include, consistent with a neo-Aristotelian fourfold causal framework, evidence of (a) a dual (parallel) or multiple identification of the competing geographies and contested lands;[64] (b) contested human agencies consisting of the historical and current actual or ontological sites where confrontations, conflict, battles and war occurred; (c) epistemic pluralism consisting of contested historical and cultural narratives[65] concerning selective suffering or grievances[66] as well as competing causes of the conflict; (d) evidence of contested outcomes, goals and the ultimate objectives of the contesting agents. This disparity results in dual (parallel) or multiple possible explanations of the conflict. Yin emphasizes the point that research can be guided in a preliminary stage by "theoretical propositions" or what Campbell describes in the foreword of Yin's book as "plausible rival hypotheses." In his foreword to Yin's book, Prof. Campbell identifies such "plausible rival hypotheses" as the very essence of science. In the context of the multiplex methodology, such "plausible rival hypotheses" are the essence, or end result, of a good case study.

Robert Yin elaborates upon the appropriateness of the case study, defining it in the following terms: "A case study is an empirical inquiry that investigates a contemporary phenomenon within its real-life context, especially when the boundaries between phenomenon and context are not clearly evident."[67] Perhaps the most famous example, which Yin cites, concerning the use of a case study to analyze contesting human agencies is Graham Allison's *Essence of Decision*, in which he uses three differing paradigms or models to analyze the Cuban missile crisis.[68]

Prof. Allison used three sequential frameworks of analysis to investigate the same data and event—namely, the Cuban missile crisis of 1962 in which the United States and the Soviet Union came to the brink of nuclear war. These three subsequent frameworks consisted of the rational actor, organizational and bureaucratic models of analysis. Allison was able to demonstrate, using these three sequential models, very different insights, explanations and outcomes concerning U.S. government policy choices actually made during this dangerous confrontation. In short, his use of the three frameworks tremendously enriched our understanding of this critical, and nearly disastrous, event. Armed with such information, we are hopefully better prepared to prevent such a dangerous confrontation spinning out of control in the future.

Though Prof. Allison obviously did not specifically use a neo-Aristotelian framework, nor did he conduct a similar investigation of the Soviet side (especially since the secrecy of that regime did not make such an investigation possible), his use of the three sequential frameworks demonstrates the *power of such multiple modeling* of the same event to reveal more fully the complexity of the choices made and their actual or potential consequences or outcomes in the most dangerous nuclear crisis so far in human history.

CONCLUSION

Elaborating upon the idea of multiple modeling found in Allison's *Essence of Decision*, I have described in this essay the need to develop competing and complimentary causal constructs in an interdisciplinary causal structure or constellation, described here as multiplex methodology, in an attempt to fully disclose and reveal more fully in the future a phenomenon as complicated as violent human conflict. All violent human conflicts end eventually, though often at much greater costs to all the participants. It is hoped that the better and more accurate understanding of such conflicts provide a first step in helping to resolving them, even after the killing begins.

BIBLIOGRAPHY

Abbott, A. *Chaos of Disciplines*. Chicago: University of Chicago Press, 2001.

Abu-Nimer, M. *Reconciliation, Justice and Coexistence: Theory and Practice*. Lanham, MD: Lexington Books, 2001.

Ahern, L. "Language and Agency." *Annual Review of Anthropology*, vol. 30 (2001): 109–137.

Alker, Haywood. *Rediscoveries and Reformulations: Humanistic Methodologies for International Studies*. Cambridge: Cambridge University Press, 1996.

Allison, G.T. *Essence of Decision: Explaining the Cuban Missile Crisis*, 1st ed. Boston: Little, Brown, 1971.

Allison, G.T., and P. Zelikow. *Essence of Decision: Explaining the Cuban Missile Crisis*, 2nd ed. Boston: Little, Brown, 1999.

Aristotle. *The Basic Works of Aristotle*, edited by Richard McKeon. New York: Random House, 1941.

Atkins, P. "Interdisciplinarity and Positionality." *Interdisciplinary Science Review* vol. 29, no. 1 (March 2004): 2–5.

Azar, E. *The Management of Protracted Social Conflict: Theory and Cases*. Aldershot: Dartmouth, 1990.

Bacon, F. *Novum Organum*. Peru, IL: Open Court Publishing, 1994.

Bandura, Albert. "Award Address at the APS Annual Convention, 2004," at www .psychologicalscince.org/observer/getArticle

Bartos, O., and P. Wehr. *Using Conflict Theory*. Cambridge: Cambridge University Press, 2002.

Bercovitch, J., ed. *Resolving International Conflicts*. Boulder, CO: Lynn Rienner, 1996.

Bondurant, Joan, and Margaret W. Fisher, eds. *Conflict: Violence and Non-violence*. New York: Lieber-Atherton, 1971.

Bose, S. *Contested Lands*. Cambridge, MA: Harvard University Press, 2007.

Boudreau, T. "Intergroup Reduction Through Identity Affirmation: Overcoming the Image of the Ethnic or Enemy Other." *Peace and Conflict Studies,* vol. 10, no. 1 (Spring 2003): 87–107.

———. *Sheathing the Sword: The Preventive Role of the United Nations Secretary-General.* Westport, CT: Greenwood Press, 1991.

———. *Universitas*. Westport, CT: Praeger Press, 1998.

Brand, M. *The Nature of Causation*. Urbana: University of Illinois Press, 1976.

Buber, Martin. *I-Thou*. New York: Free Press, 1971.

Burton, J. *Conflict: Resolution and Prevention Theory*. London: MacMillian, 1990.

Byrne, Sean, and Cynthia Irvin, eds. *Reconcilable Differences: Turning Points in Ethnopolitical Conflict.* West Hartford, CT: Kumarian Press, 2000.

Byrne, Sean, and N. Carter. "Social Cubism: Six Social Forces of Ethnoterritorial Politics in Northern Ireland and Quebec." *Peace and Conflict Studies*, vol. 3, no. 2 (1996): 52–72.

Campbell, D.T. "Reforms as Experiments." *American Psychologist*, vol. 24, no. 6 (1969): 402–429.

Campbell, D.T., and D.W. Fiske. "Convergent and Discriminate Validation by the Multitrait-multimethod Matrix." *Psychological Bulletin*, vol. 56 (1959): 81–105.

Camus, A. *Neither Victims Nor Executioners*. Chicago: World Without War Publications, 1972.

Cheldelin, S., D. Druckman, and L. Fast, eds. *Conflict: From Analysis to Intervention.* New York: Continuum, 2003.

Christie, Dan, Richard Wagner, and Deborah Winter, eds. *Peace, Conflict and Violence: Peace Psychology for the 21st Century*. Upper Saddle River, NJ: Prentice Hall, 2001.

Cook, T.D., and D.T. Campbell. *Quasi-Experimentation: Design & Analysis for Field Settings*. Boston: Houghton Mifflin Company, 1979.

Coser, L. *The Functions of Social Conflict*. Glencoe, NY: Free Press, 1956.
Deutsch, Morton, and Peter T. Coleman, eds. *The Handbook of Conflict Resolution: Theory and Practice*. San Francisco: Jossey-Bass, 2000.
Diamond, L., and A.J. McDonald, eds. *Multi-track Diplomacy: A System Approach to Peace*. West Hartford, CT: Kumarian Press, 1996.
Druckman, D. *Doing Research: Methods of Inquiry for Conflict Analysis*. Thousand Oaks, CA: Sage Publications, 2005.
Durkheim, E. *The Division of Labor in Society*. New York: Free Press, 1964.
Durkheim, E., and A. Giddens. *Emile Durkheim: Selected Writings*. Cambridge: Cambridge University Press, 1972.
Ferris, D.S. "Post-modern Interdisciplinarity: Kant, Diderot and the Encyclopedic Project." Project Muse, The John Hopkins University Press. *MLN*, vol. 118, no. 5 (2003): 1251–1277.
Friedman, M. *Essays in Political Economy*. Chicago: University of Chicago Press, 1966.
Fisher, R.J. *Interactive Conflict Resolution: Pioneers, Potential and Prospects*. Syracuse, NY: Syracuse University Press, 1996.
Foucault, M.I. *Power/Knowledge: Selected Interviews and Other Writings 1972–1977*. New York: Pantheon Books, 1980.
———. *The Archeology of Knowledge*. New York: Vintage, 1982.
Gadamer, H.G. *Truth and Method*. New York: Continuum, 2004.
Galtung, Johan. *Peace By Peaceful Means: Peace and Conflict Development and Civilization*. London: Sage, 1996.
———. *There Are Alternatives! Four Roads to Peace and Security*. Nottingham: Spokesman, 1984.
George, A.L., and T.J. McKeown. "Case Studies and Theories of Organizational Decision Making," in *Advances in Information Processing in Organizations*, A.L. George, ed. Greenwich, CT: JAI Press, 1985, 21–58.
Giddens, A. *The Constitution of Society: Outline of the Theory of Structuration*. Berkeley: University of California Press, 1984.
Heidegger, M. *Being and Time*. New York: Harper & Row, 1962.
———. *Being and Time*. Albany: State University of New York Press, 1996.
———. *The Question of Technology and Other Essays*. New York: Harper Torchbooks, 1977.
Homer-Dixon, T.F. *Environment, Scarcity and Violence*. Princeton, NJ: Princeton University Press, 2001.
———. *Strategies for Studying Causation in Complex Ecological Systems*. Toronto: University College Press, 1995.
Homer-Dixon, T.F., and J. Blitt, eds. *EcoViolence: Links Among Environment, Population and Security*. Boulder, CO: Rowman & Littlefield Publishers, 1998.
Hume, D. *Essay on Human Understanding*. Indianapolis, IN: The Library of Liberal Arts, 1955.
Kelman, Herbert. "Group Processes in the Resolution of International Conflicts: Experiences From the Israeli-Palestinian Case." *The American Psychologist*, vol. 52, no. 3 (1997): 212–220.

———. "Negotiating National Identity and Self-Determination in Ethnic Conflict: The Choice Between Pluralism and Ethnic Cleansing." *Negotiation Journal*, vol. 13, no. 4 (1997): 327–340.

Klare, M.T. *The Resource Wars: The New Landscape of Global Conflict*. New York: Henry Holt & Co. Publishers, 2002.

Kuhn, T. *The Structure of Scientific Revolutions*. Chicago: University of Chicago Press, 1970.

Lau, L., and M.W. Pasquini. "Meeting Grounds: Perceiving and Defining Interdisciplinarity across the Arts, Social Sciences and Sciences." *Interdisciplinary Science Review,* vol. 29, no. 1 (March 2004): 49–64.

LeVine, Robert A., and Donald T. Campbell. *Ethnocentrism: Theories of Conflict, Ethnic Attitudes and Group Behavior.* New York: John Wiley & Son, 1972.

MacIntyre, Alasdair. *After Virtue.* South Bend, IN: University of Notre Dame Press, 2007.

McDonald, J.W., and D.B. Bendahmane, eds. *Conflict Resolution: Track Two Diplomacy*. Washington, DC: Foreign Service Institute, Department of State, 1987.

Merleau-Ponty, M. *The Structure of Behavior*, trans. by Alden Fisher. Boston: Beacon Press, 1963.

Miall, H., O. Ramsbotham, and T. Woodhouse. *Contemporary Conflict Resolution: The Prevention, Management and Transformation of Deadly Conflicts*, 2nd ed. Cambridge, MA: Polity Press, 2005.

Nietzche, F. *The Gay Sciences*, trans. by Walter Kaufman. New York: Random House, 1974.

Nissani, Moti. "Ten Cheers for Interdisciplinarity: The Case for Interdisciplinary Knowledge and Research." *Social Science Journal*, vol. 34, no. 2 (1997): 201.

O'Leary, Rosemary, ed. *Pushing the Boundaries: New Frontiers in Conflict Resolution and Collaboration.* Bingley, UK: Emerald Group Publishing Limited, 2008.

Osgood, Charles E. *An Alternative to War or Surrender*. Urbana: University of Illinois Press, 1962.

Palmer, R. *Hermeneutics*. Chicago: Northwestern University Press, 1969.

Phillips, M. *Contested Geographies*. Burlington, VT: Ashgate Publishing, 2005.

Popper, K. *Objective Knowledge An Evolutionary Approach*. Oxford: Clarendon Press, 1979.

Quine, W.V. *Methods of Logic*, 4th ed. Cambridge, MA: Harvard University Press, 2006.

Rabinow, Paul, and William Sullivan, eds. *Interpretive Social Science: A Reader*. Berkeley: University of California Press, 1979.

Rovane, C. *The Bounds of Agency: An Essay in Revisionary Metaphysics*. Princeton, NJ: Princeton University Press, 1998.

Pruitt, G.D., and S.H. Kim. *Social Conflict: Escalation, Stalemate, and Settlement*, 3rd ed. Boston: McGraw-Hill, 2004.

Sandole, D. "A Comprehensive Mapping of Conflict Resolution: A Three-Pillar Approach," *Peace and Conflict Studies*, vol. 5 (1998): 1–25

Sandole, Dennis, Sean Byrne, Ingrid Sandole-Staroste, and Jessica Senehi, eds. *Handbook of Conflict Analysis and Resolution*. London: Routledge, 2009.

Segal, J.M. *Agency and Alienation: A Theory of Human Presence*. Lanham, MD: Rowman & Littlefield, 1991.

Senehi, Jessica. "Language, Culture and Conflict: Storytelling As A Matter of Life and Death." *Mind and Human Interaction*, vol. 7, no. 3 (1996): 150–164

Shelling, Thomas. *The Strategy of Conflict*. Cambridge, MA: Harvard University Press, 1960.

Sherif, Muzafer, and Carolyn W. Sherif, eds. *Interdisciplinary Relationships in the Social Sciences*. Chicago: Aldine Publishing Company, 1969.

Simmel, G. *Conflict and the Web of Group-Affiliations*. New York: The Free Press, 1955.

Smelser, N.J. "On Comparative Analysis, Interdisciplinarity, and Internationalization in Sociology." *International Sociology*, vol. 18, no. 4 (2003): 643–657.

Sumner, W.G. *Folkways*. Boston: Ginn Publishers, 1906.

Tilly, C., D. McAdam, and S. Tarrow. *Politics of Collective Violence*. Cambridge: Cambridge University Press, 2003.

Van Evera, S. *Guide to Methods for Students of Political Science*. Ithaca, NY: Cornell University Press, 1997.

Volkan, V. *Bloodlines: From Ethnic Pride to Ethnic Terrorism*. Boulder, CO: Westview Press, 1998.

Wehr, Paul. *Conflict Regulation*. Boulder, CO: Westview Press, 1979.

Wheelwright, Philip. *Aristotle*. Rochester, NY: Odyssey Press, 1951.

Yin, Robert. *Case Study Research: Design and Methods*, 3rd ed. Thousand Oaks, CA: Sage Publications, Inc., 2003.

Zartman, William I., and Guy Olivier Faure, eds. *Escalation and Negotiation in International Conflict.* Cambridge: University of Cambridge Press, 2006.

NOTES

1. J. Galtung, *Peace By Peaceful Means: Peace and Conflict Development and Civilization* (London: Sage, 1996); C. Tilly, D. McAdams, and S. Tarrow, *Politics of Collective Violence* (Cambridge: Cambridge University Press, 2003).

2. T. Boudreau and B. Polkinghorn, "Reversing the Destructive Discourses of Dehumanization: A Model for Reframing Narratives Through Identity Affirmation," in *Pushing the Boundaries: New Frontiers in Conflict Resolution and Collaboration*, edited by Rosemary O'Leary (Bingley, UK: Emerald Group Publishing Limited, 2008).

3. T. Boudreau, "Intergroup Reduction Through Identity Affirmation: Overcoming the Image of the Ethnic or Enemy Other," *Peace and Conflict Studies*, vol. 10, no. 1 (Spring 2003): 87–107; D. Druckman, *Doing Research: Methods of Inquiry for Conflict Analysis* (Thousand Oaks, CA: Sage Publications, 2005).

4. Aristotle, *The Basic Works of Aristotle*, edited by Richard McKeon (New York: Random House, 1941).

5. D. Hume, *Essay on Human Understanding* (Indianapolis, IN: The Library of Liberal Arts, 1955).

6. T.D. Cook and D.T. Campbell, *Quasi-Experimentation: Design & Analysis for Field Settings* (Boston: Houghton Mifflin Company, 1979).

7. J. Galtung, *Peace By Peaceful Means: Peace and Conflict Development and Civilization* (London: Sage, 1996).

8. Boudreau, "Intergroup Reduction."

9. Joan Bondurant and Margaret W. Fisher, eds., *Conflict: Violence and Non-violence* (New York: Lieber-Atherton, 1971).

10. Dan Christie, Richard Wagner, and Deborah Winter, eds, *Peace, Conflict and Violence: Peace Psychology for the 21st Century* (Upper Saddle River, NJ: Prentice Hall, 2001), 314–323.

11. T. Boudreau, "Human Agonistes: Interdisciplinary Inquiry into Contested Agency and Human Conflict," in *Handbook of Conflict Analysis and Resolution,* Dennis Sandole, Sean Byrne, Ingrid Sandole-Staroste, and Jessica Senehi, eds. (London: Routledge, 2009).

12. Michel Foucault, *Power/Knowledge: Selected Interviews and Other Writings 1972–1977* (New York: Pantheon Books, 1980).

13. T. Boudreau, *Sheathing the Sword: The Preventive Role of the United Nations Secretary-General* (Westport, CT: Greenwood Press, 1991).

14. Cook and Campbell, *Quasi-Experimentation.*

15. S. Bose, *Contested Lands* (Cambridge, MA: Harvard University Press, 2007).

16. M. Phillips, *Contested Geographies* (Burlington, VT: Ashgate Publishing, 2005).

17. T. Kuhn, *The Structure of Scientific Revolutions* (Chicago: University of Chicago Press, 1970).

18. T.F. Homer-Dixon, *Environment, Scarcity and Violence* (Princeton, NJ: Princeton University Press, 2001); A.L. George and T.J. McKeown, "Case Studies and Theories of Organizational Decision Making," in *Advances in Information Processing in Organizations*, A.L. George, ed. (Greenwich, CT: JAI Press, 1985), 21–58.

19. W.V. Quine, *Methods of Logic,* 4th ed. (Cambridge, MA: Harvard University Press, 2006).

20. K. Popper, *Objective Knowledge: An Evolutionary Approach* (Oxford: Clarendon Press, 1979).

21. Aristotle, *Basic Works.*

22. Cook and Campbell, *Quasi-Experimentation*; Quine, *Methods of Logic*; Popper, *Objective Knowledge.*

23. Boudreau, "Human Agonistes."

24. Boudreau and Polkinghorn, "Reversing the Destructive Discourses."

25. M. Friedman, *Essays in Political Economy* (Chicago: University of Chicago Press, 1966).

26. Boudreau, "Human Agonistes."

27. M. Friedman, *Essays in Political Economy* (Chicago: University of Chicago Press, 1966).

28. C. Geertz, "From the Native's Point of View," in *Interpretive Social Science: A Reader*, Paul Rabinow and William Sullivan, eds. (Berkeley: University of California Press, 1979); A. Giddens, *The Constitution of Society: Outline of the Theory of Structuration* (Berkeley: University of California Press, 1984).

29. Graham Allison, *Essence of Decision: Explaining the Cuban Missile Crisis,* 1st ed. (Boston: Little, Brown, 1971).

30. M. Heidegger, *The Question of Technology and Other Essays* (New York: Harper Torchbooks, 1977).

31. Hayward Alker, *Rediscoveries and Reformulations: Humanistic Methodologies for International Studies* (Cambridge: Cambridge University Press, 1996); Alasdair MacIntyre, *After Virtue* (South Bend, IN: University of Notre Dame Press, 2007).

32. M. Heidegger, *Being and Time*, trans. by John Macquarrie and Edward Robinson (New York: Harper & Row, 1962); also see Heidegger, *Being and Time*, trans. by Joan Stambaugh (Albany: State University of New York Press, 1996).

33. Boudreau, "Human Agonistes."

34. From Aristotle's *Physics* (Wicksteed and Cornford translation), Loeb Classical Library series, as quoted in "Aristotle to Plotinus," *The Classical Review*, vol. 6, issue 1 (1956): 45.

35. Philip Wheelwright, *Aristotle* (Rochester, NY: Odyssey Press, 1951).

36. M. Heidegger, *The Question of Technology and Other Essays* (New York: Harper Torchbooks, 1977).

37. L. Coser, *The Functions of Social Conflict* (New York: Free Press); G. Simmel, *Conflict and the Web of Group-Affiliations* (New York: Free Press, 1955).

38. Michel Foucault, *Power/Knowledge: Selected Interviews and Other Writings 1972–1977* (New York: Pantheon Books, 1980).

39. Boudreau and Polkinghorn, "Reversing the Destructive Discourses."

40. Martin Buber, *I-Thou* (New York: Free Press, 1971).

41. Buber, *I-Thou.*

42. F. Nietzsche, in *The Gay Sciences*, trans. by Walter Kaufman (New York: Random House, 1974); Merleau-Ponty, *Structure*.

43. R. Palmer, *Hermeneutics* (Chicago: Northwestern University Press, 1969); H.G. Gadamer, *Truth and Method* (New York: Continuum, 2004).

44. Boudreau and Polkinghorn, "Reversing the Destructive Discourses."

45. William I. Zartman and Guy Olivier Faure, eds., *Escalation and Negotiation in International Conflict* (Cambridge: University of Cambridge Press, 2006).

46. Herbert Kelman, "Group Processes in the Resolution of International Conflicts: Experiences From the Israeli-Palestinian Case," *The American Psychologist,* vol. 52, no. 3 (1997): 212–220. Kelman, "Negotiating National Identity and Self-Determination in Ethnic Conflict: The Choice Between Pluralism and Ethnic Cleansing," *Negotiation Journal*, vol. 13, no. 4 (1997): 327–340.

47. L. Diamond and A.J. McDonald, eds., *Multi-track Diplomacy: A System Approach to Peace* (West Hartford, CT: Kumarian Press, 1996); J.V. Montville, "The Arrow and the Olive Branch: The Case for Track Two Diplomacy," in *Conflict Resolution: Track Two Diplomacy*, J.W. McDonald and D.B. Bendahmane, eds. (Washington, DC: Foreign Service Institute, Department of State, 1987).

48. Sean Byrne and Cynthia Irvin, *Reconcilable Differences: Turning Points in Ethnopolitical Conflict* (West Hartford, CT: Kumarian Press, 2000); M. Abu-Nimer, *Reconciliation, Justice and Coexistence: Theory and Practice* (Lanham, MD: Lexington Books, 2001).

49. Morton Deutsch and Peter Coleman, eds., *The Handbook of Conflict Resolution: Theory and Practice* (San Francisco: Jossey-Bass, 2009).

50. Boudreau, *Sheathing.*

51. Charles E. Osgood, *An Alternative to War or Surrender* (Urbana: University of Illinois Press, 1962).

52. R.J. Fisher, *Interactive Conflict Resolution: Pioneers, Potential and Prospects* (Syracuse, NY: Syracuse University Press, 1996).

53. J. Bercovitch, *Resolving International Conflicts* (Boulder, CO: Lynn Rienner, 1996); D. Sandole, "A Comprehensive Mapping of Conflict Resolution: A Three-Pillar Approach," *Peace and Conflict Studies,* vol. 5 (1998): 1–25.

54. Thomas Schelling, *The Strategy of Conflict* (Cambridge, MA: Harvard University Press, 1960).

55. H. Miall, O. Ramsbotham, and T. Woodhouse, *Contemporary Conflict Resolution: The Prevention, Management and Transformation of Deadly Conflicts,* 2nd ed. (Cambridge, MA: Polity Press, 2005).

56. Brian Polkinghorn, "The Social Roots of Environmental Conflicts," in *Reconcilable Differences: Turning Points in Ethnopolitical Conflict,* Sean Byrne and Cynthia Irvin, eds. (West Hartford, CT: Kumarian Press, 2000).

57. Paul Wehr, *Conflict Regulation* (Boulder, CO: Westview Press, 1979); D. Sandole, "A Comprehensive Mapping of Conflict Resolution: A Three-Pillar Approach"; D. Sandole, "Typology," in *Conflict: From Analysis to Intervention*, S. Cheldelin, D. Druckman, and L. Fast (New York: Continuum, 2003).

58. Boudreau, "Human Agonistes."

59. Kuhn, *The Structure of Scientific.*

60. Robert Yin, *Case Study Research: Design and Methods,* 3rd ed. (Thousand Oak, CA: Sage Publications, Inc., 2003).

61. Yin, *Case Study Research.*

62. Yin, *Case Study Research*; Boudreau and Polkinghorn, "Reversing the Destructive Discourses."

63. Yin, *Case Study Research.*

64. Bose, *Contested Lands*; Phillips, *Contested Geographies.*

65. Jessica Senehi, "Constructive Storytelling in Inter-Communal Conflicts: Building Community, Building Peace," in *Reconcilable Differences: Turning Points in Ethnopolitical Conflict*, Sean Byrne and Cynthia Irvin, eds. (West Hartford, CT: Kumarian Press).

66. V. Volkan, *Bloodlines: From Ethnic Pride to Ethnic Terrorism* (Boulder, CO: Westview Press, 1998).

67. Yin, *Case Study Research.*

68. G.T. Allison and P. Zelikow, *Essence of Decision: Explaining the Cuban Missile Crisis,* 2nd ed. (Boston: Little, Brown, 1999).

Chapter 3

Post-Intervention Stability of Civil War States

Frederic Pearson and Marie Olson Lounsbery

In the growing literature on the causes, courses, and conclusions of civil wars, the question of post-war peacebuilding and re-stabilization has loomed large. A number of studies have examined the correlates of lasting rather than transient and failed peace agreements and settlements.[1] Though findings have varied depending on the population of cases considered and the definitions of key variables, they have tended to highlight the importance of factors such as decisive victories, international security guarantees, power sharing and reconciliation agreements, state capacity building, democratic reforms, and economic reconstruction.[2]

One of the most interesting questions regarding the outcome of civil wars is the role played by outside parties-states, powers, and organizations—in either promoting or dampening the combat and facilitating solutions. Indeed outside forceful intervention or meddling in such wars is proscribed under international law as a violation of state sovereignty, save for the presumed authority of state governments to invite assistance by other states. Intervention on behalf of rebels or insurgents generally is considered illegitimate, though in some circumstances, such as South Africa's *Apartheid* struggles, the international community and international governmental organization resolutions favored the "justness" of the liberation struggle. Few studies, however, have looked systematically and in detail at the question of whether foreign intervention, and particularly forceful or military intervention in the wars themselves, generally increase or decrease the odds of what might be considered favorable outcomes and post-war stability.

There is reason to think that either outcome might be the case. While civil wars themselves are notoriously destructive to social and political conditions, all too frequently entailing depraved acts of genocide, homicide, rape and victimization (as with child soldiers), we are as yet unsure whether outside interventions in such wars, aside from the question of their legality, lessen or worsen such disruptions. Regan discovered that military interventions seem to lengthen or at least correspond to longer civil wars.[3] International military brigades from abroad might tend to strengthen one side in the fighting to the point of shortening the war and helping reestablish order, or they might prolong the carnage by allowing the parties to fight on, and they might themselves become parties to the death dealing. NATO and, to a degree, Russian moves in Bosnia and Kosovo may have created conditions for at least prolonged effective ceasefires, if not actual settlement of outstanding grievances and stable democratic outcomes.

Interventions can take many forms and have a variety of motives, which might account for varied effects on war outcomes. Some interventions have been aimed at pacifying the situation and promoting peace settlements, as when arms or troops are supplied to the weaker party to encourage stalemates and negotiations. Such arms supply strategies, through Iran, were supposedly supported by the United States and Western powers as a way to aid the Muslim forces in Bosnia and bring them into a more favorable power balance with their Serb opponents.[4] Multilateral organizations such as the United Nations or regional IGOs such as the African Union can send troops meant for peacekeeping or reassurance, or to help fight against violent factions. On the other hand, some interventions, as in U.S. fighting in Afghanistan after 2001, can be designed to tip the scales and win a civil war for a favored side or party. Here the interveners might become parties to the conflict subject to the same potential for losses, blame, entrapment or terrorism as the parties they favor.

It is difficult to sort out singular or clear motives in any military involvement, as interests can range from preserving favored clients to cornering the market on lucrative resources (diamonds, gold, oil, etc.). One compelling concern might be to affect the geopolitical balance in the region in which the intervention occurs, especially given the tendency of civil wars to spread across boundaries and destabilize neighboring states.[5] Overall power and influence might be the underlying motivation common to all such interests. Yet one presumes hypothetically that multilateral interventions by world organizations generally would be aimed less at such self-interested outcomes and more at stabilization and peacemaking than those of unilateral interveners. The test of such presumptions though is in the examination of actual cases and data.

The entire subject of external intervention has been rendered topical by moves of powers such as the United States since the end of the Cold War to engineer desired outcomes in various disrupted and warring states such as Iraq and Afghanistan. One might argue that American and subsequently NATO Afghani involvement began as an effort to hunt down and capture those responsible for the September 11, 2001, terrorist attacks in New York and Washington. However, in the process, whether wisely or not, the interveners also set their sights on displacing ruling regimes in Baghdad and Kabul and subsequently on shoring up favored, if apparently corrupt, replacement regimes and keeping hostile forces such as the Taliban from regaining power some nine or ten years later. The interveners came to be viewed as occupiers in some quarters, and resistance persisted and grew, further postponing the target country's re-stabilization. Military campaigns and attendant "collateral" damage and killing among the civilian populations added to the instability. The interveners then embraced further goals of finding an honorable exit or undertaking sufficient "nation-building" to create institutions capable of surviving, at least for a "decent interval," without intervention (on the shifting intra-war patterns of intervener interests, see Miller, 2004).[6] The motives of war shift with the tides of war, and the footing can indeed be slippery in such tides.

Thus, the prospect of intervening in civil wars and even civil conflicts short of full-scale wars can be extremely challenging, as both Vietnam and Afghanistan have shown Americans and Western forces, and as the Russians, British, and others learned in Afghanistan in earlier times. The intervener affects the war and the state undergoing the war, but the war certainly affects the intervener as well for years to come. These effects might not, however, be uniformly negative, although Joseph Rudolph famously observed in 1995 that no successful intervention had ever occurred in an ongoing civil war.[7] Sometimes, as in the worst civil war conditions of West Africa during the 1990s, desperate people and parties on the spot in locations such as Liberia and the Ivory Coast yearn for foreign interveners to save them from the depredations of local governments and insurgents. In many instances, such interventions and relief are long delayed or never arrive; even the impact of multilateral peacemaking interventions might be disillusioning.[8] But in some instances, as in Britain's purported role in Sierra Leone, improved conditions can finally result. Thus, one might hope for more or less international intervention with the expectation of salubrious effects on post-war prospects. It is our task in this paper to determine whether and under what circumstances the outcomes of such involvements generally qualify as constructive or destructive.

Prior studies regarding intervention effects have concentrated either on overall trends in both civil wars and non-war contexts,[9] on impacts for war settlement,[10] and on differing effects of unilateral and multilateral, or hostile versus supportive interventions either on peace prospects or on target states.[11]

On the latter point for example, Walter and Snyder[12] note the key question of psychological underpinnings for peace, and that outside interveners or security guarantors can bolster such reassurance and offset the "security dilemma" as it, along with parties' "predatory goals," drives internal wars. They can do this either by monitoring threats and providing early warning or by penalizing and disabling would be predators and violators.

Yet we are left to wonder what impact can be expected on reestablishing viable state institutions and social progress. This question is complicated, because it hinges in part on whether interveners undertake missions such as: disarming warring factions; empowering or disempowering local elites; training civil servants, police, and armed forces; reestablishing independent judicial institutions; fostering entrepreneurs and investments; assuring more just redistribution of resources and benefits to various national regions; and creating institutions to intertwine the fates of the parties in some mutually reassuring ways.

Indeed, studies have yet to hone in specifically on civil war intervener effects on target state stability over time in the subsequent years. Yet such impacts are crucial in an age when interveners still seem tempted to indulge in nation-building strategies in hopes of long-term target and regional stabilization. Pickering and Kisangani came closest to this consideration when they measured intervention effects subsequently on states' economic growth rates, governing institutions, and physical quality of life.[13] The only consistent effect they found was in stimulating democratic development in previously autocratic states. Rival interventions by more than one power also seemed to foster relative long-term economic growth. However the authors utilized data on intervention, not on civil wars with intervention. We propose to take the alternative perspective, while incorporating and retesting many of the explanatory and dependent variables for success that they employed, thus promoting cumulative findings along with new interpretations of what interventions work best, when and for what purpose in resolving civil wars.

METHODOLOGY

In order to assess the short and long term impact of military intervention on civil war states, we first identify all civil wars occurring between 1944 and 1999 using data provided by Regan.[14] This results in 151 civil wars (i.e., intrastate conflicts involving at least 200 battle related deaths in a given year). We distinguish those that experienced military intervention from those that did not using Regan's military intervention variable (defined as intervention involving military assistance or military support). Cases are then dichotomized into those receiving such support, compared to those without. Regan also identifies the direction of military intervention. Pickering and Kisangan[15] have found that intervention direction matters in terms of post-intervention stability generally (i.e., they examined all foreign military interventions occurring in war and non-war states). Therefore, we compare "hostile" interventions (opposing the government or supporting the rebels) with those that are "supportive" (supporting the government or opposing the rebels). Civil war states that experience simultaneous supportive and hostile interventions are considered to have "rival" interventions. Interventions can also be designed to be neutral in nature, as in evacuations of foreign citizens. There were nine neutral interventions occurring in the midst of civil war in our population of cases, all but two of which occurred in the same country year as either a hostile or supportive intervention, or both. The two unrivaled neutral interventions are not included in the directional analyses.

We consider the possibility that multilateral military interventions occurring by international organizations potentially impact target states differently than unilateral interventions, or combined coalitional interventions.[16] In order to examine this possibility, we utilize the international organization variable created by Regan.[17] We would also expect that civil wars that are particularly intense, involving elements of genocide or politicide, are potentially more devastating to the state, subsequently, than less intense wars. Cases of genocide have been identified by Barbara Harff and coded dichotomously here. Harff defines genocide/politicide as "the promotion, execution, and/or implied consent of sustained policies by governing elites or their agents—or, in the case of civil war, either of the contending authorities—that are intended to destroy, in whole or part, a communal, political, or politicized ethnic group."[18]

We suggest that the lingering impact of civil war and concomitant military intervention is most likely felt on a state's subsequent regime status, political stability and economic growth. Military interventions into civil conflicts of late tend to trumpet the need to democratize target countries in order to produce long-term "stability." As a result, we use Polity IV[19] measures of a target state regime type to determine whether outcomes are indeed democratizing. The majority of civil wars occur, not surprisingly, in previously non-democracies (only 20 of the 151 civil war states receive democracy-autocracy regime scores of six or better). We then identified regime scores five years and ten years following the last year of the war. Those that receive regime scores of six or better are considered post-conflict democracies and all others are not.

In order to examine a target state's economic growth, we identified gross domestic product (GDP) per capita using Penn World Tables 6.3,[20] which are available for 188 countries for the period 1950 to 2004. We calculate the percentage change in GDP per capita five and ten years from the end of each war. Using these cumulative change calculations, we generate an ordinal level variable identifying post-war countries as exhibiting negative growth (i.e., change in GDP/capita less than zero), weak growth (0–10 percent change over five years), moderate growth (10.1–50 percent change), or strong growth (over 50 percent change).

We are also interested in examining the impact of military intervention on target state corruption. It is possible that military intervention into civil wars, particularly interventions of the hostile nature opposing or toppling formerly repressive regimes, could force post-conflict governments into becoming more transparent and less corrupt. Then again, the dislocation of war and intervention might produce increased corruption due to the loss of conventional economies. To assess this possibility, we utilize Transparency International's corruption index (n.d.), which provides scores for 150 countries beginning in 1995 (although not all countries are surveyed each year from that point). The Corruption Perception Index (CPI) measures the perceived level of public sector corruption derived through a series of surveys. Scores range from 0 to 10, with lower scores indicating more corruption. Regan's civil war data set ends in 1999; as a result, we chose to focus on civil wars occurring in the 1990s for this set of analyses. Corruption scores are identified 10 years later, allowing us to determine whether those wars experiencing military intervention fared better (i.e., receive higher scores) than their non-intervention counterparts.[21]

In order to analyze the impact of foreign military intervention in civil wars on a target states regime, economy, and corruption levels, we present a series of bivariate cross-tabulations. Tests of significance (chi-square distribution tests in this case) are presented for informational purposes although the entire population of cases is included in the analysis.

FINDINGS

Regime Status

Generally, intervention into civil war states does not appear to generate more democracy in either the short or long term (Table 3.1). Roughly the same percentages of non-democracies in civil wars remained non-democratic five years later whether or not intervention had occurred. Of the 109 civil wars occurring in non-democracies (for which we have data), the vast majority, more than 80 percent, of the post-war countries remained either autocracies or anocracies (i.e., semi-democracies) five years following the war's conclusion.

Table 3.1. Military Intervention and Target State Post-War Regime

	Five Years		
Five Years Post-War Regime	*No Intervention*	*Military Intervention*	*Total*
Non-democracy	34 (82.93%)	57 (83.82%)	91 (83.49%)
Democracy	7 (17.07%)	11 (16.18%)	18 (16.51%)
Total	41 (100%)	68 (100%)	109 (100%)

Pearson chi2(1) = 0.0149 Pr = 0.903

Table 3.2. Military Intervention and Target State Post-War Regime

	Ten Years		
Ten Years Post-War Regime	*No Intervention*	*Military Intervention*	*Total*
Non-democracy	24 (77.42%)	41 (74.55%)	65 (75.58%)
Democracy	7 (22.58%)	14 (25.45%)	21 (24.42%)
Total	31 (100%)	55 (100%)	86 (100%)

Pearson chi2(1) = 0.0887 Pr = 0.766

The same was basically true for cases ten years following wars and interventions. Based on previous research,[22] our expectation is that the direction of intervention matters in such findings. Those that are supportive are likely to solidify the regime at the time, decreasing our expectation that a non-democratic state would transition to a democratic one. Conversely, a hostile intervention into a non-democracy would be more likely to generate a democratic aftermath. We examine this possibility in Tables 3.3–3.4.

First we note a general tendency for interventions to be governmentally supportive (as international law would sanction) rather than hostile, and the majority of regime outcomes in all types of interventions remained authoritarian. However, our expectation of improved regime status from the hostile intervention cases appears to be somewhat supported. After five years, 40 percent of the hostile intervention post-war states were democracies, as compared to 25 percent for non-intervention cases and 36 percent for supportive moves. Supportive

Table 3.3. Military Intervention Direction and Target State Post-War Regime

		Five Years			
Five Years Post-War Regime	*No Intervention*	*Supportive Intervention*	*Hostile Intervention*	*Rival Intervention*	*Total*
Non-democracy	39 (75%)	18 (64.29%)	9 (60%)	31 (88.57%)	97 (74.62%)
Democracy	13 (25%)	10 (35.71%)	6 (40%)	4 (11.43%)	33 (25.38%)
Total	67 (100%)	28 (100%)	15 (100%)	35 (100%)	130 (100%)

Pearson chi2(1) = 6.8722 Pr = 0.076

Table 3.4. Military Intervention Direction and Target State Post-War Regime

		Ten Years			
Ten Years Post-War Regime	*No Intervention*	*Supportive Intervention*	*Hostile Intervention*	*Rival Intervention*	*Total*
Non-democracy	30 (71.43%)	14 (63.64%)	7 (70%)	22 (78.57%)	73 (71.57%)
Democracy	12 (28.57%)	8 (36.36%)	3 (30%)	6 (21.43%)	29 (28.43%)
Total	42 (100%)	28 (100%)	10 (100%)	328 (100%)	102 (100%)

Pearson chi2(1) = 1.3676 Pr = 0.713

intervention does not appear to have quite the negative effect on democratic status that we anticipated, as some 36 percent of these cases ended as democracies after five years. Interestingly, though not surprisingly, the largest percentage of non-democratic outcomes were in civil war states that experienced rival interventions (i.e., both supportive and hostile and sometimes neutral interventions).

These differences do not necessarily maintain themselves in the long term, however (much less significant probability scores for Table 3.4). Rival intervention post-war states continue to exhibit the fewest democratic outcomes. Supportive interventions have the largest share of democracies after ten years (36.36 percent) followed by hostile intervention states (30 percent) and non-intervention states (28.57 percent). That said, it does appear that of the 29 post-war states that were democratic after ten years, those experiencing some sort of intervention represent the majority (17 of the 29).

Pickering and Kisangani likewise found hostile foreign military interventions in non-democratic developing states (regardless of the presence of civil war) to be associated with democratization.[23] Consistent with our findings, hostile interventions resulted in more democratization in the short term. Over time, however, this difference does not maintain itself. The difference between our two studies may be that we have extended the duration of analysis to ten years and concentrated on civil war cases.

Economic Growth

Instability in post-civil war states is not simply about regime status. Economic challenges have plagued such nations in post-war reconstruction as well.[24] If military intervention tends to lead to more democracies or tends to shorten wars or lessen dislocations, perhaps it also fosters states that are economically in a better position to be viable in the post-war years. We examine this possibility five and ten years down the road from each civil war.

Here we find traces of evidence that intervention can lead to improved economies at least for the first five post-war years and perhaps longer, although the significance levels of our findings taper off (Tables 3.5–3.6).

Table 3.5. Military Intervention and Target State Post-War Economic Growth

Five Years

Five Years Post-War Cumulative Growth	*No Intervention*	*Military Intervention*	*Total*
Negative or No Growth	21 (42%)	32 (35.16%)	53 (37.59%)
Weak Growth	7 (14%)	20 (21.98%)	27 (19.15%)
Moderate Growth	22 (44%)	31 (34.07%)	53 (37.59%)
Strong Growth	0	8 (8.79%)	8 (5.67%)
Total	50 (100%)	91 (100%)	141 (100%)

Pearson chi2(3) = 6.7165 Pr = 0.082

Table 3.6. Military Intervention and Target State Post-War Economic Growth

Ten Years

Ten Years Post-War Cumulative Growth	*No Intervention*	*Military Intervention*	*Total*
Negative or No Growth	12 (37.50%)	19 (31.15%)	31 (33.33%)
Weak Growth	9 (28.12%)	14 (22.95%)	23 (24.73%)
Moderate Growth	11 (34.38%)	23 (37.70%)	34 (36.56%)
Strong Growth	0	5 (8.20%)	5 (5.38%)
Total	32 (100%)	61 (100%)	93 (100%)

Pearson chi2(3) = 3.679 Pr = 0.366

Civil war states experiencing military intervention do appear to exhibit stronger growth rates in the short and long term. In fact, all of the states with strong cumulative growth levels were civil war intervention states. Non-intervention civil war states also appear to be comparatively more prone to negative or no growth (37.50 percent compared to 31.15 percent).

Again, all military interventions are not alike. We expect that findings will vary, depending on direction of intervention. Unlike our expectations about regime change, however, we have reason to suspect that hostile interventions are potentially more disruptive of the economy than supportive intervention, in part because the possibility of regime change can lead to prolonged fighting and at least temporary economic dislocations. Tables 3.7 and 3.8 focus on the direction of interventions and their impact on post-war economic growth.

Non-intervention cases appear to exhibit weaker economic growth after both five and ten years. Rival interventions also appear potentially destabilizing, not surprisingly. Of the 30 post-war states with rival interventions, 13 (43 percent) experienced negative growth after ten years. The same amount, however, experienced moderate or strong growth. Supportive and hostile intervention post-war states did better. Half of the 18 supportive intervention post-war states exhibited moderate to strong growth, while 60 percent of the

Table 3.7. Military Intervention Direction and Target State Post-War Economic Growth

Five Years					
Five Years Post-War Cumulative Growth	*No Intervention*	*Supportive Intervention*	*Hostile Intervention*	*Rival Intervention*	*Total*
Negative or No Growth	23 (43.40%)	8 (26.67%)	4 (21.05%)	17 (47.22%)	52 (37.68%)
Weak Growth	7 (13.21%)	6 (20%)	7 (36.84%)	6 (16.67%)	26 (18.84%)
Moderate Growth	23 (43.40%)	12 (40%)	7 (36.84%)	11 (30.56%)	53 (38.41%)
Strong Growth	0	4 (13.33%)	1 (5.26%)	2 (5.56%)	7 (5.07%)
Total	53 (100%)	30 (100%)	19 (100%)	36 (100%)	138 (100%)

Pearson chi2(1) = 15.6572 Pr = 0.074

hostile intervention post-war states did so. Thus far, it seems we can conclude that military intervention prolongs civil war, but may also democratize in the short term, and boost states economically in the short and long term. It also appears that direction of intervention matters with rival interventions creating the most disruption and hostile (anti-government) interventions associated with the greatest post-war economic revival over ten years.

Genocide

One troubling aspect of many civil wars (as well as some international ones) is the tendency for degeneration into what can be termed genocide. This tendency has been driven home especially in recent years in places as diverse as Cambodia, Bosnia, and Rwanda. If such cases are the most challenging in terms of social, political and economic stability, then we should not be surprised that countries experiencing genocide, or for that matter politicide, emerge from civil war and external intervention politically and economically

Table 3.8. Hostile Military Intervention and Target State Post-War Economic Growth

Ten Years					
Ten Years Post-War Cumulative Growth	*No Intervention*	*Supportive Intervention*	*Hostile Intervention*	*Rival Intervention*	*Total*
Negative or No Growth	12 (34.29%)	4 (22.22%)	2 (20%)	13 (43.33%)	31 (33.33%)
Weak Growth	12 (34.29%)	5 (27.78%)	2 (20%)	4 (13.33%)	23 (24.73%)
Moderate Growth	11 (31.43%)	7 (38.89%)	4 (40%)	12 (40%)	34 (36.56%)
Strong Growth	0	2 (11.11%)	2 (20%)	1 (3.33%)	5 (5.38%)
Total	35	18 (100%)	19 (100%)	30 (100%)	93 (100%)

Pearson chi2(1) = 12.7370 Pr = 0.175

Table 3.9. Military Intervention and Target State Post-War Economic Growth in Genocide Cases

	Five Years		
Five Years Post-War Growth	*No Intervention*	*Military Intervention*	*Total*
Negative/No Growth	3 (37.50%)	6 (30.00%)	9 (32.14%)
Weak Growth	0	4 (20.00%)	4 (14.29%)
Moderate Growth	5 (62.50%)	7 (35.00%)	12 (42.86%)
Strong Growth	0	3 (15.00%)	2 (10.71%)
Total	8 (100%)	20 (100%)	26 (100%)

Pearson chi2(3) = 3.9083 Pr = 0.272

challenged five or ten years down the road. In order to examine this possibility, we look at political and economic change following wars with and without genocide occurring during the conflict.

There were 28 cases of civil wars in which genocide (or politicide) occurred at some point during the conflict. Military intervention occurred in 20 of those with 11 hostile interventions. None of the post-genocide countries were democratic after five years following the war's end regardless of military intervention experience, and only two were considered democratic after ten years (one with intervention and one without). Genocide in the midst of war is clearly problematic in terms of subsequent political stabilization, and intervention does not appear to alleviate post-war concerns in this regard. This issue too is troubling since the international community sometimes posits timely intervention as a way of staving off or rectifying genocidal situations. Military intervention seems to have been less successful in the more challenging wars involving genocide than in all civil wars when we focus on post-civil war economies (Tables 3.9 and 3.10). Of the eight genocidal cases

Table 3.10. Military Intervention and Target State Post-War Economic Growth in Genocide Cases

	Ten Years		
Ten Years Post-War Growth	*No Intervention*	*Military Intervention*	*Total*
Negative/No Growth	2 (25.00%)	7 (43.75%)	9 (37.50%)
Weak Growth	2 (25.00%)	3 (18.75%)	5 (20.83%)
Moderate Growth	4 (50.00%)	5 (31.25%)	9 (37.50%)
Strong Growth	0	1 (6.25%)	1 (4.17%)
Total	8 (100%)	16 (100%)	24 (100%)

Pearson chi2(3) = 1.600 Pr = 0.659

Table 3.11. Military Intervention and Target State Post-War Corruption

Ten Years			
Corruption Perceptions Index	*No Intervention*	*Military Intervention*	*Total*
Most Corrupt	3 (17.65%)	9 (42.86%)	12 (31.58%)
Moderately Corrupt	12 (70.59%)	9 (42.86%)	21 (55.26%)
Least Corrupt	2 (11.76%)	3 (14.29%)	5 (13.16%)
Total	17 (100%)	21 (100%)	38 (100%)

Pearson chi2(2) = 3.2435 Pr = 0.198

without intervention five post-war economies (62.5 percent) exhibited moderate growth. (See Table 3.9.) Comparatively, ten of the 20 intervention cases (50 percent) experienced moderate or strong growth. This difference does not maintain itself over the long term as Table 3.10 indicates; weaker subsequent economic growth is seen for intervention cases following genocides.

Post-War Corruption

An additional set of analyses explores the stability-related impact of foreign military intervention in the midst of civil war on corruption in the post-war years. Focusing on civil wars occurring in the 1990s, we compare intervention to nonintervention cases for CPI scores ten years later. Findings are presented in Table 3.11.

Post-civil war states generally appear to have fairly high levels of corruption (at least perceived corruption), and military interventions appear to do little to obviate that tendency. The highest score (and therefore the seemingly least corrupt) was 4.7 (out of 10) received by South Africa, which did not experience military intervention. The rest of the post-war states in the 1990s sample received scores less than 4.0. Those receiving scores less than 2 are considered the most corrupt; those with scores between 2 and 3 are considered moderately corrupt, and those with scores higher than 3 are the least corrupt. Civil war states that experienced military intervention appear to be over represented among the most corrupt subsequent regimes (43 percent), while nonintervention civil war states appear more likely to experience moderate levels of corruption, recognizing again that even moderately corrupt scores are not very impressive when we consider the scaling.

International Organizations

Both unitary actors and multilateral groups of states intervene in civil wars. Intervention motives are likely to vary depending on the type and identity of

Table 3.12. International Organizations and Target State Post-War Regime

		Five Years		
Five Years Post-War Regime	*No Intervention*	*IO Intervention*	*Non-IO Intervention*	*Total*
Non-democracy	36 (73.47%)	13 (72.22%)	50 (76.92%)	99 (75%)
Democracy	13 (26.53%)	5 (27.78%)	15 (23.08%)	33 (25%)
Total	49 (100%)	18 (100%)	65 (100%)	132 (100%)

Pearson chi2(1) = 0.2635 Pr = 0.877

intervener, which may in turn impact the target state's stability in the short and long term.[25] As a result, we compare military interventions by international organizations to those committed (even in tandem) by single states.

There were 23 military interventions by international organizations into civil wars during the time period under study. None of these IO interventions occurred in democratic states. In cases for which we have complete regime data (N=18), 27.78 percent became democracies after five years following the war's end, only slightly more than the 23.08 percent of the non-IO interventions and 26.53 percent of nonintervention cases. After ten years (Table 3.13), the democratization record of IO interventions (whether or not democratization was on their mission agenda) was even worse in comparison to both non-IO interventions and non-interventions.

IOs fared markedly better however in relation to post-war economic growth (Tables 3.14 and 3.15), especially at the moderate growth level. As with unilateral interventions in civil war, military intervention again appears to improve a post-civil war state's economic performance. Both in the short and long term, the majority of IO interventions have resulted in moderate or strong economic growth. Roughly the same can be said for non-IO interventions (although at ten years the IO cases performed better), and in contrast to non-intervention cases; the latter did tend to be associated with weak to moderate growth levels.

Table 3.13. International Organizations and Target State Post-War Regime

		Ten Years		
Ten Years Post-War Regime	*No Intervention*	*IO Intervention*	*Non-IO Intervention*	*Total*
Non-democracy	27 (69.23%)	10 (83.33%)	36 (70.59%)	73 (71.57%)
Democracy	12 (30.77%)	2 (16.67%)	15 (29.41%)	29 (28.43%)
Total	90 (100%)	12 (100%)	51 (100%)	102 (100%)

Pearson chi2(1) = 0.9451 Pr = 0.623

Table 3.14. International Organizations and Target State Post-War Growth

Five Years				
Five Years Post-War Growth	*No Intervention*	*IO Intervention*	*Non-IO Intervention*	*Total*
Negative/No Growth	21 (42.00%)	7 (30.43%)	25 (36.76%)	53 (37.59%)
Weak Growth	7 (14.00%)	4 (17.39%)	16 (23.53%)	27 (19.15%)
Moderate Growth	22 (44.00%)	7 (30.43%)	24 (35.29%)	53 (37.59%)
Strong Growth	0	5 (21.74%)	5 (21.54%)	8 (5.67%)
Total	50 (100%)	23 (100%)	68 (100%)	141 (100%)

Pearson chi2(3) = 16.4405 Pr = 0.012

Table 3.15. International Organizations and Target State Post-War Growth

Ten Years				
Ten Years Post-War Growth	*No Intervention*	*IO Intervention*	*Non-IO Intervention*	*Total*
Negative/No Growth	12 (37.50%)	2 (18.18%)	17 (34.00%)	31 (33.33%)
Weak Growth	9 (28.12%)	1 (9.09%)	13 (26.00%)	23 (24.73%)
Moderate Growth	11 (34.38%)	7 (63.64%)	16 (32.00%)	34 (36.56%)
Strong Growth	0	1 (9.09%)	4 (8.00%)	5 (5.38%)
Total	32 (100%)	11 (100%)	50 (100%)	93 (100%)

Pearson chi2(3) = 7.3754 Pr = 0.288

CONCLUSION

Contrary to previous findings in the literature, foreign military intervention, whether by individual states or international organizations, does not appear to help create political stability in the target state, nor does it appear to result in less corrupt states over the long term. In fact, at times it appears to make matters worse or exacerbate disruption, corruption and instability. That said, military intervention can and does, at times, help post-civil war states achieve economic growth. This potential for growth seems particularly true of multilateral intergovernmental organization interventions. There is no apparent difference in these effects, however, for hostile and supportive interventions.

Understanding what distinguishes successful endeavors from failures is key, as not all interventions are alike. Although our research here suggests that international organizations do not necessarily foster better post-war outcomes than unilateral states and their interventions, what we did not explore was the level and commitment of the intervention, or the missions and goals of intervention. We did look at intervention direction (hostile/supportive), however, and contrary to previous findings in the literature cannot detect many significant differences or improved conditions one way or the other over the long term. Hostile interventions proved marginally more associated with subsequent democratic outcomes in the five-year analysis, but proved less so over ten years. Hostile interventions also seemed effective in promoting significant post-war economic growth, and, along with supportive intervention, did far better on this score than non-intervention or rival intervention cases.

Olson Lounsbery and Cook have suggested that in order for external *diplomatic* intervention into civil wars to be effective, intervention needs to be overwhelming and committed.[26] Future research on military intervention in such wars, therefore, might benefit from a similar focus expanding beyond simply whether intervention of various forms occurs to look at how those interventions unfold and the level and direction of commitment involved. For now, however, one can expect civil war intervention to lead to considerably better economic than political outcomes.

BIBLIOGRAPHY

Aning, Emmanuel Kwesi. "War to Peace: Dilemmas of Multilateral Intervention in Civil Wars." *African Security Review,* vol. 9, no. 3 (2000): 26–51.

Balch-Lindsay, Dylan, Andrew J. Enterline, and Kyle A. Joyce. "Third Party Intervention and the Civil War Process." *Journal of Peace Research,* vol. 45, no 3 (2008): 345–363.

Collier, Paul. "On the Economic Consequences of Civil War." *Oxford Economic Paper,* vol. 51, no. 1 (1999): 168–183.

Easterly, William, and Ross Levine. "Africa's Growth Tragedy: Policies and Ethnic Divisions." *Quarterly Journal of Economics,* vol. 112, no. 4 (1997): 1203–1250.

Harff, Barbara. "No Lessons Learned from the Holocaust? Assessing Risks of Genocide and Political Mass Murder since 1955." *American Political Science Review,* vol. 97, no. 1 (2003): 57–73.

Hartzell, Caroline, Matthew Hoddie, and Donald S. Rothchild. "Stabilizing the Peace After Civil War: An Investigation of Some Key Variables." *International Organization*, vol. 55, no. 1 (2003): 1–46.

Heston, Alan, Robert Summers, and Bettina Aten. "Penn World Table Version 6.3." Center for International Comparisons of Production, Income and Prices at the University of Pennsylvania, August 2009.

Kathman, Jacob. "The International Relations of Civil War Intervention." Paper presented at the annual meeting of the American Political Science Association, Marriott Wardman Park, Omni Shoreham, Washington Hilton, Washington, DC, 2001.

Knight, Malcolm, Norman Loayza, and Delano Villanueva. "The Peace Dividend: Military Spending Cuts and Economic Growth." *IMF Staff Papers,* vol. 43, no. 1 (1996): 1–37.

Marshall, Monty G., and Keith Jaggers. "Polity IV Project: Political Regime Characteristics and Transitions, 1800–2002." 2003. www.systemicpeace.org/polity/polity4.htm.

Miller, Jordan. "External Military Intervention in Civil Wars: A Quantitative Study of the Initiation and Escalation of Third-Party State Interventions." Paper presented at the annual meeting of the Midwest Political Science Association, Palmer House Hilton, Chicago, Illinois, April 15, 2004.

Olson Lounsbery, Marie, and Alethia Cook. "What's on the Table? Bargaining Progression in the Midst of Civil War," in *Unraveling Internal Conflicts in East Asia and the Pacific: Incidence, Consequences and Resolutions*, Jacob Bercovitch and Karl DeRouen, eds. Lanham, MA: Lexington Books, 2010, 162–187.

Olson Lounsbery, Marie, and Frederic Pearson. *Civil Wars: Internal Struggles, Global Consequences*. Toronto: University of Toronto Press, 2009.

Olson Lounsbery, Marie, Andrea Talentino, and Frederic S. Pearson. "Unilateral and Multilateral Military Intervention: Effects on Stability and Security." Paper presented at annual meeting of the Academic Council on the United Nations System, Rio de Janeiro, Brazil, June 2006.

Pickering, Jeffrey, and Emiset F. Kisangani. "Political, Economic, and Social Consequences of Foreign Military Intervention." *Political Research Quarterly*, vol. 59, no. 3 (2006): 363–376

Regan, Patrick M. "The Short-Term Effects of Military Interventions in Civil Conflict." *International Negotiation*, vol. 7, no. 3 (2002): 299–311.

Rudolph, J. "Intervention in Communal Conflicts." *Orbis*, vol. 39, no. 2 (1995): 295.

Transparency International. Corruption Perceptions Index. http://www.transparency.org/policy_research/surveys_indices/cpi/2009, June 21, 2010.

Walter, Barbara. *Committing to Peace: The Successful Settlement of Civil Wars*. Princeton, NJ: Princeton University Press, 2002.

Walter, Barbara, and Jack Snyder. *Civil Wars, Insecurity and Intervention*. New York: Columbia University Press, 1999.

Williams, Daniel, and Thomas W. Lippman. "U.S. Allowed Iran to Supply Bosnian Muslims with Arms." *Washington Post*, April 14, 1999.

NOTES

1. Barbara Walter, *Committing to Peace: The Successful Settlement of Civil Wars* (Princton, NJ: Princeton University Press, 2002); Caroline Hartzell, Matthew Hoddie, and Donald S. Rothchild, "Stabilizing the Peace After Civil War: An Investigation of Some Key Variables," *International Organization*, vol. 55, no. 1 (2003): 1–46.

2. See, for example, Marie Olson Lounsbery and Frederic Pearson, *Civil Wars: Internal Struggles, Global Consequences* (Toronto: University of Toronto Press, 2009), chapter 6.

3. Patrick M. Regan, "The Short-Term Effects of Military Interventions in Civil Conflict," *International Negotiation*, vol. 7, no. 3 (2002): 299–311.

4. Daniel Williams and Thomas W. Lippman, "U.S. Allowed Iran to Supply Bosnian Muslims with Arms," *Washington Post*, April 14, 1999.

5. Jacob Kathman, "The International Relations of Civil War Intervention," paper presented at the annual meeting of the American Political Science Association, Marriott Wardman Park, Omni Shoreham, Washington Hilton, Washington, DC, 2001.

6. Jordan Miller, "External Military Intervention in Civil Wars: A Quantitative Study of the Initiation and Escalation of Third-Party State Interventions," paper presented at the annual meeting of the Midwest Political Science Association, Palmer House Hilton, Chicago, Illinois, April 15, 2004.

7. J. Rudolph, "Intervention in Communal Conflicts," *Orbis,* vol. 39, no. 2 (1995): 295; Transparency International. Corruption Perceptions Index. http://www.transparency.org/policy_research/surveys_indices/cpi/2009 (June 21, 2010).

8. Emmanuel Kwesi Aning, "War to Peace: Dilemmas of Multilateral Intervention in Civil Wars," *African Security Review,* vol. 9, no. 3 (2000): 26–51.

9. Jeffrey Pickering and Emiset F. Kisangani, "Political, Economic, and Social Consequences of Foreign Military Intervention," *Political Research Quarterly,* vol. 59, no. 3 (2006): 363–376.

10. Regan, "Short-Term Effects"; Dylan Balch-Lindsay, Andrew J. Enterline, and Kyle A. Joyce, "Third Party Intervention and the Civil War Process," *Journal of Peace Research,* vol. 45, no. 3 (2008): 345–363.

11. Olson Lounsbery and Pearson, *Civil Wars.*

12. Barbara Walter and Jack Snyder, *Civil Wars, Insecurity and Intervention* (New York: Columbia University Press, 1999).

13. Pickering and Kisangani, "Political, Economic, and Social Consequences."

14. Regan, "Short-Term Effects."

15. Pickering and Kisangani, "Political, Economic, and Social Consequences."

16. See Marie Olson Lounsbery and Alethia Cook, "What's on the Table? Bargaining Progression in the Midst of Civil War," in *Unraveling Internal Conflicts in East Asia and the Pacific: Incidence, Consequences and Resolutions*, Jacob Bercovitch and Karl DeRouen, eds. (Lanham, MA: Lexington Books, 2010), 162–187.

17. Regan, "Short-Term Effects."

18. Barbara Harff, "No Lessons Learned from the Holocaust? Assessing Risks of Genocide and Political Mass Murder since 1955," *American Political Science Review* vol. 97, no. 1 (2003): 57–73.

19. Monty G. Marshall and Keith Jaggers, "Polity IV Project: Political Regime Characteristics and Transitions, 1800–2002," 2003. www.systemicpeace.org/polity/polity4.htm.

20. Alan Heston, Robert Summers, and Bettina Aten, Penn World Table Version 6.3, Center for International Comparisons of Production, Income and Prices at the University of Pennsylvania, August 2009.

21. Given data time limitations, we were unable to assess whether corruption scores improved. We can, however, make a general comparative assessment using data that are available for the 2000s.

22. Pickering and Kisangani, "Political, Economic, and Social Consequences."

23. Pickering and Kisangani, "Political, Economic, and Social Consequences."

24. Malcolm Knight, Norman Loayza, and Delano Villanueva, "The Peace Dividend: Military Spending Cuts and Economic Growth," *IMF Staff Papers,* vol. 43, no. 1 (1996): 1–37; William Easterly and Ross Levine, "Africa's Growth Tragedy: Policies and Ethnic Divisions," *Quarterly Journal of Economics,* vol. 112, no. 4 (1997): 1203–1250; Paul Collier, "On the Economic Consequences of Civil War," *Oxford Economic Paper,* vol. 51, no. 1 (1999): 168–183.

25. Marie Olson Lounsbery, Andrea Talentino, and Frederic S. Pearson, "Unilateral and Multilateral Military Intervention: Effects on Stability and Security," paper presented at annual meeting of the Academic Council on the United Nations System, Rio de Janeiro, Brazil, June 2006.

26. Olson Lounsbery and Cook, "What's on the Table?"

Chapter 4

The Social Cube Analytical Model and Protracted Ethnoterritorial Conflicts[1]

Sean Byrne and Amos Nadan

Ethnoterritorial conflicts are often those disputes in which diverse groups lay claim to same pieces of territory based on arguments of primordial rights. Explanations of the causes and the escalation of ethnoterritorial conflicts run the risk of being either too simple to accurately depict the situation or too complex to be very useful in helping us understand its dynamics. Analysts often focus on either the psychological and cultural aspects of ethnoterritorial conflict or they emphasize the material, religious, demographic, political, or economic dimensions.[2] We believe that there is no specific dimension (e.g., politics) that encompasses an explanation for causes, escalation, and the de-escalation of ethnoterritorial conflicts. Rather, there are six relevant encompassing dimensions (those of the social cube model discussed below). We suggest that studying these dimensions in ethnoterritorial conflicts will give conflict resolution practitioners and policymakers better knowledge to be able to act constructively to reduce tension. The scope of this chapter, as well as the limitation of our expertise, encouraged us to deal with the six dimensions in the Israeli–Palestinian and Northern Irish conflicts (excluding international and regional actors). In order to emphasize the broader picture and to encourage the use of the social cube analytical model in other studies, a provisional guideline is provided in this chapter.

Social cubism is an interactive and diagnostic analytical model combining the study of the influence of demographics, history, religion, economics, politics, and psychocultural dynamics in protracted ethnic conflicts.[3] These facets of conflict are not isolated from one another. Indeed, it is the particular interaction among these faces of the social cube that produces the specific trajectory of the conflict. Protracted ethnic conflicts pose a multifaceted puzzle that necessitates concentrating on all six sides of the puzzle to produce a complete analytical picture of the problem.[4]

Only when practitioners and policymakers consider the interrelations among the faces of the puzzle can they progress toward a more holistic solution. Similarly, we isolate six forces and some of their key internal factors to show how they combine to form complex patterns of ethnic conflicts. In the wake of the tragedy of Gaza and escalating violence by dissident Republicans and Loyalists in Northern Ireland, we use the social cube as an analytical framework to examine the Israeli–Palestinian and Northern Ireland conflicts. In this comparison, we highlight some of the most salient issues of both of these complex conflicts.

There are several ways in which ethnoterritorial conflicts can develop, and the six facets of the social cube will look quite different across cases. Given the development of a multitude of studies that focus on one facet or another, we need to develop a greater sense of the dynamics within each side of the cube. We must thus go inside the social cube to develop a better sense of how these factors can influence conflict and develop structural changes. This is not a study of all the internal, or indeed, none of the external aspects of both ethnoterritorial conflicts, rather it is a demonstration of how the social cube can be used for this comparative case study. This chapter, therefore, illustrates dynamics of the six forces of the social cube: (1) historical, (2) religious, (3) political, (4) psychocultural, (5) demographic, and (6) economic. In each part, there is an outline of *some* factors—and therefore the paper has to be viewed as a standpoint for further, detailed, research.

HISTORICAL FORCE

The historical experience of groups is formed and constructed to legitimate each group's "golden past."[5] In this process, the historical experience of the other is devalued, marginalized, and is completely written out of the metahistorical narratives.

Exclusion and Independence: Each group creates its own independent historical framework that excludes minorities. By virtue of birthright and belonging to the nation, someone who is outside that experience can never be an integral part of that volk. One must be born Basque, it is a virtue of blood and the historical experience of a nation. There is an existential element to the conflict as each group sees itself as a historical nation. This leads to misunderstanding and mythologizing, which isn't far removed from the objective source of conflict. While there is some debate about civic and ethnic nationalism, intergroup conflict often relies heavily on group boundaries that have rigidified through historical re-creations of events, and this often produces a set of characteristics defining group membership.[6] Quite often, Palestinians deny that Israelis have a right to return home, as it would make them aliens in the land, while Israel denies the dispossession of an indigenous Palestinian people. Otherwise the 1948 state of Israel would have been born in sin.[7] Protestants signed their covenant to the Queen in blood during the 1916 Battle of the Somme when thousands of Ulster Protestants perished on the battlefields of France.[8] Catholics point to the 1916 rising in Dublin, the 1918 All-Ireland elections, and the Irish Republican Army (IRA's) 1919–1921 War of Independence, in which the Catholic Nationalists used violence to strike for Irish self-determination.

Folklore and Stories: A local folklore builds up in each community about the conflict and the atrocities carried out by the other side, as well as the goodness of the in-group.[9] Tales of past violence create future violence so that the conflict becomes enduring and intractable.[10] Leaders in both communities may have a vested interest in the continuation of the conflict. Thus, stories of hostile relationships in the past ensure hostile relationships in the present.[11] Destructive stories serve to effect the group's perceptions of the conflict while increasing moral hazards of continuing violence.[12] For the in-group, retelling histories can improve self-esteem, increase group solidarity, and give hope since other members of the group have accomplished great things in the past.[13] A culture of violence in Israel, Palestine, and Northern Ireland increases the intensity of feeling within each group as fear, suspicion, and threat evoke a demonization and hatred of the other.[14]

Golden Age: Each group looks into its past to find its Golden Age for a sense of efficacy, identity, belonging, and value in the present.[15] Invoking and remembering this glorious past creates an important connection with the present. This process is critical for elites in forging nostalgia for an authentic ethnic past, developing an ethnonational identity, enveloping a victim mentality, and creating unity within the group. Folklorists, archaeologists, and historians sift through the records to rediscover and reappropriate a genuine "ethno-history" in which the culture is purified and the other is excluded.[16] The chosen people are thus on a sacred mission to purify the historic homeland. Israelis would point to the fact that Israel has a history in which God's chosen people had a special relationship to the land, while Palestinians refer, from time to time, to the Philistinians as their ancestors.[17] Similarly, Irish Catholics extort a rich historical past, tracing their roots back two thousand years to the arrival of the Bronze Age, the Celts, and the Viking and the Norman invasion of the twelfth century.

Gender and Inequality: Women's voices are generally excluded from the historical narrative within ethnic communities locked in internal strife.[18]

The patriarchy frames the historical narrative in terms of male power and privilege. The gendered relationship increasingly pushes women in each community to the margins. The ensuing patriarchal war culture takes on a more negative guise as women's voices are disempowered.[19] The extent of disempowerment may vary, however, and women can sometimes make use of their marginal status in order to conduct political acts that might have been severely punished were they conducted by men. For example, Republican women in Northern Ireland would bang garbage bin lids as both a warning to the Provisional PIRA and as a sign of protest. In Israel women complete military service while Palestinian women have become more intensively involved in the Israeli–Palestinian conflict including becoming suicide bombers serving as *shahedah* (woman holy martyrs).[20]

Divided Communities: Neighborhoods and schools are segregated as the historic textbooks in the schools only cover the history of each group while the history of the other community is excluded, ensuring that children grow up in a divided society.[21] Children develop conflicting views of the past, and identify with different historical figures. In Israel and Northern Ireland neighborhoods are segregated so that they are territorially defensible and so that terrorist groups can launch attacks against the other group.[22]

Transgenerational Transmission of Trauma: Ethnic groups select events from the past in which they have been victimized. This traumatic experience is passed orally from one generation to the next, and is used to legitimate the destructive behavior of the in-group.[23] The collapse of time, whereby past and present become inextricably interlinked, ensures that competing narratives and victimization become ingrained within the collective memory of each group.

Marches, historical dates, Golden Ages, historical birthrights, martyrs, and blood sacrifices are the stories and historical narratives that are handed down from one generation to the next.[24] The Israeli Law of Return ensures that Israel is the state for Jewish people; while Gaza and the West Bank are often seen as the Palestinian state.[25] Many Palestinians argue for the right of return to Israel and the Palestinian territories.[26] Catholics look to the 1848 Irish famine and the apartheid Penal Laws that took away their political and economic rights after the 1690 Battle of the Boyne. For Protestants, continued Catholic insurrection and Protestant resistance is ingrained in the stories of the Unionists.[27]

RELIGIOUS FORCE

Religion has served to further divide communities and escalate tensions in protracted ethnoterritorial conflicts, as elites use religion as a political instrument to demonize the other because it follows a "false" God.[28] Religious conformism eliminates heresy and validates beliefs and practices that influence politics and ethnonational identity.[29] Not surprisingly, religion also becomes a badge of identity or a cultural marker for groups embroiled in protracted group conflicts.[30]

True Believers: True Believers believe that their religion is the only true religion as they are God's chosen people. The religion of the other is evil and bad because the other group's religion is perceived as heretical.[31] For example, within Northern Ireland some members of the ultra-Protestant Free Presbyterian Church believe the Catholic religion is the anti-Christ. Consequently, how could Protestants commingle and share power with Catholics? Fundamentalists contribute to keeping the communities divided.

God's Chosen People: The hegemonic group creates a mystique that it is God's "chosen people" who are given a divine right to the land and the territory.[32] In essence, it does not have to share that land with any other usurper group it constructs as savage and uncivilized.[33] The Afrikaners of South Africa, Jews of Israel, and Protestants of Northern Ireland have in the past portrayed themselves in this light. The most intractable conflicts exist when two ethnoreligious groups with separate identities compete for the same territory.[34]

Intra-Group Conflict: Conflict also exists within ethnoreligious communities. Intra-group conflict divides up groups between extremists who don't want any contact with members of the other group, and moderates who favor an ecumenical approach based on that religion's teachings of compassion, reconciliation, and forgiveness.[35] In Northern Ireland there is heterogeneity within the Protestant community as conflict envelops relationships between the Church of Ireland, Methodist, Presbyterian, and Free Presbyterian believers while Catholics remain a homogenous community. Conflict between Palestinian Sunni Muslims and Christians has forced many Christians to leave the holy land, as political and religious identities coincide and conflict between Orthodox and Liberal Jews, which revolves around the point that all of Palestine is part of the Jewish homeland versus the need to disengage from Palestine.[36]

POLITICAL FORCE

Unequal distribution of power within society pushes out-groups to the fringes of political irrelevancy.[37] The out-group remains at the margins of political life and does not constitute any real threat to the hegemonic status quo. The manifestation of political divisions continues to emphasize the persistence of conflictual relations between the in-group and out-group.

Exclusion From Power: The minority community (the out-group), even while elections are part of the status quo, is often excluded from the political process and is framed as a group of disloyal citizens who cannot be trusted. The exclusion of the minority elites from political power forces them to mobilize their group members to protest for social justice while at the same time setting up parallel political structures within the community. The conflicting ideologies of the groups provide a separate vision of what is possible politically and is at the heart of both conflicts.[38] Protestant Unionists vote for pro-British parties while Catholic Nationalists vote for pro-Irish parties. In Israel, Israeli Jews tend to vote for "Zionist parties," unlike Israeli Arabs.

Minority Scapegoating: The hegemonic political elite scapegoats the minority as disloyal citizens while the state turns its legal and political apparatuses towards containing the other.[39] Special powers are decreed by the state, which allows the security forces generally made up entirely by the in-group to forcefully police the minority group.[40] This policing in turn exacerbates tensions and hostility within the minority community, as the police and army begin to

exceed their power. Hence, one can see many Israelis perceiving Palestinians as militant and untrustworthy while Protestants see Catholics as a disloyal fifth column who are a threat to Northern Ireland's political position within the United Kingdom.

Nationalism: A pan-nationalist front unites all shades of political opinion within both the in-group and the out-group while a nationalist ideology becomes the goal for each ethnoterritorial group.[41] However, nationalists are also divided over what shape the future nation state should take; should it include or exclude constitutional members of the other community? An ensuing tussle between moderates and extremists witnesses competing nationalist discourses within each community.

Israel has more power over the Palestinians. According to foreign reports, Israel has also about 100–150 tactical nuclear weapons to deal with external threats while the Arab world has more human and material resources to throw into any conflict with Israel.[42] For Israel, terrorist attacks and three regional wars demonstrate the Arab intention to annihilate their state. Abu Mazan's Fatah is trying to negotiate a two-state solution with Israel while the militant nationalism of Hamas refuses to recognize Israel and the Jewish settlements in Gaza and the West Bank. Moderate Unionists and Nationalists are working together within the framework of the 1998 Good Friday Agreement (GFA) to negotiate a devolved power sharing administration while breakaways from the more militant PIRA and UDA and Ulster Volunteer Force (UVF) refuse to negotiate with the other side believing that the use of violence is more pragmatic than politics.[43]

Paramilitaries: Paramilitaries initially form to protect their communities against violence directed against the people by both the security forces and/or rival paramilitaries or to take the ethnic war to the other group. Paramilitaries also serve the interests of the political elites within their own communities. They use political violence to keep the conflict at an escalated level because they fear that to end the political violence their political leaders will give too much away when they negotiate and compromise with the political leaders in the other community.[44] Hamas's use of suicide bombers in Israel leads to a lack of security and a siege mentality within Israel. Ariel Sharon built the separation wall to deter suicide bombers from crossing into Israel and to offer some kind of security to Israeli citizens.[45] Rogue Loyalist and Republican paramilitary splinter groups' efforts to destabilize the political process and bring down the GFA through the tactical use of bombings and targeted assassinations continue, as the majority of citizens have bought into the peace process.[46]

Structural Violence: The hegemonic group ensures that the political structure of the state discriminates against the out-group and that hidden, as well as overt violence, is built into the very structures of society.[47] Structural violence stunts the optimal development of every human being within the out-group on the basis of his or her ethnoterritorial identity. Individuals from the out-group cannot serve in public office, the civil service, or the security forces because they are construed as enemies of the state.

Minority members might be given marginal roles in the political institutions and in the structure of society, so that the majority can claim that some members of the minority are included, and thus inclusion is a matter of merit rather than identity.[48] However, even if minorities may be included in the institutions, there remains much to fight for because it does little good to be included in the institutions unless one can make a difference. Members of the minority often seek to have at least a voice, that is, to be consulted in the policymaking stage. They desire to have input and some control over some policies, especially those that particularly affect them.

The Northern Ireland Civil Rights Association (NICRA) came about in 1968 because Catholics were discriminated against in terms of employment, housing, and voting in elections. Today segregated housing and schools polarize both communities and make compromise difficult. Sectarianism continues to trickle down invisibly through the institutions, discriminating against Protestants and Catholics in terms of employment and housing.[49] In Israel Arab citizens are not Jewish and the state is a Jewish state. Although Arabs enjoy most of the privileges of Jewish citizens they have a different type of status.[50] The structural violence is more extreme in cases of different levels of discrimination. The resistance of Israeli Arabs was always much lower than that of Palestinians in the West Bank and Gaza Strip.

PSYCHOCULTURAL FORCE

Psychocultural issues are critical to the escalation and de-escalation of ethnic conflicts. As interaction continues, emotions are likely to shape future interaction and to affect attribution of the other's motives while cultural markers serve the purpose of marking out-group boundaries, making it clear to which group one belongs.[51]

Identity: Individuals need to belong to a group, especially under the conditions of protracted ethnoterritorial conflict. Group identity assists the individual in developing a self-definition and sense of self-esteem, and requires both a sense of belonging and a sense of differentiation from others. Identity serves to exclude those who do not fit within the cultural traits of the in-group. Group-identity boundaries also drive a wedge between communities, thus escalating tensions.[52] A distorted identity develops as individuals' moral values and identity disappear and attachment to the ideology intensifies.[53] Stereotypes are used to create the other and leaders can emphasize different identities in their appeals to constituents. As leaders face new opportunities or challenges, they may shift group labels or levels of inclusiveness in their discourse. Appeals to identity enable the leaders to overcome the free-rider problem by encouraging individuals to view group goals as their own.

When two ethnic groups compete for the same territory, an intractable conflict ensues. Israelis and Palestinians as well as Protestants and Catholics believe that each group has an exclusive legitimacy to hold their respective lands, each one portraying itself as an indigenous group while the other is construed as an illegitimate invader who wants to steal the in-group's land.[54] This reality leads to threats and insecurity because any concession to the other side is perceived as a loss. Hence, the cries of "not an inch" and "no surrender" shape the relations of the rival groups.

Self-Esteem and Self-Efficacy: Individuals in the out-group are objectified and abandoned by friends, which creates a tremendous potential of individual trauma.[55] The victim develops a diminished sense of self and perceives the world as a dangerous place while the in-group begins to devalue the out-group, and over time this behavior intensifies as the motivation toward instrumental violence increases.[56] As conflict escalates, members of the in-group increasingly view the out-group as homogenous, and the dehumanization that occurs leads members of the in-group to see themselves as superior to the others.

Israelis and Palestinians, and Protestants and Catholics, attribute positive traits and values to their own group, portraying themselves as brave, courageous, determined, hardworking, and intelligent. The in-group believes that its goals are just and that the out-group has no legitimacy, which in effect denies the right of the out-group to exist.

Frustration, Anger and Fear: As members of groups come to see themselves as deprived of things others get, they may lose hope and become frustrated with the current system, develop a sense of injustice, and then choose to engage in violent conflict. As the conflict develops, frustration develops into anger and fear of the other group. Members of groups locked in highly escalated conflict fear genocide, and believe that the other group will wipe it out it. The media play a significant role in distorting the image of the other. Also, "conversion specialists" use local issues to spark intergroup tensions at both the micro and macro levels.[57] All members of the out-group are clumped together, and stripped of their individuality. The anger of the in-group is then directed against the other, as individuals become detached from their individual affective thinking processes.

Palestinians, Israelis, Catholics, and Protestants feel persecuted and mistrustful, which leads to a lack of security and a siege mentality. The Holocaust, terrorism, massacres, expulsions, and raped homelands are used as each group's self-presentation as victims of the other side.[58]

Perceptions: Misperceptions arise regarding the perceived behavior of the other group. As tension increases, the behavior of the other is construed as increasingly hostile, even if their behavior is not threatening. Each act of the out-group is interpreted in negative terms, which serves to escalate tensions between both groups. As part of the interactions from other elements in the social cube, misperceptions eventually lead to a zero-sum confrontation. Palestinians and Catholics argue that foreigners invaded and occupied the land and dispossessed them. Some Palestinians refuse to believe that Israelis are returning to their homeland after 2,000 years while Catholics refuse to recognize that Protestants have been living in Northern Ireland for over 400 years.

Symbols: Cultural symbols serve to reinforce group boundaries, and group identity.[59] Folklore, language, flags, national anthems, and cultural events give a distinctive flavor to the group's identity. These trappings of culture allow the dominant group to develop a "culture of superiority" as it works to eradicate the cultural symbols of the other society in a process that Anthony Smith terms "ethnocide."[60]

Voluntary and Forced Segregation: As a result of conflict, ethnic groups may begin to move into enclaves to protect their cultural way of living, leading to some kind of cultural tranquility.[61] Alternatively, the government might establish policies that produce segregated areas in housing, workplace, and schools to ensure little contact so that stereotypes cannot be challenged empirically on a day-to-day basis.[62] Mixed neighborhoods disappear as people from the other group are forcibly removed from the area. Once the process of ethnic cleansing starts, it is extremely difficult to reverse. Palestinians travel through the checkpoints to work in Israel with the wall separating Israel from the Palestinian Authority while in Israel Jews and Israeli Arabs live within their own enclaves.[63] In Northern Ireland neighborhoods are segregated, as each community strives to protect its culture, way of life, and security for its people.

DEMOGRAPHIC FORCE

Demography (the size of ethnic groups) certainly affects conflict. Minority groups have to mimic the behavior of the dominant group to survive while the dominant group does not have to learn the cultural mores and historical experience of the other. Rapid changes in the size of groups relative to each other can produce attributions of threat or opportunity; indeed, minorities may view the "revenge of the cradle" as their best option for long-term security.[64]

Double Minority: When geographical contexts are shifted an ethnic group, which is in the majority, may find itself in the minority, and an ethnic group in the minority may become the majority group. For example, Catholics in Northern Ireland are a minority in both the United Kingdom and Northern Ireland, but they are in the majority if the context is the island of Ireland. Both groups may claim they are discriminated against and threatened because of the other's superior numbers. The numbers game has a wide range of implications for ethnic groups who are trapped in protracted conflict, ranging from being a minority without political power to fear of cultural ethnocide, fear of genocide, and feeling under siege among others.[65] In Israel, excluding the West Bank and Gaza Strip, it is estimated that between 75 and 80 percent of the population are Israeli Jews[66] while Israelis are a minority in the Middle East. In Northern Ireland Catholics are 45 percent of the population and 70 percent within a united Ireland context.[67]

Political Geography: Everyone is aware of the dangers of passing through the territory of the other community as one can be beaten, interrogated, and even killed for straying into the enclave of the enemy.[68] Cultural signposts such as political wall murals, footpaths painted with group colors, and flags signify the territory of each community. There is also an urban-rural dichotomy that allows the conflict to take on many shapes and forms. Some geographical boundaries between communities tend to be less stringent than others, as there is a lot of variation within the conflict.

Cognitively, individuals are aware of the geographical space and what is and what is not safe for them to do. Majority groups use cultural ceremonies to march through the territory of the other, essentially marking out territory.[69] Such events can lead to confrontation, as the other uses violence to protect its community against what it perceives as cultural encroachment and triumphalism. For example, flashpoint areas, such as the Garvaghy Road in Portadown, and the Ormeau Road in Belfast, serve to escalate conflict between Protestants and Catholics during the marching season in Northern Ireland. A "chill factor" serves to prevent a member of one group from working in or traveling into the spatial territory of the other community.

Palestinians rejected the UN 1947 two-state solution and the resulting war between Israel and its Arab neighbors resulted in Israel expanding its borders and the displacement of Palestinian refugees. As a result of the 1967 war, Gaza Strip and the West Bank were taken from Egypt and Jordan. Today, most Palestinians refuse to recognize Jewish settlements in the West Bank, while the case for the 1948 borders is different.[70]

Genocide and *Differential Growth*: The Holocaust, the Nakbah, Bloody Sunday, and the Enniskillen Remembrance Day bombing leads to a lack of security, trust, and a siege mentality, as each group presents itself as the victim of the other side so that each group's needs are non-negotiable.

ECONOMIC FORCE

Economic power is harnessed by the dominant ethnic group to maintain the loyalty of the working class within its community, excluding the other group from access to resources. Class differences are also integrated into nationalist protest.

Discriminatory Policies: Discriminatory policies are set up by the elites within the dominant group to exclude the minority group from employment and housing while opening up these opportunities for the working class within its own group. Further, these policies also serve to force the unemployed in the out-group to immigrate to other countries, so that the birth rate is lowered in the out-group and it never has the numbers to become a majority.

In Mandate Palestine, Arabs employed in the Jewish economy earned significantly less than Jews in the same position. This was due to the Zionist policy to limit Arab employment and keep Jewish wages high in order to encourage Jewish immigration.[71] These Palestinian workers receive no welfare or health benefits from the state. In Northern Ireland, the McBride Principles, coupled with the Fair Employment Agency, ensure that the economic policies adopted by the government are not discriminatory.[72] However, sectarianism as a practice continues in non-skilled and semi-skilled employment.

Poverty and Political Violence: Consequently, the impoverished and unemployed working class within the out-group become alienated and disenchanted with their lot. This alienated group forms paramilitary organizations dedicated to the use of political violence to achieve economic and political goals. Young people join the organizations in part because they have nothing to lose, but also because the Marxist-nationalist ideologies of these movements appeals to their sense of spirit, adventure, excitement, grievance, and future society.

In the 1970s young unemployed Catholics flocked to join the PIRA in the long war with Britain; after Bloody Sunday, the ranks of the PIRA burgeoned with new recruits.[73] Similarly, young, unemployed Palestinians or those trapped in dead-end jobs tended to join the Palestinian national uprisings of 1936 and 1987[74] and the people who joined the ranks of Fatah and Hamas as part of the militant and violent struggle with Israel were, specifically, from the same stratum.[75]

Colonizer-Colonized Relationship: The out-group is treated within the context of a colonizer-colonized relationship. The colonizer or the in-group sets up a racist apparatus to justify, legitimate, and protect its economic privileges.[76] The state has a strong police force to police the "wicked native," a government to rule the "backward and ignorant native," and a judicial system to punish the native. The dialectical relationship between the colonizer and the colonized allows the native to both admire and hate the colonizer at the same time.[77] However, it is the ultimate dream of the persecuted to become the persecutor and the out-group turns to political violence to rid itself of the in-group. This relationship can be seen in both cases of Northern Ireland and Israel.

Diaspora: The ethnic diaspora and external forces increasingly send economic aid and munitions to support the out-group's armed struggle against the hegemonic state.[78] For example, over the past thirty years Irish Americans sent millions of dollars through NORAID and Libya's Colonel Gadhafi supplied seven shiploads of weapons and munitions to support the PIRA's long war within Northern Ireland. Within the ethnic conflict, the in-group is forced to provide more economic resources to its security forces to protect the community against the political violence of the out-group. Israel has wide Jewish diasporas supporting it. Palestinians who worked in Israel, as well as in the Gulf countries, provided economic resources to ensure a decent quality of life for family members living in Palestine. Similarly, Catholics and Protestants who work abroad have provided a source of economic infusion into their respective communities in Northern Ireland.

CONCLUSION

There is a strong role for external, economic assistance in an interim period in the political, economic, and psychological (self-esteem and self-efficacy) of working-class Palestinians and Israelis, Catholics and Protestants. The social cubism analytical model illustrates the underlying driving forces in both the Israeli–Palestinian and the Northern Ireland conflicts. Historical symbolism combined with religious differences, fear and misperception, political identities, economic discrimination, and a culture of violence has ensured little contact among the ethnic groups as stereotypes and prejudices structure bipolar relationships.

We acknowledge that a comprehensive, long-term peace plan must approach the conflict system from multimodal and multilevel interventions, which includes a strong economic dimension, to facilitate constructive interaction, to solve problems, and to get all of the key issues on the table in order to encourage the groups to share their hopes, fears, and needs. Thus, a new paradigm of engagement built on a trusting and peaceful relationship can forge a vision of peace so that the ethnoterritorial groups can negotiate territory, power, and wealth. It is hoped that further research would explore these spheres, external actors and structures to provide a wider analysis alongside the method of the cube. Hopefully, this would bring about better understanding and successful peacebuilding.

BIBLIOGRAPHY

Abu-Nimer, Mohammad. *Conflict Resolution and Change: The Case of Arabs and Jews in Israel.* Albany, NY: SUNY Press, 1999.

Bar-On, Dan. *Tell Your Life Story: Creating Dialogue Among Jews And Germans, Israelis And Palestinians.* Budapest: Central European University Press, 2006.

Bekerman, Zvi. "The Ethnography of Peace Education: Some Lessons Learned from Palestinian-Jewish Integrated Education in Israel," in *Handbook of Conflict Analysis and Resolution,* Dennis Sandole, Sean Byrne, Ingrid Sandole-Staroste, and Jessica Senehi, eds. London: Routledge, 2009, 142–154.

Ben-Ami, Shlomo. *Scars of War, Wounds of Peace: The Israeli-Arab Tragedy.* London: Phoenix, 2005.

Bew, Paul. *Ireland: The Politics of Enmity 1789–2006.* Oxford: Oxford University Press, 2007.

Bollens, Scott. *On Narrow Ground: Urban Policy and Conflict in Jerusalem and Belfast.* Binghamton: State University of New York Press, 2000.

Bose, Sumantra. *Contested Lands: Israel-Palestine, Kashmir, Bosnia, Cyprus and Sri Lanka.* Boston: Harvard University Press, 2007.

Bryan, Dominic, T.G. Fraser, and Seamus Dunn. *Political Rituals: Loyalist Parades in Portadown.* Coleraine: University of Ulster, 1995.

Brynen, Rex. *A Very Political Economy: Peace Building and Foreign Aid in the West Bank and Gaza.* Washington, DC: USIP Press, 2000.

Byrne, Sean. *Economic Assistance and the Northern Ireland Conflict: Building the Peace Dividend.* Cranbury, NJ: Associated University Press, 2009.

———. "The Politics of Peace and War in Northern Ireland," in *Regional and Ethnic Conflicts Perspectives from the Front Lines*. Judy Carter, George Irani, and Vamik Volkan, eds. New York: Prentice Hall, 2009, chapter 9

———. "Mired in Intractability: The Roles of External Ethno-Guarantors and Primary Mediators in Cyprus and Northern Ireland," *Conflict Resolution Quarterly* vol. 24, no. 3 (2007): 149–172.

———. "Toward Tractability: The 1993 South African Record of Understanding and the 1998 Northern Ireland Good Friday Agreement," *Irish Studies in International Affairs* vol. 13, no. 1 (2002): 135–149.

———. "Consociational and Civic Society Approaches to Peace Building in Northern Ireland," *Journal of Peace Research,* vol. 38, no. 3 (2001): 327–352.

———. "Power Politics as Usual: Divided Islands and the Roles of External Ethno-Guarantors," *Nationalism and Ethnic Politics,* vol. 6, no. 1 (2000): 1–24.

———. *Growing Up in a Divided Society: The Influence of Conflict on Belfast Schoolchildren*. Cranbury, NJ: Associated University Presses, 1997.

Byrne, Sean, and Neal Carter. "Social Cubism: Six Social Forces of Ethnoterritorial Politics in Northern Ireland and Quebec," *Peace and Conflict Studies*, vol. 3, no. 2 (1996): 52–72.

Byrne, Sean, Neal Carter, and Jessica Senehi. "Social Cubism and Social Conflict: Analysis and Resolution," *International and Comparative Law*, vol. 8, no. 3 (2002): 725–740.

Byrne, Sean, and Loraleigh Keashly. "Working with Ethno-Political Conflict: A Multi-Modal and Multi-Level Approach to Conflict Intervention," *International Peacekeeping,* vol. 7, no. 1 (2000): 97–120.

Carter, Judy, George Irani, and Vamik Volkan, eds. *Regional and Ethnic Conflicts: Perspectives from the Front Lines*. New York: Prentice Hall, 2009.

Cox, Michael, Adrian Guelke, and Fiona Stephen. "Introduction: A Farewell to Arms? From Long War to Uncertain Peace in Northern Ireland," in *A Farewell to Arms? From "Long War" to Long Peace in Northern Ireland,* Michael Cox, Adrian Guelke, and Fiona Stephen, eds. Manchester: Manchester University Press, 2000, 1–11.

Darby, John. *The Effects of Violence on Peace Processes*. Washington, DC: United States Institute of Peace Press, 2001.

Enloe, Cynthia. *Manoeuvres: The International Politics of Militarizing Women's Lives*. Berkeley: University of California Press, 2000.

Fanon, Frantz. *The Wretched of the Earth*. Jackson, TN: Grove Press, 1965.

Fisk, Robert. *The Great War for Civilization: The Conquest of the Middle East*. New York: Knopf, 2005.

Galtung, Johan. *Peace by Peaceful Means: Peace and Conflict Development and Civilization*. London: Sage, 1996.

Gavron, Daniel. *The Other Side of Despair: Jews and Arabs in the Promised Land*. Boulder, CO: Rowman and Littlefield, 2004.

Guelke, Adrian. *Northern Ireland: The International Perspective*. Dublin: Gill and Macmillan, 1988.

Hechter, Michael. *Internal Colonialism: The Celtic Fringe in British National Development, 1536–1966*. London: Routledge and Kegan Paul, 1975.

Horowitz, Donald L. *The Deadly Ethnic Riot*. Berkeley: University of California Press, 2001.

Jeong, Ho-Won. *Peacebuilding in Postconflict Societies: Strategy and Process*. Boulder, CO: Lynne Rienner, 2005.

Kaufman, Edy, and Manuel Hassassian. "Understanding Our Israeli-Palestinian Conflict and Searching for its Resolution," in *Regional and Ethnic Conflicts: Perspectives From the Front Lines*, Judy Carter, George Irani, and Vamik Volkan, eds. Upper Saddle River, NJ: Pearson/Prentice Hall, 2009, 87–129.

Kelman, Herb. "Group Processes in the Resolution of International Conflicts: Experiences from the Israeli-Palestinian Case." *American Psychologist*, vol. 52, no. 3 (1997): 212–220.

Kimmerling, Baruch, and Joel Migdal. *The Palestinian People: A History*. Boston: Harvard University Press, 2003.

Kriesberg, Louis. *Constructive Conflicts: From Escalation to Resolution*. Lanham, MD: Rowman and Littlefield, 1998.

Kriesberg, Louis, and Bruce Dayton. *Conflict Transformation and Peacebuilding: Moving From Violence to Sustainable Peace*. London: Routledge, 2009.

Lederach, John Paul. *Building Peace: Sustainable Reconciliation in Divided Societies*. Washington, DC: United States Institute of Peace, 1997.

———. *Preparing for Peace: Conflict Transformation Across Cultures*. Syracuse, NY: Syracuse University Press, 1995.

Levitt, Matthew. *Hamas: Politics, Charity and Terrorism in the Service of Jihad*. New Haven, CT: Yale University Press, 2006.

Memmi, Albert. *The Colonizer and the Colonized*. London: Souvenir Press, 1974.

Miall, Hugh, Oliver Ramsbotham, and Tom Woodhouse. *Contemporary Conflict Resolution: The Prevention, Management and Transformation of Deadly Conflicts*. Cambridge, MA: Polity Press, 1999.

Nadan, Amos. "From the Arab Revolt to the Al-Aqsa Intifada: The Economic and Social Dimensions," *Skirot*, vol. 131 (2003): 53–85.

———. *The Palestinian Peasant Economy under the Mandate: A Story of Colonial Bungling*. Boston: Harvard University Press, 2006.

O'Leary, Brendan, and John McGarry. *The Politics of Antagonism: Understanding Northern Ireland*. Atlantic Highlands, NJ: Athlone, 1996.

Olson-Lounsberry, Marie, and Fred Pearson. *Civil Wars: Internal Struggles, Global Consequences*. Toronto: University of Toronto Press, 2009.

Pearson, Fred. "Dimensions of Conflict Resolution in Ethnopolitical Disputes," *Journal of Peace Research*, vol. 38, no. 2 (2001): 275–288.

Rabie, Mohamed. *Conflict Resolution and Ethnicity*. Westport, CT: Praeger, 1994.

Ross, Marc Howard. *Cultural Contestation in Ethnic Conflict*. Cambridge: Cambridge University Press, 2007.

Rothman, Jay. *Resolving Identity Based Conflicts*. San Francisco: Jossey-Bass, 1997.

Rouhana, Nadim. *Palestinian Citizens in an Ethnic Jewish State: Identities in Conflict*. New Haven, CT: Yale University Press, 1997.

Ryan, Stephen. *The Transformation of Violent Intercommunal Conflict*. Aldershot: Ashgate, 2007.

Salem, Walid and Edy Kaufman. "From Diagnosis to Treatment: Towards New shared Principles for Israeli-Palestinian Peacebuilding," in *Handbook of Conflict Analysis and Resolution*, Dennis Sandole, Sean Byrne, Ingrid Sandole-Staroste, and Jessica Senehi, eds. London: Routledge, 2009, 435–453.

Schirch, Lisa. *Ritual and Symbol in Peacebuilding*. West Hartford, CT: Kumarian Press, 2004.

Senehi, Jessica. "Building Peace: Storytelling to Transform Conflicts Constructively," in *Handbook of Conflict Analysis and Resolution*, Dennis Sandole, Sean Byrne, Ingrid Sandole-Staroste, and Jessica Senehi, eds. London: Routledge, 2009, 199–212.

———. "The Role of Constructive Transcultural Storytelling in Ethnopolitical Conflict Transformation in Northern Ireland," in *Regional and Ethnic Conflicts: Perspectives From the Front Lines*, Judy Carter, George Irani, and Vamik Volkan, eds. Upper Saddle River, NJ: Prentice Hall, 2009, 227–237

———. "Constructive Storytelling: A Peace Process." *Peace and Conflict Studies* vol. 9, no. 2 (2002): 41–63.

———. "Constructive Storytelling in Inter-Communal Conflicts: Building Community, Building Peace," in *Reconcilable Differences: Turning Points in Ethnopolitical Conflict,* Sean Byrne, Cynthia Irvin, Paul Dixon, Brian Polkinghorn, and Jessica Senehi, eds. West Hartford, CT: Kumarian, 2000, 96–115.

———. "Language, Culture and Conflict: Storytelling as a Matter of Life and Death," *Mind and Human Interaction,* vol. 7, no. 3 (1996): 150–164.

Senehi, Jessica, and Sean Byrne. "From Violence Toward Peace: The Role of Storytelling for Youth Healing and Political Empowerment After Conflict," in *Troublemakers or Peacemakers? Youth and Post-Accord Peace-Building*, Siobhan McEvoy-Levy, ed. South Bend, IN: University of Notre Dame Press, 2006, 235–258.

Smith, Anthony D. *Chosen Peoples: Sacred Sources of National Identity*. Oxford: Oxford University Press, 2003.

———. "Culture, Community and Territory: The Politics of Ethnicity and Nationalism," *International Affairs,* vol. 72, no. 3 (1996): 445–458.

Sylvester, Christine. *Feminist International Relations: An Unfinished Journey*. Cambridge: Cambridge University Press, 2002.

Staub, Ervin. *The Roots of Evil: The Origins of Genocide and Other Group Violence*. Cambridge: Cambridge University Press, 1992.

Volkan, Vamik. *Blood Lines: From Ethnic Pride to Ethnic Terrorism*. Boulder, CO: Westview, 1998.

Whyte, John. *Interpreting Northern Ireland*. Oxford: Clarendon, 1990.

Wolff, Stefan. *Ethnic Conflict: A Global Perspective*. Oxford: Oxford University Press, 2006.

Zartman, William I. "Ethnic Conflicts: Mediating Conflicts of Need, Greed, and Creed," *Orbis,* vol. 44, no. 2 (Spring 2000): 255–266.

NOTES

1. Acknowledgments: Research on this project was supported by a grant from the Canadian Friends of the Hebrew University of Jerusalem in honor of Dr. Arthur V. Mauro.

2. Sean Byrne and Loraleigh Keashly, "Working with Ethno-Political Conflict: A Multi-Modal and Multi-Level Approach to Conflict Intervention," *International Peacekeeping*, vol. 7, no. 1 (2000): 97–120.

3. Sean Byrne and Neal Carter, "Social Cubism: Six Social Forces of Ethnoterritorial Politics in Northern Ireland and Quebec," *Peace and Conflict Studies*, vol. 3, no. 2 (1996): 52–72.

4. Sean Byrne, Neal Carter, and Jessica Senehi, "Social Cubism and Social Conflict: Analysis and Resolution," *International and Comparative Law*, vol. 8, no. 3 (2002): 725–740.

5. Anthony D. Smith, "Culture, Community and Territory: The Politics of Ethnicity and Nationalism," *International Affairs,* vol. 72, no. 3 (1996): 445–458.

6. Stefan Wolff, *Ethnic Conflict: A Global Perspective.* Oxford: Oxford University Press, 2006.

7. Nadim Rouhana, *Palestinian Citizens in an Ethnic Jewish State: Identities in Conflict.* New Haven, CT: Yale University Press, 1997.

8. Paul Arthur, *Special Relationships: Britain, Ireland and the Northern Ireland Problem*, 2000.

9. Jessica Senehi, "Constructive Storytelling in Inter-Communal Conflicts: Building Community, Building Peace," in *Reconcilable Differences: Turning Points in Ethnopolitical Conflict,* Sean Byrne, Cynthia Irvin, Paul Dixon, Brian Polkinghorn, and Jessica Senehi, eds. (West Hartford, CT: Kumarian, 2000), 96–115.

10. Jessica Senehi, "Building Peace: Storytelling to Transform Conflicts Constructively," in *Handbook of Conflict Analysis and Resolution*, Dennis Sandole, Sean Byrne, Ingrid Sandole-Staroste, and Jessica Senehi, eds. (London: Routledge, 2009), 199–212.

11. Jessica Senehi, "Constructive Storytelling: A Peace Process," *Peace and Conflict Studies,* vol. 9, no. 2 (2002): 41–63.

12. Jessica Senehi, "The Role of Constructive Transcultural Storytelling in Ethnopolitical Conflict Transformation in Northern Ireland," in *Regional and Ethnic Conflicts: Perspectives From the Front Lines*, Judy Carter, George Irani, and Vamik Volkan, eds. (Upper Saddle River, NJ: Prentice Hall, 2009), 227–237.

13. Jessica Senehi and Sean Byrne, "From Violence Toward Peace: The Role of Storytelling for Youth Healing and Political Empowerment After Conflict," in *Troublemakers or Peacemakers? Youth and Post-Accord Peace-Building*, Siobhan McEvoy-Levy, ed. (South Bend, IN: University of Notre Dame Press, 2006), 235–258.

14. Stephen Ryan, *The Transformation of Violent Intercommunal Conflict* (Aldershot: Ashgate, 2007).

15. Smith, "Culture."

16. Anthony D. Smith, *Chosen Peoples: Sacred Sources of National Identity* (Oxford: Oxford University Press, 2003).

17. Daniel Gavron, *The Other Side of Despair: Jews and Arabs in the Promised Land* (Boulder, CO: Rowman and Littlefield, 2004).

18. Cynthia Enloe, *Manoeuvres: The International Politics of Militarizing Women's Lives* (Berkeley: University of California Press, 2000).

19. Christine Sylvester, *Feminist International Relations: An Unfinished Journey* (Cambridge: Cambridge University Press, 2002).

20. Matthew Levitt, *Hamas: Politics, Charity and Terrorism in the Service of Jihad* (New Haven, CT: Yale University Press, 2006).

21. Zvi Bekerman, "The Ethnography of Peace Education: Some Lessons Learned from Palestinian-Jewish Integrated Education in Israel," in *Handbook of Conflict Analysis and Resolution*, Dennis Sandole, Sean Byrne, Ingrid Sandole-Staroste, and Jessica Senehi, eds. (London: Routledge, 2009), 142–154.

22. Sean Byrne, "Mired in Intractability: The Roles of External Ethno-Guarantors and Primary Mediators in Cyprus and Northern Ireland, "*Conflict Resolution Quarterly*, vol. 24, no. 3 (2007): 149–172.

23. Vamik Volkan, *Blood Lines: From Ethnic Pride to Ethnic Terrorism* (Boulder, CO: Westview, 1998).

24. Jessica Senehi, "Language, Culture and Conflict: Storytelling as a Matter of Life and Death," *Mind and Human Interaction,* vol. 7, no. 3 (1996): 150–164.

25. Mohammad Abu-Nimer, *Conflict Resolution and Change: The Case of Arabs and Jews in Israel* (Albany, NY: SUNY Press, 1999).

26. Brauch Kimmerling and Joel Migdal, *The Palestinian People: A History* (Boston: Harvard University Press, 2003).

27. Senehi, "Building Peace."

28. John Darby *The Effects of Violence on Peace Processes* (Washington, DC: United States Institute of Peace Press, 2001).

29. Smith, "Culture, Community, and Territory."

30. John Whyte, *Interpreting Northern Ireland* (Oxford: Clarendon, 1990).

31. Sumantra Bose, *Contested Lands: Israel-Palestine, Kashmir, Bosnia, Cyprus and Sri Lanka* (Boston: Harvard University Press, 2007).

32. Scott Bollens, *On Narrow Ground: Urban Policy and Conflict in Jerusalem and Belfast* (Binghamton, NY: State University of New York Press, 2000).

33. Marc Howard Ross, *Cultural Contestation in Ethnic Conflict* (Cambridge: Cambridge University Press, 2007).

34. Marie Olson-Lounsberry and Fred Pearson, *Civil Wars: Internal Struggles, Global Consequences* (Toronto: University of Toronto Press, 2009).

35. Sean Byrne, "Consociational and Civic Society Approaches to Peace Building in Northern Ireland," *Journal of Peace Research,* vol. 38, no. 3 (2001): 327–352.

36. Edy Kaufman and Manuel Hassassian, "Understanding Our Israeli-Palestinian Conflict and Searching for its Resolution," in *Regional and Ethnic Conflicts: Perspectives From the Front Lines*, Judy Carter, George Irani, and Vamik Volkan, eds. (Upper Saddle River, NJ: Pearson/Prentice Hall, 2009), 87–129.

37. Donald L. Horowitz, *The Deadly Ethnic Riot* (Berkeley: University of California Press, 2001).

38. Louis Kriesberg, *Constructive Conflicts: From Escalation to Resolution* (Lanham, MD: Rowman and Littlefield, 1998).

39. Hugh Miall, Oliver Ramsbotham, and Tom Woodhouse, *Contemporary Conflict Resolution: The Prevention, Management and Transformation of Deadly Conflicta* (Cambridge, MA: Polity Press, 1999).

40. Brendan O'Leary and John McGarry, *The Politics of Antagonism: Understanding Northern Ireland* (Atlantic Highlands, NJ: Athlone, 1996).

41. Smith, *Chosen Peoples.*

42. Robert Fisk, *The Great War for Civilization: The Conquest of the Middle East* (New York: Knopf, 2005).

43. Sean Byrne, "Toward Tractability: The 1993 South African Record of Understanding and the 1998 Northern Ireland Good Friday Agreement," *Irish Studies in International Affairs,* vol. 13, no. 1 (2002): 135–149.

44. Ho-Won Jeong, *Peacebuilding in Postconflict Societies: Strategy and Process* (Boulder, CO: Lynne Rienner, 2005).

45. Walid Salem and Edy Kaufman, "From Diagnosis to Treatment: Towards New shared Principles for Israeli-Palestinian Peacebuilding," in *Handbook of Conflict Analysis and Resolution*, Dennis Sandole, Sean Byrne, Ingrid Sandole-Staroste, and Jessica Senehi, eds. (London: Routledge, 2009), 435–453.

46. Sean Byrne, "The Politics of Peace and War in Northern Ireland," in *Regional and Ethnic Conflicts Perspectives from the Front Lines*, Judy Carter, George Irani, and Vamik Volkan, eds. (New York: Prentice Hall, 2009b), chapter 9.

47. Johan Galtung, *Peace by Peaceful Means: Peace and Conflict Development and Civilization* (London: Sage, 1996).

48. Judy Carter, George Irani, and Vamik Volkan, eds., *Regional and Ethnic Conflicts: Perspectives from the Front Lines* (New York: Prentice Hall, 2009).

49. Sean Byrne, *Economic Assistance and the Northern Ireland Conflict: Building the Peace Dividend* (Cranbury, NJ: Associated University Press, 2009).

50. Bekerman, "Ethnography."

51. Lisa Schirch, *Ritual and Symbol in Peacebuilding* (West Hartford, CT: Kumarian Press, 2004).

52. Fred Pearson, "Dimensions of Conflict Resolution in Ethnopolitical Disputes," *Journal of Peace Research,* vol. 38, no. 2 (2001): 275–288.

53. Byrne, "Consociational and Civic Society."

54. Bollens, *Narrow Ground.*

55. Ervin Staub, *The Roots of Evil: The Origins of Genocide and Other Group Violence* (Cambridge: Cambridge University Press, 1992).

56. Volkan, *Blood Lines.*

57. Staub, *Roots of Evil.*

58. Smith, *Chosen Peoples.*

59. John Paul Lederach, *Preparing for Peace: Conflict Transformation Across Cultures* (Syracuse, NY: Syracuse University Press, 1995).

60. Smith, "Culture, Community, and Territory."

61. Sean Byrne, "Power Politics as Usual: Divided Islands and the Roles of External Ethno-Guarantors," *Nationalism and Ethnic Politics,* vol. 6, no. 1 (2000): 1–24.

62. Byrne, *Growing Up in a Divided Society: The Influence of Conflict on Belfast Schoolchildren* (Cranbury, NJ: Associated University Presses, 1997).

63. Amos Nadan, "From the Arab Revolt to the Al-Aqsa Intifada: The Economic and Social Dimensions," *Skirot,* vol. 131 (2003): 53–85.

64. Wolff, *Ethnic Conflict.*

65. Bose, *Contested Lands.*

66. Shlomo Ben-Ami, *Scars of War, Wounds of Peace: The Israeli-Arab Tragedy* (London: Phoenix, 2005).

67. Sean Byrne, "The Politics of Peace and War in Northern Ireland," in *Regional and Ethnic Conflicts Perspectives from the Front Lines*, Judy Carter, George Irani, and Vamik Volkan, eds. (New York: Prentice Hall, 2009), chapter 9.

68. Lederach, *Building Peace.*

69. Dominic Bryan, T.G. Fraser, and Seamus Dunn, *Political Rituals: Loyalist Parades in Portadown* (Coleraine: University of Ulster, 1995).

70. Kimmerling and Migdal, *The Palestinian People.*

71. Amos Nadan, *The Palestinian Peasant Economy under the Mandate: A Story of Colonial Bungling* (Boston: Harvard University Press, 2006).

72. Sean Byrne, *Economic Assistance and the Northern Ireland Conflict: Building the Peace Dividend* (Cranbury, NJ: Associated University Press, 2009).

73. David Bloomfield, *Peacemaking Strategies in Northern Ireland: Building Complementarity in Conflict Management* (London: Palgrave Macmillan, 1997).

74. Nadan, "From the Arab Revolt."

75. Rouhana, *Palestinian Citizens.*

76. Albert Memmi, *The Colonizer and the Colonized* (London: Souvenir Press, 1974).

77. Frantz Fanon, *The Wretched of the Earth* (Jackson, TN: Grove Press, 1965).

78. Carter, Irani, and Volkan, *Blood Lines.*

Chapter 5

Ethnic Genocide, Trauma, Healing, and Recovery

The Case of Identity Ruptures and Restoration among Bosnian Refugees

Ousmane Bakary Bâ and Brenda A. LeFrançois

This chapter focuses on sociological and ethno-anthropological understandings of identity in the context of war, migration, and intercultural dynamics. Covering the traumatic trajectories of ethnic war refugees through their exile from Bosnia-Herzegovina to Quebec, the fundamental concepts of "identity ruptures" and "cultural bereavement" are addressed, and their role in the refugees' integration and adaptation processes are examined.

War and genocide violently and deeply uproot men, women, and children who were socially and culturally signified and structured by a common original identity. Their common identity already broken, refugees move through new traumatic exile experiences after migration. Carrying their memory as the only cultural heritage left to them, they are constantly confronted not only by loss and by duality of culture and language but also by other critical family rifts and new sociocultural divergences.

Thus the experience of migration across societies and cultures tends to be punctuated by multiple irreversible losses and separations. Those losses and separations may impose a deep psychoaffective experience, a persistent existential state of uncertainty and identity anxiety, which questions the ultimate sense of belongingness. Such hardships are not only about an individual disparity of people, objects, or idiosyncratic expressions of identity, but also, more specifically, about a vaster and collective set of sociocultural, sociosymbolic, and structural components. The collective form of these hardships comprises the type of bereavement conceptualized as cultural bereavement or cultural mourning,[1] applicable to various contexts of vital physical and symbolic losses at a broader societal level.

Ethnic genocide perpetrated against individual and collective identities, as well as socioethnic, cultural, or religious belongingness, may also lead to what has been conceptualized as identity ruptures[2] when refugees face hardships related to exile and cumulative cultural shocks experienced during the integration process. Living within and being assimilated by the different and unknown linguistic, sociocultural, political, and economic systems of their new host societies, refugees must start over on the basis of the only legacy that survived the chaos of genocide: the traumatic memory of irreversible individual and collective loss and separation.

Such traumatic memory usually carries with it two psychosocial tendencies affecting the process of integration or adaptation. Individual potential and experiences of social exclusion in the new host society may impact these tendencies. The first, renunciation, consists of a self-construction of meaningfulness attributed to the experiences of irreversible loss and separation. Renunciation allows a new cultural personality and identity to assimilate the receptive values and spaces available in the new host society into the recollection of the basic values carried from the culture of origin. The second, traumatic fixation and regression, may occur if the individual potential for renunciation is impaired or absent or if the host society's receptivity is low. Traumatic fixation and regression may find expression in the conversion phenomena of identity anxiety, aggravated by a deep crisis of ontological security and ultimately leading to various psychosomatic, physical, or mental health problems.

THEORETICAL FRAMEWORK

The current proliferation of wars fueled by radical nationalism—from Bosnia-Herzegovina to Rwanda, Tchetchenia, and elsewhere—has resulted in more than 130 million immigrants, including more than 19 million refugees, comprising a massive demographic amplification of exile phenomena. Migration due to war and genocide cannot be reified and reduced to a simplistic expression of mechanical displacement. It fully incorporates, through the duality of life and death, the crucial issues of survival afterward and it contains the whole ontological value of human identity and its discovery process of "otherness" or alterity. As Grinberg and Grinberg[3] emphasize, any migration comprises a crisis and a traumatic experience.

Permanently de-structuring and restructuring into an unrecognizable configuration the historical sites of many peoples' cultural origins and, hence, collective identities,[4] the contemporary human ecology of exile experiences nevertheless also demonstrates our capacity to survive the intense and ongoing struggles associated with such catastrophes.[5] The theoretical frameworks of sociology, ethno-anthropology, and social work help illustrate the relationship between exile experiences and issues of identity. Many authors count exile experiences among the foundations of human culture and history. Its historicity is recorded by most of the ancient religious texts, such as those in Judaism, Christianity, and Islam. Gomez Mango considers the example of Moses in exile and notes, "exodus is the preservation of origins" and "the state of exile is an appeal to open-mindedness, it is a source of culture."[6]

The notion of identity generally refers to the state of individuality and its uniqueness. Human culture and social organization gives to uniqueness—biologically and symbolically, at every stage of its evolution—the vital means of its own survival, reproduction, and sense of belonging within what sociologists such as Durkheim, Marx, and Weber called a "social totality." In the philosophical approach, "identity" has no reality and cannot be defined without any relationship with otherness. Socially, self-identity and self-consciousness are the same results of the relationship with otherness.[7] In the psychological approach, self-identity appears through many authors as the profound unity of an individual personality who identifies and assimilates the different states of self-consciousness.[8]

Nevertheless, all these authors have emphasized the sociological genesis of identity. In the sociological approach, culture appears as the social basis of the whole psychological dynamic, providing self-identity through otherness. For example, according to Mead,[9] identity is the result of the whole relationship sustained by any individual with the entireness of social processes. In the light of these reflections, "identity" is a consciousness of belonging to a social and cultural entity. That entity provides the ontological attributes and existential justifications rendering members signified and significant. Thus an individual is a social being whose reality, according to Marx, cannot be anything other than the result of the whole social relationship.[10]

The interactions of exile and bereavement have likewise been examined from many perspectives. Sociology of culture examines rituals as social institutions or structures, particularly as regards death and mourning phenomena.[11] These studies have mostly influenced other social sciences in that field, providing them with theoretical frameworks and empirical bases, which enabled their own scientific evolution.[12] From an anthropological or ethno-psychiatric perspective, Thomas and Nathan[13] parse the semantics of mourning, noting the variety of expressions reflecting its many psychological and social manifestations. For example, they note that psychoanalysts refer to the "work of mourning" to indicate an individual's escape from depression and return to enjoyment; while "to carry mourning" refers to external, socially mandated and recognized signs of a state of mourning.

Cultural sociologists and cultural anthropologists have revealed the dialectical relationship between exile and mourning. The same critical psychic processes characterizing the state of mourning for an individual or group having lost a cherished person also affects an exiled individual separated from the original culture, homeland, family members, and sense of belonging. The mourning process, by its disorganization of references and certainties, incorporates a state of exile very similar to territorial and cultural exile. To confirm the dialectical relationship within which the state of exile resides in the state of mourning and vice versa, Monette calls the public funerary ritual "a gathering of exiled people" and notes, "as a ceremonial of memory, the funerary ritual, private or collective, initiates the separation and struggles against it."[14]

Indeed, exile is an integral part of the mourning experience and any act of exile necessarily implies a mourning experience. But cultural mourning is more total and durable, more multidimensional and afflicting, more abstract and historical than the mortal loss of a loved person. It includes mortal loss, but it also transcends it through the trauma and potentially violent events that have been lived through and kept in gestation. The war refugee is a human and social category fundamentally and qualitatively different from any other kind of immigrant. Gomez Mango describes the interactions of mourning and exile and their common ability and predisposition to global cultural rebirth. The exiled individual can be conceived, "not only as a figure of misery, of nostalgia, as a desperate uprooting and hopeless, but also as propitious new form of spirit life."[15]

In addition to the viewpoints of cultural sociology and anthropology, the diachronic and synchronic temporality of the relationships between exile and culture are particularly relevant for this study. The diachronic temporality translates here as the whole historicity of origins, even the most mythical ones, of human society's evolution. As noted above, "exile as the founding principle of cultures"[16] signified key figures through Abraham, the patriarch, Moses, and others such as Oedipus. Even more broadly, the perspective of prehistorical anthropology on the migration of the anthropoids from the African forest to the savannah through the rift valley reveals a major foundational exile experience as the underlying basis of humankind's anthropogenesis and ethnogenesis. The synchronic temporality is marked by radical movements of self-determination leading to cultural, ethnic, religious, and linguistic oppression and resistance. Such "racial," religious, and even linguistic homogenization practices fully materialize the complete tragic sense of ethnic genocide as crime against humanity.[17]

CONTEXT AND METHODOLOGY

To better understand "identity ruptures," "cultural mourning phenomena," and their consequences on war refugees' integration and adaptation process within foreign host societies, the case of Bosnian refugees living in Quebec since 1992 is used as an example.

In 1990 the national question in Bosnia placed in opposition three major nations, three major religions and three major ethnic groups: Orthodox Serbians, Catholic Croatians and Muslim Bosnians. Since their arrival between 1990 and 1992, Bosnian refugees have built a community of more than one thousand members. Being welcomed at the same time and in the same way as other refugees, particularly Serbians and Croatians, Bosnian refugees have developed integration strategies within Quebec Francophone society. But among refugees groups entering Quebec since the 1970s, Bosnians are the least manageable, calling into question the traditional political model and paradigm of immigration management in Canada (Quebec). Their political system (socialism), their social collectivism, and their traditional and religious background (officially atheism but historically Islam), as well as cultural and linguistic discontinuities, separate them from Canadian society. In addition, most documentary sources indicate that Quebec society has never before been confronted by such war events as ethnocide.[18]

Bosnian refugees have experienced relational difficulties with most institutional levels of their integration process and also with host society members. Their trauma expressed as identity ruptures could be worsened by culture shock, the stress of cultural integration, and the hardships of cultural bereavement. In order to theoretically and empirically deepen this research into complex historical and contemporary facets of exile phenomena, it is important to know these refugees' perceptions—their lived experiences, sense of culture, collective identity, massive and violent fragmentation through war, and trajectories during integration and adaptation.

Chaufrault-Duchet and Desmarais defined "life histories" as a global research process where the narrator organizes through his own speech the meaningfulness of his true life experience.[19] This process gives the researcher access to life experiences encompassing the relationships between the individual and his community. Among the typological varieties of life histories such as autobiography or psychobiography, the sociological and cultural orientation of ethnobiography is most appropriate to this research. This approach consists of situating the narrator as the mirror of his culture, his society, his belonging group, and the significant events that marked the individual and collective identity throughout his representations.[20]

The present ethnographic study details the lived experiences of three Bosnian refugee men. The selection criteria are based on participants' lived experiences and hardships as representative informants of ethnic genocide. The non-probabilistic process of sample constitution is limited to the three brothers of the Kuckovic family. Their ethnobiographical life histories were the basis of category and semantic content analysis: the global corpus of five hundred pages in three volumes respectively, collected as ethnobiographical data from these three brothers, revealed the whole sociological and ethno-anthropological scope of their experiential, sociocultural, and discursive representativity.

THE KUCKOVIC BROTHERS

The Kuckovic brothers' ethnobiographies were examined with a variety of goals in mind. One such goal was to understand the basic cultural and collective traditions of peace and their state and definitions of their identity before the war. Another was to identify cultural forms and endogenous knowledge and practices of conflict ritualization, as well as the traditional and endogenous forms of, and healing practices for, cultural mourning within the original society. A further aim was to draw up an inventory of events—that is, individual and collective trajectories during the war, during the exile, and in consequence of their integration and adaptation within the host country. Ultimately as discussed in the next section, the analysis sought input to the formulation of original new research leads and social intervention frameworks that would take into account all of the above and encompass a global contribution to the reconstruction of new cultural references and to ethnocultural diversity in the host society.

To these ends, data analysis focused in the first instance on the configuration of diachronic and synchronic temporality scales in the ethnobiographical histories of the Kuckovic brothers. Their ethno-anthropological scope is recurrently translated through the intergenerational and ancestral experience of exile across the Kuckovic family genealogy all along the ethnobiographical narratives. The temporality scales of the brothers themselves were operationalized and subdivided into four major periods.

First, the pre-war period was examined to better understand the sudden occurrence of ethnic genocide and the complex mechanisms and nature of identity ruptures and cultural bereavement as traumatic consequences of genocide. Analysis focused on the anthropological configuration of the culture and structure of the ethnic group. It revealed specific ways by which individual and collective identities were generated in Bosnian society before the war. Examination of this period revealed the family's previous states, the impacts of the socialization process, and its different stages. During this period, the cultural ethnogenesis of identity formation emerged in the context of the family and the traditions, values, expectations, and aspirations of its belonging community.

Analysis of the war period shows the sudden outbreak of war, specifically marked by the massive and systematic destruction of Bosnian ethnic, religious, cultural, and national identity. This period, as described and analyzed through the life histories, was crucially affected by tragic attempts perpetrated by Serbian military forces and militias to dismantle the Bosnians' individual and collective identity. Tactics included collective expropriation of families' properties, massive exterminations, racial and ethnic cleansing, population displacements and deportations into concentration camps, public rapes, and sophisticated tortures. Specific dehumanization practices were based on a systematic application of scientific methods of human personality destruction inspired by Nazi traditions of the Holocaust.

With an approximate death toll of 800,000 victims and more than 1,000,000 refugees, the survival principle of the exile period was to fly or to die. During this period the international community and international organizations became involved in the discovery of mass concentration and death camps. They established refugee settlement camps where former Bosnian prisoners and other asylum seekers were protected and organized for exile. Analysis reveals the experience of exile was lived through a contradictory emotional duality: the happiness and the guiltiness of survival. From their homeland to their new host societies, the brothers' exile trajectory through different countries was marked by fear and culture shocks, language barriers, and other stresses, in addition to their other eventful experiences. Their previous substantial traumas were instantaneously revived by the presence of any officer wearing a military or police uniform, for example, upon their arrival at Quebec City airport as well as at many other points through their journey.

The arrival, settling, and integration period included the welcoming, the provision of housing, and the brothers' first contacts with immigrant and refugees agencies managing their adjustment and integration process. It is also the period during which, after their registration in the social welfare program, they had to attend French immersion school in the same classes with other Serbian refugees still perceived as their aggressors and enemies. During this period their long-repressed and suspended trauma suddenly re-emerged. It affected, through multiple types of psychological, emotional and physical disorders and distresses, their ability to face the hardships of integration into their new host society. Their experience of this war trauma was aggravated by the lack of psychosocial assessment and the non-existence of services specializing in psychotherapy and sociotherapy of refugee victims of ethnic genocide.

In light of these temporality scales, analysis of the ethnobiographies revealed the anthropological issues of the Kuckovic brothers' culture, religion, and history in the context of a particular ideological and sociopolitical system which was strongly denying their community's collective identity and ethnicity. The ethnobiographies emphasize the importance of the collective as well as the personal sense of their identity and history as members of an oppressed family in the pre-war period. The brothers faced identity challenges of birthright statute in the family. This question occurred within the macro-sociological context of the political and cultural prescription of a new ethnonymy to their ethnic group which confused and reduced a religious belonging to a nationality (triggered by the revision of Yugoslavia's constitution in 1963 by Tito). Within this context, the identity significance of accidental occurrence appeared as a marking and structuring factor in the subjects' life history. The ethnobiographies illustrate that a duality exists between social and family projections on an individual identity and the eventful contingency phenomena of factual history. Such divergence from initial expectations found expression within the accidental occurrence of two major symbolically structuring events in the cultural formation of individual identity though the narrators' life histories. It showed the modality by which representations (i.e., interpretations) are inscribed, recorded, and internalized in the collective and mythical imaginary of identity archetypes specific to their culture and society.

The first event revealed that the first names of the three brothers were perceived as the nominal metaphor of a survival myth through the contingency of the coincidental or accidental choice of their first names. The parents' choice of names through the family maternal line was coincidently inspired by a Turkish film based on a real historical war event. In it, three brothers survived a massive extermination of all the population of a village. The attribution of these three survivor brothers' first names respectively to the three Kuckovic brothers is symbolically meaningful, representing a type of psycho-cultural transference of "potential inherited capacity," or survival skills, from the first set of brothers to the second. The cultural interpretation of such transfer is based on a spiritual premonition implying the occurrence of eventful and deadly hardships that the Kuckovic brothers will overcome through their gift of survival skills. Note that the anthropological significance of the ontological transposition of first names within genealogical relationships—from dead ancestors to living descendants—appears to be a fundamental taboo and prohibition within their culture. In contrast to the cultural and symbolic significance of the transference of survivors' first names to living human beings, the transposition of dead ancestors' first names to living descendants is interpreted as a phenomenal transposition that will quickly precipitate the tragic destiny of the first ones and will shorten the starting life of their young descendants.

The second event involved circumcision, considered as a very important ritual of socialization in which sacrificial value and sociosymbolic stature are generally inscribed with religious and cultural justification and significance. As an experience embodying the skill of survival, the circumcision tradition is collectively perceived as a crucial rite of passage and as an empowering instance of cultural and religious socialization for individuals. Within this, the three Kuckovic brothers had to acquire a vital sense of endurance and resilience enabling them to overcome and transcend eventual hardships in life, such as the tragic events they finally lived through during the war, as confirmation of the premonitory and anticipatory experiences noted above. Among the three brothers, the circumcision of the eldest spontaneously occurred when he was three years old, while sleeping alone and without intervention by any family member or other person. It was culturally and religiously integrated into a special ritual which signified it as a sign of divine protection through the action of an entity called "Mellecci," the angel.

Among other decisive traditional instances of the socialization process that engendered the Kuckovic brothers' personal identity within the family, ethnic community, and culture, the ritual of baptism remains the most foundational one. It stands out among the collective rites which forge and mark the individual's sense of group belonging. This major socialization event is essentially marked by the cultural importance and social presence of Zadruga, meaning the much extended and largely inclusive family community. It reveals the social structuring value of the socialization process of the Kuckovic brothers, their family and ethnic group, based upon four founding customs.

Pobratimstvo (fraternity) comprises a very inclusive brotherhood relationship applied broadly across diverse elements of the society, including members of different religions and ethnic groups. It is a preventive custom against conflicts between families, communities, and ethnic or religious groups and plays a vital role in the ritualization of conflict.

Posestrimstvo (the blood's sorority) is a blood ritual of which the sociocultural and historical role in preceding war periods was to seal a blood brotherhood between enemies. They would therefore respect and preserve the peace by considering themselves as brothers in mutual and collective protection. This value was still preserved and applied before the war in Bosnian society as a major cultural tradition and component of conflict ritualization and resolution between Bosnians, Croatians, and Serbians.

Kumstvo (the godfatherhood) allows any member of any non-Bosnian ethnic or religious group to become the godfather of a Bosnian child. For instance, any previously unknown person from those groups, passing near the family house where a child is being born or was recently born or even where a child is sick, will be called and invited by the family to became the child's godfather. This value was, prior to the war, the social and cultural mechanism for the development and enlargement of kinship. It not only enriched the child's diverse socialization models, but also reinforced and promoted individual and collective responsibility for global social peace and harmony.

Komsiluk (good neighborhood values) appears in Bosnian culture as the integrative model for the whole value system presented above. It emphasizes the social, cultural, and interpersonal centrality of the neighborhood relationship system as the source of extended families through intermarriage and mixture between Bosnians and different ethnic and religious groups. This value system explicitly reflects the social and cultural stature of the Bosnian matrilineal exogamic structure. Such structure plays a crucial role in constant social reproduction through the development and renewal of the extension of large family communities (i.e., Zadruga) in a spirit of a collective cohesion. Before the war there was no Bosnian family ceremonial instance in the center of which neighborhood was not celebrated for the re-actualization of their collective historical memory. The purpose as an important traditional form of conflict ritualization is still to remind them that despite the genocide all the different groups fighting each other (Bosnians, Croatians and Serbians) came from the same Slavic origin.

In light of the marking events and fundamental cultural values described above, two major socialization trajectories are discernable through the ethnobiographies: the traditional trajectory and the modern trajectory. Analysis of both trajectories elucidated the founding models by which collective ethnic identity was acquired. It also revealed elements by which the Bosnian community's collective identity became the central target of the war, as lived and witnessed by the three Kuckovic brothers. These included socioeconomic, geopolitical, and ideological oppression as well as instrumentalization of ethnic rivalries.

The three Kuckovic brothers' experience of the trajectory of traditional socialization provided them with the essential core of their personal and collective identity. Their individual symbolic appropriation of the collective founding models occurred in a family and ethnocultural context. Analysis of their life histories showed several important cultural traits. These included the memory of their history, as well as traditions and rituals related to migration and bereavement. More specifically, cultural memory and traditions were transmitted by a key figure, the grandmother, including the experiences and traditions of past family migrations. The Kuckovic brothers' memory and consciousness are paradoxically vivacious, as they recall the historical and cultural anchorage of their genealogical and kinship relationships within their family and ethnic group lineage. Representations and interpretations of their survival within and beyond their experience in concentration camps evoke the sense of their first names, their circumcision experience, and the spirit of Melleci, the protective angel. Key ceremonial traits of their traditional socialization include conjuration and protection rituals against illnesses, misfortunes, and bad luck along travelers' journeys. Cultural mourning rituals and customs related to the experience of loss and separation emphasize the importance of the ritual of water during the departure of travelers in order to prevent misfortunes on their journey.

The three brothers' experiences of the trajectory of modern socialization highlight their educational path and profile in the military, as well as their experiences as industrial technicians. These were lived through various institutional forms of oppression targeting ethnic and religious identity and belonging. As victims, they witnessed the ideological process of ethnic identity racialization through the violent rejection of any kind of cultural mixing. With the eruption of genocidal war came the macro-sociological configuration of collective fractured identities. These were precipitated by massacres, torture and other forms of genocidal ethnic purification and violence as described for the war period above. This trajectory was also marked by the reminiscence movement of collective traditions of the Komsiluk values system. In the face of racist xenophobia and ethnic and linguistic cleansing perpetrated by Serbian military forces during the war, Catholics and Muslims allied through massive and constant public demonstrations and strikes to advocate for the active restoration and rehabilitation of the collective memory of the interethnic faith of the Komsiluk ritual of peace and sociocultural cohesion between rival groups.

DISCUSSION AND CONCLUSION

The representativity of the Kuckovic brothers' trauma stands in metonomy to the social totality of refugees from ethnic genocide. Heuristically, the ethnobiographical analysis of their life histories reveals modalities by which a culture incorporates contingent events of high social and identity significance in order to register them within its sociosymbolic system. The analysis also shows that for refugees of ethnic genocide, the resorption mechanism—processing the devastations of identity ruptures and cultural mourning—remains the basic symbolic material necessary to psychosocial reconstruction. In exile, not forgetting but rather memory, as the only receptacle of true-life experiences, is the faculty from which the creation or reconstruction of new cultural paradigms is truly possible.

The global and qualitative reconstruction of ethnic war refugees' identity ruptures and their integration or adaptation depends principally on two factors. One of these, as noted above, derives chiefly within individual refugees and their communities; namely, the capacity for completion of cultural mourning and the usefulness of cultural endogenous patrimony, original values, and available knowledge and practices. The other, though, derives from perceptions and attitudes of acceptance and solidarity or of exclusion and rejection by host society members. As social and cultural standardization, mostly in the name of economic and political gains, becomes the dominant sociological and political paradigm of modern societies, the survival of ethnic minorities' culture can be crucially endangered. Specifically, this can occur when currently ruling forces within an unequal democracy interplay majority and minority on a simplistic statistical and quantitative basis, placing them in vicious opposition. War diasporas, when badly integrated in their host countries and left to themselves, can turn into a potential source of intrinsic or extrinsic reproduction and transposition of historical traumas and frustrations previously lived. Like most host societies, Quebec has become the receptacle of new social and cultural mutations demanding from both refugees and host members a strong ability to cope with a new sociological context of multiculturalism and interculturalism.

Toward that end, this study has application for both theory and practice. It suggests new research leads for theoretical and empirical exploration from sociological, anthropological and cross-cultural social work perspectives. Similarly, the study has relevance for the comprehensive and phenomenological paradigm in the approaches of social work to war or genocide trauma, as well as to the areas of critical theory, community studies, and anti-oppressive social work.

In social and practical application, on one level it provides cultural empowerment for war refugee communities. Further, it points toward a practical framework of consistent interdisciplinary intervention strategies for social workers, sociologists, anthropologists, psychologists, and others working on immigration issues. Such a framework also has application in conflicts studies, promoting peaceful integration of communities while taking into account the endogenous beliefs, knowledge, practices, expectations of dignity, and real life experiences of refugees.

A methodologically sensitive approach could help individuals, families, and rival ethnic groups to heal, to self-forgive, and to forgive and reconcile with their antagonist ethnic group, acknowledging their common historical, geographic, cultural, and genetic origins. This process could include the psychosocial assessment of trauma by former refugees or immigrant professionals with similar life experiences. Helped through a comprehensive methodological approach that fosters renunciation as defined above and a consequent new cultural identity, war refugees would be empowered to realize—here, now—their investment in the present and future, situating them at the first rank in achievement of their own individual and collective aspirations.

BIBLIOGRAPHY

Bâ, O.B. *Récits ethnobiographiques des Frères Samir, Amir et Alis Kuckovic.* Sainte-Foy, Québec: Presses de l'Université Laval, 2010.

———. *Exil et culture: Génocide ethnique, fractures, deuil et reconstruction identitaire.* Sainte-Foy, Québec: Presses de l'Université Laval, 2009.

———. *La créolisation dans les contextes coloniaux.* Ottawa-Bruxelles: Éditions Muhoka, 2009.

———. "Exil et culture: Fracture d'identité, deuil culturel et processus d'intégration chez les réfugiés victime de génocide ethnique, Tome I-II." PhD diss., l'Université Laval, Québec, 2003.

———. "Etude exploratoire des facteurs culturels influençant l'utilisation ou la sous-utilisation des services de sante modernes par la communauté des nomades peuhls du Borgou, Nord-Benin (Afrique de l'Ouest)." Thèse de Maitrise en Service social, l'Université Laval, Québec, 1994.

Chaufrault-Duchet, M.F. "Récit de vie: Donnée ou texte." *Cahiers de recherché sociologique* vol. 5, no. 2 (1987): 11–30.

Desmarais, D. "Chômage, travail salarié et vie domestique: Esquisse d'une trajectoire sociale," in *Les récits de vie,* D. Desmarais and P. Grell, eds. Montréal: Éditions Saint-Martin, 1986, 55–83

Durkheim, E. *De la division du travail social.* Paris: Lib. F. Alcan, 1983.

———. *Les formes élémentaires de la vie religieuse.* Paris: Lib. F. Alcan, 1912.

Fédida, P. "Preface," in *La survivance: Traduire le trauma collectif,* Janine Altounian. Paris: Dunod, 2000.

Freud, S. *Totem et tabous.* Paris: Éditions Payot, 1912.

Gaussen, F. "L'exil." *Le Monde,* Hors série 1 (1993): 15–20.

Gomez Mango, E. *La place des mères.* Paris: Gallimard, 1999.

———. *L'expérience de l'exil et la culture.* Luxembourg: SDI Publications, 1988.

Griaule, M. *Dieux d'eau: Entretiens avec Ogotommêli. 1947.* Paris: Fayard, 1975.

Grinberg, L., and R. Grinberg. *Psychanalyse du migrant et de l'exilé.* Paris: Césura Lyon, 1986.

Hegel, G.W.F. *La phénoménologie de l'esprit.* Paris: P.U.F., 1806.

———. "L'identité," in *La communication interculturelle,* Jean-René Ladmiral and E.M. Lipiansky, eds. Paris: Armand Colin, 1989, 119–133.

Levy-Strauss, C. *Anthropologie structurale.* Paris: Plon, 1958.

Lipiansky, E.M. *La communication interculturelle.* Paris: Éditions Armand Colin, 1989.

Malinowski, B. *Une theorie scientifique de la culture. Traduction française, 1968 réédité en 1970.* Paris: François Maspero, 1944.

Marx, K. and Engels, F. *Thèse sur Feuerbach: Æuvres choisies.* Thèse Vl, Tome. l. Moscow: Éditions du Progrès, 1978.

Mauss. M. *Sociologie et anthropologie.* Paris: Presses Universitaires de France, 1950.

Mead. G.H. *L'esprit de soi et la société.* Paris: Presses Universitaires de France, 1963.

Mead. M. *Co-Operation and Competition Among Primitive Peoples.* London: McGraw-Hill, 1937.

Monette, L. *Séparer, se réparer seul ou avec les autres.* Québec: Frontières, printemps-été, 1991, 18–21.

Morfaux, L.M. *Vocabulaire de philosophie.* Paris: Armand Colin, 1980.

Poirier, J., S. Clapier-Vallandon, and P. Raybaut. *Les récits de vie: Théorie et pratique.* Paris: Presses Universitaires de France, 1983.

Sartre, J.P. *L'être et le néant: Essai d'ontologie phénoménologique.* Paris: Gallimard, 1970.

Simon, G. *Géodynamique des migrations internationales dans le monde.* Paris: Presses Universitaires de France, 1995.

Spitz, R.A. *De la naissance a la parole.* Paris: Presses Universitaires de France, 1968.

Thomas, L.V., and T. Nathan. "Leçon pour l'Occident: Ritualité du chagrin et du deuil en Afrique noire," in *Rituels de deuil, travail du deuil.* Nouvelle Revue d'Ethnopsychiatrie no. 10, Grenoble: La Pensée sauvage, 1988, 11–44

Tremblay, M.A. *L'afflux des réfugiés politiques au Canada: Les enjeux sociopolitiques.* Québec: Conseil Québécois de la Recherche Sociale, 1988.

NOTES

1. O.B. Bâ, "Etude exploratoire des facteurs culturels influençant l'utilisation ou la sous-utilisation des services de sante modernes par la communauté des nomades peuhls du Borgou, Nord-Benin (Afrique de l'Ouest)," *Thèse de Maitrise en Service social* (l'Université Laval, Québec, 1994); "Exil et culture: Fracture d'identité, deuil culturel et processus d'intégration chez les réfugiés victime de génocide ethnique, Tome I-II," PhD diss. (l'Université Laval, Québec, 2003); *Exil et culture: Génocide ethnique, fractures, deuil et reconstruction identitaire* (Sainte-Foy, Québec: Presses de l'Université Laval, 2009); *La créolisation dans les contextes coloniaux* (Ottawa-Bruxelles: Éditions Muhoka, 2009); Amir Samir et Alis Kuckovic, *Récits ethnobiographiques des Frères* (Sainte-Foy, Québec: Presses de l'Université Laval, 2010).

2. O.B. Bâ, "Etude exploratoire des facteurs culturels influençant l'utilisation ou la sous-utilisation des services de sante modernes par la communauté des nomades peuhls du Borgou, Nord-Benin (Afrique de l'Ouest)," Thèse de Maitrise en Service social (l'Université Laval, Québec, 1994); "Exil et culture," 2003; *Exil et culture*, 2009; *La créolisation*; Samir et Kuckovic, *Récits Ethnobiographiques*.

3. L. Grinberg and R. Grinberg, *Psychanalyse du migrant et de l'exilé* (Paris: Césura Lyon, 1986)

4. G. Simon, *Géodynamique des migrations internationales dans le monde* (Paris: Presses Universitaires de France, 1995), 107.

5. F. Gaussen, "L'exil," *Le Monde,* Hors série 1 (1993): 15–20.

6. Mango Gomez, *L'expérience de l'exil et la culture* (Luxembourg: SDI Publications, 1988), 4–5.

7. G.W.F. Hegel, "L'identité," In *La communication interculturelle,* Jean-René Ladmiral and E.M. Lipiansky, eds. (Paris: Armand Colin, 1989), 119–133; C. Levy-Strauss, *Anthropologie structural* (Paris: Plon, 1958); E.M. Lipiansky, *La communication interculturelle* (Paris: Éditions Armand Colin, 1989).

8. E.g.: S. Freud, *Totem et tabou* (Paris: Éditions Payot, 1912); L.M. Morfaux, *Vocabulaire de philosophie* (Paris: Armand Colin, 1980); R.A. Spitz, *De la naissance a la parole* (Paris: Presses Universitaires de France, 1968).

9. G.H. Mead, *L'esprit de soi et la société* (Paris: Presses Universitaires de France, 1963).

10. K. Marx and F. Engels, *Thèse sur Feuerbach: Æuvres choisies*, Thèse VI, Tome. I. (Moscow: Éditions du Progrès, 1978), 8.

11. E. Durkheim, *Les formes élémentaires de la vie religieuse* (Paris: Lib. F. Alcan, 1912); M. Mauss, *Sociologie et anthropologie* (Paris: Presses Universitaires de France, 1950), 331–362; M. Griaule, *Dieux d'eau: Entretiens avec Ogotommêli. 1947* (Paris: Fayard, 1975).

12. B. Malinowski, *Une theorie scientifique de la culture: Traduction française, 1968 réédité en 1970* (Paris: François Maspero, 1944); M. Mead, *Co-Operation and Competition Among Primitive Peoples* (London: McGraw-Hill, 1937); Levy-Strauss, *Anthropologie structurale*.

13. L.V. Thomas and T. Nathan, "Leçon pour l'Occident: ritualité du chagrin et du deuil en Afrique noire." In *Rituels de deuil, travail du deuil: Nouvelle Revue d'Ethnopsychiatrie* no. 10 (1988): 11–44.

14. L. Monette, *Séparer, se réparer seul ou avec les autres* (Québec: Frontières, printemps-été, 1991), 21

15. Mango E. Gomez, *L'expérience de l'exil et la culture* (Luxembourg: 1988), 8–12.

16. Grinberg and Grinberg, *Psychanalyse du migrant et de l'exilé*; Mango E. Gomez, *La place des mères* (Paris: Gallimard, 1999).

17. P. Fédida, "Preface," in *La survivance: Traduire le trauma collectif*, Janine Altounian (Paris: Dunod, 2000).

18. M.A. Tremblay, *L'afflux des réfugiés politiques au Canada: Les enjeux socio-politiques* (Québec: Conseil Québécois de la Recherche Sociale, 1988).

19. M.F. Chaufrault-Duchet, "Récit de vie: Donnée ou texte," *Cahiers de recherché sociologique,* vol. 5, no. 2 (1987): 11–30; D. Desmarais, "Chômage, travail salarié et vie domestique: Esquisse d'une trajectoire sociale," in *Les récits de vie,* D. Desmarais and P. Grell, eds. (Montréal: Éditions Saint-Martin, 1986), 55–83.

20. J. Poirier, S. Clapier-Vallandon, and P. Raybaut, *Les récits de vie: Théorie et pratique* (Paris: Presses Universitaires de France, 1983).

Chapter 6

Disability and Conflict

Untold Stories from the North of Ireland

Myrtle Hill and Nancy Hansen

> "In times of war, disabled people are even more neglected. During conflicts, where there is so much destruction of life, society and the economy, communities rarely consider the care and protection of disabled people"[1]

People with disabilities make up around 10 percent of the world's population—an estimated 500 million people worldwide. However, as a consequence of fear, social stigma, poverty and lack of access to services, they are often located on the fringes of society and the reality of their lives, both historical and contemporary, remains largely unknown and unexplored. While we are not suggesting that persons with disabilities make up a homogeneous group, for "disability is complex [and] multifactoral [as well as] common,"[2] until very recently their experiences have been thought unworthy of record or analysis and therefore they face similar marginalization in the academic literature. Over the past few decades, however, the issue of disability has slowly emerged as an area of interest in a range of disciplines, including peace and conflict studies, and the aim of this chapter is to draw on the albeit limited research to highlight the ways in which periods of conflict impact on the lives of disabled people.

Given that violent social disruption is itself a major cause of disablement, we would perhaps expect that its greater visibility at such times would impact on attitudes and behaviors by, for example, raising public awareness, changing social perceptions and influencing social policy. This expectation seems an assumption worthy of investigation. Moreover, we know very little of the experiences of people with disabilities who live through periods of violent conflict and to what extent and in what ways those experiences differ from the experiences of their non-disabled peers. To facilitate a more detailed exploration of these various issues, this chapter, following a brief review of relevant literature, will move to a specific focus on the six counties that make up Northern Ireland—a region with a significant percentage of people with disabilities in its population—which is just emerging from a protracted period of conflict.

Conflict and disability has emerged relevantly recently as a theme in the literature of humanitarian agencies and, to a more limited degree, within the academic disciplines of both disability and conflict studies. Geographically, and reflecting the history of war and political upheaval in the second half of the twentieth century, the main focus has been on Eastern Europe, South America, Africa, and the Middle East. Discussion mainly centers on the increase in numbers of the disabled population during periods of conflict, and on the consequences of civil conflict for their health and well-being. In terms of the former, a 1990 report estimated that "non-fatal outcomes of war resulted in 4.8 million disability adjusted life years worldwide, about the same as fires and more than half that caused by road traffic injuries,"[3] and there is general agreement that disabled people are disproportionately affected by conflict. With the relationship between poverty and disability well documented, it is clear that persons with disabilities already exist on the edges of society with limited access to power and resources. Their vulnerability is significantly heightened in times of crisis, particularly because of the targeting of civilians, which is so characteristic of modern civil conflict and from which the weakest members of society have little protection. Thus, for example, "Disabled children have greater difficulty escaping during attacks . . . Parents may have to make difficult decisions about who to leave behind when fleeing. . . . A Lebanese man admitted that he fled his home taking a cow rather than his disabled daughter, because the cow was of more use."[4] This account underscores the tenuous nature by which people with disabilities are often forced to live their lives and demonstrates the economic and cultural realities of Third World and low-income nations where a disability, whether pre-existing or newly acquired, impacts on the family as a whole. Moreover, Kett and others argue that emergency plans for those living in crisis situations "are not inclusive or accessible," citing findings which demonstrated that "many factors contributed to the inaccessibility of relief services: the collapse of basic infrastructures, family displacement, ignorance of disability issues among mainstream relief agencies and the tendency for people to be treated as passive victims."[5]

Although various humanitarian agencies have drawn up guidelines for just such circumstances,

> "There is little evidence that these guidelines [for inclusion] are used to any effect with people with disabilities, in part because of a lack of standards and indicators to monitor inclusion but also because of the lack of awareness and training at field level. Local disabled people's organizations are rarely included in planning and coordination meetings, particularly in crises. Thus the opportunity is missed to improve coordination and inclusion of people with disabilities in humanitarian aid. . . . Humanitarian agencies are not immune from widely held social perceptions about disability, consequently disabled peoples access issues are rarely considered in matters such as education, employment or the need for goods and services. As a result, in such circumstances, disabled people often die."[6]

But, although cultural stereotypes appear to be magnified when the existing infrastructure begins to crumble, other research reveals potentially more positive influences. Thus Mark Priestly in his review of the literature on disability and conflict cites Montero's example of the many Nicaraguans disabled during revolution: "veterans experienced disability in very different ways to those who were disabled before the revolution." Making comparisons with Vietnam veterans in the United States, Montero notes how "these disabled people were practically considered national heroes and were given all the opportunities possible to develop and strengthen their own organizations."[7] It is also possible that the call for social inclusion, usually voiced during peace negotiations, has at least the potential to bring about change for those on the margins of society. So, for example, Brichtova argues that in the political reformations following the break of the Soviet Union, "the vision of democracy" spread to those with disabilities: "Maybe for the first time in our history their views and desires for real civil involvement and participation have been heard in public."[8] However, while Santos Zingale notes a more general shift in attitudes over the past two decades, from a welfare approach to disability issues to a human rights approach, which "has greatly increased the involvement of people with disabilities at all levels of society,"[9] she goes on to point out that "the struggle for equal citizenship has remained within the borders of developed Western societies . . . disability issues are at the end of priority lists in most developing nations."[10] We will now turn our attention from the broad realities of living with a disability in war zones to a more focused discussion on the specificities of Northern Ireland.

The conflict in the north of Ireland, locally known as "the Troubles" (1969–1994), marks only the most recent period in a long history of violence characterizing the disputed relations within and between the islands of Britain and Ireland. These turbulent years saw the total breakdown of social, civil and political life during which over three and a half thousand people lost their lives and an estimated 40,000 were injured as a direct result of the violence.

Following the announcement of a paramilitary ceasefire in 1994, a series of political initiatives was launched in an attempt to bring a measure of stability to a province torn apart by communal strife. Despite frequent setbacks and recurring crises, a prolonged and often contested "peace process" has gradually unrolled which, while not fully resolving the key constitutional question of whether Northern Ireland should remain part of the United Kingdom or be incorporated into the Republic of Ireland, has so far resulted in the decommissioning of paramilitary weapons, the return of devolved government and a welcome degree of normality in the everyday lives of the local population. That "normality," and the desired progress towards a more equal society has, however, been shaped by the nature and legacy of the conflict itself, which continues to cast its shadow over the hoped-for transformation in the daily lives of the people of Northern Ireland. And for some that transformation, with its promise of equality of treatment and opportunity, is more elusive than for others.

Although there are important internal divisions in each faction, this conflict has generally been characterized as a struggle between Irish Republicanism/nationalism and British/Ulster Unionism/loyalism, and the religious creeds with which each are associated (Irish-Catholic and Ulster-Protestant). More recently, however, scholars have been concerned to draw attention to other divisions within Northern Irish society and other inequalities which have hitherto been masked by the political focus on nationalist and religious ideologies. Thus McLaughlin et al, in an exploration of "Eighty Years of Talking about Equality in Northern Ireland," have demonstrated how debates around gender, "race"/ethnicity, sexual orientation, and disability, while present from the 1970s, were marginalized by the concentration on religious and political identity and evolved slowly out of a contested and divided society, to emerge only in the late 1990s as part of a broader equality discourse, whose values were enshrined in the 1998 Good Friday or Belfast Agreement.[11]

This settlement, which restored devolved government in Northern Ireland, sought to address the roots of the conflict between unionism and nationalism by providing a framework within which physical warfare could be transformed into a political conflict characterized by negotiation and communication. Moreover, the Agreement addressed two equality agendas; a national equality agenda in which equal respect for the two different allegiances, Irish and British, were reflected in the institutional arrangements put in place and also a social equality agenda.[12] Thus Section 75 places a statutory requirement on public authorities to carry out their duties with due regard to the need to promote equality across nine categories: people of different gender, age, ethnic origin, religious belief, or political opinion; married and unmarried people; disabled and non-disabled people; people with or without dependants; and people of differing sexual orientation.

However, while this new concentration on equality, "the most extensive positive duty imposed in the UK,"[13] has been welcomed as "both unique and world leading,"[14] no one doubts that the prospect of sustained peace in the north remains precarious and tentative. Indeed, many would also argue that the political settlement has, so far at least, failed to realize its potential or fulfill its promise of justice and equality, particularly for the most vulnerable sections of society. Having provided an, albeit brief, introduction to the context in which their lives were lived, the remainder of this chapter will focus on the experiences of people with disabilities in Northern Ireland, both during and after the conflict. Although in many ways they suffered the same fears, anxieties and traumas as wider society, some of the challenges they faced were uniquely linked to their physical, sensory or mental capabilities yet, during decades of intense media coverage of their locality, they have received little attention from observers or commentators.

With around 20 percent of the population having some form of disability, the rates of disability and impairment in the small province of Northern Ireland are the highest in the United Kingdom, to which it remains constitutionally, though controversially, linked. As is the case elsewhere, there are clear links between disability and poverty both in terms of causes and consequences, the latter including poorer education and employment prospects. A recent survey indicates that 70 percent of people with disabilities in the province live on or about the poverty line, are twice as likely as the able-bodied to have no qualifications and three times as likely to be unemployed.[15] Despite the prevalence of disability, and its serious consequences, however, Northern Ireland has historically lacked the kind of robust disability movement which evolved elsewhere in the United Kingdom. Though, as mentioned above, there have been a number of organized groups whose demands were overshadowed by the central political debate, a range of other factors further inhibited their development and effectiveness.

As Acheson points out, decades of government by direct rule from Westminster meant that "the ideological struggle between the Left and Right and between local and central government that provided the context of the emergence of the disability movement in Britain, was simply absent."[16] In addition, the social services community provision in Northern Ireland started from a lower base than that in Great Britain and from a less independent philosophy. Acceptance of institutionalization, dependency and care for people with impairments was unquestioned by both social services and promoters of 'special' education. Again, the weakness of a general culture of social rights in Northern Ireland may have weakened the ground for group specific demands, as has the tendency of professionals to "seek individual solutions to what are seen primarily as individual problems."[17]

This kind of attitude fits squarely into the traditional medical, or social welfare, model which disempowers people with disabilities by defining them primarily by their illness or medical condition, using medical diagnoses to regulate and control their access to social benefits, housing, education, leisure and employment. This approach assumes that the disabled persons are themselves the "problem" and that they must be cured or cared for, put into the hands of professionals and "experts." It also tends to elicit sympathy rather than promote activism from the non-disabled and from those who are in a position to bring about change; as Michael Morgan puts it, "politically, in effect, to be seen as supporting disabled people is viewed as important, and unquestionably, reflects a huge groundswell of public sympathy." What he defines as the "rent a crib" syndrome inevitably reinforces the culture of dependency already discussed.[18] This position contrasts with the social model which argues that it is the responsibility of society, not the disabled individual, to remove the barriers to participation that result in discrimination against disabled people. These models are not merely academic abstractions but provide frameworks for thinking about disability which deeply influence policy and practice and thus the everyday lives of large sectors of the population. Thus, for example, the charity ethic inherent in the medical model, which appears to be deeply entrenched in Northern Ireland, sits in opposition to the approach of the social model which frames its understanding of disability within a discourse of equality and human rights. It is against the background of such attitudes and values that we now turn to explore how a protracted period of civil conflict impacted on an already marginalized, if not silenced, sector of Northern Irish society.

As evidence from other war zones makes clear, people with disabilities, often lacking access not only to power but to many of the taken-for-granted rights of citizenship, can find their personal, social and economic circumstances severely challenged by the consequences of civil conflict. The element of risk brought to daily life by the threat of bombs, bullets and the various activities of legal and illegal armies, the weakening of infrastructures as the result of social disruption, and the general breakdown of law and order impact, of course, on all members of society, but the experiences of disabled people are all too often missing in the "remembering" process, which often characterizes the immediate post-conflict period. In the north of Ireland, where equality and social inclusion are seen as central to the process of reconciliation and conflict transformation, the absence of these stories is particularly regrettable. However, despite the dearth of scholarship in this area, our preliminary research brought to light some key issues of interest to people with disabilities, the able-bodied and, perhaps most importantly, to those with the power to shape policy and practice.

When the discontents within Northern Ireland, which had long simmered beneath the surface, erupted into bloodshed on the streets of Belfast and Derry in the summer of 1969, it could not have been foreseen that the subsequent descent into sectarian violence and the total breakdown of social, civil, and political life would persist for over thirty years. With republicans and nationalists challenging the basic legitimacy of the Unionist-controlled state within which they were denied many of the fundamental rights of citizenship, pro- and anti-civil rights demonstrations marked the beginning of what became euphemistically known as "the Troubles." Physical force republicanism and loyalist paramilitarism, the presence of the British army, internment, the collapse of the regional government, and political stalemate provided the backdrop to more than three decades of politically motivated violence. While the scale and intensity of the violence is difficult to appreciate in retrospect, so too the statistical details of the dead and injured fail to evoke the emotionally charged atmosphere which it generated.

This is not the place to revisit the catalogue of deaths and injuries, kidnappings, and beatings suffered by men, women, and children. Images of death and destruction dominated the news, with sobbing family members following a seemingly endless series of funeral processions. With no warning—or brief warning—bombs were perhaps the most frightening phenomena of this period, the normal pursuits of everyday life thrown into panic and confusion and the danger, of course, heightened for those with mobility problems. As one wheelchair user put it, "If you're sitting somewhere—even inside or outside a shop—and there's a bomb scare, you can't just get up and leg it like everyone else!"[19] Similarly, the inability to use elevators in times of danger could leave such individuals with no clear means of escape—heavily dependent on others, themselves focused on fleeing the scene. Those with hearing problems were also vulnerable, unable to respond to calls/alarms to evacuate buildings—and thus put at extreme risk. This reality undoubtedly contributed significantly to the degree of isolation and inviability experienced by disabled people in Northern Ireland's society.

There were also more indirect consequences. For example, the practice of placing bombs in parked cars led to strict parking restrictions in most towns and villages, so that those with mobility issues faced considerable difficulty in going about their business—"so I would just sit in the car and wait or stay at home."[20] Negotiating roads and pavements in the aftermath of bombs or riots was also severely challenging for those with mobility or visual impairments. The closure of public toilets, the body searches on entering shops, and the ransacking of homes during police or army raids—all disruptive to able-bodied—had the potential to be particularly distressing and problematic for those with bodily or other impairments.

Perhaps more serious than the disruption to daily routines (in lives where stability and routine were particularly important) was the increased dependency and social isolation that commonly resulted from life in this strife-ridden community. Awareness of their vulnerability and fear of not being able to escape riots or bombs left many individuals trapped in their homes, as did the constant disruptions to both public and private transport resulting from bomb scares and hoaxes and from both military and paramilitary activities. Searches, diversions, and delays made travelling from one place to another unreliable and hazardous. A community worker related the story of two profoundly deaf young men who were stopped by the army when driving a fast car—their inability to quickly and articulately respond to short, sharp questioning raised the suspicions of the young soldiers and placed the young men in an extremely difficult, potentially dangerous situation. The vulnerability of the security forces to ambush or attack was inevitably their first consideration when dealing with the public, but there are also examples of responses that pointed to harassment rather than insensitivity.

Community tensions were particularly high during the early 1970s, especially in nationalist areas, and relations between the armed forces and local people were strained, if not hostile. It was in this context that Joe Hughes, disabled from birth—a wheelchair user who could not walk, speak or fully use his hands—approached the local army barracks with a note from his deaf father to inquire about his brother, whom they believed to have been lifted by troops in an army raid. Their reaction to this individual was brutal: they "said he was a madman, tore up the note, pushed him out of the wheelchair and punched him in the stomach." This was not the only instance of harassment he suffered during his life; however, Hughes, a lifelong disability activist and fund-raiser who was awarded many honors in the course of his life, including an MBE, was not prepared to accept such treatment, and was later awarded £150 in damages.[21] Although this individual appears to have been quite exceptional (and thus his story was recorded), there must have been many such incidents of abuse against those regarded as weak in a society characterized by violence and brutality, and where instances of hate crime against the disabled was in any case not uncommon. Thus, a June 2009 Report from the Institute for Conflict Research (Belfast) cites incidences of disabled people experiencing physical violence, verbal taunting and damage to property. The report also documents similar instances in England, Scotland, the United States, and Canada. Perhaps most disturbing is the lack of awareness of law enforcement agencies of such activities coupled with an unwillingness to prosecute such crimes.[22]

Access to required services and supports was also disrupted during these years, especially for those who lived in rural areas for whom transport to schools or for hospital appointments was frequently interrupted, if not cancelled, by bomb scares, hoaxes, army searches or other activities within the locality. This was particularly true during periods of high social tension. Thus, during the Holy Cross School dispute in Belfast in 2000, a day center for people with learning difficulties was subjected to occasional closure at short notice, while during the Drumcree dispute, a bus setting out to bring a group of disabled people to their local day center was stopped at barricades by protesters who threatened to burn it down.[23] The community workers, to whom the protesters were known, were able to negotiate a safe passage through, but the incident was a clear warning that the right to travel through a neighborhood could not be taken for granted. Social workers themselves were vulnerable to attack; arriving as strangers in areas where representatives of officialdom were both feared and resented, they could easily be suspected of being plain-clothes police or army personnel. Indeed, in some districts of a region where Catholic/nationalist and Protestant/unionist communities were increasingly polarized, even the appearance of laborers from outside the area could provoke violent intervention. Thus, "it [became] necessary to mark buses clearly 'Handicapped People' in order to avoid confusion with workmen's buses which could be ambushed."[24]

In this divided society, with issues of religious and political identity central to the conflict, the majority of schoolchildren were both socially and educationally segregated—separate housing estates and schooling for Protestants and Catholics—a situation exacerbated by the volatile situation. Those with disabilities, however, were often subjected to a different type of exclusionary practice—educated in "special" schools, separate from the able-bodied, while "mixed" in terms of religion/political identity—a type of social exclusion rarely mentioned in heated debates about equal citizenship. Michael, who attended a special school for eleven years during the Troubles, said, "You just didn't talk about those things"—meaning the political/religious identity which was so heatedly debated elsewhere. Little attention has been paid to the possible social and political consequences of being thus segregated from mainstream society during the formative years of schooling, but it seems that, both literally and figuratively, disabled people are remote from the larger cultural identity.

The continuity of care and provision for disabled people by health and social service agencies was further affected by the displacement of many families and individuals who were intimidated from their homes, particularly during the 1970s. One nurse told of her helplessness in the face of local paramilitary activity while caring for her husband who had suffered a stroke: "I was so frightened because, what would I do? How would I get my husband sorted out? They wouldn't give us time to get out, they would set the house on fire before I could get him out!"[25]

The widespread trauma and distress generated by fear and anxiety during this prolonged period of violence had particularly negative effects for those with existing mental health problems. Already vulnerable to discrimination or abuse in everyday life,[26] they were even more at risk at times of heightened community tension. Moreover, the impact on existing conditions could affect other aspects of life. Thus, Peter, a schoolboy at the time, explained that tension and anxiety so exacerbated his epilepsy that he was unable to attend school for long periods of his childhood.

These few examples skim the surface and are merely suggestive of some of the problems faced by disabled people in this time and place. Mostly, however, like those in the able-bodied community, they simply tried "to get on with things." One group I spoke with said that they felt their situation was no different from others struggling with the daily dangers of social conflict, though others noted that their life was "abnormal" anyway—that coping with day-to-day difficulties overwhelmed other considerations. The main impression gained from our discussions was that few, if any of them, had considered or reflected on their personal experiences. It nonetheless became clear that their lives were marked by higher than usual levels of dependency and social isolation. Given the perceived (and actual) risks generated by the "Troubles," it is perhaps not surprising that the first concern of the families of those with disabilities was to shield them from harm. Keeping them "safe" in the circumstances of the north, however, meant keeping them at home and limiting their activities. This increased dependency on family members inevitably worked to infantilize disabled people, further inhibiting opportunities for empowerment, already few and far between.

So far we have looked at how conflict impacted on those with existing disabilities, but what of those for whom the conflict was the cause of impairment or disablement—"the forgotten victims of the Troubles."[27] Although there is "no reliable central register of the injured, or measure of the long-term economic and other effects of their injuries."[28] Research estimates that "around 100,000 people in Northern Ireland live in households where someone has been injured in a troubles-related incident. Some of these injuries were relatively minor, but some have been severely disabling."[29] It is difficult to summarize or provide an overview of these experiences; as Smyth and Darby point out, like the bereaved, "the constituency of those . . . injured was a fragmented one, divided by politics and geography, and isolated within a culture of silence and a lack of support services."[30] REAL nonetheless concludes that "there is no room for doubt that this has involved much enduring impairment—blindness, loss of hearing, disfigurement, single or multiple amputation as well as high levels of mental ill-health."[31] The chief executive of the victim's group WAVE claims that more than forty thousand injured in political violence in Northern Ireland were "left to pick up the pieces of their lives, suffering trauma and debilitating injuries, with little support," and notes that "this entire area remains under-researched and under-funded."[32]

The 1970s was the most violent decade of all, with almost one third of injuries suffered between 1972 and 1977 in incidents such as the Abercorn bombing, in March 1972, which killed two and left 139 people injured or maimed—many lost several limbs. Jennifer McNern, for example, a twenty-one-year-old out shopping for her wedding dress, wakened in a local hospital to find she had lost both her legs, as had her sister, who also lost an arm. The numbers involved and the extent of their injuries on this occasion left a vivid impression on the wider population, but, more generally speaking, once removed from the newspaper headlines and apart from when anniversaries roll around, there is little public record of how individuals coped with the dramatic changes so suddenly wrought in their lives—in personal relationships, employment opportunities or leisure activities. As mentioned above, families are also affected by disability, so for parents, children, partners, and siblings, life must often have changed course in ways previously unimagined. While battles for financial compensation and justice became part of the wider political debate, the personal biographies are largely forgotten.

Despite the large numbers suffering disablement, however, it is difficult to say there is a "disabled community." It would appear that people permanently disabled in the conflict have not been "smoothly integrated into the broader disability sector."[33] There are several reasons why these individuals may not wish to readily identify with those who have disabilities from birth or early onset. Their early socialization might have been very different; they may wish to distance themselves from the social stigma so often associated with the latter group, whom they feel may not have acquired social worth as compared to those who have disabilities as a result of the conflict. And while support groups have been put in place for groups such as injured members of the police service, the nature of the conflict has ensured that divisions among combatants are reflected in differing attitudes to those disabled by violence.

Indeed, it could be argued that the development of victim politics also serves to set these individuals apart from the wider disability community, with the "discourse of victimhood" reinforcing the ethno-religious/sectarian concerns which have dominated and continue to dominate the social, political and cultural agenda. Thus, a clear hierarchy of victims has emerged. For example, paramilitaries injured "in action" against the British army or the opposing paramilitary grouping are often lauded as heroes in their own communities and reviled in others, while those randomly injured by bombs or bullets are labeled innocent victims of "terrorist" warfare. This categorizing has inevitably become one of the most difficult aspects of the current discourse of peacemaking, with those at the helm stressing the importance of acceptance and forgiveness. However, and while this is an area requiring further, and indeed urgent, research, a few examples indicate that people disabled in conflict are as diverse as any other group.

Journalist Suzanne Breen provides examples of three men disabled during the Troubles—a former part-time soldier of the Ulster Defence Regiment, a former policeman, and a former member of a paramilitary group. Despite the terrible nature of their injuries and the loss of their occupations, they each retained their political allegiances—one by "marching" on a motorized scooter for example, while the former republican activist claimed that he "played a full and active role," even as a paraplegic. His actions against the British army led to a period of imprisonment where he found he had nothing in common with the disabled ex-security force members he met during hospital treatment: "the reality is I'd have put them in a wheelchair, and they'd have put me in a wheelchair if they'd had the chance. It was a war. We were on different sides." On the other hand, the group Disability Think Tank, founded in 2004 to promote the interests of both categories of disabled, highlighted their commonality in an appeal for sensitivity for a sector of the community "for whom insensitivity at the hands of others is an everyday problem with no religious or cultural boundaries."[34] Similarly, an adult from the same group, disabled by shooting during the Troubles, argued that "when you're in a place like here [Artability, a disabled person's group] or the likes of Fleming Fulton [a segregated or disability only or 'special' school for disabled people], you are among both Catholics and Protestants. Our disabilities are what brings us together, and what is important to us all. Being of different religion isn't important."[35] So it is clear that numerous factors are at work here that connect and intersect and that while some people feel they are defined by their disability, this is not the case for all. Identity is complex, multi-layered and fluid and there is a need to recognize and reflect a far more complex reality of life with disability beyond the tragic/brave/heroic/victim binaries that have led to a simplistic reductionist understanding of the experiences of a large sector of the population.

Northern Ireland is a particularly interesting case study, not least because of the important equality legislation which is central to the ongoing peace process. Those involved with disability issues, however, recognize that disabled people are still in the midst of social citizenship acquisition; Section 75 has not yet delivered. Jennifer McNern, one of the disabled survivors of the Troubles discussed above, argued in a radio interview in June 2010 that provisions made for people like herself were "piecemeal and ad hoc"; compensation levels were pitifully inadequate and while various schemes to support survivors were put in place, they were insufficiently thought through.[36] At the same time, a disability activist, voicing her frustration at the culture of dependency resulting from the overprotection experienced by many disabled people, claimed that "the state is disabling people further in the post-conflict situation." Despite the setting up of a Victims' Commission and a series of reports, even the promised Bill of Rights is still not in place, and indeed, when a draft was recently put out to consultation, disability groups voiced their anger that in terms of disability it proposes to treat Northern Ireland in the same way as the rest of the United Kingdom.[37] They point to the distinctiveness of Northern Ireland's issues, particularly following the troubles. Higher levels of economic inactivity and lack of investment in economic and social policy initiatives in comparison with the neighboring island have a real impact on day-to-day life and promoters of disability rights are emphatic about the need for the relevant authorities to move from a needs-based to a rights-based focus. Clearly, whatever the source of the disablement, much remains to be done: "The inclusion of people with disabilities is a matter of social justice and an essential investment in the future of society. It is not based on charity or goodwill but is an integral element of the expression and realization of universal human rights."[38]

This approach is the one taken by the UN Convention on the Rights of Persons with Disabilities (2006), Article 11 of which states, "States parties shall take, in accordance with their obligations under international law, including international humanitarian law and international human rights law, all necessary measures to ensure the protection and safety of persons with disabilities in situations of risk, including situations of armed conflict, humanitarian emergencies and the occurrence of natural disasters."[39] Ratified by ninety-one states across the world, this approach has the potential to heighten public awareness of the experiences of disabled people during conflicts or humanitarian emergencies, and affirms their rights as citizens. The extent to which reality reflects the commitments enshrined in the Convention is something which should be closely monitored by society as a whole.

BIBLIOGRAPHY

Acheson, N. *Voluntary Action, Disability and Citizenship: Evidence from Northern Ireland.* Belfast: University of Ulster, 2003.

Bloomfield, Kenneth. *We Will Remember Them: Report of the Northern Ireland Victims' Commission.* CAIN, 1998. http://cain.ulst.ac.uk/issues/violence/victims.htm

Breen, Suzanne. "The Forgotten Victims of the Troubles." *SAOIRSE,* vol. 32 (2006). http://saoirse32.blogsome.com/2006/05/31/the-forgotten-victims-of-the-troubles//saoirse32.blogsome.com/2006/05/31/the-forgotten-victims-of-the-troubles/ (September 9, 2010).

CBR News. *The International Newsletter on Community-based Rehabilitation and the Concerns of Disabled People,* no. 32 (December–March 2002).

Darby, John, and Arthur Williamson. "Social Welfare Services," in *Violence and the Social Services in Northern Ireland,* John Darby and Arthur Williamson, eds. London: Heinman, 1978.

Donaghy, T. "Mainstreaming: Northern Ireland's Participative-Democratic Approach." *The Policy Press*, vol. 32 (2004): 49–62.

Fay, Marie Therese, Mike Morrissey, Marie Smyth, and Tracy Wong. *Cost of the Troubles Study: Report on the Northern Ireland Survey: the Experience and Impact of the Troubles.* Belfast: Incore, 1999.

Hall, Michael. *Look at Me, Not at My Disability: An Exploration by the Disability Think Tank.* Newtownabbey: Island Pamphlets, 2004.

Harknett, Steve. "Disability and War." *CBR News,* no. 32 (December–March 2000).

Harvey, C. "Northern Ireland in Transition: An Introduction," in *Human Rights, Equality and Democratic Renewal in Northern Ireland*, C. Harvey, ed. Oxford and Portland: Hart Publishing, 2001.

Kett, Maria, Sue Stubbs, and Rebecca Yeo. *Disability in Conflict and Emergency Situations: Focus on Tsunami-affected Areas*. IDDC Research Report (June 2005).

Kett, M., and M. van Ommeren. "Disability: Beyond the Medical Model." *The Lancet,* vol. 374, no. 9704 (November 28–December 4, 2009): 1801–1803.

King, R., and N. Ryan. *Joe Hughes: A Life Less Ordinary.* Belfast: Glandore Publishing, 2000.

McCrudden, C. "Equality and the Good Friday Agreement," in *After the Good Friday Agreement, Analysing Political Change in Northern Ireland,* J. Ruane and J. Todd, eds. Dublin: University College Dublin Press, 1999.

McLaughlin, Eithne, Myrtle Hill, Caroline McAuley, and Fran Porter. *Eighty Years of Talking about Equality in Northern Ireland: A History of Equality Discourses and Practices.* Belfast: University of Ulster, 2005.

McNern, Jennifer. *The Stephen Nolan Show*. June 2010. http://www.bbc.co.uk/northern ireland/nolan/specialreports/victims/, September 7, 2010.

Morgan, Michael. "The Disability Movement in Northern Ireland." *Disability & Society*, vol. 10, no. 2 (June 1995): 233–236.

Murray, C.J.L., G. King, A.D. Lopez, N. Tomijima, and E.G. Krug. "Armed Conflict as a Public Health Problem." *BMJ,* vol. 324 (February 2002): 346–349.

O'Cinneide, C. "Beyond the Limits of Equal Treatment: The Use of Positive Duties in Equality Law," in *Mainstreaming Equality: Models for a Statutory Duty*, Kate Hayes, ed. Dublin: University College Dublin Press, 2003.

Parnes, Penny. "The Global Issue of People with Disabilities." http://www.icdr.utoronto.ca, September 9, 2010.

Priestly, Mark. *Disability and the Life Course: Global Perspectives.* Cambridge: Cambridge University Press, 2001.

The REAL (Rights, Empowerment, Action, Lobbying) Network. *Response to the Northern Ireland Office's Consultation on a Bill of Rights*, March 26, 2010.

Santos-Zingale, Myriam dos, and Mary Ann McColl. "Disability and Participation in Post-conflict Situations: the Case of Sierra Leone." *Disability & Society*, vol. 21, no. 3 (May 2006): 243–257.

Smyth, Marie, and John Darby. "Does Research Make any Difference? Northern Ireland." in *Researching Violently Divided Societies: Ethical and Methodological Issues*, Marie Smyth and Gillian Robinson, eds. London: Pluto Press, 2001, 34–54.

Smyth, Marie, Mike Morrissey, and Jennifer Hamilton. *Caring through the Troubles: Health and Social Services in North and West Belfast*. Belfast: EHSSB, 2001.

UN Convention on Human Rights, http://www.un.org/disabilities/convention/conventionfull.html (September 24, 2010).

Vincent, Fred, Katy Radford, Neil Jarman, Agnieszka Martynowicz, and Mary-Katherine Rallings. *Hate Crime Against People with Disabilities: A Baseline Study of Experiences in Northern Ireland*. Belfast: Institute for Conflict Research, 2009.

NOTES

1. With thanks to Bronagh Byrne for her input and comments, and to Anne McGlone and the members of the Willow Bank Community Resource Centre, Dungannon; Steve Harknett, "Disability and War," *CBR News,* no. 32 (December–March 2000), 2.

2. Maria Kett and M. van Ommeren, "Disability: Beyond the Medical Model," *The Lancet,* vol. 374, no. 9704 (November 28–December 4, 2009): 1801–1803.

3. C.J.L. Murray, G. King, A.D. Lopez, N. Tomijima, and E.G. Krug, "Armed Conflict as a Public Health Problem," *BMJ,* vol. 324 (February 2002): 346–349.

4. CBR News, *The International Newsletter on Community-based Rehabilitation and the Concerns of Disabled People,* no. 32 (December–March 2002): 5.

5. Maria Kett, Sue Stubbs, and Rebecca Yeo, "Disability in Conflict and Emergency Situations: Focus on Tsunami-affected Areas," *IDDC Research Report* (June 2005).

6. Kett and van Ommeren, "Disability," 1801.

7. Mark Priestly, *Disability and the Life Course: Global Perspectives* (Cambridge: Cambridge University Press, 2001), 11.

8. Priestly, *Disability*, 11.

9. Myriam dos Santos-Zingale and Mary Ann McColl, "Disability and Participation in Post-conflict Situations: The Case of Sierra Leone," *Disability & Society*, vol. 21, no. 3 (May 2006): 244–245.

10. Santos-Zingale, "Disability," 245.

11. Eithne McLaughlin, Myrtle Hill, Caroline McAuley, and Fran Porter, *Eighty Years of Talking about Equality in Northern Ireland: A History of Equality Discourses and Practices* (Belfast: University of Ulster, 2005).

12. C. McCrudden, "Equality and the Good Friday Agreement," in *After the Good Friday Agreement, Analysing Political Change in Northern Ireland,* J. Ruane and J. Todd, eds. (Dublin: University College Dublin Press, 1999), 106.

13. C O'Cinneide, "Beyond the Limits of Equal Treatment: The Use of Positive Duties in Equality Law," in *Mainstreaming Equality: Models for a Statutory Duty*, Kate Hayes, ed. (Dublin: University College Dublin Press, 2003).

14. T. Donaghy, "Mainstreaming: Northern Ireland's Participative-Democratic Approach," *The Policy Press,* vol. 32 (2004): 49–62.

15. The REAL (Rights, Empowerment, Action, Lobbying) Network, *Response to the Northern Ireland Office's Consultation on a Bill of Rights*, March 26, 2010, 4.

16. N. Acheson, *Voluntary Action, Disability and Citizenship: Evidence from Northern Ireland* (Belfast: University of Ulster, 2003), 238.

17. Michael Morgan, "The Disability Movement in Northern Ireland," *Disability & Society*, vol. 10, no. 2 (June 1995): 233.

18. Morgan, "Disability Movement," 234.

19. Michael Hall, *Look at Me, Not at My Disability: An Exploration by the Disability Think Tank* (Newtownabbey: Island Pamphlets, 2004), 14.

20. Hall, *Look*, 14.

21. R. King and N. Ryan, *Joe Hughes: A Life Less Ordinary* (Belfast: Glandore Publishing, 2000).

22. Fred Vincent, Katy Radford, Neil Jarman, Agnieszka Martynowicz, and Mary-Katherine Rallings, *Hate Crime Against People with Disabilities: A Baseline Study of Experiences in Northern Ireland* (Belfast: Institute for Conflict Research, 2009).

23. The Holy Cross Dispute involved outbreaks of sectarian violence in 2001 and 2002 between parents and pupils of a Roman Catholic school and loyalist residents of an area en route to the school. The Drumcree dispute concerned an annual parade between loyalist marchers opposed by nationalist residents of the marching route.

24. John Darby and Arthur Williamson, "Social Welfare Services," in *Violence and the Social Services in Northern Ireland*, John Darby and Arthur Williamson, eds. (London: Heinman, 1978), 83.

25. Marie Smyth, Mike Morrissey, and Jennifer Hamilton, *Caring through the Troubles: Health and Social Services in North and West Belfast* (Belfast: EHSSB, 2001), 70.

26. UN Convention on Human Rights, "Mental Health Review," http://www.un.org/disabilities/convention/conventionfull.html, September 24, 2010.

27. Suzanne Breen, "The Forgotten Victims of the Troubles," *SAOIRSE,* vol. 32 (2006), http://saoirse32.blogsome.com/2006/05/31/the-forgotten-victims-of-the-troubles//saoirse32.blogsome.com/2006/05/31/the-forgotten-victims-of-the-troubles/ (September 9, 2010).

28. Kenneth Bloomfield, *We Will Remember Them: Report of the Northern Ireland Victims' Commission,* CAIN, 1998, http://cain.ulst.ac.uk/issues/violence/victims.htm, September 24, 2010.

29. Marie Therese Fay, Mike Morrissey, Marie Smyth, and Tracy Wong, *Cost of the Troubles Study: Report on the Northern Ireland Survey: the Experience and Impact of the Troubles* (Belfast: Incore, 1999).

30. Marie Smyth and John Darby, "Does Research Make any Difference? Northern Ireland," in *Researching Violently Divided Societies: Ethical and Methodological Issues*, Marie Smyth and Gillian Robinson, eds. (London: Pluto Press, 2001), 43.

31. REAL, *Response,* 3.

32. Breen, "Forgotten Victims."

33. REAL, *Response*, 4.

34. Hall, *Look,* 3.

35. Hall, *Look*, 17.

36. Jennifer McNern, *The Stephen Nolan Show*, June 2010, http://www.bbc.co.uk/northern ireland/nolan/specialreports/victims/ (September 7, 2010).

37. REAL, *Response*, 7.

38. Penny Parnes, *The Global Issue of People with Disabilities*, http://www.icdr.utoronto.ca (September 9, 2010).

39. UN Convention on Human Rights, 2006.

Chapter 7

Emancipatory Peacebuilding

Critical Responses to (Neo)Liberal Trends

Charles Thiessen

Post–Cold War civil warfare and, more recently, the elevated fear of terrorist activity have motivated the burgeoning support for foreign intervention into war-affected contexts. Supported by international permissions, a reduction in the scope of Westphalian national sovereignty, and an emboldened UN system, the world community has responded to civil violence across the globe with complex peacebuilding projects incorporating a diverse troupe of UN, military, and other governmental and nongovernmental actors. Recent peacebuilding projects, such as those in Afghanistan, Kosovo, East Timor, and Sierra Leone have been large scale multi-dimensional ventures, incorporating approaches aimed at rapid liberalization and the establishment of the "liberal peace" through (neo)liberal peacebuilding strategies.

This chapter will briefly survey the (neo)liberal peacebuilding project and the emerging critique of its methodology and values. Initial efforts at identifying and elaborating upon an alternative, viable, and localized peacebuilding paradigm have highlighted the centrality of local participation and "emancipation" for local war-affected populations. This emerging paradigm, labelled here as "emancipatory peacebuilding," has been primarily defined in the literature by what it is not. Thus, this chapter ventures beyond the critique of the (neo)liberal peacebuilding project and investigates some philosophical underpinnings to the emerging emancipatory peacebuilding alternative, and explores its implications for peacebuilding practice and coordination.

(NEO)LIBERAL PEACEBUILDING

Two prominent features of current peacebuilding interventions are exposed by labelling them as "(neo)liberal"—the integration of neoliberal economic policy and liberal political structures in the creation of a market democracy in war-torn contexts. Neoliberal economic policy has required rapid Adam Smith–style marketization and the adoption of market economics complete with limited government intrusion in the economy and expanded freedoms for individual economic actors.[1] Liberal political policy aims to institutionalize the "highest" liberal principles of individualism, universalism, egalitarianism, meliorism, human rights, and democracy within democratic state structures and processes.[2] This has necessitated aggressive democratization schemes, hurried democratic elections, and intensive state-building projects. Securing these unsettling economic and political transformations has warranted a highly interventional program of confidence building, combat against insurgent groups, DDR (demobilization, disarmament, and reintegration), and security sector reform. Methodologically, the (neo)liberal peacebuilding project has maintained a focus on upper-level reconciliation strategies, "outside-in" official processes, prescriptions by international "experts," and has thus resembled more a system of governance as opposed to a reconciliatory process.[3]

The legitimacy of (neo)liberal peacebuilding has increasingly come under scrutiny. In his book *At War's End*, Roland Paris systematically critiques all fourteen major peacebuilding operations between 1989 and 1999. Paris points out major peacebuilding "missteps"—for example, the failure of postwar elections to secure sustainable peace in Angola (1992), Rwanda (1994), and Cambodia (1993), and the manner in which economic liberalization in El Salvador and Nicaragua exacerbated the very socio-economic inequalities that served to initiate conflict in the first place. Paris's conclusion asserts, "The case studies do suggest that the liberalization process either contributed to a rekindling of violence or helped to recreate the historic sources of violence in many of the countries that have hosted these missions—a conclusion that casts doubt on the reliability of the peace-through-liberalization strategy as it has been practiced to date."[4] In response to its failures, the UN revised its statebuilding practice in Sierra Leone (1999), Kosovo (1999), and East Timor (1999) and subsequently met with moderate success. However, efforts to replicate these strategies in Afghanistan (2001) and Iraq (2003) have suffered from insufficient international and local legitimacy and continued local resistance and violence.[5]

The changing global political and economic climate has also served to de-legitimate (neo)liberal peacebuilding processes. The rise in power of China, Russia, Iran, and India, as well as regional organizations, such as the Organization of American States (OAS), the African Union (AU), and the Arab League, has certainly impacted the Western-dominated (neo)liberal consensus—particularly within the UN Security Council.[6]

A body of deeper, more philosophical critiques has also emerged that assesses the underlying values of the (neo)liberal peacebuilding project. The reaction of the United States to 9/11, and in particular its declared "war on terror," has "given liberalism an aggressive face in global politics" and has called into question its appeal as the purported carrier of human rights and democracy.[7] Furthermore, the "war on terror" has failed to address human security concerns, and has rather given way to traditional heavy-handed security operations and, consequently, provoked local distrust and resistance.

The "war on terror" has also served to strengthen another critique—that Western peacebuilding is simply a form of neo-colonialism or liberal imperialism. Jabri and Williams analyze peacebuilding discourse and believe that the liberal peace project is centrally projected as a "rescue" mission, primarily using the tools of security to manipulate developing populations to secure the security of the West.[8] In this way, the (neo)liberal project has become a project of war and inherently concerned about the propogation of the Western liberal self into the social realms of the "other." Williams tends to agree, and notes how indigenous forms of social and political organization are written off as "tribal," "clan-based" and lacking in modern functionality, thus justifying the embedding of Western versions of organization into non-Western contexts.[9]

Jacoby takes a sharply critical stance toward U.S. hegemony and its motivations in leading the charge in many post-war reconstruction projects—particularly in Iraq. He perceives the U.S. role in Iraq as clearly defending and propagating U.S./Western hegemony.[10] The "shock and awe" destruction and consequent rebuilding of the country is intended to warn potential adversaries from aspiring to power in the current world system. Furthermore, Jacoby accuses post-war reconstruction as being a technology for ensuring Western prosperity by limiting state sovereignty in order that the country can be taken advantage of by Western corporations and the world market.

Other critiques question whether (neo)liberal peacebuilding methods are socially and culturally appropriate in many contexts.[11] For example, in communally based social structures, democracy and competitive economic structures may be viewed with suspicion. This may be partly because of the neoliberal-motivated omission of much needed welfare schemes in devastated war zones. In the Cambodian context, Richmond and Franks note that the peacebuilding effort has established only a "virtual peace"—one having limited impact on citizens and recognized mainly by internationals.[12] This could be partly due to the liberal propensity for "top-down" peace processes, all the while giving inadequate attention to grassroots actors. Other commentators are concerned with the extensive control international actors exert over local populations. Duffield (borrowing from Foucault) labels liberal methods as "biopolitics"—"a form of politics that entails the administration of the processes of life at the aggregate level of population"—in this case by foreign intervening powers.[13]

Emancipatory Peacebuilding

As evidenced in the above critique, a growing body of literature is arguing that the (neo)liberal peacebuilding project is in crisis and uncertain how it will proceed.[14] Despite reports on the steady reduction in war-related deaths over the last decade (e.g., see the *Human Security Report Project*),[15] there appears to be significant dissatisfaction with, and increasing resistance to, the liberal peace as experienced by local populations around the world.[16] It is seen as "ethically bankrupt, subject to double standards, coercive and conditional, acultural, unconcerned with social welfare, and unfeeling and insensitive towards its subject."[17]

These inherent contradictions have spurred on a growing body of peacebuilding theory that proposes major revisions to (neo)liberal theory and practice and suggest the need for the construction of a new peacebuilding agenda.[18] Being situated much more in the critical tradition, emerging peacebuilding theory works toward emancipation and the pursuit of justice for all actors—state and non-state.[19] It is much more concerned with peace as experienced at the local and the "everyday" level, as well as at upper levels.[20] It is aware that the liberal peace "looks far more coherent from the outside than from the inside," and has tended to focus on the shell of the state while ignoring the relationship of the state to its constituents.[21] It insists that (neo)liberal peacebuilding processes become attentive to, supportive of, and emancipatory in regard to the local culture and its inherent social processes, traditions, and conceptions of peace. Thus, the liberalized peace is to be situated in a "localized, contextual, and hybridised form."[22]

Furthermore, emerging theory proposes that peacebuilding actors not work from universal blueprints, but engage in caring and empathetic multilevel consultation in order to provide the grassroots with a voice, operate on the norms they are trying to instill (e.g., democracy, equality, social justice), and place local community concerns before liberal/neoliberal goals.[23] Thus, peacebuilding actors are required to conduct continual critique of their activities, be well aware of their "baggage" they bring to peace activities, and work as "enablers for localized dynamics of peace" at the grassroots level of society.[24]

The critique of (neo)liberal methodology points to the urgently needed reformation of the (neo)liberal peacebuilding project, or perhaps its abandonment. Peacebuilding theorists are divided on this point. A minority of scholars call for the termination of the (neo)liberal peacebuilding project, but for various reasons. For authors such as Duffield and Jacoby, the imperialist nature of (neo)liberal peacebuilding justifies its replacement by a fundamentally different strategy.[25] Others point out that the "victor's peace"—that is, allowing a clear and dominant victor to gain power—has historically shown itself to be more sustainable, and thus civil conflicts should be allowed to "work themselves out" without foreign interference. Realist scholars invoke different reasons for abandoning the project. They are fundamentally critical of intervening for the sake of humanitarianism as opposed to national interests.

Most current critical scholarship, however, calls for reformation of the (neo)liberal peacebuilding project as opposed to its abandonment. For example, Paris believes that even though the critical analysis of the project has laid bare important challenges, there is nothing in the current critique that justifies the jettisoning of (neo)liberal peacebuilding and its replacement with an entirely "post-liberal" alternative.[26] However, he proposes that the (neo) liberal critique does point to a much-needed reformation of approaches and methodology, but not of the underlying liberal orientation of the project.

Even though Richmond, in places, labels the emerging emancipatory peacebuilding paradigm as "post-liberal," he does not call for the abandonment of the project but rather describes a liberal-hybridized alternative which places more weight on "bottom up" policies, peace at the "everyday" level, and the participation of local actors.[27] Donais, also, believes that sole reliance on either grassroots or upper-level peacemaking resources will lead to failure—thus forcing the necessity of a "negotiated hybridity."[28] Tadjbakhsh too, calls for reform.[29] She proposes that central to any peacebuilding alternative should be an expansion of the prevailing, but constricted conceptions of human security that simply allow the maintenance of the status quo in the international system of power. Current conceptions of human security have lost sight of their original purpose as an international movement to emancipate populations and ensure global justice and equity.

PHILOSOPHICAL AND ETHICAL BASES FOR EMANCIPATORY PEACEBUILDING

The emancipatory peacebuilding project is undergirded by at least two philosophical and ethical themes—local ownership and agency, and embracing the guidance of critical theory.

LOCAL OWNERSHIP AND AGENCY

The first theme concerns the voice and ownership of the "local" (and often "indigenous") in peacebuilding processes. On the surface, the theme of local ownership may seem like nothing new since "local ownership" discourse is present in the orthodox (neo)liberal project. However, in practice, (neo)liberal goals have by necessity restricted local ownership to domestic elites and their cooperation with the overall peacebuilding scheme. Thus, the liberal project has been unable to transcend its top-down bias.[30]

Emancipatory peacebuilding has as a central dilemma the elusive objective of reconciling "its 'global' objectives and the local conditions for their realization."[31] Because some form of external intervention is necessary in many conflict-affected contexts to secure the space for meaningful local ownership and the adoption of indigenous peacemaking practices, it becomes vital to consider the feasibility of a complimentary relationship between external and local actors. In order to unpack this insecure relationship, this section first investigates the philosophical and ethical imperatives allowing this tedious relationship to flourish and, second, surveys four revisionist proposals that claim to re-conceptualize the role of the "local" in the mission of the "international."

Emancipatory Discourse

Central to the international-local dilemma is the prevailing discourse of peacebuilding. In similar fashion to a parallel and more matured discussion in development studies,[32] the manner in which war-affected contexts are written about, conceived of, and narrated in mainstream peacebuilding text and discourse serves to frame these contexts as dysfunctional, failed, weak, irrational, and immature.[33] This mainstream discourse props up the West as the peacebuilding authority and savior, and situates expertise solely in the laps of experts from Western countries. The discourse also serves to legitimize therapeutic action whereby the international community assumes responsibility for a population no longer able to care for themselves and in need of rescue.[34] Paternalistic attitudes abound as locals are viewed with pity and as incapable of meaningful agency—certainly not without careful and overbearing supervision.

Emancipatory peacebuilding calls for a fundamental change in voice and tone. Scholars such as Cockell and Lederach eschew international-centered language and insist on viewing the "local" as both a vital source of peacebuilding resources and instrumental in shaping peacebuilding methodology.[35] Cockell is quite exclusive: "Sustainable peace can only be founded on the indigenous, societal resources for intergroup dialogue, cooperation and consensus."[36] Emancipatory peacebuilding requires an elicitive stance whereby resources are not imported and imposed by outsiders, but draws upon local knowledge and processes.[37] Such a stance will prove dissonant with the disempowering nature of "failed state" discourse and the manner in which it silences alternative voices and visions. Rather, it will be receptive to locally-legitimated social and political structuring leading to peace.[38]

"Everyday" Welfare and Bottom-Up Agency

Driving down the discussion of peacebuilding to the level of the local will invariably raise important but difficult questions—not least of which is what the local population envisions as crucial peacebuilding work, and who will best fulfil these visions. Richmond insists that the liberal peacebuilding project has "failed to deliver on their promise of a liberal peace for all," but has created only shells of institutions and benefited predatory domestic elites.[39] Conversely, benefits have not had significant or adequate impact on the everyday life of populations. Emancipatory peacebuilding, however, is comprehensive and relational,[40] and focuses on individual and communal perceptions of needs, aspirations, and opportunities, while rejecting the central status of models, states, and institutions as the objects and subjects of peace. Thus, the politics of peacebuilding should "spring organically from the agency of the people involved."[41] For example, Pugh points out that neoliberal, economic intervention policies have ignored socially and historically embedded welfare arrangements, and have assaulted welfare as a social contract in many conflict-affected contexts.[42] In response, the emancipatory peacebuilding project must engage in elicitive negotiations with local communities where local voices are taken seriously, and reconceptualize "atomised societies as collectives."

What role for the "local"? Hemmer, et al., and Van Tongeren, et al., investigate how grassroots citizen peacebuilders are able to influence upper level peacebuilding processes.[43] In order to achieve this difficult stance with the upper level, Hemmer, et al., integrate theories of Track II diplomacy, citizen peacebuilding, civic democratization, and social movements to present a case for the agency of a grassroots "peacebuilding organism." This organism would consist of a broad network of peacebuilding organizations and would be able to influence diplomatic negotiations by transforming the local political landscape. Pugh, however, is more skeptical of locally inspired transformation, unless it is accompanied by massive global economic restructuring.[44] This change would seem extremely unlikely, however, in the short-term. However, opportunities may arise from within the current global economic turmoil.

Communitarian Basis

The emancipatory peacebuilding project is being identified as communitarian in character.[45] As a reaction against liberalism and, in particular, its universalist pretensions and its devaluation of community, communitarianism argues that both tradition and social context prove essential to moral and political decision-making and action.[46] Whereas the (neo)liberal peacebuilding project argues for the universal nature of its central tenants, communitarianism suggests that any peacebuilding solutions must be derived from the potentially non-liberal local populations affected by the conflict who should, consequently, be granted the power to make their own choices regardless of their dissonance with (Western) international norms.[47]

Four Revisionist Proposals

A growing body of literature documents the inadequacies of the "liberal peace" and its rapid push for liberal market democracies in countries emerging from civil war. However, the criticisms of the vast majority of peacebuilding scholars do not call for an outright termination of interventional action, but rather point to potential revisions to current theory and practice to make international intervention more efficient and increasingly sustainable. To this end, this section presents four revisionist proposals that are largely liberal in their stance, but do not all adopt the universalist assumptions of the currently fashionable (neo)liberal model. The proposals are presented and arranged in an order that reflects the magnitude of control granted to local populations by international interveners—starting with the lowest.

First, Roland Paris's *At War's End* concludes that, while the end goals of liberalization need not be dropped, the rapid liberalization processes in countries recently emerging from civil war have tended to endanger the fragile peace that liberalization was intended to consolidate.[48] What he proposes is an *institutionalization before liberalization* (IBL) strategy. IBL mandates a strong-handed foreign intervention along with the strategic minimizing of the destabilizing effects of liberalization by delaying the introduction of democratic and market-oriented reforms until local institutions have been established and strengthened. Institutions must first be strengthened because strong and coercive institutions are better able to absorb the destabilizing competition resulting from democratic elections and economic reforms.

Second, Michael Barnett proposes a coercive *republican peacebuilding* methodology similar to Roland Paris's IBL, but with slightly different means and ends in mind—that is, the use of the republican principles of deliberation, constitutionalism, and representation to help states recovering from violence garner stability and legitimacy.[49] Innovative in the republican approach is its focus on limiting and distributing political power in order to restrain the exertion of arbitrary power and "spoiling" faction groups. The modest pace and deliberative processes inherent to republicanism do not force elections too quickly, and it is willing to utilize nonelected but locally-led government structures in precarious transitional periods. Most importantly, republicanism "views the essence of legitimacy as the state's use of proper means to achieve collectively accepted goals"[50]—even non-liberal goals, although unlikely given the broadly liberal means used to incorporate the interests of citizens.

Third, Richmond and Lidén describe an emancipatory (Lidén labels it "social") peacebuilding methodology.[51] Unlike IBL and republican revisionist forms, emancipatory peacebuilding diverges significantly from the (neo) liberal project. It is much less coercive (particularly in regard to international actors), is not evangelistic in regard to universal liberal conceptions of politics, economics, and human rights, and may not birth liberal market democracies (although this is certainly a possibility). Emancipatory peacebuilding, in short, broadens the narrow top-down state-building focus of liberal peacebuilding, and holistically redirects the project as a grassroots, bottom-up activity—engaging with the local and the marginalized. Local decision-making processes are allowed to determine basic political, economic, and social developments in the post-violence period.[52] As such, emancipatory peacebuilding is intimately interested in the "everyday" needs of a conflict-affected population (similar to Burton's "basic needs"),[53] and the culturally adapted provision of vital resources, political agency, and economic opportunity.[54] Political organization and any state-building activities are negotiated between local and international actors—a process void of pre-determined political models and outcomes. Furthermore, versions of human rights and rule-of-law should be included in the "local peace" that reflect the consensus of local groupings as well as broader international expectations.[55] In this way, emancipatory peacebuilding allows local conditions and capacities to determine what type of peace will emerge in a particular context.[56]

The above emancipatory agenda requires that international peacebuilding actors subject themselves to requirements that prevent them from treating every peacebuilding context in the same way. Richmond states that emancipatory peacebuilding actors are inherently concerned about care and welfare, are empathetic, eschew standardized blueprints, seek open and free communication with local groups, and operate on the basis of the norms and systems they are trying to instill in the local context.[57]

Fourth, Mac Ginty describes a system of indigenous peacebuilding that rests solidly on traditional peacemaking processes.[58] Locally inspired peacebuilding processes such as consensus decision-making, restoring human-environmental systems and balance, traditional rituals, and reciprocal compensation and gifts are propped up and viewed as far removed from, and dissonant with, foreign ideologies of peace. Any international role, if any, is wary of imposing a foreign culture onto the local culture. Indigenous peacemaking, though, despite its current popularity in emerging policy, is starting to come under serious criticism as being unable to deal with post-war vacuums of domestic authority, unable to stand its ground in the face of any foreign influence, unable to prevent the empowering of local spoilers, and preventing local cultural identities from flourishing in locally legitimated and desired modernizing contexts.[59]

THE VOICE OF CRITICAL THEORY

A second philosophical theme emerging from the emancipatory peacebuilding literature is the project's grounding in critical theory. This theme is certainly related to the previous "local" theme in that critical theory accuses (neo)liberal peacebuilding of not addressing local interests. However, critical theory broadens the scope of the critique of (neo)liberal peacebuilding through its focus on the global dimensions of peacebuilding.[60]

Critical theory responses to international peacebuilding and peacekeeping have arisen in response to recent revisions to official UN peacebuilding and peacekeeping policy—most notably in the Brahimi Report that focused on how to better manage peacekeeping personnel to produce more effective peacekeeping results; the focus on "human security"; the UN's *Millennium Development Goals*; and the *Responsibility to Protect* doctrine that attempted to reconcile conceptions of national sovereignty with human rights protection. While seeing positive movement in these revisions toward care of the "local," some peacebuilding scholars believe that this rethinking of theory and practice is not going nearly far enough; it is failing to interrogate the role of (neo)liberal peacekeeping and peacebuilding in the wider processes of global politics. These scholars have initiated a more radical discourse in the challenge of rethinking peacebuilding/peacekeeping practice, and utilize critical perspectives to both deconstruct orthodox practice and construct a more critical agenda for peace operations.

Pugh proposes that (neo)liberal peacebuilding serves as a "management device" to maintain the current version of global politics and economics "that privileges the rich and powerful states in their efforts to control or isolate unruly parts of the world."[61] As such, peacebuilding is viewed as serving a narrow purpose—"to doctor the dysfunctions of the global political economy within a framework of liberal imperialism."[62] Thus, while (neo)liberal structures are inherently interested in maintaining the status quo of the world system with its embedded instabilities and inequalities, critical theory is able to expose injustices that stem from (neo)liberalism and provides a philosophical and ethical basis for the construction of structural transformations to emancipate conflict-affected societies. Pugh contends that many conflict resolution and peacekeeping efforts simply "smooth the functioning of the system" and serve the purposes of existing world system powers.[63] More radical critical work is needed that spotlights larger issues such as globalization-induced inequality and global economic structural violence.

For Bellamy and Williams, a critical response starts with a new peacekeeping agenda intensely focused on hearing the voices of locals in the planning and execution of peace operations.[64] They point out, however, that this agenda must be situated within a program focused on local democratization, the creation of local nonviolent conflict resolution structures, and structured cooperation across political borders. Beyond this, a critical agenda needs to move its eyes outward and upward. The hegemonic position of the United States in the global system must be addressed, in particular its willingness to act unilaterally without international support, and its ambivalence to international law and the International Criminal Court (ICC).[65]

A critical agenda must come to terms with the predominant "failed state" discourse. This discourse does not make evident the fact that in most cases conflict-affected states are not void of state power; however, it may be obscured because of the state's illiberal methodology. Thus, peacebuilding strategies may need to be directed at civil society and the opening up of space for dialogue.[66]

Pugh proposes UN Security Council reform such as its replacement by a revamped population-weighted UN General Assembly—thus making intervention decisions democratic at the global level.[67] He also proposes the outright replacement of international financial institutions (IMF, World Bank, and the WTO) with more democratic structures that are more relevant to the poor. In terms of peacekeeping forces, Woodhouse and Ramsbotham suggest the creation of a permanent UN force that would align, not with the interests of the world powers, but rather with the powerless inside conflict zones.[68]

EMANCIPATORY PEACEBUILDING PRIORITIES

In order to flesh out the above formulations of emerging conceptions of emancipatory peacebuilding, this section investigates revisionist proposals in the four priority areas of orthodox (neo)liberal peacebuilding—security, political transition, economic and social development, and reconciliation and justice.[69] Furthermore, it explores the implications of the emancipatory project on peacebuilding coordination.

Security and Emancipation

Booth, shortly after the end of the Cold War, stated, "Emancipation, theoretically, is security."[70] Booth identified a post–Cold War transformation in security thought, a movement past realism and neorealism and the adoption of a more critical stance to security—primarily expressed through the human security doctrine. The human security narrative has served to awaken some traditional security actors to the plight of oppressed populations, highlighting the manner in which poverty and underdevelopment leads to insecurity for all. However, human security is coming under increased scrutiny. Duffield views human security as simply another "technology of governance," enacted by the North over the South for ultimately self-serving ends.[71] Christie argues that human security has lost its critical edge, has become a new orthodoxy, is unable to amplify the voice of peoples in the South, and is thus unfit as a basis for necessary systemic change.[72]

Not so with emancipatory conceptions of security. Emancipation, as a chief aim of security, requires bottom-up approaches where individuals are empowered to voice, negotiate, and develop forms of human security tailored to their particular situation. Local agency becomes central to security work, resulting in increased legitimacy and effectiveness. For example, Jabri believes that the "enemy" of the people in Afghanistan (the Taliban) is being defined by the liberal intervenors, thus providing the Taliban with an inflated political and social agency, all the while precluding any form of localized resistance to the Taliban, which inadvertantly denies the population political agency.[73] A more appropriate and progressive emancipatory response would be to support local nonviolent resistance and extend "solidarity to progressive forces of emancipation in that society."[74]

Political Transition and Local Participation

Emancipatory transitional political structures allow local voices expression and participatory power in the transformation of cultural and political foundations as part of any state-building process—even if the processes do not result in Western-style democracy or integration into the capitalist world system. Chopra and Hohe propose a democratic system of participatory intervention where indigenous paradigm(s) are allowed to coexist with, or evolve during, the establishment of modern institutions.[75] Central to this process is the active local participation of local administrative structures, which should ensure representation upward throughout the government structure, thus increasing the likelihood of its social viability, as well as local identification and ownership.

While Chopra and Hohe's system is inherently democratic, Brown, et al., resist mandating a "democratic" requirement and put forward the concept of "hybrid political orders"—the coexistence of different models of governance and government.[76] Stemming from both Western models and local indigenous traditions, hybrid political orders are shaped by both globalization and societal fragmentation (ethnic, tribal, religious). As opposed to the usual and dominant discourse of statebuilding, which is derived from modernization and the ideal "stages of growth," the authors believe that hybrid political orders may be better able to allow for the establishment of viable, participatory, and democratic political community in the aftermath of violent conflict. By labelling these hybrid political orders as "fragile states" or "weak," Western governments and peacebuilding actors may miss crucial opportunities for constructive peacebuilding, as established and locally legitimated local political forms underpinning the fragile peace in post-war contexts are ignored.[77]

Rethinking Economic and Social Development

Emancipatory economic and social development refocuses the means and broadens the narrowed ends of (neo)liberal economic and social development. In regard to economic development, scholars are increasingly arguing for a break-up of the marriage between economic development policy and neoliberal economic policy. Galtung argues for an eclectic development that would broaden its American capitalist roots and incorporate socialist and "African local" structures.[78] Others argue that Western development actors should eschew "historical templates for new and evolving situations" and allow for locally generated reconstruction programs even if they fall short of the high, and perhaps ethno-cultural-centric, standards set by the "liberal peace."[79] Other authors, such as Duffield, offer a harsher critique.[80] Duffield believes that development has been reinvented as a strategic tool in managing conflict-affected contexts and their populations and hence development aid has become "securitized." Thus, aid and development actors ultimately serve the purposes of the dominating North—leading to the conclusion that the entire enterprise should be revamped or perhaps dropped.

Pierce and Stubbs use a case study of UNDP project work in the town of Travnik in central Bosnia to illustrate the linked concepts of social development and hegemony.[81] They envision peacebuilding processes moving past an "inventory approach" with the usual mix of peacebuilding activities, and propose that social development's central role is challenging hegemony in the local social context. They propose that conflict/post-conflict zones need to be viewed as "highly complex structures, rather than simply as places where warmongering 'hard-liners' have ensured the acquiescence of the population."[82] Peacebuilding processes are thus conceived of as a counter-hegemonic project inside this complex social structure.

Reconciliation and Justice

Peacebuilding theorists such as Lederach, Mani, Philpott, and Sriram propose that the liberal restriction of "reconciliation" to rule-of-law and human rights work is inadequate.[83] While the rule-of-law and human rights are certainly crucial in ensuring justice in a post-war context, the liberal peace will struggle to attend to the deep wounds inflicted by war and political violence. Further, rule-of-law and human rights work will fall short in the empowerment and healing of victims, prove inadequate in reforming and reintegrating perpetrators, and avoid the powerful legacy of emotions that can lead to revenge and renewed violence.[84]

Emancipatory peacebuilding pushes for the centrality of reconciliation in the politics of peacebuilding theory and practice, and for deeper healing than possible through trials, Truth and Reconciliation Commissions, and human rights work. Reconciliation activities should be located at the community level and be aimed at reasserting established social codes and processes, healing communal trauma, and regaining trust, unity, and peaceful coexistence. To this end, scholars such as Kelman, Fisher, and Rothman have been developing the conflict resolution methodology of dialogue groups and problem-solving workshops.[85] Dialogue-based strategies aim to build bridges by creating a safe space for antagonists to engage with each other in a constructive and controlled manner. Other conflict resolution practitioners interested in initiating community reconciliation processes are increasingly recognizing the power of storytelling, narrative, and proverbs.[86]

Another strand of important reconciliation theory is emerging from the field of restorative justice. Restorative justice theorists and practitioners propose revisions to criminal justice processes—eschewing the dominant conceptions of criminal justice as being primarily retributive in nature and rather adopting the vindication of victims as a central priority.[87]

CHALLENGES AND PROGRESS IN EMANCIPATORY PEACEBUILDING COORDINATION

Strategic coordination of the (neo)liberal peacebuilding project is heavily invested in hierarchy, Western outlooks, expressions of Western power, upper-level control, and ignorance of local wisdom. This structure proves to be dissonant with the emancipatory project. The emancipatory project will resist direct transfer of (neo)liberal coordination methodology because of its fundamental epistemological and ontological differences. As opposed to being primarily concerned with the horizontal integration of activities among international actors, emancipatory coordination concerns will be largely vertical in nature—between the "international" and the "local." It is interested in how internationally assisted peacebuilding can be controlled, directed, or guided by the "local." Thus, a discussion of emancipatory coordination will tackle "multi-level" challenges, and be interested in projections of power and conceptions of culture at each level.

There does not, at this point, exist any literature dealing directly and systematically with the coordination of the emancipatory project, which certainly reflects the ambiguity regarding the role of international actors in the paradigm, and because the paradigm has not been adopted in practice to a large extent. However, at an even more fundamental level, there may be widespread hesitancy to explore practicalities such as peacebuilding coordination because the theoretical requirements of an emancipatory stance have not been fully explored. There remain significant challenges within the model that may prove unbearable for the model—stemming not from inherent contradictions, but from a shortage of political willingness to make the tough choices necessitated by the model. Pugh is one of the few peacebuilding theorists venturing into this contentious territory. He believes that Northern peacebuilding powers have shown themselves unwilling to "consider fundamental questions about the extent to which the statist structure and neoliberal value system fosters the kinds of political and social instability that require policing, protection or exclusion."[88] Thus, peacebuilding operations have become "vehicles of system management" for oppressive global politico-economic structures, with peacebuilding actors serving as managers within a system that is primarily interested in the security of the North and the maintenance of its way of life.

The interface between the international and the local is situated within a dominant (neo)liberal politico-economic-cultural milieu, where Western-based "universals" are embedded in localized developing contexts. Thus, emancipatory peacebuilding coordination is dependent on retooled global liberal political and neoliberal capitalist economic structures, and an end to the exploitative relationship between the North and the South—no small task indeed. Without such changes, the emancipatory project will consistently be ground down and burdened with insupportable amounts of (neo)liberal baggage.

However, many scholars are more hopeful, and believe that humanitarians cannot be paralyzed by daunting and necessary global economic and political structural transformations, and concentrate on reformist steps (even if small and inadequate) that make a better world more likely for war-affected populations. Booth describes this slow reformation as "process utopian" (a phrase coined by Joseph Nye)—"At each political crossroad, there is always one route that seems more rather than less progressive in terms of global community-building."[89] Many of the authors surveyed in this chapter hint at inherent coordination necessities in the emancipatory project that can be achieved or pushed for despite the disempowering politico-economic systems within which we live. The essential item they struggle with is the manner in which the international community can work alongside the local community, all the while granting the local community power over and voice in peacebuilding decisions.

John Paul Lederach has constructed a theory of "multi-level" action that is much more reliant on grassroots forces for change than (neo)liberal peacebuilding theories.[90] Central to his theory is the elite-grassroots nexus—strategies at the upper national level must feed on the energy of processes at the grassroots level and, concurrently, national level policies can ameliorate tensions at the community level. In negative terms, transformative progress at the grassroots level will be significantly impeded with insecurity at the national elite level, while a failure to address basic needs at the grassroots level will create societal instability and threats of violence which handicap macro-level transformative activities. Lederach's "multi-level" theory is important for the coordination of emancipatory peacebuilding processes. International actors must serve as facilitators for elite-grassroots interaction. International actors must not dictate the outcome of this interaction, however, but use their resources and power to ensure its occurrence—perhaps justifying the use of coercion in some cases. Further, his theory highlights the necessity of coordination structures engaging all levels of society.

Fast, Neufeldt, and Schirch deal more directly with the ethics of international-local interactions undergirding the emancipatory peacebuilding coordination project.[91] They construct a theory of international-local interactions based on: (1) the individualist human rights of inherent worth and dignity and the right to make decisions that affect their lives; and (2) the communally relativist principles of the ability of communities to define their own common good, and the value of authentic relationships. Purposeful international-local interactions guided by these principles should, according to the authors, result in decision-making structures that are open to communal expertise, guided by local leadership, and inclusive of all parties, even extremists.

Other authors are starting to address another thorn in the side for any attempts at coordination in the emancipatory project—the tension between international standards/norms (e.g., human rights, environmental, accountability, justice, etc.) and competing local conceptions and systems.[92] The central tension is the extent to which international rights/norms are considered "universal" as opposed to being "relative." It seems that scholars are increasingly resisting either extreme in the debate and are emphasizing a healthy tension between the two. Theory in the debate is starting to converge, however. Attempts at reconciling local ownership with international norms require the eschewal of conceptions of culture as static and unchangeable, and rather culture is viewed as changing and socially constructed, and as holding transformative power.[93] Emancipatory coordination efforts, therefore, need to avoid romanticizing the "traditional," not blindly equate everything traditional with "good," and not label everything stemming from the West as harmful and culturally inappropriate.[94]

CONCLUSION

International (neo)liberal peacebuilding has begun to expose its inherent contradictions and struggles. As a technology of the global liberal politico-economic system, it is certainly creating conflict and dependency.[95] Thus, it appears necessary to critically transcend current peacebuilding practice and strive for more emancipatory and culturally empowering methodologies. To this end, a couple of imperatives in regards to international interventionist practice seem instructive.

First, the international community cannot become paralyzed by the "emancipatory" critique—it is imperative that we not abandon conflict-affected citizens. Inaction has serious consequences as evident in the Rwandan and Darfurian cases—it is clearly inhumane to leave whole societies vulnerable to suffering. Second, international actors must increasingly adopt a critical(ly) self-reflective stance—being honest with local populations in regard to their interests (they will always hold some), being particularly sensitive to any attachments to current versions of global capitalism, democracy, and our Western mindset and way of living, being empathetic and compassionate in their practice, and intensely dedicated to the improvement of life-chances for war-affected individuals and communities. Third, and perhaps related to the previous point, international actors must be "thinking" and "judging" actors—deeply aware of becoming simply a "cog in the administrative machinery."[96] The emancipatory paradigm requires actors embedded within the peacebuilding system to avoid abdicating their individual responsibility to think and judge in order to maintain their transformative potential. In a similar vein, Galtung calls for the rejection of the traditional division of labor between those who establish the values (ideologists), those who establish the trends (scientists), and those who form the means to the ends (politicians), and the implementation of a more unified approach.[97] Those who act must also be the ones who think about and judge the action.

BIBLIOGRAPHY

Avruch, Kevin. "Culture, Relativism, and Human Rights," in *Human Rights and Conflict: Exploring the Links between Rights, Law, and Peacebuilding*, Julie Mertus and Jeffrey W. Helsing, eds. Washington, DC: United States Institute of Peace Press, 2006.

Barnett, Michael. "Building a Republican Peace: Stabilizing States after War." *International Security,* vol. 30, no. 4 (2006): 87–112.

Barnett, Michael, et al. "Peacebuilding: What Is in a Name?" *Global Governance,* vol. 13, no. 1 (2007): 35–58.

Bell, Daniel. "Communitarianism." *The Stanford Encyclopedia of Philosophy*, 2009. http://plato.stanford.edu/archives/spr2009/entries/communitarianism/ (June 14, 2010).

Bellamy, Alex J., and Paul Williams."Conclusion: What Future for Peace Operations? Brahimi and Beyond." *International Peacekeeping,* vol. 11, no. 1 (2004): 183–212.

Biggar, Nigel. "Making Peace or Doing Justice: Must We Choose?" in *Burying the Past: Making Peace and Doing Justice after Civil Conflict*, Nigel Biggar, ed. Washington, DC: Georgetown University Press, 2003.

Booth, Ken. "Security and Emancipation." *Review of International Studies,* vol. 17, no. 4 (1991): 313–326.

Brown, Anne, et al. "Challenging Statebuilding as Peacebuilding: Working with Hybrid Political Orders to Build Peace," in *Palgrave Advances in Peacebuilding: Critical Developments and Approaches*, Oliver Richmond, ed. New York: Palgrave MacMillan, 2010.

Burton, John W. *Violence Explained: The Sources of Conflict, Violence and Crime and Their Provention*. Manchester, NY: Manchester University Press, 1997.

Chopra, Jarat, and Tanja Hohe. "Participatory Intervention." *Global Governance,* vol. 10, no. 3 (2004): 289–305.

Cockell, John G. "Conceptualising Peacebuilding: Human Security and Sustainable Peace," in *Regeneration of War-Torn Societies*, Michael Pugh, ed. New York: St. Martin's Press, 2000.

Coulter, David, and John Wiens. "Educational Judgement: Linking the Actor and the Spectator." *Educational Researcher,* vol. 31, no. 4 (2002): 15–25.

Crush, Jonathan Scott. "Introduction," in *Power of Development*, Jonathan Scott Crush, ed. New York: Routledge, 1995.

Donais, Timothy. "Empowerment or Imposition? Dilemmas of Local Ownership in Post-Conflict Peacebuilding Processes." *Peace & Change,* vol. 34, no. 1 (2009): 3–26.

Duffield, Mark. *Development, Security and Unending War: Governing the World of Peoples*. Malden, MA: Polity, 2007.

Escobar, Arturo. *Encountering Development: The Making and Unmaking of the Third World*. Princeton, NJ: Princeton University Press, 1995.

Fast, Larissa A., Reina C. Neufeldt, and Lisa Schirch. "Toward Ethically Grounded Conflict Interventions: Reevaluating Challenges in the 21st Century." *International Negotiation,* vol. 7, no. 2 (2002): 185–207.

Fisher, Ronald J. "Interactive Conflict Resolution: Dialogue, Conflict Analysis, and Problemsolving," in *Handbook of Conflict Analysis and Resolution,* Dennis Sandole, Sean Byrne, Ingrid Sandole-Staroste, and Jessica Senehi, eds. New York: Routledge, 2009.

Galtung, Johan. "On the Future of the International System." *Journal of Peace Research,* vol. 4, no. 4 (1967): 305–333.

———. *Peace by Peaceful Means: Peace and Conflict, Development and Civilization*. Thousand Oaks, CA: Sage Publications, 1996.

Hemmer, Bruce, et al. "Putting the 'Up' In Bottom-up Peacebuilding: Broadening the Concept of Peace Negotiations." *International Negotiation,* vol. 11, no. 1 (2006): 129–162.

Human Security Report Project. "Human Security Report." 2009. http://www.hsrgroup.org/human-security-reports/2009/overview.aspx (June 10, 2010).

Jabri, Vivienne. "War, Government, Politics: A Critical Response to the Hegemony of the Liberal Peace," in *Palgrave Advances in Peacebuilding: Critical Developments and Approaches*, Oliver Richmond, ed. New York: Palgrave Macmillan, 2010.

Jacoby, Tim. "Hegemony, Modernisation and Post-War Reconstruction." *Global Society: Journal of Interdisciplinary International Relations,* vol. 21, no. 4 (2007): 521–537.

Jeong, Ho Won. *Peacebuilding in Postconflict Societies: Strategy and Processes*. Boulder: Lynne Rienner Publishers, 2005.

Kelman, Herbert C. "The Role of an International Facilitating Service for Conflict Resolution." *International Negotiation,* vol. 11, no. 1 (2006): 209–223.

Lederach, John Paul. *Building Peace: Sustainable Reconciliation in Divided Societies*. Washington, DC: United States Institute of Peace Press, 1997.

———. *Preparing for Peace: Conflict Transformation across Cultures*. Syracuse, NY: Syracuse University Press, 1995.

Lekha Sriram, Chandra. "Justice as Peace? Liberal Peacebuilding and Strategies of Transitional Justice." *Global Society: Journal of Interdisciplinary International Relations,* vol. 21, no. 4 (2007): 579–591.

Lekha Sriram, Chandra. "Resolving Conflicts and Pursuing Accountability: Beyond "Justice Versus Peace." in *Palgrave Advances in Peacebuilding: Critical Developments and Approaches*, Oliver Richmond, ed. New York: Palgrave Macmillan, 2010.

Lidèn, Kristoffer. "Building Peace between Global and Local Politics: The Cosmopolitical Ethics of Liberal Peacebuilding." *International Peacekeeping,* vol. 16, no. 5 (2009): 616–634.

———. "Whose Peace? Which Peace? On the Political Architecture of Liberal Peacebuilding." Masters Thesis. Oslo: University of Oslo, 2006.

Lidèn, Kristoffer, Roger Mac Ginty, and Oliver Richmond. "Introduction: Beyond Northern Epistemologies of Peace: Peacebuilding Reconstructed?" *International Peacekeeping,* vol. 16, no. 5 (2009): 587–598.

Mac Ginty, Roger. "Indigenous Peace-Making Versus the Liberal Peace." *Cooperation and Conflict,* vol. 43, no. 2 (2008): 139–163.

Mani, Rama. "Rebuilding an Inclusive Political Community after War." *Security Dialogue,* vol. 36, no. 4 (2005): 511–526.

———. "The Rule of Law or the Rule of Might? Restoring Legal Justice in the Aftermath of Conflict," in *Regeneration of War-Torn Societies*, Michael Pugh, ed. New York: St. Martin's Press, 2000.

Merry, Sally Engle. *Human Rights and Gender Violence: Translating International Law into Local Justice*. Chicago: University of Chicago Press, 2006.

Milliken, Jennifer, and Keith Krause. "State Failure, State Collapse, and State Reconstruction: Concepts, Lessons and Strategies." *Development & Change,* vol. 33, no. 5 (2002): 753.

Narten, Jens. "Dilemmas of Promoting 'Local Ownership': The Case of Postwar Kosovo," in *The Dilemmas of Statebuilding: Confronting the Contradictions of Postwar Peace Operations*, Roland Paris and Timothy D. Sisk, eds. New York: Routledge, 2009.

Paris, Roland. *At War's End: Building Peace after Civil Conflict*. Cambridge: Cambridge University Press, 2004.

———. "Saving Liberal Peacebuilding." *Review of International Studies,* vol. 36, no. 2 (2010): 337–365.

Philpott, Daniel. "An Ethic of Political Reconciliation." *Ethics & International Affairs,* vol. 23, no. 4 (2009): 389–407.

Pierce, Philip, and Paul Stubbs, "Peacebuilding, Hegemony and Integrated Social Development: The UNDP in Travnik," in *Regeneration of War-Torn Societies*, Michael Pugh, ed. New York: St. Martin's Press, 2000.

Pugh, Michael. "Peacekeeping and Critical Theory." *International Peacekeeping,* vol. 11, no. 1 (2004): 39–58.

———. "The Political Economy of Peacebuilding: A Critical Theory Perspective." *International Journal of Peace Studies,* vol. 10, no. 2 (2005): 23–42.

———. "Welfare in War-Torn Societies: Nemesis of the Liberal Peace?" in *Palgrave Advances in Peacebuilding: Critical Developments and Approaches*, Oliver Richmond, ed. New York: Palgrave Macmillan, 2010.

Richmond, Oliver. "A Geneology of Peace and Conflict Theory," in *Palgrave Advances in Peacebuilding: Critical Develoments and Approaches*, Oliver Richmond, ed. New York: Palgrave Macmillan, 2010.

———. "A Post-Liberal Peace: Eirenism and the Everyday." *Review of International Studies,* vol. 35, no. 03 (2009): 557–580.

———. "Becoming Liberal, Unbecoming Liberalism: Liberal-Local Hybridity Via the Everyday as a Response to the Paradoxes of Liberal Peacebuilding." *Journal of Intervention and Statebuilding,* vol. 3, no. 3 (2009): 324–344.

———. "Emancipatory Forms of Human Security and Liberal Peacebuilding." *International Journal,* vol. 62, no. 3 (2007): 458–477.

Richmond, Oliver, and Jason Franks. "Liberal Hubris? Virtual Peace in Cambodia." *Security Dialogue,* vol. 38, no. 1 (2007): 27–48.

Rothman, Jay. *Resolving Identity-Based Conflict in Nations, Organizations, and Communities*. San Francisco: Jossey-Bass, 1997.

Ryerson, Christie. "Critical Voices and Human Security: To Endure, to Engage or to Critique." *Security Dialogue,* vol. 41, no. 2 (2010): 169–190.

Schwarz, Rolf. "Post-Conflict Peacebuilding: The Challenges of Security, Welfare and Representation." *Security Dialogue,* vol. 36, no. 4 (2005): 429–446.

Stacy, Helen. *Human Rights for the 21st Century: Sovereignty, Civil Society, Culture.* Stanford, CA: Stanford University Press, 2009.

Tadjbakhsh, Shahrbanou. "Conflicted Outcomes and Values: (Neo)Liberal Peace in Central Asia and Afghanistan," *International Peacekeeping,* vol. 16, no. 5 (2009): 635–651.

———. "Human Security and the Legitimisation of Peacebuilding," in *Palgrave Advances in Peacebuilding: Critical Developments and Approaches*, Oliver Richmond, ed. New York: Palgrave MacMillan, 2010.

Tadjbakhsh, Shahrbanou, and Michael Schoiswohl. "Playing with Fire? The International Community's Democratization Experiment in Afghanistan." *International Peacekeeping,* vol. 15, no. 2 (2008): 252–267.

Taylor, Ian. "What Fit for the Liberal Peace in Africa?" *Global Society: Journal of Interdisciplinary International Relations,* vol. 21, no. 4 (2007): 553–566.

Van Tongeren, Paul, et al., eds. *People Building Peace II: Successful Stories of Civil Society*. Boulder, CO: Lynne Rienner Publishers, 2005.

Williams, Andrew. "Reconstruction: The Missing Historical Link," in *Palgrave Advances in Peacebuilding: Critical Developments and Approaches*, Oliver Richmond, ed. New York: Palgrave Macmillan, 2010.

Woodhouse, Tom, and Oliver Ramsbotham. "Cosmopolitan Peacekeeping and the Globalization of Security." *International Peacekeeping,* vol. 12, no. 2 (2005): 139–156.

Woolford, Andrew, and R.S. Ratner. "Mediation Frames/Justice Games." in *Handbook of Conflict Analysis and Resolution*, Dennis Sandole, Sean Byrne, Ingrid Sandole-Staroste, and Jessica Senehi, eds. New York: Routledge, 2009.

NOTES

1. Roland Paris, *At War's End: Building Peace after Civil Conflict* (Cambridge: Cambridge University Press, 2004).

2. Kristoffer Lidèn, "Whose Peace? Which Peace? On the Political Architecture of Liberal Peacebuilding," Masters Thesis (Oslo: University of Oslo, 2006).

3. Oliver Richmond, "A Geneology of Peace and Conflict Theory," in *Palgrave Advances in Peacebuilding: Critical Develoments and Approaches*, Oliver Richmond, ed. (New York: Palgrave Macmillan, 2010).

4. Paris, *At War's End.*

5. Kristoffer Lidèn, Roger Mac Ginty, and Oliver Richmond, "Introduction: Beyond Northern Epistemologies of Peace: Peacebuilding Reconstructed?" *International Peacekeeping,* vol. 16, no. 5 (2009): 587–598.

6. Lidèn, Mac Ginty, and Richmond, "Beyond Northern Epistemologies," 587–598.

7. Lidèn, Mac Ginty, and Richmond, "Beyond Northern Epistemologies," 587–598.

8. Vivienne Jabri, "War, Government, Politics: A Critical Response to the Hegemony of the Liberal Peace," in *Palgrave Advances in Peacebuilding: Critical Developments and Approaches*, Oliver Richmond, ed. (New York: Palgrave Macmillan, 2010); Andrew Williams, "Reconstruction: The Missing Historical Link," in *Palgrave Advances in Peacebuilding: Critical Developments and Approaches*, Oliver Richmond, ed. (New York: Palgrave Macmillan, 2010).

9. Williams, "Reconstruction."

10. Tim Jacoby, "Hegemony, Modernisation and Post-War Reconstruction," *Global Society: Journal of Interdisciplinary International Relations,* vol. 21, no. 4 (2007): 521–537.

11. Shahrbanou Tadjbakhsh, "Conflicted Outcomes and Values: (Neo)Liberal Peace in Central Asia and Afghanistan," *International Peacekeeping,* vol. 16, no. 5 (2009): 635–651; Ian Taylor, "What Fit for the Liberal Peace in Africa?" *Global Society: Journal of Interdisciplinary International Relations,* vol. 21, no. 4 (2007): 553–566.

12. Oliver Richmond and Jason Franks, "Liberal Hubris? Virtual Peace in Cambodia," *Security Dialogue,* vol. 38, no. 1 (2007): 27–48.

13. Mark Duffield, *Development, Security and Unending War: Governing the World of Peoples* (Malden, MA: Polity, 2007).

14. Oliver Richmond, "A Post-Liberal Peace: Eirenism and the Everyday," *Review of International Studies,* vol. 35, no. 03 (2009): 557–580; Roger Mac Ginty, "Indigenous Peace-Making Versus the Liberal Peace," *Cooperation and Conflict,* vol. 43, no. 2 (2008): 139–163; Duffield, *Development, Security*; Kristoffer Lidèn, "Building Peace between Global and Local Politics: The Cosmopolitical Ethics of Liberal Peacebuilding," *International Peacekeeping,* vol. 16, no. 5 (2009): 616–634; Jabri, "War, Government, Politics."

15. Human Security Report Project, *Human Security Report,* 2009. http://www.hsrgroup.org/human-security-reports/2009/overview.aspx (June 10, 2010).

16. Taylor, "What Fit"; Shahrbanou Tadjbakhsh and Michael Schoiswohl, "Playing with Fire? The International Community's Democratization Experiment in Afghanistan," *International Peacekeeping,* vol. 15, no. 2 (2008): 252–267.

17. Richmond, "A Post-Liberal Peace."

18. Richmond, "A Geneology of Peace and Conflict Theory."

19. Michael Pugh, "The Political Economy of Peacebuilding: A Critical Theory Perspective," *International Journal of Peace Studies,* vol. 10, no. 2 (2005): 23–42; Duffield, *Development, Security.*

20. Richmond, "A Geneology of Peace and Conflict Theory"; Richmond, "A Post-Liberal Peace."

21. Richmond, "A Geneology of Peace and Conflict Theory."

22. Richmond, "A Geneology of Peace and Conflict Theory."

23. Richmond, "A Post-Liberal Peace."

24. Richmond, "A Geneology of Peace and Conflict Theory."

25. Duffield, *Development, Security*; Jacoby, "Hegemony, Modernisation."

26. Roland Paris, "Saving Liberal Peacebuilding," *Review of International Studies,* vol. 36, no. 2 (2010): 337–365.

27. Oliver Richmond, "Emancipatory Forms of Human Security and Liberal Peacebuilding," *International Journal*, vol. 62, no. 3 (2007): 458–477; Richmond, "A Geneology of Peace and Conflict Theory"; Richmond, "A Post-Liberal Peace."

28. Timothy Donais, "Empowerment or Imposition? Dilemmas of Local Ownership in Post-Conflict Peacebuilding Processes," *Peace & Change,* vol. 34, no. 1 (2009): 3–26.

29. Shahrbanou Tadjbakhsh, "Human Security and the Legitimisation of Peacebuilding," in *Palgrave Advances in Peacebuilding: Critical Developments and Approaches*, Oliver Richmond, ed. (New York: Palgrave MacMillan, 2010).

30. Mac Ginty, "Indigenous Peace-Making."

31. Lidèn, "Building Peace between Global and Local Politics."

32. Jonathan Scott Crush, "Introduction," in *Power of Development*, Jonathan Scott Crush, ed. (New York: Routledge, 1995); Arturo Escobar, *Encountering Development: The Making and Unmaking of the Third World* (Princeton, NJ: Princeton University Press, 1995).

33. Donais, "Empowerment or Imposition."

34. Donais, "Empowerment or Imposition."

35. John G. Cockell, "Conceptualising Peacebuilding: Human Security and Sustainable Peace," in *Regeneration of War-Torn Societies*, Michael Pugh, ed. (New York: St. Martin's Press, 2000); John Paul Lederach, *Preparing for Peace: Conflict Transformation across Cultures* (Syracuse, NY: Syracuse University Press, 1995).

36. Cockell, "Conceptualising Peacebuilding."

37. Lederach, *Preparing for Peace.*

38. Jennifer Milliken and Keith Krause, "State Failure, State Collapse, and State Reconstruction: Concepts, Lessons and Strategies," *Development & Change,* vol. 33, no. 5 (2002): 753.

39. Oliver Richmond, "Becoming Liberal, Unbecoming Liberalism: Liberal-Local Hybridity Via the Everyday as a Response to the Paradoxes of Liberal Peacebuilding," *Journal of Intervention and Statebuilding,* vol. 3, no. 3 (2009): 324–344.

40. John Paul Lederach, *Building Peace: Sustainable Reconciliation in Divided Societies* (Washington, DC: United States Institute of Peace Press, 1997).

41. Tadjbakhsh, "Human Security."

42. Michael Pugh, "Welfare in War-Torn Societies: Nemesis of the Liberal Peace?" in *Palgrave Advances in Peacebuilding: Critical Developments and Approaches*, Oliver Richmond, ed. (New York: Palgrave Macmillan, 2010).

43. Bruce Hemmer, et al., "Putting the 'Up' In Bottom-up Peacebuilding: Broadening the Concept of Peace Negotiations," *International Negotiation,* vol. 11, no. 1 (2006): 129–162; Paul Van Tongeren, et al., eds., *People Building Peace II: Successful Stories of Civil Society* (Boulder: Lynne Rienner Publishers, 2005).

44. Pugh, "Welfare in War-Torn Societies."

45. Donais, "Empowerment or Imposition"; Lidèn, "Whose Peace?"; Lidèn, "Building Peace"; Tadjbakhsh, "Human Security."

46. Daniel Bell, "Communitarianism," *The Stanford Encyclopedia of Philosophy*, 2009. http://plato.stanford.edu/archives/spr2009/entries/communitarianism/ (June 14, 2010).

47. Donais, "Empowerment or Imposition."

48. Paris, *At War's End.*

49. Michael Barnett, "Building a Republican Peace: Stabilizing States after War," *International Security,* vol. 30, no. 4 (2006): 87–112.

50. Barnett, "Building a Republican Peace."

51. Lidèn, "Building Peace between Global and Local Politics"; Richmond, "Becoming Liberal"; Richmond, "A Post-Liberal Peace."

52. Richmond, "A Post-Liberal Peace."

53. John W. Burton, *Violence Explained: The Sources of Conflict, Violence and Crime and Their Provention* (Manchester, NY: Manchester University Press, 1997).

54. Lidèn, "Building Peace between Global and Local Politics."

55. Richmond, "A Post-Liberal Peace."

56. Lidèn, "Building Peace between Global and Local Politics."

57. Richmond, "A Post-Liberal Peace."

58. Mac Ginty, "Indigenous Peace-Making."

59. Lidèn, "Building Peace between Global and Local Politics"; Mac Ginty, "Indigenous Peace-Making"; Jens Narten, "Dilemmas of Promoting 'Local Ownership': The Case of Postwar Kosovo," in *The Dilemmas of Statebuilding: Confronting the Contradictions of Postwar Peace Operations*, Roland Paris and Timothy D. Sisk, eds. (New York: Routledge, 2009).

60. Lidèn, "Whose Peace?"

61. Michael Pugh, "Peacekeeping and Critical Theory," *International Peacekeeping,* vol. 11, no. 1 (2004): 39–58.

62. Pugh, "Peacekeeping and Critical Theory."

63. Pugh, "Peacekeeping and Critical Theory."

64. Alex J. Bellamy and Paul Williams, "Conclusion: What Future for Peace Operations? Brahimi and Beyond," *International Peacekeeping,* vol. 11, no. 1 (2004): 183–212.

65. Bellamy and Williams, "Conclusion."

66. Bellamy and Williams, "Conclusion."

67. Pugh, "Peacekeeping and Critical Theory."

68. Tom Woodhouse and Oliver Ramsbotham, "Cosmopolitan Peacekeeping and the Globalization of Security," *International Peacekeeping,* vol. 12, no. 2 (2005): 139–156.

69. Ho Won Jeong, *Peacebuilding in Postconflict Societies: Strategy and Processes* (Boulder, CO: Lynne Rienner Publishers, 2005); Michael Barnett, et al., "Peacebuilding: What Is in a Name?" *Global Governance,* vol. 13, no. 1 (2007): 35–58.

70. Ken Booth, "Security and Emancipation," *Review of International Studies,* vol. 17, no. 4 (1991): 313–326.

71. Duffield, *Development, Security.*

72. Christie Ryerson, "Critical Voices and Human Security: To Endure, to Engage or to Critique," *Security Dialogue,* vol. 41, no. 2 (2010): 169–190.

73. Vivienne Jabri, "War, Government, Politics: A Critical Response to the Hegemony of the Liberal Peace," in *Palgrave Advances in Peacebuilding: Critical Developments and Approaches*, Oliver Richmond, ed. (New York: Palgrave Macmillan, 2010).

74. Jabri, "War, Government, Politics."

75. Jarat Chopra and Tanja Hohe, "Participatory Intervention," *Global Governance,* vol. 10, no. 3 (2004): 289–305.

76. Anne Brown, et al., "Challenging Statebuilding as Peacebuilding: Working with Hybrid Political Orders to Build Peace," in *Palgrave Advances in Peacebuilding: Critical Developments and Approaches*, Oliver Richmond, ed. (New York: Palgrave MacMillan, 2010).

77. Brown, et al., "Challenging Statebuilding."

78. Johan Galtung, *Peace by Peaceful Means: Peace and Conflict, Development and Civilization* (Thousand Oaks, CA: Sage Publications, 1996).

79. Andrew Williams, "Reconstruction: The Missing Historical Link," in *Palgrave Advances in Peacebuilding: Critical Developments and Approaches*, Oliver Richmond, ed. (New York: Palgrave Macmillan, 2010).

80. Duffield, *Development, Security.*

81. Philip Pierce and Paul Stubbs, "Peacebuilding, Hegemony and Integrated Social Development: The UNDP in Travnik," in *Regeneration of War-Torn Societies*, Michael Pugh, ed. (New York: St. Martin's Press, 2000).

82. Pierce and Stubbs, "Peacebuilding, Hegemony."

83. Lederach, *Building Peace*; Daniel Philpott, "An Ethic of Political Reconciliation," *Ethics & International Affairs,* vol. 23, no. 4 (2009): 389–407; Chandra Lekha Sriram, "Justice as Peace? Liberal Peacebuilding and Strategies of Transitional Justice," *Global Society: Journal of Interdisciplinary International Relations,* vol. 21, no. 4 (2007): 579–591; Chandra Lekha Sriram, "Resolving Conflicts and Pursuing Accountability: Beyond 'Justice Versus Peace,'" in *Palgrave Advances in Peacebuilding: Critical Developments and Approaches*, Oliver Richmond, ed. (New York: Palgrave Macmillan, 2010); Rama Mani, "The Rule of Law or the Rule of Might? Restoring Legal Justice in the Aftermath of Conflict," in *Regeneration of War-Torn*

Societies, Michael Pugh, ed. (New York: St. Martin's Press, 2000); Rama Mani, "Rebuilding an Inclusive Political Community after War," *Security Dialogue,* vol. 36, no. 4 (2005): 511–526.

84. Philpott, "An Ethic of Political Reconciliation."

85. Herbert C. Kelman, "The Role of an International Facilitating Service for Conflict Resolution," *International Negotiation,* vol. 11, no. 1 (2006): 209–223; Ronald J. Fisher, "Interactive Conflict Resolution: Dialogue, Conflict Analysis, and Problemsolving," in *Handbook of Conflict Analysis and Resolution,* Dennis Sandole, Sean Byrne, Ingrid Sandole-Staroste, and Jessica Senehi, eds. (New York: Routledge, 2009); Jay Rothman, *Resolving Identity-Based Conflict in Nations, Organizations, and Communities* (San Francisco: Jossey-Bass, 1997).

86. Lederach, *Preparing for Peace.*

87. Mani, "Rebuilding an Inclusive Political Community"; Nigel Biggar, "Making Peace or Doing Justice: Must We Choose?" in *Burying the Past: Making Peace and Doing Justice after Civil Conflict*, Nigel Biggar, ed. (Washington, DC: Georgetown University Press, 2003); Andrew Woolford and R.S. Ratner, "Mediation Frames/Justice Games," in *Handbook of Conflict Analysis and Resolution*, Dennis Sandole, Sean Byrne, Ingrid Sandole-Staroste, and Jessica Senehi, eds. (New York: Routledge, 2009).

88. Pugh, "Peacekeeping and Critical Theory."

89. Booth, "Security and Emancipation."

90. Lederach, *Building Peace.*

91. Larissa A. Fast, Reina C. Neufeldt, and Lisa Schirch, "Toward Ethically Grounded Conflict Interventions: Reevaluating Challenges in the 21st Century," *International Negotiation,* vol. 7, no. 2 (2002): 185–207.

92. Donais, "Empowerment or Imposition?"; Lidèn, "Building Peace between Global and Local Politics"; Mac Ginty, "Indigenous Peace-Making"; Kevin Avruch, "Culture, Relativism, and Human Rights," in *Human Rights and Conflict: Exploring the Links between Rights, Law, and Peacebuilding*, Julie Mertus and Jeffrey W. Helsing, eds. (Washington, DC: United States Institute of Peace Press, 2006); Helen Stacy, *Human Rights for the 21st Century: Sovereignty, Civil Society, Culture* (Stanford, CA: Stanford University Press, 2009); Rolf Schwarz, "Post-Conflict Peacebuilding: The Challenges of Security, Welfare and Representation," *Security Dialogue,* vol. 36, no. 4 (2005): 429–446.

93. Sally Engle Merry, *Human Rights and Gender Violence: Translating International Law into Local Justice* (Chicago: University of Chicago Press, 2006).

94. Mac Ginty, "Indigenous Peace-Making."

95. Lidèn, "Building Peace between Global and Local Politics"; Duffield, *Development, Security.*

96. David Coulter and John Wiens, "Educational Judgement: Linking the Actor and the Spectator," *Educational Researcher,* vol. 31, no. 4 (2002): 15–25.

97. Johan Galtung, "On the Future of the International System," *Journal of Peace Research,* vol. 4, no. 4 (1967): 305–333.

Part Two

Practice

Chapter 8

Ripeness, Readiness, and Grief in Conflict Analysis[1]

Arnaud Stimec, Jean Poitras, and Jason J. Campbell

Social conflicts are a strong challenge for researchers and practitioners because they involve, among others, multiple issues, actors, cultures, or decision-making processes. Once the strategy to resolve the underlying problem has been selected, a second challenge is to determine at what point a conflict resolution strategy may be applied. It is a matter of timing the resolution efforts, in particular, evaluating how ripe a conflict is and whether the protagonists are ready to make an effort at reconciliation. Such effort, however, is contingent on various motivating factors, which move the parties through the process of reconciliation.

In assessing the pertinence of a conflict resolution effort, one of the most frequently used explanatory frameworks is ripeness theory.[2] In short, this theory identifies some key factors which must be present for a conflict to be considered ripe for an attempt at resolution (e.g., negotiation). Despite its popularity, ripeness theory has some limitations: poorly established generalization outside international situations, empirical validation is difficult to objectify, limited consideration of non-rational factors, and low predictability or risk of tautology.[3]

Growing out of ripeness theory, readiness theory,[4] based on ripeness is a recent effort to overcome the limits of ripeness theory. Among other things, readiness theory is more flexible and encompassing, and it makes it easier to apply ripeness theory as a conflict management tool. We believe that enriching readiness theory by bringing in the theory of grief developed by Elisabeth Kubler-Ross[5] would even further our understanding of ripeness theory. This paper explores how grief theory can be used to expand ripeness and readiness theories.

RIPENESS THEORY

A major challenge of any effort to resolve a conflict is to pinpoint the right time for initiating a negotiation: acting too early could lead to failure, while acting too late generates needless social costs. The notion of ripeness has emerged in studying international intractable conflicts where international efforts may come too early or push the wrong trigger. Thus, this notion is important in pinpointing the moment when dialogue can begin anew or the timing is right for action.[6] Ripeness theory stipulates that the parties in a conflict will not agree to negotiate until they have reached an uncomfortable impasse and perceived a way out of the stalemate.[7]

Hurting Stalemate

According to Zartman's theory, parties agree to negotiate because they cannot resolve the conflict unilaterally (e.g., by force), and the costs associated with it are too large to keep it going. Sometimes it is the risk associated with the enduring conflict that will motivate parties to negotiate.[8] An impasse can also be linked to the existence of an imminent mutual catastrophe that would occur if the conflict were to continue.[9] In theory, any intervention that occurs before the parties have reached the hurting stalemate point is unlikely to succeed, as the parties still have a power-based competitive attitude (i.e., they think they can win at a reasonable cost).

Perceived Way Out of the Conflict

The second necessary ripeness condition is that parties see a way out of the conflict. According to this concept, parties will initiate talks only when they can reasonably believe a negotiated compromise is possible. The condition might be induced by introducing new opportunities for joint gain in a negotiation.[10] Dean G. Pruitt and Sung H. Kim define this concept more broadly as optimism.[11] With this extended version of the concept, the perception that the other is willing to talk seriously is enough (i.e., there is no need to foresee a potential compromise as with the strict version of the theory).

For example, during the Vietnam War, between the Tet offensive of 1968 and the Paris Peace Talks of 1968 and 1973, the conflict in Vietnam transitioned from an escalated conflict to resolution within a five-year period. The key factor in analyzing the negotiation between the United States and the Republic of Vietnam (RVN), on the one hand, and the Democratic Republic of Vietnam (DRV) and the National Liberation Front (NLF), on the other, is to recognize that the Democratic Republic of Vietnam, after the Tet offensive of 1968, could rearm itself by protracting the conflict, which could have elicited an escalated offensive from the United States.[12] However, by this time the citizens of the United States, especially students and academics, were in total opposition to the war.[13] After the Tet offensive failed, North Vietnam and the Democratic Republic of Vietnam forces remained vulnerable to further attack, but for the United States to seize this opportunity to attack would incite further anti-war protests back home. Thus, both parties to the conflict had much to lose.

The conflict, then, was "ripe" for resolution, because both parties had much to lose and the perceived way out for both the United States and North Vietnam involved very complex negotiations, wherein the United States recognized that it could regain its prisoners of war and the Democratic Republic of Vietnam forces could possibly gain a unified Vietnamese coalition between the Democratic Republic of Vietnam, the Republic of Vietnam, and the National Liberation Front.[14] Thus, one interpretation of the effectiveness of the Paris Peace Talks was precisely the recognition that both parties to the conflict were overextending themselves (financially, socially, and militarily) by continuing to escalate the conflict, and both parties could potentially gain what they wanted by leaving the conflict.

Limits of Ripeness Theory

Despite empirical evidences and strong analysis power, ripeness theory is essentially a "necessary condition" model with the consequence that it may not lead to a move. It has several limitations: poorly established generalization outside international situations, empirical validation that is difficult to objectify, limited consideration of non-rational factors, and low predictability or risk of tautology.[15] Moreover, because there is a subjective interpretation, some situations that may be a hurting stalemate or offer a way out from the observer point of view may not be perceived as such by key leaders or influential stakeholders. This subjectivity is where ripeness theory offers new possibilities.

READINESS THEORY: EXPANDING RIPENESS THEORY

Readiness is mainly, in the intention of its author, a reformulation of ripeness theory to make it more amenable.[16] The first change is to consider each condition as a psychological state and not a necessary condition. The hurting stalemate condition becomes a "motivation" variable and the perceived way out becomes an "optimism" variable. The second change is to consider the psychological state of each party separately and not as a mutual state. Two parties might be both ready, but for two different reasons. One can be highly motivated with little optimism while the other is optimistic but has little motivation. Using motivation and optimism adds flexibility to ripeness theory.

Motivation

The perceived mutually hurting stalemate is reframed as a degree of motivation to end conflict. This stalemate can be the result of the perception that the conflict is dysfunctional and/or has third-party pressures. A conflict is perceived as dysfunctional when it appears that it may not be won or to a higher degree it may be lost. The full perception of the costs (that includes previously hidden costs) is a second key point. If the more damaging costs are only potential, the higher degree of the perception of the risk, and the higher the motivation is to end conflict. The pressure of strong third parties is another type of motivation. It could be the fear of a loss of support or of any type of sanction. Although this was discarded for intractable conflict, we suggest that the enticing opportunity model[17] should be added there as it could be, following the famous experience of Sherif on superordinate goals, a positive motivation to stop escalation.

Optimism

The perceived way out is reframed as optimism. Three factors might favor the perception that there is a potential for agreement. First is the perception of the other side's motivation to negotiate, indicating a better chance of success. For example, it could be a public declaration showing the opponent's willingness to come to a compromise. Moreover, if the other side's representatives are credible and have enough power to commit, the degree of optimism should be higher. Second, it may also be based on an evaluation of the situation by a strategic analysis of the negotiation context. For example, decreased distance between positions increases the power to negotiate. Third, the presence of powerful or credible third parties could reinforce optimism by making the other side's commitments more binding.[18]

In discussing the Tet offensive and the Paris Peace Talks of 1973, one can also analyze the nature of the resolution using readiness theory. It is our stance that the analysis of international conflict is better served using readiness theory than ripeness theory for four reasons. First, in examining the Vietnam War using readiness theory, one is better suited to analyze the motivation of ceasing to fight if one looks at mutually hurting stalemates as conditions for motivation (i.e., the motive to stop the conflict in Vietnam resulted from the financial, social, and military overextension of the United States, the Democratic Republic of Vietnam, and the Republic of Vietnam). Both parties were motivated to stop because they each wanted to secure what they had remaining. Second, readiness theory gives primacy to the difference in motivations for potentially resolving the conflict and recognizes that each party will likely have different reasons for conflict resolution. In the example of the Vietnam War, the failure of the Tet offensive contributed to motivating North Vietnam to seek resolution and the antiwar protests in the United States contributed to motivating American forces. Finally, readiness theory serves as a better theoretical tool of analysis because of the inherent flexibility gained in considering both parties' respective motivations. Negotiators can incentivize party participation by tailoring the resolution to meet the specific desires of each party, without having to consider shared justifications for resolution.

Contribution and Limits of Readiness Theory

Readiness theory is a strong move toward a psychological view of ripeness. One consequence of this new framework is to envision a compensatory model where more of one state may compensate for another. It is not motivation + optimism, but motivation × optimism that measures readiness. Furthermore, using the psychological state, it is possible to envision measuring a degree of motivation and optimism, and therefore we are better ready to assess readiness more accurately than with the ripeness condition.

But is motivation and optimism enough to explain why parties would be ready to negotiate a way out to a conflict? For example, two spouses may well realize that their marital dispute is costly to them and their children and that a divorce is a viable alternative. However, until both spouses accept that the relationship is over, any attempt to mediate this divorce is likely to fail or at least drag on for a long time. Sometime, parties are not truly ready to negotiate a way out until they accept that the past is over and that there is no way back. It is from this perspective that grief theory becomes an interesting alternative or complement to the classical models.

GRIEF THEORY AND CONFLICT RESOLUTION

According to Dwight Golann, the experience of giving up goals and settling below expectations is very painful; the predominant feeling of many disputants as they negotiate toward resolution appears to be one of loss. Thus, conflict resolution is by definition a grieving process.[19] One basic principle of grief is that when a person is not allowed or encouraged to express feelings of emotional loss, the emotion lingers and it makes any effort to move forward difficult.

Philippe Ariès discusses how grief lingers through a social mandate to be happy.[20] In some societies the grief-stricken party is socially obligated to implement coping mechanisms that mask grief. We are arguing, however, that the suppressed presence of grief, be it socially obligated or self-imposed, is precisely the inhibitor that prevents members of the PACS community from assisting parties in resolving their conflict.

With respect to grief management, Jessica Mitford argues that an inability to manage one's grief results in a greater inability to manage conflict. This inability could potentially result in higher frequencies of conflict for bereft persons. As a result, only when grieving is completed would a person be ready to resolve a conflict permanently. Unfortunately, this is not further modeled in conflict management theory.

Thus, practitioners must investigate the role of grief in the conflict resolution process, since it has been shown that grief can inhibit reconciliation. Thus, understanding the stages of the grief process will facilitate a greater recognition of the relationship between grief and conflict resolution.

Stages of the Grief Process

Based on research on support for the dying, psychiatrist Elisabeth Kubler-Ross proposed a five-stage model of grieving: denial, anger, bargaining, depression, and acceptance. According to the Kubler-Ross model, a person must go through these stages to be able to emerge from mourning and move on. Table 8.1 below describes the model's five stages.

The shock of the bad news tends to produce denial. This stage of grief is characterized by a refusal to see things as they are. Individuals tend not to want to admit the underlying problem. Denial seems in many regards consistent with theoretical issues on "impediments to recognizing and acting on objective elements of ripeness."[21]

Table 8.1. Five Stages of the Grief Cycle

Phase	*Description*
1. Denial	The subject refuses to recognize the situation.
2. Anger	The subject realizes the loss and does not accept the situation.
3. Bargaining	Searching for the lost object (desperate bargaining attitude), the subject strives desperately to get back to the way things were.
4. Depression	The subject realizes that things will never be as they were again.
5. Acceptance	A new beginning—the subject begins to take steps to reorganize his life differently.

After a denial period of some length, anger begins. At that time, the parties realize that they are dealing with an underlying problem and become very aggressive with each other. They realize the seriousness of the problem, but not necessarily their own role or contribution to the issue. At this stage, the dynamic can be very escalatory, harkening to the escalation model described in the previous section. Frequently, parties also focus their attention on scapegoats.[22]

Next comes the bargaining phase. It is very similar to negotiation, but it is primarily a desperate search for what has been lost. The negotiations are regularly accompanied by unrealistic promises. This phase of negotiation is often doomed to fail because people are not trying to build the future, but rebuild the past. The solutions chosen are generally not appropriate to the new situation and do not hold up. Either the negotiations are never-ending or the agreement does not produce the expected results.

After the failure of the pseudo-negotiations there is a time of dejection that is also described as depression. People then realize that there is no going back. It is at this phase that the individuals realize the full scope of the problem. They are also confronted with the fact that things will never be the same.

The last phase is acceptance and openness prevails. Individuals are now ready to start fresh. This results in new negotiations that are now actually based on the future and suited to the new situation. The new negotiations then bear fruit and can result in original agreements.

Although Kubler-Ross's model was developed in the framework of human psychology, it can be applied to many situations. For example, the model has been transposed to the individual context for job loss situations,[23] the community context for organizational change situations and merger and acquisition situations.[24]

APPLICATION OF GRIEF THEORY TO CONFLICT RESOLUTION

Grief theory is complex and has many implications for conflict resolution.[25] Nevertheless, two points stick out from our analysis as to the application of this theory to ripeness theory and readiness theory. First, in attempting to apply grief theory to conflict resolution, one must first recognize that denial (phase I) and anger (phase II) inhibit the progression of resolution by contributing to the escalation of conflict. Without acknowledging grief, by denying its existence, the party attempts to cope with grief by deferring the pain and suffering associated with the process of grieving. Negotiation efforts, however, will be severely hampered by this deferment. Thus, when parties have not been able to let go of the past or status quo, grief theory predicts that the negotiation effort will aim at restoring or preserving the status quo and thus fail.

Second, grief theory predicts that only when parties accept that something is over will they be truly willing to negotiate an agreement that is a new start as opposed to an agreement aiming at restoring or preserving the status quo. In a word, grief theory indicates a final stage where parties might be ready to move negotiation forward. In this regard, Frankl discusses the importance of addressing one's suffering and pain as a precondition to changing one's attitude and interpretation of the event.[26] One must, in effect, recognize grief and grieve. This recognition is cathartic, and purgative. Such recognition naturally results in anger, but to remain angry, to harbor a grudge or seek vengeance for perceived injustices, only escalates the conflict. Thus, it is only during the acceptance phase that a party is cognitively ready to begin the process of resolving the conflict.

The association then, between an inability to overcome grief and mounting tension between parties is perfectly demonstrated in the ongoing conflict between the Hutu and Tutsi tribes. The Burundi genocide of 1972, where Tutsis killed Hutus, only fuelled an already toxic climate of fear and hatred. The inability of the Hutus to properly grieve for the attempted extermination of their people incited decades of anger, which eventually resulted in the 1994 Rwanda genocide, where Hutus, now in power, killed Tutsis. Jazen discusses in a section titled "'Normal grieving in a land of genocide': The indifference and 'emotionless responses to atrocities,'" where any semblance of grief was totally absent.[27] We then assert that the inability to successfully transition through the stages of grief can and does result in the escalation of anger and conflict between parties. The ongoing conflict between the Hutus and Tutsis serves as an indication of how violent unresolved grief can become. Integrating grief theory into readiness theory is critical.

We believe that grief theory should not be viewed as an expansion of readiness theory, but as a complement. More specifically, grief theory points to an additional third element of Pruitt's model: transition. According to William Bridges, transition is the process of accepting the ending that one has to make to leave the old situation behind.[28] Failure to identify and get ready for endings and losses is the largest difficulty for people in transition. According to our proposed model (see Figure 8.1 below), the degree of transition could be a hidden part of readiness, and by extension ripeness. In other words, we believe that transition was an implicit factor in ripeness and readiness. The contribution of grief theory is to make this part of ripeness and readiness explicit.

Because we consider transition as a third psychological state, it should work as motivation and optimism in the readiness model. Consequently, a poor transition might be compensated by very high motivation and high optimism. For example, someone thinks "the opportunity is too good to pass on," even if transition is incomplete. Likewise, high levels of transition might compensate for low motivation. There might not be much advantage to reach a negotiated agreement

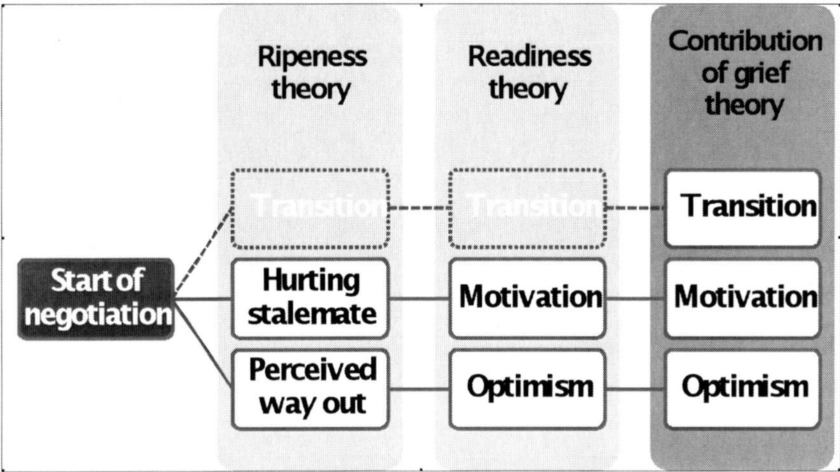

Figure 8.1.

(low motivation), but parties might be ready to move on (high transition). However, when any of the three variables is near zero, readiness would be near zero.

Thus, when neither the first party nor the second party acknowledges the grievance, the possibility for a meaningful negotiation will be thwarted. As a result, there is no possibility for reconciliation, since the transitional element between crisis and consensus is negotiating. Readiness, then, is stymied by an inability to negotiate a new start. In several severe community conflicts such as South Africa, or Hutu and Tutsi slaughters, Truth and Reconciliation grievance processes were initiated.[29] In Truth and Reconciliation processes, amnesty frees the possibility of expression. "The person or the family needs to recount the traumatic experience in detail, and express the emotions it produced. This permits integration into a coherent history of events that were necessarily disassociated, allowing the person to feel the pain of the losses experienced. It opens up the possibility for grief and mourning, and facilitates the development of a more coherent self-image."[30] A major issue for readiness is that the reconciliation process not only affects participants but also extends to ordinary people.[31] Therefore, it is a collective grieving process.

THEORETICAL AND PRACTICAL IMPLICATIONS FOR FURTHER RESEARCH

Readiness theory would be improved by considering "transition" if this new item provides a higher level of reliability in detecting true readiness. For example, transition could help explain false positives (i.e., the situation looks ripe and ready, but there is no real meaningful start of negotiation). Without including transition in the analysis, it might be difficult to explain why such a ripe situation does not lead to a successful negotiation effort. However, with transition, things might appear clearer. Parties are not ready to start negotiation, because they have not completed the grief process (i.e., low transition).

Although transition is well defined in accordance with grief, it remains important to precisely define its role and effects in readiness. The fact that grief has been described by a phase model has different implications. It is not certain that the next phase produces a higher degree of readiness (transition). For instance, the fourth phase (depression) may lead to less readiness to negotiate than the third (bargaining). And precisely, the third phase may push, as it was shown, to a hopeless negotiation because it refers to an attempt to avoid facing reality. There may be at this stage an apparent motivation to negotiate but in the wrong direction (past oriented). A theoretical issue is consequently to identify if transition may be measured as a linear or threshold variable and if one can identify the direction of negotiation (restoring the status quo or a new beginning.

Applying grief theory to conflict resolution not only increases the power to detect if a situation is ripe or if parties are ready to start a conflict management effort, but it also points out to strategies to help parties get ready for such efforts. When parties have not accepted that the past or status quo is over, they are probably not ready to negotiate and the situation is probably not ripe for conflict resolution. In such cases, the main task of a conflict resolution process will be to help parties through the "grieving process," before initiating a conflict resolution effort. It may increase the power of ripeness-readiness theory for situations where things seem to be ripe but lead to no movement. In the example of the prospect of a divorce, each spouse may need to be ready, emotionally, for the prospect of living separately whatever the hurting stalemate and the perceived way out is (such as a new job, a buyer for the house . . .).

Several strategies can be used to help parties move through transition. For example, approaches like a conflict analysis workshop,[32] joint expertise, or a regulation from a powerful third party may help. Grief also implies emotional issues that negotiators have sometimes difficulties to deal with,[33] whether at an individual level or at the collective level. Processes like "truth and reconciliation"[34] may also be helping the emotional transition needed. Finally, the debate over agreement building strategies may be enriched by a contingency approach including the different dimensions of readiness. For example, it might be better to use an agreement on a principle approach when parties are not through with the grief process (i.e., transition is low). This strategy allows parties to move forward without being confronted with a final agreement, which would be stressful to a party that is still early in the grief process. When grieving is advanced enough that parties could negotiate a new beginning, it would then be possible to negotiate the details of the agreement.

CONCLUSION

A peace or reconciliation process is so fragile that it is essential to avoid spoiling the peacebuilding efforts by using the wrong approach at the wrong time. Assessing ripeness before acting is thus essential to any conflict resolution process. But until now, ripeness theory has been more a theory to analyze past situations than to guide action. Prolonging ripeness theory, readiness theory offers an adapted frame that may match more situations and help practitioners and researchers to follow the waves of conflict more precisely. Grief theory enriches the model by integrating better the emotional side of ripeness.

But further research is needed to make more attainable the vow of knowing when and how to act in a conflict situation. For our purpose, the development of indicators or measuring tools is a next step to be experimented with. In this prospect, the question is if we can expect to integrate a general theory of readiness into conflict resolution or if strong contingent factors persist.

BIBLIOGRAPHY

Ariès, P. *Western Attitudes toward Death: From the Middle Ages to the Present*. Baltimore: The John Hopkins University Press, 1974.

Bareil, C. *Les modèles dynamiques, une façon renouvelée de comprendre les réactions des individus en situation de changement organisationnel*. Centre d'études en transformation des organisations, HEC Montréal. Booklet #04–08, 2004.

Betts, R.K. "Comments on Mueller: Interests, Burdens, and Persistence: Asymmetrics between Washington and Hanoi." *International Studies Quarterly*, vol. 24, no. 4 (1980): 520–524.

Bridges, W. *Managing Transitions: Making the Most of Changes*. London: Nicholas Brealy Publishing, 2003.

Carpenter, S.L., and W.J.D. Kennedy. *Managing Public Disputes: A Practical Guide for Government, Business, and Citizens' Group*. San Francisco: Jossey-Bass, 2001.

Castelbajac (de), B. *Le différend franco-espagnol à propos de la pêche dans le golfe de Gascogne*. Doctoral dissertation, IEP de Bordeaux, 1984.

Druckman, D. "Turning Points in International Negotiation: A Comparative Analysis." *The Journal of Conflict Resolution*, vol. 45, no. 4 (2001): 519–544.

Druckman, D., and M. Olekalns. "Emotions in Negotiation." *Group Decision and Negotiation*, vol. 17, no. 1 (2008): 1–11.

Errante, A. "Peace Work as Grief Work in Mozambique and South Africa: Post Conflict Communities as Context for Child and Youth Socialization." *Peace and Conflict,* vol. 5, no. 3 (1999): 261–281.

Frankl, V. *Man's Search for Meaning*. Boston: Beacon Press, 1959.

Gibson, L. *Overcoming Apartheid: Can Truth Reconcile a Divided Nation?* New York: HSRC Press, 2004.

Girard, R. *La violence et le sacré*, 1st ed, trans. by Hachette-Pluriel (*Violence and the Sacred*) Paris: Johns Hopkins, 1995.

Golann, D. "Death of a Claim: The Impact of Loss Reactions on Bargaining." *Negotiation Journal*, vol. 20, no. 4 (2004): 539–553.

Hampson, F. "Belligerent Reprisal and the 1977 Protocols to the Geneva Conventions of 1949." *The International and Comparative Law Quarterly*, vol. 37, no. 4 (1988): 818–843.

Jazen, J. "Historical Consciousness and a 'Prise De Conscience' in Genocidal Rwanda." *Journal of African Cultural Studies*, vol. 13, no. 1 (2000): 153–168.

Joanette, N., and M.L. Brunel. "Identification des étapes émotionnelles liées à la perte d'emploi des cadres à l'aide du modèle du deuil de Kübler-Ross." *Carriérologie,* vol. 8, nos. 1–2 (2001): 234–249.

Kriesberg, L. "Timing and the Initiation of De-Escalation Moves." *Negotiation Journal,* vol. 3, no. 3 (1987): 375–383.

Kubler-Ross, E. *On Death and Dying*. London: Tavistock Publication, 1978.

McMahan, J. "The Ethics of Killing in War." *Ethics,* vol. 114, no. 4 (2004): 693–733.

Minow, M. "Between Vangeance and Forgiveness: South Africa's Truth and Reconciliation Commission." *Negotiation Journal,* vol. 14, no. 4 (1998): 319–355.

Mirvis, P.H. "Negotiations after the Sale: The Roots and Ramifications of Conflict in an Acquisition." *Journal of Occupational Behaviour,* vol. 6, no. 1 (1985): 65–84.

Mitchell, C. "The Right Moment: Notes on Four Models of Ripeness." *The Kent Journal of International Relations,* vol. 9, no. 2 (1995): 35–52.

Mitford, J. *The American Way of Death Revisited.* New York: Buccaneer, 1998.

Mooradian, M., and D. Druckman. "Hurting Stalemate or Mediation? The Conflict over Nagorno-Karabakh." *Journal of Peace Research,* vol. 36, no. 6 (1999): 709–727.

Perlman, D., and G.J. Takacs. "The 10 Stages of Change." *Nursing Management,* vol. 21, no. 4 (1990): 33–38.

Poitras, J., R.E. Bowen, and S.J. Byrne. "Bringing Horses to Water? Overcoming Bad Relationships in the Pre-Negotiating Stage of Consensus Building." *Negotiation Journal,* vol. 19, no. 3 (2003): 251–263.

Pruitt, D.G. "Ripeness Theory and the Oslo Talks." *International Negotiation,* vol. 2 (1997): 237–250.

———. "Whither Ripeness Theory." Institute for Conflict Analysis and Resolution, George Mason University. Working Paper no. 25, 2005, http://www.gmu.edu/departments/ICAR/wp_25_pruitt.pdf.

———. "Back-Channel Communication in the Settlement of Conflict." *International Negotiation,* vol. 13 (2008): 37–54.

Pruitt, D.G., and S.H. Kim. *Social Conflict: Escalation, Stalemate, and Settlement,* 3rd ed. Boston: McGraw-Hill, 2008.

Rashford, N., and S. Coghlan. "Phases and Levels of Organisational Change." *Journal of Managerial Psychology,* vol. 4, no. 3 (1989): 17–22.

Rubin, J.Z. "Psychological Traps." *Psychology Today Magazine,* vol. 15 (1981): 52–63.

Schreiber, E.M. "Opposition to the Vietnam War among American University Students and Faculty." *The British Journal of Sociology,* vol. 24, no. 3 (1973): 288–302.

Stimec, A., P. Guillotreau, and J. Poitras. "Ripeness and Grief in Conflict Analysis." *Group Decision and Negotiation*, published online, 2009. www.springerlink.com/content/p04213635523p653/.

Zagare, F.C. "A Game-Theoretic Analysis of the Vietnam Negotiations: Preferences and Strategies 1968–1973." *The Journal of Conflict Resolution,* vol. 21, no. 4 (1977): 663–684.

Zartman, I.W. "Conflict and Resolution: Contest, Cost, and Change." *Annals of the American Academy of Political and Social Science, Issue 518, Resolving Regional Conflicts: International Perspectives,* 1991, 11–22.

———. *Ripe for Resolution: Conflict Resolution in Africa,* 2nd ed. New York: Oxford University Press, 1989.

———. "Ripeness: The Hurting Stalemate and Beyond," in *International Conflict Resolution After the Cold War*, P.C. Stern and D. Druckman, eds. Washington, DC: National Academy Press, 2000.

Zartman, I.W., and M. Berman. *The Practical Negotiator.* New Haven, CT: Yale University Press, 1982.

NOTES

1. This communication is an extension of an earlier empirical work—Stimec, Guillotreau, and Poitras, 2009, "Ripeness and Grief in Conflict Analysis" (www.springerlink.com/content/p04213635523p653/)—which is reframed and prolonged within readiness theory.

2. I.W. Zartman and M. Berman, *The Practical Negotiator* (New Haven, CT: Yale University Press, 1982); L. Kriesberg, "Timing and the Initiation of De-Escalation Moves." *Negotiation Journal,* vol. 3, no. 3 (1987): 375–383; I.W. Zartman, *Ripe for Resolution Conflict Resolution in Africa,* 2nd ed. (New York: Oxford University Press, 1989).

3. M. Mooradian and D. Druckman, "Hurting Stalemate or Mediation? The Conflict over Nagorno-Karabakh," *Journal of Peace Research,* vol. 36, no. 6 (1999): 709–727; D. Druckman, "Turning Points in International Negotiation: A Comparative Analysis," *The Journal of Conflict Resolution,* vol. 45, no. 4 (2001): 519–544; D.G. Pruitt, "Whither Ripeness Theory," Institute for Conflict Analysis and Resolu-

tion, George Mason University. Working Paper no. 25, 2005, http://www.gmu.edu/departments/ICAR/wp_25_pruitt.pdf.

4. Pruitt, "Whither Ripeness Theory."

5. Elisabeth Kubler-Ross, *On Death and Dying* (London: Tavistock Publication, 1978).

6. I.W. Zartman, "Ripeness: The Hurting Stalemate and Beyond," in *International Conflict Resolution after the Cold War*, P.C. Stern and D. Druckman, eds. (Washington, DC: National Academy Press, 2000).

7. Zartman, *Ripe for Resolution.*

8. D.G. Pruitt and S.H. Kim, *Social Conflict: Escalation, Stalemate, and Settlement,* 3rd ed. (Boston: McGraw-Hill, 2008).

9. C. Mitchell, "The Right Moment: Notes on Four Models of Ripeness," *The Kent Journal of International Relations,* vol. 9, no. 2 (1995): 35–52; J.Z. Rubin, "Psychological Traps," *Psychology Today Magazine,* vol. 15 (1981): 52–63.

10. Rubin, "Psychological Traps."

11. Pruitt and Kim, *Social Conflict: Escalation.*

12. R.K. Betts, "Comments on Mueller: Interests, Burdens, and Persistence: Asymmetrics between Washington and Hanoi," *International Studies Quarterly,* vol. 24, no. 4 (1980): 520–524.

13. E.M. Schreiberm, "Opposition to the Vietnam War among American University Students and Faculty," *The British Journal of Sociology,* vol. 24, no. 3 (1973): 288–302.

14. F.C. Zagare, "A Game-Theoretic Analysis of the Vietnam Negotiations: Preferences and Strategies 1968–1973," *The Journal of Conflict Resolution,* vol. 21, no. 4 (1977): 663–684.

15. Mooradian and Druckman, "Hurting Stalemate"; Druckman, "Turning Points"; Pruitt, "Whither Ripeness Theory."

16. D.G. Pruitt, "Ripeness Theory and the Oslo Talks," *International Negotiation,* vol. 2 (1997): 237–250; Pruitt, "Whither Ripeness Theory."

17. Pruitt and Kim, *Social Conflict.*

18. J. Poitras, R.E. Bowen, and S.J. Byrne, "Bringing Horses to Water? Overcoming Bad Relationships in the Pre-Negotiating Stage of Consensus Building," *Negotiation Journal,* vol. 19, no. 3 (2003): 251–263.

19. A. Errante, "Peace Work as Grief Work in Mozambique and South Africa: Post Conflict Communities as Context for Child and Youth Socialization," *Peace and Conflict,* vol. 5, no. 3 (1999): 261–281.

20. P. Ariès, *Western Attitudes toward Death: From the Middle Ages to the Present* (Baltimore: The John Hopkins University Press, 1974), 93–94.

21. Pruitt, "Turning Points," 3–4.

22. R. Girard, *La violence et le sacré*, 1st ed., trans. Hachette/Pluriel (*Violence and the Sacred*) (Paris: Johns Hopkins, 1995).

23. N. Joanette and M.L. Brunel, "Identification des étapes émotionnelles liées à la perte d'emploi des cadres à l'aide du modèle du deuil de Kübler-Ross," *Carriérologie*, vol. 8, nos. 1–2 (2001): 234–249.

24. N.S. Rashford and S. Coglan, "Phases and Levels of Organisational Change," *Journal of Managerial Psychology*, vol. 4, no. 3 (1989): 17–22; D. Perlman and G.J. Takacs, "The 10 Stages of Change," *Nursing Management,* vol. 21, no. 4 (1990): 33–38; P.H. Mirvis, "Negotiations after the Sale: The Roots and Ramifications of Conflict in an Acquisition," *Journal of Occupational Behaviour,* vol. 6, no. 1 (1985): 65–84.

25. Stimec, Guillotreau, and Poitras, "Ripeness and Grief."

26. V. Frankl, *Man's Search for Meaning* (Boston: Beacon Press, 1959).

27. J. Jazen, "Historical Consciousness and a 'Prise De Conscience' in Genocidal Rwanda," *Journal of African Cultural Studies,* vol. 13, no. 1 (2000): 153–168.

28. William Bridges, *Managing Transitions: Making the Most of Changes* (London: Nicholas Brealy Publishing, 2003).

29. L. Gibson, *Overcoming Apartheid: Can Truth Reconcile a Divided Nation?* (New York: HSRC Press, 2004).

30. M. Minow, "Between Vengeance and Forgiveness: South Africa's Truth and Reconciliation Commission," *Negotiation Journal,* vol. 14, no. 4 (1998): 319–355.

31. Gibson, *Overcoming Apartheid*; see also South African Reconciliation Barometer on www.ijr.org.za.

32. Poitras, et al., "Bringing Horses."

33. D. Druckman and M. Olekalns, "Emotions in Negotiation," *Group Decision and Negotiation,* vol. 17, no. 1 (2008): 1–11.

34. Minow, "Between Vengeance and Forgiveness"; Errante, "Peace Work as Grief Work in Mozambique and South Africa," 261–281.

Chapter 9

Children, Youth, and Peacebuilding

Siobhan McEvoy-Levy

This chapter explores some of the different ways in which children and young people are critical issues for conflict resolution in both theory and practice. The first part of the chapter discusses the politics of defining "children" and "youth." The next section examines four discourses about youth that currently frame global policy. These four discourses can be summarized as follows: (1) children have rights and should be protected; (2) youth are a development asset; (3) youth are a threat to security; and (4) youth are agents of change. It asks how well these discourses help us to accurately see "children" and "youth" within their own shifting political, economic, social, moral, and developmental contexts. Finally, the chapter moves to a discussion of what can be learned from young people's own views of "youth" and "peacebuilding," with special attention given to the views of young Palestinians interviewed in 2009, and to the importance of identities and systems. The chapter draws on interviews and focus groups with young people, youth workers, policymakers, and other youth and conflict experts in several countries, as well as on background research in secondary sources.

An initial critical issue for peace scholars and practitioners interested in the connections between young people, conflict, and peace is this: Who are "children" and "youth"? This question is important for peace scholars and practitioners for two reasons: first, definitions and frames shape approaches to intervention, and vice versa. Ideas about young people shape policies and programs which, in turn, shape local and global understandings about youth. Significant consensus exists about the desirability of practicing "elicitive" peacebuilding.[1] This means using methods of preventing violence and resolving or transforming conflicts that are culturally appropriate, and that authentically reflect the ideas, needs and wishes of people on the ground in conflict zones. There are additional challenges to "elicitive" peacebuilding when oriented to children and youth. Adult gatekeepers often limit youth involvement and protect their own turf; ideas of "children" and "youth" can be contested, manipulated, and politicized.

A general consensus holds that international interventions will be both unethical and ineffective if they assume superior knowledge on the part of interveners about what peace is and how it can be achieved. But when it comes to drawing on the knowledge, ideas, and motivations of youth, no consensus exists on what genuine participation is and how to measure it. Very little systematic thought has been given to what such a condition as "peace" entails, either. These challenges suggests a second reason for critically exploring how "children" and "youth" are understood in the academic and policy discourses about armed conflict and peacebuilding. A characteristic of peace and conflict studies as a field is that it is normative and prescriptive, as well as descriptive and analytical. Many students of peace, conflict, development, and human rights are not only intellectually interested in issues of youth and violence, but are also motivated by a desire to effect positive change for children and young people. Yet they may have little opportunity for critical reflection on the frames and underlying ideologies of their own potential practice.

The consequences of this absence can be easily seen among some practitioners. Naive idealism; a stubborn, even paternalist, belief in the superiority of certain practitioner ideas; disconnection from youth, rather than solidarity with them; and a lack of realism about the policy process promote vulnerability to disillusionment and cynicism that sometimes turns sour. Youth and aid workers, young teachers, and police officers, for example, are often found to have stereotypical and derogatory views of the young people they work with. There are structural explanations for this dynamic among people working with youth that can be addressed. These practitioners often are overburdened, under-resourced, and feel marginalized from higher-level decision-making processes.

However, this chapter argues that an additional area for focus is how peace work with youth is framed and understood. The frames, ideological images, and discourses of youth that have emerged in the conflict and development field in the last two decades, shape the global policy process. They emerge from historical patterns of the use and abuse of children and childhood for military and political ends. In many ways contemporary frameworks for peace and youth practice, such as rights and development, are reactions against this history, but not invariably or completely so. Knowledge of and competencies in negotiating these different organizing frameworks and discourses may provide a source of power and resilience for professionals and would-be professionals in the field.

THE GLOBAL-LOCAL POLITICS OF YOUTH—CHALLENGES FOR PEDAGOGY AND PRACTICE

Contemporary peace practitioners are exposed to a confusing array of discourses about children and youth that are mostly emotive and/or reductionist. Are we to be concerned about "stolen childhoods" and "lost generations" (youth as victims) or "youth bulges" and the "demographic of insurgency" (youth as threats)? Should we think about "generations stalled in transition" or "youth as agents of change" (youth as deficit or resource)? These images and ideas about youth currently shape the global academic and policy debate. At the local level, within countries in conflict, images of youth in part mirror these discourses and also diverge from them. In different contexts, youth are seen as a revolutionary vanguard, as moral guardians, as amoral thugs, and, in some places, they are seen as a mix of all of these, and more, over time. At the local/national level, children and youth have an emotional meaning and power that is not conveyed by the global frameworks we use of youth as threat, victim, or agent. They may come to symbolize the nation's suffering and existential peril, or its triumph and hope for the future. As symbols "the child," "youth," or "next generation" may justify continued hatred and aggression. They can also come to represent a rationale for concessions, negotiations, and peace.

In all contexts, ideas of who is a "child," "youth," or "adult" reflect tradition, as well as struggles for recognition and rights, change over time and vary across and within cultures. David Rosen argues, "The child-soldier crisis is part of the contested domain of international politics in which childhood serves as a proxy for other political interests."[2] Rosen's claim is also relevant when considering youth and conflict more broadly than the child soldier issue. In fact, both history and more contemporary events suggest that ideas about children and their rights, potentials, and dangers shift in many settings due to economic contingency, violence, and the politics and expediency of local and global elites.

Why is an American fifteen-year-old called a "youth gang member" and not a "child soldier?" What complex, contradictory politics are in play in detaining sixteen-year-olds at Guantanamo Bay prison, but giving them a special wing called Camp Iguana? Why are some categories of vulnerable children higher on the international agenda—such as refugees, AIDs orphans, or child soldiers—than others? Who defines what peacebuilding is, and how are model youth peacebuilders identified and cultivated by the international community? These and many other questions about the politics of children and youth in conflict and peacebuilding have complex, multi-layered answers. We need to look in national and institutional histories, in patterns of discrimination, and in the dynamics and needs of war and warriors, as well as among a host of other political actors and their policies for protecting and developing young people and societies.

A recently developed sub-field in scholarly international relations theorizes the child in global politics.[3] One of the reasons this literature is important is that it highlights continuity in the uses of children and childhood by states and sub-state groups for military and political ends. Drawing on numerous historical examples, Helen Brocklehurst demonstrates how children have been "central to the practices of militarization and nationalization across the world and throughout history."[4] In detailed case studies of youth in Nazi Germany, Mozambique, Northern Ireland, and South Africa, Brocklehurst argues both that "children's bodies have a political function and that children are a political 'body' or group." Children are "used as an emotional sphere against which to normalize and legitimize violence." They are kept separate from adults, but they can be "brought into the political sphere at times of national interest," according to Brocklehurst.[5]

Brocklehurst notes that children are "embodiments or potential vessels of national security or strength and also a conveniently mobile collective body."[6] One example she cites is of the British government's "forced or arranged mass migration" of children from "the slums" to their dominions in the nineteenth and early twentieth centuries. This transfer of children was both an empire- and nation-building strategy and a "safety valve" for social discontent at home.[7] British children were "exported" to Australia and New Zealand by charities as late as 1967, reports Brocklehurst. The "mass baby-lift" of Vietnamese orphans by the U.S. military on their exit from the war in 1975, and who were then to be adopted in the United States, is another example of this treatment of children as a "mobile collective body." "Social cleansing" of street children in Latin America, Turkey, India, Bulgaria, and Kenya, and the war strategies of rape and forced impregnation of women, and of sterilization and castration of men in the Balkans, suggest a long global history of the use and abuse of children, youth, and human reproduction for international and domestic political ends. Perhaps this history is one reason for skepticism among some scholars and practitioners about international actors today "harnessing" youth as a "resource" for peace. Framing matters. As an example, R. Charli Carpenter shows in her work on children born of sexual violence and exploitation in war, that the "framing of atrocity" by transnational networks of human rights organizations has impacted who is seen as vulnerable, innocent, or aggrieved and, therefore, deserving of policy interventions.[8]

Local-level framing also matters. In conflict zones, for example, both adults and children may find scholarly categories and purported ethics distracting: "our children are like adults," stated one young Palestinian translator in response to concerns about a child's understanding of research ethics protocols. This statement does not mean people in war zones do not wish to protect their children or value their rights. It suggests, rather, that local notions of children and their *agency* can change, or evolve differently, under conditions of occupation or armed conflict. War and deprivation can change local and global understandings of "children" and "childhood" in ways that affect peacemaking and pose a challenge for research and practice.

NEGOTIATING FRAMEWORKS

The main international actors involved with youth are identified in Yael Ohana's *The International Youth Sector: Mapping and Directory.*[9] In this very useful resource, Ohana describes four categories of actors: (1) intergovernmental and supranational organizations (e.g., the United Nations system, the World Bank); (2) the governmental and nongovernmental aid community (e.g., USAID, CIDA, International Red Cross, Save the Children); (3) the international nongovernmental youth sector (e.g., American Field Service International, Global Youth Alliance, World Association of Girl Guides); and (4) international foundations that financially support youth projects (e.g., Ashoka, Ford and Kellogg Foundations). Another important resource is Yvonne Kemper's *Youth in War to Peace Transitions.*[10] Kemper identifies three broad approaches to work with youth in conflict zones by international organizations. These are the rights-based, economic, and socio-political approaches. In addition to the actors and approaches documented by Ohana and Kemper, various parts of the global security sector are also increasingly interested in youth.[11]

The next section of this chapter explores four discourses about the objectives and orientation of youth work. These discourses help frame interventions within the rights, development, and security approaches mentioned above. These are as follows: (1) children have rights and should be protected; (2) youth are a development asset; (3) youth are a threat to security; and (4) youth are agents of change. In practice, no single agency or organization truly acts according to one worldview. These discourses cut across the different actor categories outlined by Ohana. The purpose of this analysis is not to thoroughly evaluate how different organizations or agencies integrate these discourses into their policies and practices. Rather, the intention is to show that these discourses are both broadly influential across the international youth sector and that they are contested. The aim is to prompt reflection on their pros and cons. These discourses have many common, but some different, ideological underpinnings and messages. The first and most obvious of these messages is the distinction that is made between children, who are in need of protection, and youth who are not. Youth are primarily considered to require development, containment, or recognition in international policy frameworks. Yet, as already discussed, definitions of child and youth are contested.

CHILDREN IN NEED OF PROTECTION

Many researchers, practitioners and policymakers who focus on young people intentionally draw on the human rights framework provided by the UN Convention of the Rights of Child (1989), which defines a child as anyone under the age of eighteen. In seeking to address children's needs from the very basic to the political, the children's rights agenda sets standards for protection of children from a variety of abuses. UNICEF, for example, as the flagship agency, sees its mission as to "help build a world where the rights of every child are realized. . . . We believe that nurturing and caring for children are the cornerstones of human progress." As a vision and framework for advocacy, this agenda has considerable power. The rights protection approach involves probably the most holistic worldview for addressing children in every aspect of their lives. But under conditions of severe deprivation and war, such a vision of rights may be difficult to enforce, relying as it does upon transparency, as well as moral and political pressures. In practice, children's rights are highly politicized, and the rigid programmatic cut-offs of the child's rights and youth policy frameworks (eighteen for children, twenty-four for youth) may be difficult to justify in the context of armed conflict, displacement and disaster.

Moreover failures of rights protection are usually more noticeable than successes, affecting the credibility of the rights approach, which is seen as "soft" by some (to use the common gendered/biased language). Others not only query the basic assumption that universal norms and definitions can exist, but also question the morality of exporting Western ideas and practices through interventions aimed at children. Appropriating children and childhood as vessels for political messages crafted in elite (Westernized) circles is a form of neo-colonialism in this worldview. This criticism also has relevance for the development assistance and education fields.

Indeed, Ohana's analysis of the international youth sector suggests that there is substantial synergy and reinforcement between values and principles of the rights and development approaches. These consensus values are "the promotion of pluralist democracy, human rights, peace, and social cohesion."[12] Further, Ohana finds that the youth sector is defined by the following common principles:

- shared decision making between governmental and nongovernmental partners;
- based on policies grounded in evidence of the condition of young people;
- empowerment oriented;
- considerate of the interdisciplinary nature of the youth field;
- underwritten by a human rights perspective; and
- guided by the belief that young people are a resource rather than a problem.[13]

The idea of "youth as a resource" is mainstreamed in the field of development, which is discussed next.

YOUTH AS DEVELOPING ASSETS

In the development sphere, working definitions of youth vary across agencies and NGOs. The World Bank, for example, uses a fifteen-to-twenty-four age range as does the United Nations in its Youth Policy, though both recognize the limitations of these definitions.[14] In many NGOs that take on both rights and development roles, the age range of twelve to thirty is more common, reflecting an anthropologically informed consensus about the social-contextual nature of "youth." The international development assistance approach emphasizes early education and health for the youngest children, and, then, identifies employment/livelihoods, entrepreneurship, and empowerment as the key areas of interest for older young people. Youth are seen as a social and economic resource that can be cultivated. An obvious Western bias and corporate influence permeates some of this discourse. For example, a strong contemporary ethos exists of "youth as assets and partners in the development process."[15] Like the rights-based approach, development practice claims to value the participation of young people, as "partners" in program design, implementation, and evaluation. Opinions vary widely on how much genuine participation of youth actually occurs across all of these tasks. A critical issue moving forward is to more clearly understand what meaningful participation in conflict zones entails and how adult territoriality at all levels affects it.

In the development assistance approach, the image of "youth as a resource" has traditionally emphasized the *potential* that youth have to steward the growth and stability of their countries and the roles they *will* have as the next generation. Education systems and interventions also operate according to the belief that youth are our future resources and need to be prepared for (real) life that they will grow into. In being converted to adulthood, children and youth rely on the guidance of their elders. As already discussed, armed conflict, displacement and serious deprivation can destabilize this idealized trajectory for young people's development. Even apart from armed conflict, it is increasingly being recognized in both policy and academic circles that by thinking only in terms of "youth as the future" we will miss the valuable knowledge, experience, and talents that young people have in the present.

Ideologically, the notion of youth as existing in a state of "becoming" suggests that people who are not able to cross the boundaries that mark the transition to adulthood will never be fully human, or at least not fully a part of society. This limitation may be an empirical reality for many young people. A recent trend involves conceptualizing the youth "crisis" or predicament in developing countries as one of being unable to complete certain rites of passage to adulthood because of economic marginalization and conflict.[16] Young people in the Middle East, for example, are characterized as a "generation in waiting,"[17] and in the interviews with young Palestinians reported on later in the chapter, this theme emerges.

However, as discussion of the "youth bulge" thesis below will reinforce, it is important to think critically about all of these frames and claims, however empirically based, because of the ideological messages they reinforce. If youth cannot fulfill their development-prescribed role as resources for the future, they become stuck in theory as well as in practice. Their agency in the present becomes invisible. As well as marginalizing youth further, the "stalled transition" diagnosis may unwittingly reinforce the moral and political separation of children from adults, the infantilization of youth and their exclusion from politics, and this provides no preparation at all for peacebuilding.[18] Thinking about youth as a social, cultural and peace resource in the present, with rights to participation and value for society even though they are stuck in transition, may help. Even then, it could certainly be argued that it is also exploitative to treat youth as a resource to be mined in order to extract knowledge about peace. So, while the "youth as resource" discourse provides a balance to the idea of "youth as threat," it is not without its own flaws and dilemmas.

YOUTH AS A THREAT TO SECURITY

The focus on conflict as an "area of concern for the situation of youth" emerged with strength in UN development discussions between 1996 and 2001, according to the UNDP Youth and Conflict report.[19] Interest was initially due to a growing recognition of the challenges that young people face when returning from armed conflict and attempting to integrate into communities and find jobs or access to education. The UN view was that "young people are disproportionately affected by violent conflict, both as victims and as active participants."[20] However, in the United States, youth have primarily been viewed as potential perpetrators, due to the influence of two intertwining agendas.

According to many U.S.-based youth and conflict experts and policy/practitioners (interviewed in Washington, DC, in 2010), the most influential idea driving an increase in interest in youth in the last decade has been the "youth bulge." The idea has been most closely associated with research by Henrik Urdal for the World Bank. Urdal has summarized his findings as: "When youth make up 35% of the adult population, which they do in many developing countries, the risk of armed conflict is 150 per cent higher than it is in countries with an age structure similar to most developed countries."[21] Illustrating the power of frames, the idea of the "youth bulge," though it was not new and only shows a correlation between youth and violence, not a guarantee of conflict, was frighteningly compelling to many political and security actors in a world where youth made up the majority of the global population.

In fact, the "youth bulge" frame has entailed benefits for development actors and youth NGOs in the form of increased interest in higher policy levels and from funders and therefore resources. But the "youth bulge" combined with the insecurity thesis has also had the negative side-effect of over-emphasizing youth as a threat. In several good critiques of the many flaws in this thesis, academics with strong field experience in Africa and other "youth bulge" locations note that it creates a very distorted picture of reality and demonizes young men as inherently violent.[22] These scholars also critique how young women are presented as a threat because of their "explosive fertility," which is blamed for breeding young terrorists.[23] The *terror lens* since 2001 has greatly shaped international youth policy too and is intricately connected with "youth bulge" concerns. Indeed, Hendrixson argues that "9/11 proved a watershed for popular and policy acceptance of the 'youth bulge' figure of speech."[24]

A third connected lens is that of *gangs and organized violence,* which links the domestic and international political violence with transnational crime, over-crowded mega-cities, and the youth bulge. Recently, comparative international research, such as that by Luke Dowdney and John Hagedorn, seeks to demystify the gang threat, and critically interrogates the image of the aggressive urban male youth, identifying gangs as important social movements.[25] Implicit in this approach is the idea that young gang members are agents of change and that the gangs they create are adaptive social forms in response to failures of states and globalization. This work is important, but also complicates research, policy, and practice, because it collapses the boxes that identify child soldiers over there, and gangsters over here, and diverts the focus from youth as the problem to indicting larger structures of global power.

The "youth as threat" idea has motivated development responses such as attention to economic opportunity and livelihoods and socio-political empowerment programs, as well as more attention at the international level to Disarmament, Demobilization, and Reintegration (DDR). The counter-terrorism response to the youth threat leads to a narrower focus on specific countries in the Middle East/South Asia and Sub-Saharan Africa or subpopulations in developed countries such as young Muslims in Europe. It also justifies militarized containment and surveillance approaches, and re-education/de-radicalization programs aimed at specific groups. These latter approaches are suspect to many rights advocates and development professionals.

Many would criticize the security approach for reducing young people to a threat to be prevented or pacified and worry that it will produce a backlash effect among both those targeted for security interventions and those young people who are being neglected because of the primacy of the security/terror vision. A critical issue for those in the peace research and practice fields is to what extent these powerful policy and discursive trends of the youth bulge and counter-terrorism are shaping their work, and whether peace studies resists, shapes or follows these perspectives? What is common to all of the approaches surveyed, to greater and lesser degrees, is a belief that youth need to be guided, shaped, pacified, or controlled. Yet elicitive peacebuilding proposes the opposite: the guidance and shape of conflict transformation and peacebuilding measures are located within, and should emerge from, the people living through war and adversity. So another critical issue for peace and conflict studies is how to address this contradiction.

YOUTH AS AGENTS OF CHANGE

A youth agency lens starts with youth themselves rather than with rights, development, or violence. It implies that youth have the capability to effect change independent of outside actors. This premise does not preclude working with adult supervision and through organizational structures. And, as Schwartz has shown about post-conflict peacebuilding, outside actors can have considerable impact on young people depending on how well they complete the key "transition functions" of protection, reintegration, and empowerment. A youth agency lens prompts consideration not just of how youth are threats to security, but also of how they are agents of peace. Applying a youth agency lens to the challenge of post-war peacebuilding and youth, McEvoy-Levy and Schwartz both note that a dichotomy between violent youth and peaceful youth is unhelpful, because it masks a complex reality where victim and perpetrator are often blurred.[26] Indeed, the shift from a position and identity that justifies violence to one that not only accepts nonviolence as a preferable stance, but also entails active peace work is an important transition to understand. One task for the peace and conflict studies community is to further document the peace activities of youth to present a stronger evidence-base, particularly of spontaneous youth-led action, that can add persuasive power to the discourse of "youth as agents of peace," perhaps making it as compelling as the "youth bulge" and insecurity connection.

Yet a "youth as agents of peace" discourse can certainly also be criticized, perhaps especially for romanticizing youth. Does this notion simply mirror other idealized forms, like youth as a revolutionary vanguard, only in this case for peace? Critics would argue that viewing youth in this way underestimates the structural challenges and asymmetries of power between youth and class/political elites that make peace action very difficult. At a practical level, attempting to popularize the idea of "youth as agents of peace" in conflict zones could raise youth expectations and lead to retaliation by elders/elites, who are invested in the status quo, or to a backlash by ultimately disappointed youth. Even a "youth as agents of peace" lens can objectify youth and be exploitative. Like other discourses and frames, it has its limitations. Each of the main contemporary discourses of youth in conflict—rights/protection, development, security, and agency—present a piece of the picture. Only young people themselves can complete the puzzle. The next sections of the chapter examine what young people themselves can teach us about definitions and discourses. It also considers the concepts of identity and systems.

YOUNG PEOPLE'S OWN SELF-CONCEPTS, COMPLEX IDENTITIES, AND SYSTEMS

Young people's own self-concepts and identities invariably will be more complicated than either local, national, or global images or dominant trends in policy and academia can capture. For example, a fourteen-year-old who has been a combatant, or who has experienced power and independence as a member of an armed group, resistance movement, or in street life, may not want to be seen as a child, turned back to school, and confined and controlled by adults. But, at the same time, he/she may not have an education or relevant skills for survival in peacetime. Moreover, he/she may be feared by elders, increasing the chances of his/her exclusion from post-war social, economic, and political life. But evidence shows that youth soldiers and others can be integrated into post-war societies, help foster reconciliation, and often desire positive social roles and involvement in peacemaking.[27] The cycle of conflict and violence, and of peace, turns in parallel with shifting meanings and identities of youth that occur in a social context.

As well as young people's own self-concepts and complex identities, peacemakers need to consider what is happening outside the youth frame, specifically the roles of youth within peer, family and community systems. The ecological model[28] is a useful theoretical approach to exploring the contexts, relationships and transactions of youth in conflict zones. Family, peer group, and wider community provide complex systems of interaction and meaning that young people can shape and sometimes control. In conflict zones, young people move between different social spaces—school, refugee camp, leisure and/or religious organizations, the street, and political or armed groups. Their experiences within overlapping and competing groups, and within complex social systems, creates knowledge, shapes their attitudes, and mediates the impact of war and other forms of violence on them. Young people's experiences and transactions within the system also influence the other components of the web, the family, school, and so on, and contribute to the development of systems of meaning as well as concrete facts-on-the-ground.

The importance of youth concepts, identities and systems may be better illustrated by closer attention to a particular case. So the next section of the paper explores the ways in which young Palestinians make meaning out of their experience of being under occupation. In interviews conducted by this author in 2009, Palestinian university students in their late teens and early twenties were asked "what are the main challenges facing youth?" Their responses suggested that "youth" is a contested concept even with a close group of peers. Some chose to answer by describing their own lives and challenges, and those of their college-aged peers. Others interpreted the question as referring to a younger age group, and discussed children throwing stones or being injured by the Israeli Defense Forces. Gender, intergenerational dynamics, and class all shaped their interpretation of who "youth" were and the challenges they faced:

> Q. What are the main challenges facing young people?
>
> A: "The Occupation [. . .] Our life is bad. We have to do so many things to improve it. Many males who do not have houses cannot get married. As a girl who has a Palestinian ID, I cannot live in Jerusalem or Haifa. I am forced to live here. I don't have the choice to live by the sea or in the mountains, unless I leave this land and go to Syria or Jordan. But I will stay here. Many boys graduate and do not have a chance to work. Many are traveling to the Gulf countries or are emigrating to Sweden and other places."

J: "In my village [. . .] soldiers killed five children throwing stones. I haven't thrown stones but I would like to. I wish to. Because it is my village! Why have I not? (Laughs). Because it is not acceptable for women to go on to the street, but I hope." (She says this wistfully with a big smile.)

H: "There is no peace for children or for all Palestinians. May be our leaders talk about peace. Peace as means of agreement. There is no security. Peace would be that you cannot ask anymore to talk about the occupation, that we can live together with soldiers and settlers. Another definition of peace—not the peace our leaders hope for—is a peace of just to live."

These interview excerpts illustrate how "child" and "youth" are contextual, flexible, shifting and overlapping categories. Describing their challenges, young people identify many variables—marriage, travel, lack of choices, work, violence, protest, gender roles, loyalty, and a lack peace—that result from the experience of occupation. They share frustrations about not easily having a social life and not being able to see relatives, and fears about not being able to start a family or find work because of the occupation. One young man sums up this situation: "My biggest fear is that I can't start any relationship." As the idea of a "generation in waiting"[29] suggests, many young Palestinians are stuck because of structures and politics beyond their control.

However, while many young people interviewed did share concerns about how they would transition to full adulthood, this was not the only way they saw themselves. Even more wanted to direct the conversation away from problems of their development and to address the outside world, to accentuate collective endurance despite obstacles, and show their agency in the present:

"Tell them [Americans and Europeans]: that we live here. We have no rights. But we have our life. We can cope with it. Even if we don't live like others, we are still alive. We go to the university, socialize, communicate. This is not a Third World country. We are somewhere in between, I think. We can be better—maybe helped by other people, maybe by ourselves. But the most important thing is that we are staying here, we will not leave our Palestine."

The young woman in this statement expresses resilience and empowerment. Recognizing a loss of rights, she is nevertheless defiant in her belief in change. She insists on her own and other's agency, as young people who study, make friendships, and "communicate"—that is, speak in community—as a form of witness.

In many conflicts, young people conceptualize their involvement in armed activism as a duty to the wider community or nation. They may see themselves as representatives for the community or nation's aspirations, or as guiding a struggle against hopelessness. For example, the few Palestinian youth I interviewed who sanctioned armed activism did so either because they considered normal rites of passage for young people to be impossible, and believed that this unacceptable state needed to be reversed, or because they positioned themselves as defenders of a wider vulnerable "we." Or, as shown in this quotation, they were motivated by both ideas:

> "I hope that in your research you write a note: I know that in the West—Europe and America—there is the idea that we are terrorists. We're not terrorists. We are just resisting. They kill our mothers, sisters, the old people. They have the power. It is a kind of resistance to make a missile. We don't want to hit public places. We want to hit soldiers, but we can't find them easily. If you slap me on one cheek and I don't do anything, you will slap the other. So I must stop you. Palestinians are very well educated, but the occupation prevents us from being free to make what we want."

Most young people did not advocate violence, but most did conceptualize themselves as being in resistance to the occupation, often simply through maintaining the routine of their daily lives. The Palestinian university students interviewed cited the struggles they face to attend college and to be on time for classes and exams as a shared experience, and one that has higher meaning, because to continue to struggle for one's education by crossing Israeli checkpoints is a form of resistance: "It is a struggle against the occupation in a nonviolent way just to go and come back [to school]." Securing access to education in this way is a form of nonviolent collective action, and an example of organic youth agency. Others who were active in community organizations were clear that local activism served a larger national purpose, for example: "If we empower young people to be engaged against drug addiction and violent action, we are making a resistance to the occupation." In fact, a very important role is fulfilled by community based organizations in providing opportunities for youth leadership, service and activism in nonviolent ways. Such organizations, while providing places for recreation and for learning, also shape a terrain of alternative opportunities for young people to have voice and to be engaged in positive social activities with their peers.

In young people's own testimony, each of the global discourses about youth in conflict examined earlier in this chapter, are reflected to some degree. The absence of protection and opportunity are clearly described. There is also insistence on both organic youth agency and agency through organizations as a vital part of community development and national identity and solidarity. The words "rights" and "empowerment" are used, reflecting the global reach of these discourses. One student wishes to throw stones, another justifies violence, but both are directed at concrete targets and have political aims, and are not a generalized expression of frustration at economic marginalization. For most, nonviolence dominates as a mode of action and the aim is "just to live." While there is insufficient evidence to draw policy conclusions from these interviews, they do show that no one framework for understanding or addressing young people in conflict exactly fits. They also show that for young people themselves, childhood, and the condition of youth, carries intense meaning that is shaped by conflict, friendships, family, gender roles, politics, and ideas both local and global.

CONCLUSION

This chapter has tried to address some of the complex theoretical, practical and pedagogical challenges that the issue of peacebuilding with youth presents, but much more research and reflection needs to be done. There is a need for continued critical reflection on the ideological underpinnings, political and cultural influences, and biases of the frames that we already use, sometimes unintentionally. To what extent are these theories, frameworks and approaches drawn from, and reality-tested by, the people they intend to explain and address? Are we missing or ignoring some important frames and failing to develop others? Informed practitioners argue that the peace and conflict studies community needs to help identify and champion a theory of youth and peaceful change that is genuinely elicitive, and that is supported by a strong body of research. Documenting young people's concrete achievements for peace and analyzing them in a theoretically rigorous way is one way in which scholars can contribute to this agenda. This agenda could also entail (re)theorizing both peace and the idea of meaningful participation using the lenses of youth as complex agents and key connectors. In ethically and effectively addressing youth needs and aspirations through policy or programmatic interventions, a key challenge remains in operationalizing awareness of the multiple identities, motivations, spaces, images, and roles of youth in global and local contexts. A youth agency lens is a good start, because it recognizes that young people live, work and act independently of organizations and programs, and in their everyday activities impact people, structures and systems in complex ways. Seeing youth as an organic social force, all the time enmeshed in cultural and conflict reproduction, should facilitate more elicitive peacebuilding. As part of this process, it may be useful for people aspiring to work in youth-related NGOs and aid agencies, as well as scholars researching and writing about children and youth, to reflect on how different distillations of research findings, and frameworks for practice, construct youth as a category for intervention. At the same time, educators, trainers, and policymakers need to be open to learning from the "untrained" and revising their worldviews and approaches in dialogue with students, young activists, and other young people on the ground in conflict zones.

BIBLIOGRAPHY

Boothby, Neil, Alison Strang, and Michael Wessells, eds. *A World Turned Upside Down: Social Ecological Approaches to Children In Armed Conflict.* Bloomfield, CT: Kumarian Press, 2006.

Brainard, Lael, and Derek Chollet. *Too Poor for Peace? Global Poverty, Conflict and Security in the 21st Century.* Washington, DC: The Brookings Institution, 2007.

Brocklehurst, H. *Who's Afraid of Children? Children, Conflict and International Relations.* Aldershot: Ashgate, 2006.

Carpenter, R. Charli. *Forgetting Children Born of War: Setting the Human Rights Agenda in Bosnia and Beyond.* New York: Columbia University Press, 2010.

Darby, John, Tristan Anne Borer, and Siobhan McEvoy-Levy. *Peacebuilding After Peace Accords: The Challenges of Violence, Truth and Youth.* South Bend, IN: Notre Dame University Press, 2006.

Dhillon, Navtej, and Tarik Yousef, eds. *Generation in Waiting: The Unfulfilled Promise of Young People in the Middle East.* Washington, DC: Brookings Institution Press, 2009.

Dowdney, Luke, ed. *Neither War nor Peace: International Comparisons of Children and Youth in Organised Armed Violence.* Rio de Janeiro: 7Letras, 2005.

Hagedorn, John M. *A World of Gangs: Armed Young Men and Gangsta Culture.* Minneapolis: University of Minnesota Press, 2008.

Hendrixson, Anne. "Angry Young Men and Veiled Young Women: Constructing a New Population Threat." *Corner House Briefing* 34, December 2, 2004.

Kemper, Yvonne. *Youth in War to Peace Transitions: Approaches of International Organizations.* Berghof Report 10. Berghof Research Center for Constructive Conflict Management, Berlin, Germany, 2005.

Making Cents International. "Youth Microenterprise and Livelihoods: State of the Field." *Lessons from the 2007 Global Youth Microenterprise Conference*, 2008.

McEvoy-Levy, Siobhan, ed. *Troublemakers or Peacemakers? Youth and Post-Accord Peacebuilding.* South Bend, IN: University of Notre Dame Press, 2006.

Ohana, Yael. *The International Youth Sector: Mapping and Directory: Prepared for the Open Society Institute Youth Initiative.* New York: Open Society Youth Initiative, 2009.

Rosen, David. *Armies of the Young. Child Soldiers in War and Terrorism.* The Rutgers Series in Childhood Studies. New Brunswick, NJ: Rutgers University Press, 2005.

Rupesinghe, K., ed. *Conflict Transformation.* New York: St. Martin's Press, 1995.

Schwartz, Stephanie. *Youth in Post-Conflict Reconstruction: Agents of Change.* Washington, DC: United States Institute of Peace Press, 2010.

UNDP. *Youth and Violent Conflict. Society and Development in Crisis?* New York: United Nations Development Program. Bureau for Crisis Prevention and Recovery, 2006, http://www.undp.org/bcpr.

USAID. *Youth and Conflict: A Toolkit for Intervention. Key Issues Lessons Learned Program Options Monitoring and Evaluation Resources*. Washington, DC: USAID, 2005.

Watson, Alison M.S. "Children and International Relations: A New Site of Knowledge?" *Review of International Studies*, vol. 32, no. 2 (2006): 237–250.

NOTES

1. John Paul Lederach, "Conflict Transformation in Protracted Internal Conflicts: The Case for a Comprehensive Framework," in *Conflict Transformation*, K. Rupesinghe, ed. (New York: St. Martin's Press, 1995), 201–202.

2. David Rosen, *Armies of the Young: Child Soldiers in War and Terrorism*. The Rutgers Series in Childhood Studies (New Brunswick, NJ: Rutgers University Press, 2005), 2.

3. H. Brocklehurst, *Who's Afraid of Children? Children, Conflict and International Relations* (Aldershot: Ashgate, 2006); Alison M.S. Watson, "Children and International Relations: A New Site of Knowledge?" *Review of International Studies*, vol. 32, no. 2 (2006): 237–250.

4. Brocklehurst, *Who's Afraid of Children?*; Watson, "Children and International Relations."

5. Brocklehurst, *Who's Afraid of Children?*, 171–172.

6. Brocklehurst, *Who's Afraid of Children?*, 27.

7. Brocklehurst, *Who's Afraid of Children?*, 26.

8. R. Charli Carpenter, *Forgetting Children Born of War: Setting the Human Rights Agenda in Bosnia and Beyond* (New York: Columbia University Press, 2010).

9. Yael Ohana, *The International Youth Sector: Mapping and Directory. Prepared for the Open Society Institute Youth Initiative* (New York: Open Society Youth Initiative, 2009).

10. Yvonne Kemper, *Youth in War to Peace Transitions: Approaches of International Organizations*, Berghof Report 10. Berghof Research Center for Constructive Conflict Management, Berlin, Germany, 2005.

11. John Darby, Tristan Anne Borer, and Siobhan McEvoy-Levy, *Peacebuilding After Peace Accords: The Challenges of Violence, Truth and Youth* (South Bend, IN: Notre Dame University Press, 2006).

12. Ohana, *The International Youth Sector.*

13. Ohana, *The International Youth Sector.*

14. Ohana, *The International Youth Sector.*

15. Making Cents International, "Youth Microenterprise and Livelihoods: State of the Field," *Lessons from the 2007 Global Youth Microenterprise Conference*, 2008, 11.

16. Marc Sommers, "In the Shadows of Genocide. Rwanda's Youth Challenge," in *Troublemakers or Peacemakers? Youth and Post-Accord Peacebuilding*, Siobhan McEvoy, ed. (South Bend, IN: University of Notre Dame Press, 2007), 81–98.

17. Navtej Dhillon and Tarik Yousef, eds. *Generation in Waiting: The Unfulfilled Promise of Young People in the Middle East* (Washington, DC: Brookings Institution Press, 2009).

18. Siobhan McEvoy-Levy, ed., *Troublemakers or Peacemakers? Youth and Post-Accord Peacebuilding* (South Bend, IN: University of Notre Dame Press, 2006).

19. UNDP, Youth and Conflict Report: "Youth and Violent Conflict: Society and Development in Crisis?" New York: United Nations Development Program, Bureau for Crisis Prevention and Recovery, 2006, 36, http://www.undp.org/bcpr.

20. UNDP, "Youth and Violent Conflict."

21. Henrik Urdal, "The Demographics of Political Violence: Youth Bulges, Insecurity and Conflict," in *Too Poor for Peace? Global Poverty, Conflict and Security in the 21st Century,* Lael Brainard and Derek Chollet, eds. (Washington, DC: The Brookings Institution, 2007), 90–100.

22. Sommers, "In the Shadows of Genocide."

23. Sommers, "In the Shadows of Genocide"; Anne Hendrixson, "Angry Young Men and Veiled Young Women: Constructing a New Population Threat," *Corner House Briefing* 34, December 2, 2004, 2.

24. Hendrixson, "Angry Young Men," 2.

25. Luke Dowdney, ed., *Neither War nor Peace: International Comparisons of Children and Youth in Organised Armed Violence* (Rio de Janeiro: 7 Letras, 2005); John Hagedorn, *A World of Gangs: Armed Young Men and Gangsta Culture* (Minneapolis: University of Minnesota Press, 2008).

26. McEvoy-Levy, *Troublemakers or Peacemakers?*; and Stephanie Schwartz, *Youth in Post-Conflict Reconstruction: Agents of Change* (Washington, DC: United States Institute of Peace Press, 2010).

27. For example, McEvoy-Levy, *Troublemakers or Peacemakers?*; Schwartz, *Youth in Post-Conflict Reconstruction.*

28. Neil Boothby, Alison Strang, and Michael Wessells, eds. *A World Turned Upside Down: Social Ecological Approaches to Children In Armed Conflict* (Bloomfield CT: Kumarian Press, 2006).

29. Dhillon and Yousef, *Generation in Waiting.*

Chapter 10

Developing Refugee Peacebuilding Capacity

Women in Exile on the Thai/Burmese Border

Anna Snyder

This chapter is a gendered analysis of peacebuilding capacity in the context of forced migration. Scholars have tended to focus primarily on potential threats from conflict-generated diasporas[1] rather than how they contribute to peace processes in their homelands. Understanding how the millions of refugees affected by armed conflicts may, as non-state actors, help to facilitate peace-making and peacebuilding not only addresses some of the needs of refugees, but also develops the new conflict resolution theory and practices necessary to address contemporary ethno-political conflict.

Despite the portrayal of migrants as security risks for Western countries and the attention given to minority militants from countries like Ireland, Iraq, and Sri Lanka, some research challenges views of migrants as warmongers. Smith and Stares[2] claim diasporas can be both peace-makers and peace-wreckers, sometimes even at "one and the same time." Diaspora groups are diverse, "stratified by class, caste, education, occupation, religious affiliation, cultural interests, urban or rural background."[3] As such, members of diasporas engaging in extremist activities are often a minority; they are not representative. Further, diasporas may develop multiple identities in host countries, changing mono-dimensional identities.[4] Diaspora responses are not static; as conflict changes, diaspora responses change.

Some of the specific ways that diasporas contribute to peace include: (1) civic-oriented activities, such as community development activities and business investments; (2) direct political involvement in the country of origin; and (3) advocacy and lobbying activities.[5] For example, members of the Irish diaspora convinced the IRA to adopt more peaceful measures acting as mediators between the IRA and Clinton administration in securing the Good Friday Agreement in 1998.[6]

Understanding the impact of diasporas on any given conflict situation, requires studying the capacities of the diaspora, as well as the broader political opportunity structures within the country of origin and the host country that might influence mobilization and engagement of diaspora groups.[7] However, very few such studies exist. This research is an attempt to fill that gap. My study examined capacity building efforts of indigenous women's refugee organizations and the implications of their work for peacebuilding.

Lederach defines capacity building as "the process of reinforcing the inherent capabilities and understandings of people related to the challenge of conflict in their context and to a philosophy oriented towards the generation of new, proactive, empowered action for desired change in those settings."[8] He maintains that at the heart of capacity building is empowerment. A fundamental challenge of peacebuilding is changing the individuals' and the communities' beliefs that they are not capable to the sense that they do have the power to effect change.

The focus of this study is women's empowerment in refugee and migrant worker camps. The empowerment is ambivalent.[9] On the one hand, as forced migrants, strategic life choices clearly narrow rather than expand. There is little doubt that women often bear a double burden, taking on unaccustomed roles such as head of household and principal income generator, because they have lost male family members and experienced displacement arising from conflict. On the other hand, alternatives which may not have been available in the homeland, arise in the new context. New spaces may open up for women's agency and leadership within changing family and community structures. Some examples do exist of women's refugee organizations leading peacemaking and/or post-agreement peacebuilding, due in part to empowering experiences in refugee camps, for example, El Salvador and Cambodia.[10]

This qualitative study of refugee women from Burma in camps on the Thai/Burmese border reinforces data on the enormous difficulties refugee women encounter documented by researchers in forced migration studies and by international NGOs working in the border areas. However, the research challenges the infantilization of refugee women by revealing the transformative influence of a grassroots network of women's NGOs on the lives of the refugees. This study shows how the social resources—the healthcare, leadership skills, and gender training—made available by women's NGOs in Thailand helped to create discursive alternatives that the interviewees maintained resulted in growing self-esteem and changes in how the sexual division of labor is conceptualized. The sense of empowerment some women discussed in the interviews conducted may indicate an increased capacity for peacebuilding among some refugee communities on the Thai/Burmese border. The research reinforces the importance of implementing policy and practice that develops women's agency and peacebuilding capacity during conflict. Promoting social emancipation, empowerment, political participation, and good governance helps to build civil society peace constituencies from the bottom up.

BACKGROUND ON MYANMAR/BURMA

The Conflicts

Since its independence from Britain in 1947, Burma has experienced civil war. In the decade after independence, Burma's fledgling democratic government was challenged by communist and ethnic groups that maintained they were under-represented in the 1948 constitution; the autonomy promised to minority states was never granted. General Ne Win took control first in 1958 and then staged a coup against Prime Minister U Nu in 1960, solidifying his position as Burma's military leader by instituting authoritarian military rule and in 1974 suspending the constitution. The main focus of the government was the military defeat of communist and ethnic-minority guerrilla groups.

In 1988 Ne Win announced he would step down and thousands of demonstrators took to the streets in the hope of escaping military rule, economic decline and routine human rights abuses. On August 8, 1988, the troops began a four-day massacre, killing at least ten thousand demonstrators across the country. In Rangoon, Aung San Suu Kyi, the daughter of the independence hero General Aung San, made public her support for the struggle for democracy. Ne Win ordered a staged coup from behind the scenes and handed power to the nineteen-member State Law and Order Restoration Council (SLORC), which in turn ordered a crackdown on the protestors.

In 1989, Aung San Suu Kyi, although committed to nonviolence, was placed under house arrest and not allowed to leave the country to receive the Nobel Peace Prize awarded to her in 1991. She remains under house arrest. Multi-party elections were held in 1990; however, when Suu Kyi's National League for Democracy party (NLD) won, SLORC refused to acknowledge the election results and have continued to rule as a military regime for the last eighteen years. Although SLORC was replaced by the State Peace and Development Council (SPDC) in 1997, government control remained with the military. Negotiations concerning a new constitution that began in the early 1990s culminated in a referendum held in the aftermath of the devastation of Cyclone Nargis in 2008; criticism of the consultation process was widespread and the new constitution clearly reinforces military dominance.

Many Burmese refugees have fled the on-going civil conflict, which is multifaceted, involving ethnic minorities, political ideology and participation, and access to resources such as oil, timber, and land. Some of the refugees fled to Thailand to live in camps on the Thai/Burmese border and have lived there for decades. Others are more recent refugees, fleeing the military campaigns and economic policies that make survival questionable in contemporary Myanmar. Thailand has not signed the 1951 Convention on the Status of Refugees or the 1967 Protocol, meaning the refugees are often dependent on maintaining the favor of local authorities and communities, as well as the government, to ensure their stay. Although the military government, the SPDC, has negotiated settlements with any number of ethnic factions, it is still involved in armed struggle with seven ethnic groups including the ethnic minorities highlighted in this study.

Women's NGOs on the Thai/Burmese Border

In the 1990s on the Thai/Burmese border, women from Burma developed a grassroots network of women's NGOs that grew out of their experiences of gendered conflict. This network of NGOs influenced the lives of most of the participants in our study. Mary O'Kane has documented how women's experiences as refugees, migrant workers, and student activists made them more aware of gender relations.[11] In the refugee camps, women leaders noticed the male control of political and military decision-making and weaponry, women's experience of rape and sex abuse, increased domestic violence, and growing maternal and infant mortality. Female activists who had helped to organize the 1988 uprising were told they could become medics or teachers. Migrant women were called to hospitals and police stations over and over again to assist women in sexually, physically, and psychologically abusive situations. Their heightened awareness led in turn to the formation of women's associations that required conflict resolution and alliance building across ethnic boundaries as well as agreement on political processes.

Eventually, in 2000, the women's activities led to the formation of the Women's League of Burma. The women activists connected with global women's movements, networking on issues like the trafficking of women. Although the international connection meant renewed opposition from male political leaders, participating in global networks presented many opportunities including the experience of attending UN international and regional conferences, increased funding, educational opportunities and new strategies from networking with women in other conflict areas. Currently, the Women's League of Burma (WLB) offers training and services in refugee and migrant worker camps and with international support conducts research on gendered violence in the Burmese context.

Methodology

This research project explored whether women experience any of their new roles and circumstances in armed conflict as empowering and how their experiences impact their involvement in and/or perception of peacebuilding. My research assistant, Dr. Brian Rice, and I conducted 35 interviews of refugee women and several men, with the assistance of interpreters in March, April and May of 2007 near Chiang Mai, Thailand in three refugee camps on the Thai/Burmese border. The refugee women are members of ethnic groups that have been forced from their lands by the civil wars in Myanmar/Burma. They were all connected in some way to the grassroots NGO, Empowering Women of Burma, which arranged for our visits to the camps. Some of the interviews were carried out in the context of focus groups.

The methodology used for the interviews was oral testimony (OT). OT is an appropriate research method for interviewing men and women in conflict, given the sensitive nature of their experiences and the possible consequences of disclosure. Research on gender and conflict using conventional social science methodology misses aspects of male and female experiences in conflict, such as the role of affect and its relationship with economic and political domains.[12] This testimonial approach gives narrators the opportunity to address sensitive political and social topics that are difficult to address through other methods. Further, research on indigenous research methodology tends to reinforce the cultural appropriateness of unstructured interviews with indigenous peoples, especially elders.[13] The interviews were supplemented by three small focus groups.

The 35 men and women interviewed left Burma for varied reasons and were living in varied contexts emphasizing the variation in the experience of refugees. All of the interviewees were members of ethnic minority groups involved in violent conflict with the Burmese military. Some had experienced direct violence from bombing, burned villages, landmines, torture and rape. Others were unable to survive when their villages were relocated to areas controlled by the Burmese military, or because of the military's demand for taxes, rice, or farm animals. Several people left because of forced labor or fears of forced labor and rape. A few talked about dreams of a better life in Thailand in the refugee camps.

The interviews were conducted in five contexts: (1) a new small Shan migrant refuge on land donated by a Buddhist temple just outside a small village, Ban Luang; (2) a large, long-established Karen camp in an isolated, mountainous region in the vicinity of Mae Sariang; (3) Karenni NGOs outside of but closely connected to a series of Karenni camps near Mae Hong Son; (4) a Kayan village useful to the Thai tourist business in Mae Hong Son; and (5) a training center for refugee camp nursery school teachers in Chiang Mai. Most of the women had lived for several years in various camps; a few had grown up in the camps never having seen Burma. The majority of the women left subsistence farming in remote mountain villages to become refugees or migrant workers in Thailand.

Defining Empowerment

Malhotra, Schuler, and Boender's study of women's empowerment as a variable in international development shows that although there are many different terms related to the concept of empowerment—such as gender equity and gender equality—there are common themes throughout the literature such as control, agency, and self-efficacy.[14] Most definitions of empowerment focus on women's ability to make decisions and achieve outcomes that are important to themselves and their families. Gita Sen defines empowerment as "altering relations of power . . . which constrain women's options and autonomy and adversely affect health and well-being."[15]

Empowerment is thought to be a process that encompasses progression from one state (gender inequality) to another state (gender equality). This process, however, is a bottom-up rather than top-down progression; in other words, women must be significant actors in the process, not simply recipients of improved outcomes. Further, a fundamental shift in perceptions—that is, an "inner transformation"—is considered essential to the formulation of choices and to the empowerment process.[16] In addition to inner transformation, feminist scholars point to the institutionalized aspects of gender inequality and call for the adoption of mechanisms and training to ensure "mainstreaming" of gender issues in order to transform structural inequity in society. As such, processes of empowerment require change at different levels: the level of the individual, the level of the family and household, and the structural level—that is, the level of the economy and state.

The existence of alternatives is crucial to women's capacity for meaningful decisionmaking, as is access to resources—economic, social, and physical. Wieringa maintains that if women become aware of their own oppression, without viable alternatives or choices available, they turn their anger inward or develop an acceptance, perhaps religious acceptance—of suffering.[17] Resources that enhance the ability to make choices include material resources, for example, economic and physical, as well as social resources such as healthcare, or various forms of training. However, Kabeer emphasizes that resources measure potential not actualized choice.[18]

Alternatives at the discursive level help people to at least imagine possibilities and are thus important for the development of a critical view of the social order that may potentially transform perspectives.[19] Choices, particularly those that appear to show compliance with norms and practices that deny women choice—for example, son preference and/or daughter discrimination, acquiescence to domestic violence, childbirth despite maternal health problems, and promotion of female circumcision—may be inscribed in taken-for-granted tradition and culture, what Bourdieu calls *doxa*. *Doxa* refers to those traditions and beliefs that are "undiscussed, unnamed, admitted without argument or scrutiny"; they are beyond discourse or documentation.[20] The journey from *doxa* to discourse becomes possible when competing ways of being and doing emerge as material and cultural possibilities to challenge the commonsense propositions and naturalized character of culture. Some choices may result in improved functioning, but do not challenge or destabilize social inequities.

Empowerment is often socially embedded; agency and choice may be inextricably linked to values which reflect the wider context. Women tend to make choices based on community values, because on the one hand women tend to gain respect within their communities when they conform to community, and, on the other hand, they are penalized if they do not conform. Access to new resources may open up new possibilities for women, but how women view these opportunities will be shaped by the intersection of social relations and individual histories. As such research on empowerment must be sensitive to the aspects of culture that women value and seek to reproduce in processes of change and those they reject or seek to modify.[21]

This study shows the social resources—healthcare, leadership skills, and gender training—made available by indigenous women's NGOs in the camps helped to create discursive alternatives that the interviewees maintained resulted in growing self-esteem and changes in their perceptions of gender relations and the sexual division of labor. Mainstreaming of individuals and the women's NGOs in camp governance structures also contributed to a new discourse of equality. At the same time, some of the women indicated they were resisting the loss of valued traditional cultural practices that became increasingly important to them as exiles and that, in some cases, increased their value as women in the eyes of their own ethnic communities as well as their Thai hosts. The indigenous women's NGOs supported this cultural resistance offering training in traditional sewing, weaving, and ceremonial practices.

Ambivalent Empowerment: Restrictions on Life Choices

The ambivalency of women's empowerment during armed conflict was reinforced. Although many of the women experienced some new opportunities, they also described an overwhelming number of intersecting concerns and restrictions as well as exploitation and oppression. They chose not to mention the most well-documented difficulties: (1) lack of healthcare and family planning resulting in high maternal morbidity from childbirth and attempted abortions; (2) rape from both the Burmese military, who use rape as a weapon, and Thai military, police, and employers, who commit rape with impunity; (3) as well as the high volume of sex trafficking of girls and women.[22] However, a few of the Karen women informed us that they had little recourse when Thai soldiers seduced their daughters and got them pregnant.

The Shan subsistence farmers who had recently been forced to leave Burma expressed deep frustration with their loss of land which meant a loss of independence. They did not like being dependent on money and forced to work for someone else for very poor wages. Many of the women interviewed in all settings mentioned they had little freedom of movement, describing the camps as prisons or cages. When they did go out of the camps, they had to hide for fear of arrest or deportation. Lack of language facility was another major obstacle; several of the Shan women described themselves as "deaf and dumb," because they did not speak Thai or English. Income generation is a major problem, particularly for female headed households, as is loss of family and social networks. Some of the interviewees talked about being tired and overworked and struggling with new kinds of worries generated by raising children in a world based on a money economy, access to modern technology, and foreign lifestyles.

A few of the female leaders maintained that even though women had new opportunities for leadership, they did not receive respect from male leaders. In the Shan camp, the elected women leaders sat at the back of the room, just like they did in the Buddhist temples. The same women expressed frustration that women were thrust into leadership positions without training or support.

Change and Empowerment

In some of the refugee and migrant camps in Thailand, some women from Burma are experiencing limited positive transformation at the same time that they experience hardship. To some extent, the women found opportunity from changes in their way of life, from dislocation; life-threatening security issues were eliminated and in refugee camps, limited food and healthcare services were provided. However, the interviewees maintained their experiences of empowerment did not come automatically from dislocation. The strongest positive impact on the lives of interviewees came from the training and leadership opportunities created by the grassroots network of women's organizations described above. Further, the interaction of the Thai context, new community structures in the Thai refugee and migrant camps, and women's NGOs has resulted in a new approach to domestic violence. As forced relocation to Thailand has threatened their traditional life and identity, their role as cultural leaders and educators has increased their own sense of importance.

INFORMAL EDUCATION AND TRAINING

In each camp that we visited on the Thai/Burmese border, the network of women's NGOs offers various types of training to women, men, and youth including human rights, women's rights, child development, healthcare, leadership, and conflict resolution. Almost all of the women interviewed thought that the training they had received from the grassroots women's NGOs provided them with new opportunities they did not receive in Burma.

The training increased their pride and self-confidence; they are "more brave," in the words of one interviewee.[23] It gave them a sense of hope, a perception that life for them as women is improving. Because many of the women are illiterate or have little education, the training represents further education and an increase in experience to them. According to an interviewee, they are learning more than had they stayed at home in Burma. With this greater experience and training, they received more respect from the wider community and as a result, a greater voice; that is, they expressed themselves more often and in public (not all of the women agreed that everything was improving for women; those who had the least contact with the NGOs were the least likely to talk about improvement).

Many of the women thought that the training had changed female and male perceptions of gender roles. A number of the interviewees maintained that women were seen as weak before coming to the camps and receiving training. Now "women work as much as men." Women ran in the camp committee elections. They also received vocational training in knitting, sewing, and haircutting so the women can generate income. Moreover, some women (although not all) thought that men's perception of male roles had changed as well so that now men were willing to cook, a role they would not have taken on without the influence of the camp training.

A Karenni nursery school administrator maintained,

> "In the past, women were looked down on because except the housework, men thought that woman couldn't do anything. Women were discriminated and more women were oppressed by men in the past. When women get more education, men have more sympathy to women. Women have more equality than the past. When women looked after their children, men cook for their family. Before that I had to work very hard and my husband didn't help me with the housework. He didn't understand me. But now when I am washing, he cooks. Wherever I go, he allows me and he understands me now."[24]

She felt strongly that her training and experience gained in the camps influenced the respect she received from her family and from community members and, as such, she had much more confidence and was comfortable speaking. In addition, she noticed that people listened to her more.

Moreover, the women's NGOs introduced a "new rule," a new way of thinking about gender relations. In the trainings, several women explained, men are taught women are equal (both men and women receive training in human rights and women's rights). As a result, they said, women can leave the home and stay out late to attend meetings or trainings. A member of the Karenni National Women's Organization said in an interview that after conducting a training on human rights and women's rights, women leaders came and talked to them, saying, "We did not know we had rights like this before, because in our traditional culture women had to stay at home."[25] Before the new rule was introduced, she added, women were afraid of men if they did not fulfill their household duties. Generally, some of the women observed that the community as a whole gave more of a chance to women to take on new roles given the framework of equality.

This new rule of equality does result in conflict in families; however, a number of the interviewees described situations where the NGO staff had intervened, helping to explain the new rule to husbands who disagreed and to wives who did not understand and thus "misused" the rights-based discourse. Further, the women's NGOs offered conflict resolution training in addition to human rights training. Few interviewees touched on the effectiveness of the conflict resolution training.

FORMAL EDUCATION

Obtaining a formal education in the camps represents an opportunity that many of the women and men did not have in Burma. Most of the women I interviewed reported that their families were too poor to send them to school for very long. For most of the women, hope for the future was embodied in the educational opportunities for their children. Their own formal education did not appear to be a viable option; generally there were no adult education classes offered in the camps and a number of women mentioned they had too many worries and responsibilities to focus on learning.

However, some of the young women/girls who came to the camps and were able to finish high school in camp, talked about the camps as a place where they could dream about a future for themselves. I met a number of young adults who came to the camps specifically to study. Through formal education, training from and work with women's NGOs, they managed to develop careers unavailable to them in Burma.

A Mon nursery school teacher who had come to the camps as a young woman to be a teacher said,

> "I can study freely here and I can dream what I want to be. I can improve my skill and knowledge because I can go to school and attend the trainings. In Burma, there is nothing to do just eat and sleep. I couldn't go to school. My parents couldn't afford me to go to school. You cannot finish high school if you don't have money even you are very clever in school. Some people who are rich they give money to their teacher and they can pass the exam easily. I am not look down on people who graduate in the university but they just have their degree, they don't have general knowledge and they don't know what happen in the world. Here I learn that about the world situation and we can get real information. If you go and ask young people in Burma, they will not know what happen in other countries and who the new and old prime minister of Thailand is. It was very different."[26]

In the camps, education had become a priority of the community; one woman maintained there was now 100% community support for the education of children.[27] Training and education was seen as important for the next generation. One interviewee noted that the community was becoming more open-minded in Thailand. She said "men say that now women have more rights to education and it is good for them."[28] Those women who came to the camps already educated were believed to have an easier time, finding work as teachers and nurses with NGOs.

NEW COMMUNITY STRUCTURES

In Thailand, forced migration to refugee and migrant worker camps resulted in different community structures which opened up new opportunities for women to participate in community life. A few interviewees assured me that the camps were run differently than their villages; for example, they were living together with people from different villages in the camps, that is, strangers. The camps were led and organized through camp committees which included formal structures, sections, sub-committees, elected leaders, conflict resolution mechanisms, healthcare, schools, and so forth. The value systems of the international NGOs running the camps[29] influenced the structure of the camps; a number of the women interviewed mentioned that the NGOs required a quota of women be elected to the camp committee, providing a few women with leadership roles. A female Karen camp committee member maintained, "Men are cooperating with women and giving women a chance to work and advice on how to work. This means equality. The advantage of women's leadership is that women understand women more."[30] In addition, the networks of women's NGOs played an active and important role in the camp structures, which in turn presented some opportunities for women in terms of employment, community participation, and training. Moreover, the camp structures included women's sections, validating the need for attention to gender-specific issues.

NEW APPROACH TO DOMESTIC VIOLENCE

Almost all of the women I interviewed identified domestic violence as the primary conflict they struggle with as women. At the same time, most interviewees pointed to ways that approaches to domestic violence had changed since migration to Thailand. A female elected leader of the Karen camp committee attributed the change to the response to training on domestic violence and human rights. Many interviewees believed that the changes concerning domestic violence had resulted in a reduction in the incidence of domestic violence (we were unaware of camp-specific data that would confirm or refute their perceptions).

The interviews revealed three ways that living in the camps and the migrant refuge had changed how communities and families respond to domestic violence. First, the conception of domestic violence transformed from a private family issue to a social problem.[31] Domestic violence is now seen as a threat to the community as a whole, because of the potential involvement of the Thai police/military. Involvement of the Thai authorities in community affairs threatens their already vulnerable status as refugees or illegal aliens. As such, according to a Shan migrant worker, camp committee pressures couples to get along, to "love and unite."[32]

Second, the camps set up specific procedures and structures to respond to domestic violence altering how domestic violence would typically be dealt with in their villages at home. The procedures differed somewhat depending on the camp but all of the systems involved women at the forefront. Most often members/staff of the women NGOs responded first to a call for help; if the first level of response was unsuccessful, then different levels of the camp hierarchy intervened, depending on the size and structure of the camp. A couple of the larger camps set up a safe house where the abused spouse could stay until everyone had calmed down and the people involved could discuss what had happened. The interviewees consistently attributed domestic violence to alcohol consumption and thought the conflict could be resolved for the most part through negotiation. Most of the women I interviewed were generally aware of how the process worked.

Third, women are now encouraged to speak up about violence in the home. The director of the Karenni National Women's Organization maintained, "Women suffer from domestic violence. Before that [in Burma], they didn't speak out because they were shy and afraid of their husbands but now they share with their friends how they suffer."[33]

One morning, I observed a woman in a central meeting place in the Shan refugee camp speaking loudly to several people standing around. My interpreter informed me she said her husband had beaten her, confirming that women are speaking more openly about domestic violence.

GENDER AND CULTURE: MAKING CHOICES

In many conflict situations when a group is under attack, the importance of social identity helps to form and transform.[34] Often it is the women who pass on cultural practices and maintain social identity. Many of the refugees I spoke to emphasized the importance of maintaining their culture and identity and expressed concern that it was changing in Thailand. The longer they had lived in Thailand, the more concern they expressed. Some thought that their children were influenced by Thai culture and practices, meaning that potentially their children would see themselves as Thai. Several stated they would never see themselves as Thai—especially when they had no Thai ID cards; in other words, they did not belong. Many thought teaching children about their ethnic culture in the school curriculum was important, as was training in weaving, music, and sewing.

Moreover, they felt their leadership in traditional ceremonies and cultural practices was key. A few women interviewed described how the women cooked for cultural events and led key aspects of spiritual ceremonies. Those who could weave expressed great pride in their weaving as a symbol of the beauty of their culture. Exposure to foreign visitors who praised their weaving reinforced their pride. Some of the women learned how to weave in the camps with the assistance of the NGOs and were provided with looms and cotton to practice their craft when resources were available.

A Kayan woman, in the context of a focus group, stated,

> "Yeah, we live in Thailand but we still use our tradition; we keep our tradition, like the long-neck. My mother wore rings around her neck, my sisters wear rings and my daughters also wear the rings to keep the culture. My mother said, 'you have to ask your daughter to wear the rings, if not then our culture will be lost.'"[35]

She felt strongly that as a Kayan woman, her choices would impact the survival of the community's identity and culture.

Most of the women felt that changes to women's traditional behavior were negative. They mentioned clothing specifically; some women no longer wore the traditional woven longyi or skirt, choosing instead "immodest" Thai clothing. Many discussed traditional marriage practices; some thought girls were getting married younger, others thought older. Most thought there was more freedom of choice (traditionally, the parents would arrange the marriage, although most often in consultation with the children) in marriage partners, but at the same time a few interviewees observed more divorce, adultery, and polygamy. Most thought girls in Burma respect their parents and traditions more than the girls in the camps.

Sentiments expressed about changes in culture resulting from their life as refugees in Thailand were mixed and complex. Some connected their new equality with changes in traditional culture, but most did not. As a young Kayan man stated in a focus group, "Women are changing. In Burma, women respect their parents and neighbors, they maintain their culture. Here women think about education. They are more confident; they see each other more often and want to talk. Foreigners talk about education and human rights. They have opportunities. There is a difference between women with confidence and experience and those without. They improve their lives. [But] the women who are afraid and scared are respectful. In one way it is good but one way it is bad for them. [laughing] I don't know what to say."[36]

The young man observed changes but noted his own preference for women who are "respectful" to men. The same Kayan woman who talked about the importance of maintaining culture responded to him, "I am happy men and women are now equal."

Analysis: Discursive Alternatives

The women in my study indicated their perceptions of themselves, gender relations, and gender roles had changed since coming from Burma as a result of the services (social resources) provided by the indigenous women's organizations. They were introduced to new ideas and opportunities that changed their perceptions of what was possible and brought about new confidence. Some of the alternatives visible to the women challenged traditional norms and values.

At the individual level, many of the women talked about an increase in confidence. Fundamental changes in perception are indicators of an inner transformation.[37] According to Amartya Sen, women's own perception of their value is as critical to increased empowerment as is their perceived value by others.[38]

At the family or household level, informal educational opportunities appeared to increase status and provide new discursive alternatives. The women maintained that the new social resources had an impact similar to that of formal education; that is, the trainings increased their status in the eyes of their husbands. Several of the women indicated that increases in educational levels were key to perceptions of equality in marriage. Their increased status and informal power assisted them in their negotiations with their husbands when it came to further attendance at trainings and camp meetings.

Furthermore, the trainings initiated the use of human rights/women's rights discourse (the "new rule" of equality), altering perceptions of gender relations and gender roles. The existence of gender equity is disputed in the Burmese context. Both Khiang and Spiro use early colonial texts to reinforce their conclusions that Burmese women experience relative equality with men.[39] The military government also claims that women in Burma are equal to men in contrast to contemporary analysis that indicates the authoritarian, conservative, military regime undermines women's status and independence.[40] However, Belak, author of the most recent comprehensive study of women originally from Burma, argues that most of the claims of gender equality are made by women with elite social status and maintains that if there were advantages that Burmese women experienced in the Victorian era, they no longer exist inside contemporary Burma or for women in exile.[41]

Nevertheless, the interviewees maintained that the new discourse changed their expectations of what was possible and/or desirable; now it was within the realm of possibility that their husbands take over typical female household chores and support their increased mobility in order to attend informal educational events available to them in the camps. The roles of women as wives and mothers across different ethnic cultures are clearly defined in Burma; women are expected to be responsible for child-rearing and most of the household work regardless of whether or not they are the primary or sole breadwinner.[42] The connection between leadership and mobility is critical in Myanmar/Burma. Nobel Peace Prize winner Daw Aung San Suu Kyi is said to have herself questioned the feasibility of women's leadership in the NLD, given the impact of mobility on the reputation of young women.[43]

Many of the women discussed their dreams of formal education for their children. Almost all of the women indicated that their families had been too poor to send them to school for long. Surveys of refugee camps indicate that less than 50% of Mon women between the ages of 20 and 30 were literate and that 50 to 60% of Karenni women of all ages were literate. Further, the survey showed rates of literacy generally decreased with age, indicating that more young women had gained access to education.[44] In Burma, teaching ethnic languages is discouraged and learning to read and write Burmese means studying a second or third language. Moreover, women's literacy in their mother tongues has not been considered important in farming communities and culturally, women are seen to belong in the home, meaning a girl's education is seen as a waste of resources.[45]

In contrast, in the Thai refugee camps, however, the interviewees stated that education for their daughters is a viable alternative; Kishor maintains that when women can dream of an education for their children, when it becomes a viable alternative, it is a direct indicator of empowerment.[46] The women believed that their communities now validated the importance of education for both boys and girls indicating, in their minds, a shift in value preferences.

The efforts of NGOs to mainstream women into governance structures at the community or camp level were perceived to be ineffective. Our informants did not believe the quota of women leaders required by outside NGOs had a concrete impact on their lives. But at the same time, they did not question that women could or should take on leadership roles in the governance structure. Whether or not visible female community leaders created a discursive alternative is debatable; did the quota transform perceptions or was that perception already an integral part of their cultural values and practices? Key studies of women from Burma indicate that women did have political power in pre-colonial Burma, although it often took an indirect form as influence on their husbands.[47] More contemporary data indicates that women from Burma experience discrimination in all aspects of political life.[48] Nevertheless, the women observed female leadership in the camp governance structure and although they questioned their viability, they did not question that women belong in key governance roles. Overall, they were very pleased with the additional opportunities to meet with and provide support to other women; opportunities facilitated by new community structures.

However, informants did feel newly empowered by the change in community level procedures that put the women's NGOs at the forefront of family conflict resolution and by new attitudes toward domestic violence. The women attributed the new attitudes and procedures in part to their precarious/ambiguous political status in Thailand. However, they attributed the decrease in incidence to the human rights and conflict resolution training for men and women offered by the women's NGOs. During armed conflict, domestic violence tends to rise.[49] Furthermore, England and Farkas's study indicates that women's empowerment may increase the level of family conflict.[50] Yet some of the women in our study indicated they have new "normative" alternatives when domestic violence occurs in their communities.

The increased importance of certain gendered cultural practices illustrates women's complex choices, as they pick and chose which cultural values they chose to modify and those they chose to retain. In the context where ethnic values and practices were endangered by forced migration resulting from armed conflict, some of the women noted that their status increased if they were able to practice and teach some visible and economically advantageous gendered cultural customs such as weaving, sewing, music, ceremonial practices, and, for the Kayan, wearing neck rings. Further, generally, the women in our study did not condone changing cultural practices that pertained to marriage and dress. The attitudes of the women may indicate compliance with traditional gendered roles. However, their perceptions may also be seen as a form of resistance, a type of agency; are they resisting loss of culture?

CONCLUSION

This study shows that on the Thai/Burmese border, networks of women's NGOs are offering training that is giving some women a new language, a new way of thinking about themselves that is empowering to them. The women's groups provide additional social resources through the trainings that increase the informal power of some women in the camps and create discursive alternatives for many. As a result, some of the women have noticed changes in gendered practices including male and female perceptions of housework and female mobility. As such, the work of the women's NGOs can be considered grassroots capacity building. They have begun to change at an individual and at a community level the sense that women are not capable to the sense that they do have the power to effect change.

The presence of transformative experiences reinforces the need for refugee policies and practices that support the potential for gender transformation and for peacebuilding during conflict. Interviewees connected experiences of empowerment to the training workshops offered by the NGO network of women from Burma and the new community structures in which they took part. According to the refugees, empowerment did not come automatically from changes in gendered roles and responsibilities brought about through dislocation. Despite limited capacities as exiles in a foreign country, the NGOs self-organized offering capacity building training as refugee organizations.

Sustainable peacebuilding requires linking bottom up and top down approaches. The work of the NGO network is contributing to a civil society peace constituency by promoting women's empowerment. Further research is needed on how grassroots efforts might be linked to political participation at the top level. None of the NGO leaders who we interviewed were informed about or involved in political negotiations conducted by the government in exile. However, my sense is that this empowerment and capacity building at the grassroots level has been instrumental in the Womens' League of Burma's belief that they are capable of being involved in the top-level negotiations regarding both Burma's governments in exile and with the military government in Myanmar. The Women's League of Burma has appealed to the United Nations Security Council for training and resources to help implement UN Resolution 1325, which calls for the inclusion of women in all aspects of peacemaking, peacebuilding, and peacekeeping.

BIBLIOGRAPHY

Afshar, Haleh, and Deborah Eade, eds. *Development, Women, and War*. Oxford: Oxfam, 2004.

Belak, Brenda. *Gathering Strength: Women from Burma on Their Rights*. Chiang Mai, Thailand: Images Asia, Nopburee Press, 2002.

Bourdieu, Pierre. *Outline of a Theory of Practice*. Cambridge: Cambridge University Press, 1977.

Burmese Border Consortium. "Educational Assessment of Mon and Karenni Refugee Camps on the Thai/Burmese Border." Report Prepared for the Burmese Border Consortium, September 1995, 13.

Cheran, Rudhramoorthy. "Diaspora Circulation and Transnationalism as Agents for Change in the Post Conflict Zones of Sri Lanka." Department of Sociology and Centre for Refugee Studies, York University, 2003, http://www.sangam.org/articles/view2/523.pdf (May 12, 2006).

Cochrane, Feargal, Bahar Baser, and Ashok Swain. "Home Thoughts from Abroad: Diasporas and Peace-Building in Northern Ireland and Sri Lanka." *Studies in Conflict and Terrorism*, vol. 32 (2009): 681–704.

Cook-Huffman. Celia. "Who Do They Say We Are? Framing Social Identity and Gender in Church Conflict." in *Social Conflicts and Collective Identities*, Pat Coy and Lynne Woehrle, eds. Lanham, MD: Rowman and Littlefield Publishers, 2000.

El-Bushra, Judy. "Transforming Conflict: Some Thoughts on a Gendered Understanding of Conflict Dynamics," in *States of Conflict: Gender, Violence and Resistance*, S. Jacobs, R. Jacobson, and J. Marchbank, eds. London: Zed Books, 2000, 66–86

England, Paula, and George Farkas. *Households, Employment and Gender: A Social, Economic and Demographic View*. Hawthorne, NY: Aldine de Gruyter, 1986.

Fagen, Patricia Weiss, and Sally Yudelman. "El Salvador and Guatemala: Refugee Camp and Repatriation Experiences," in *Women and Civil War: Impact, Organizations, and Action*, Krishna Kumar, ed. Boulder, CO: Lynne Reinner, 2001, 79–96

Kabeer, Naila. "The Conditions and Consequences of Choice: Reflections on the Measurement of Women's Empowerment." United Nations Research Institute of Social Development Discussion Paper No. 108, August 1999, http://www.unrisd.org/UNRISD/website/document.nsf (July 7, 2008).

Kabeer, Naila. "Reflections on the Measurement of Women's Empowerment," in *Discussing Women's Empowerment—Theory and Practice*, Sida Studies No. 3. Stockholm: Novuum Grafiska AB, 2001.

Kachin Women's Association Thailand. *Driven Away: Trafficking of Kachin Women on the China-Burma Border*, 2005, http://www.womenofburma.org (May 12, 2006).

Khiang, Mi Mi. *The World of Burmese Women*. London: Zed Books, 1984.

Kishor, Sunitra. "Empowerment of Women in Egypt and Links to the Survival and Health of Their Infants," in *Women's Empowerment and Demographic Processes: Moving Beyond Cairo*, Harriet Presser and Gita Sen, eds. New York: Oxford University Press, 2000.

Kriesberg, Louis. *Social Conflicts*. Englewood Cliffs, NJ: Prentice-Hall, 1982.

Kumar, Krishna, ed. *Women and Civil War: Impact, Organizations, and Action*. Boulder, CO: Lynne Reinner, 2001.

Kumar, Krishna, and Hannah Baldwin. "Women's Organizations in Postconflict Cambodia," in *Women and Civil War: Impact, Organizations, and Action*, Krishna Kumar, ed. Boulder, CO: Lynne Reinner, 2001, 129–148

Lederach, John Paul. *Building Peace: Sustainable Reconciliation in Divided Societies*. Washington, DC: United States Institute of Peace, 1997.

Malhotra, Anju, Sidney Schuler, and Carol Boender. "Measuring Women's Empowerment as a Variable in International Development." *Gender and Development Group of World Bank*, 2002, http://www.aed.org/LeadershipandDemocracy/upload/MeasuringWomen.pdf (September 8, 2006).

Meintejes, Sheila, Anu Pillay, and Meredith Turshen, eds. *The Aftermath: Women in Post-Conflict Transformation*. London: Zed Books, 2001.

Mills, Janell. "Militarism, Civil War and Women's Status: A Burma Case Study," in *Women in Asia: Tradition, Modernity and Globalization*, Louise P. Edwards and Mina Roces, eds. Ann Arbor: The University of Michigan Press, 2000, 265–290.

O'Kane, Mary. "Gender, Borders and Transversality: The Emerging Women's Movement in the Burma-Thailand Borderlands," in *Gender, Conflict and Migration*, Navnita C. Behera, ed. New Delhi: Sage Publications, 2006.

Panos Institute. *Giving Voice: A Practical Guide to Implementing Oral Testimony Projects*. London: Panos Oral Testimony Programme, Panos Institute, 2001.

Pirkkalainen, Paivi, and Abdile Mahdi. "The Diaspora—Conflict—Peace—Nexus: A Literature Review," *Diaspeace*, Working Paper No. 1, 2009.

Rajasingham-Senanayake, Darini. "Ambivalent Empowerment: The Tragedy of Tamil Women in Conflict," in *Women, War and Peace in South Asia: Beyond Victimhood to Agency*, Rita Manchanda, ed. New Delhi: Sage Publications, 2001, 102–130.

Rice, Brian. *Native Voices in Research*. Winnipeg: Aboriginal Issues Press, 2004.

Sen, Amartya. *Development as Freedom*. Oxford: Oxford University Press, 1999.

Sen, Gita. "Women's Empowerment and Human Rights: The Challenge to Policy." Paper Presented at the Population Summit of the World's Scientific Academies, 1993.

Smith, Hazel, and Paul Stares, eds. *Diasporas in Conflict: Peace-Makers or Peace-Wreckers?* Tokyo: United Nations University Press, 2007.

Spiro, Melford. *Gender Ideology and Psychological Reality: An Essay on Cultural Reproduction*. New Haven, CT: Yale University Press, 1997.

Turpin, Jennifer. "Many Faces: Women Confronting War," in *The Women and War Reader*, Lois Ann Lorentzen and Jennifer Turpin, eds. New York: New York University Press, 1998.

Werbner, Pnina. "Global Pathways: Working Class Cosmopolitans and the Creation of Transnational Ethnic Worlds." *Social Anthropology*, vol. 7, no. 1 (1999): 17–35.

Wieringa, Saskia. "Measuring Women's Empowerment: Developing a Global Tool," in *Engendering Human Security*, Thanh-Dam Truong, Saskia Wieringa, and Amrita Chhachhi, eds. London: Zed Books, 2006.

Women's League of Burma. *A Shadow Report to the Beijing Plus Five Report*. 2000, http://www.womenofburma.org (May 12, 2006).

NOTES

1. Conflict-generated diasporas are defined as diasporas that originate in conflict and emerge through forced migration.

2. Hazel Smith and Paul Stares, eds., *Diasporas in Conflict: Peace-Makers or Peace-Wreckers?* (Tokyo: United Nations University Press, 2007).

3. Pnina Werbner, "Global Pathways: Working Class Cosmopolitans and the Creation of Transnational Ethnic Worlds," *Social Anthropology*, vol. 7, no. 1 (1999): 24.

4. Rudhramoorthy Cheran, "Diaspora Circulation and Transnationalism as Agents for Change in the Post Conflict Zones of Sri Lanka," Department of Sociology and Centre for Refugee Studies, York University, 2003, http://www.sangam.org/articles/view2/523.pdf.

5. Paivi Pirkkalainen and Mahdi Abdile, "The Diaspora—Conflict—Peace—Nexus: A Literature Review," *Diaspeace*, Working Paper No. 1, 2009.

6. Feargal Cochrane, Bahar Baser, and Ashok Swain, "Home Thoughts from Abroad: Diasporas and Peace-Building in Northern Ireland and Sri Lanka," *Studies in Conflict and Terrorism*, vol. 32 (2009): 681–704.

7. Pirkkalainin and Abdile, *Diaspora*.

8. John Paul Lederach, *Building Peace: Sustainable Reconciliation in Divided Societies* (Washington, DC: United States Institute of Peace, 1997), 109.

9. Darini Rajasingham-Senanayake, "Ambivalent Empowerment: The Tragedy of Tamil Women in Conflict," in *Women, War and Peace in South Asia: Beyond Victimhood to Agency*, Rita Manchanda, ed. (New Delhi: Sage Publications, 2001), 105.

10. Patricia Weiss Fagen, Patricia Weiss, and Sally Yudelman, "El Salvador and Guatemala: Refugee Camp and Repatriation Experiences," in *Women and Civil War: Impact,*

Organizations, and Action, Krishna Kumar, ed. (Boulder, CO: Lynne Reinner, 2001): 79–96; Krishna Kumar and Hannah Baldwin, "Women's Organizations in Postconflict Cambodia," in *Women and Civil War: Impact, Organizations, and Action*, Krishna Kumar, ed. (Boulder, CO: Lynne Reinner, 2001): 129–148.

11. Mary O'Kane, "Gender, Borders and Transversality: The Emerging Women's Movement in the Burma-Thailand Borderlands," in *Gender, Conflict and Migration*, Navnita C. Behera, ed. (New Delhi: Sage Publications, 2006).

12. Judy El-Bushra, "Transforming Conflict: Some Thoughts on a Gendered Understanding of Conflict Dynamics," in *States of Conflict: Gender, Violence and Resistance*, S. Jacobs, R. Jacobson, and J. Marchbank, eds. (London: Zed Books, 2000), 66–86.

13. Brian Rice, *Native Voices in Research* (Winnipeg: Aboriginal Issues Press, 2004).

14. Anju Malhotra, Sidney Schuler, and Carol Boender, "Measuring Women's Empowerment as a Variable in International Development," *Gender and Development Group of World Bank* 2002, http://www.aed.org/LeadershipandDemocracy/upload/MeasuringWomen.pdf (September 8, 2006).

15. Gita Sen, "Women's Empowerment and Human Rights: The Challenge to Policy," paper presented at the Population Summit of the World's Scientific Academies, 1993.

16. Amartya Sen, *Development as Freedom* (Oxford: Oxford University Press, 1999); Gita Sen, "Women's"; Naila Kabeer, "Reflections on the Measurement of Women's Empowerment," in *Discussing Women's Empowerment—Theory and Practice,* Sida Studies No. 3 (Stockholm: Novuum Grafiska AB, 2001).

17. Saskia Wieringa, "Measuring Women's Empowerment: Developing a Global Tool," in *Engendering Human Security*, Thanh-Dam Truong, Saskia Wieringa, and Amrita Chhachhi, eds. (London: Zed Books, 2006).

18. Nail Kabeer, "The Conditions and Consequences of Choice: Reflections on the Measurement of Women's Empowerment," United Nations Research Institute of Social Development Discussion Paper No. 108, August 1999, http://www.unrisd.org/UNRISD/website/document.nsf (July 7, 2008).

19. Kabeer, "Conditions."

20. Pierre Bourdieu, *Outline of a Theory of Practice* (Cambridge: Cambridge University Press, 1977).

21. Kabeer, "Conditions."

22. Women's League of Burma, *A Shadow Report to the Beijing Plus Five Report,* 2000, http://www.womenofburma.org (May 12, 2006); Kachin Women's Association Thailand, *Driven Away: Trafficking of Kachin Women on the China-Burma Border*, 2005, http://www.womenofburma.org (May 12, 2006).

23. Interview, Ban Luang (March 2007).

24. Interview, Chiang Mai (April 2007).

25. Interview, Chiang Mai.

26. Interview, Chiang Mai.

27. Interview, Mae Sariang (May 2007).

28. Interview, Mae Hong Son (April 2007).

29. UNHCR and the Thai/Burmese Border Consortium ran the camps. Burmese Border Consortium, "Educational Assessment of Mon and Karenni Refugee Camps on the Thai/Burmese Border," report prepared for the Burmese Border Consortium, September 1995, 13.

30. Interview, Mae Sariang.

31. Fieldnotes, 18.

32. Interview, Ban Luang (March 2007).

33. Interview, Mae Hong Son.

34. Louis Kriesberg, *Social Conflicts* (Englewood Cliffs, NJ: Prentice-Hall, 1982); Celia Cook-Huffman, "Who Do They Say We Are? Framing Social Identity and Gender in Church Conflict," in *Social Conflicts and Collective Identities*, Pat Coy and Lynne Woehrle, eds. (Lanham, MD: Rowman and Littlefield Publishers, 2000).

35. Interview, Mae Hong Son.

36. Interview, Mae Hong Son.

37. Amartya Sen, *Development*; Gita Sen, "Women's"; Kabeer, "Reflections."

38. Sen (1993).

39. Mi Mi Khiang, *The World of Burmese Women* (London: Zed Books, 1984); and Melford Spiro, *Gender Ideology and Psychological Reality: An Essay on Cultural Reproduction* (New Haven, CT: Yale University Press, 1997).

40. Janell Mills, "Militarism, Civil War and Women's Status: A Burma Case Study," in *Women in Asia: Tradition, Modernity and Globalization*, Louise P. Edwards and Mina Roces, eds. (Ann Arbor: The University of Michigan Press, 2000), 265–290.

41. Brenda Belak, *Gathering Strength: Women from Burma on Their Rights* (Chiang Mai, Thailand: Images Asia, Nopburee Press, 2002), 8.

42. Belak, *Gathering*, 44.

43. Belak, *Gathering*.

44. Burmese Border Consortium, 13.

45. Belak, *Gathering*.

46. Sunitra Kishor,"Empowerment of Women in Egypt and Links to the Survival and Health of Their Infants," in *Women's Empowerment and Demographic Processes: Moving Beyond Cairo*, Harriet Presser and Gita Sen, eds. (New York: Oxford University Press, 2000).

47. Khiang, *World*; Spiro, *Gender*.

48. Belak, *Gathering*.

49. Jennifer Turpin, "Many Faces: Women Confronting War," in *The Women and War Reader*, Lois Ann Lorentzen and Jennifer Turpin, eds. (New York: New York University Press, 1998).

50. Paula England and George Farkas, *Households, Employment and Gender: A Social, Economic and Demographic View* (Hawthorne, NY: Aldine de Gruyter, 1986).

Chapter 11

Relationships with Human and Non-Human Species and How They Apply toward Peacebuilding and Leadership in Indigenous Societies

Brian Rice

Relationships with human and non-human species as they pertain to peacebuilding are essential to keeping harmony within indigenous societies. They derive from a holistic worldview and are necessary in maintaining balance within the society. Indigenous societies depend on balance in order to survive; therefore, it requires coexistence between humans and the other forms of life that surround them. Developing and maintaining that relationship is a form of peacebuilding.

HOW DO INDIGENOUS PEACEBUILDERS BECOME LEADERS?

The Rotinonshonni, also known as Six Nations Iroquois, developed its governing institutions on the following premise and its government still functions so to this day at Onondaga in Rotinonshonni traditional territory, now the State of New York. Years ago, Cadwallader Colden[1] mentioned that it was only by way of merit that a member could become a leader. Those who were selected were said to not have accepted any salary or made any profit from their positions. Most were selected by how they were able to relate to the needs of their people. If they did not live up to their responsibilities, they were removed from their positions of leadership. Contrast this with many of the indigenous leaders in the federal government imposed on Canadian band councils and American tribal councils today, and we can see that there has been a dramatic shift in worldview in the present-day leadership in many indigenous communities. In order to be a leader, one had to be able to keep the peace in his or her society. Traditionally, part of keeping the peace was ensuring that they were accountable not only to members of the society, but also to non-humans that lived in the environments surrounding them.

Before the imposed systems of government came into effect, the Rotinonshonni had leaders who acted on the decisions of their people. Leadership evolved from an equal distribution of power between men and women by way of consensus. Women chose the male representatives of the people and if the men did not do the will of the people after three warnings given to them by the women, they had the power to dismiss them. At Onondaga, it is still up to the women to ensure that the voice of the people is heard.

One of the qualities expected of a leader is generosity. Colden[2] mentioned that their greatest leaders remained poorer than most of the rest of the society by giving away much of their wealth, leaving little for themselves. Even to this day, traditional leaders at both Onondaga and at Six Nations Territory in Ontario lead a sparse existence, as they are not paid for their positions. At Six Nations, unlike at Onondaga, the traditional functioning government was deposed by the government of Canada in 1924; but now, the people are governed by a federal government-imposed band council. Nonetheless, the traditional governing council still meets at various longhouses to discuss issues of importance with their people. At Onondaga, thankfully, they were never replaced.

Leaders are also required to lead by example. As the late chief, Jacob Thomas, noted, to be a leader one has to have skin seven spans thick so as not to show anger.[3] They have to be persons who can reason things out at all times. Furthermore, to be a leader, one has to be married, have children, and show that he or she could provide for a family. It was believed that if leaders could not keep the peace in their own family, they were not capable of keeping the peace among their people. The name of a traditional leader is *Royan:er*, "He of the Good Mind." Leaders were said to be like trees. To be a leader, one needs to always be of a good mind and stout like a tree if they are to lead their people. They may bend but not break. Once chosen to represent their people, they may never take up the weapons of war, as they then have an obligation to keep the peace.

Leaders are not allowed to coerce their people into doing things they don't want to do. Every person is free to choose their own path, as long as their decisions don't have an injurious effect on the whole. It was only through reason and calm that leaders would be able to direct their own people. If not, the people would immediately forsake them.[4] Adario, a leader of the Huron, explained many years ago that their leaders had no more power than anyone else. This equality alleviated any jealousy or quarrelling. It was through the wisdom of the leaders that decisions were made and the leaders found respect among their people.[5] Much of this was dependent on how well they could maintain the peace.

In building relationships toward peacebuilding with others, an important quality in becoming a leader is that of showing respect for all living things. During councils, either a pipe ceremony takes place or words are given for all the things essential within the people's world. During a pipe ceremony, when tobacco is put in a pipe, thanks is given to all forms of life, thereby acknowledging their contributions to the world. In this way, communication takes place between the one bestowed with the pipe and the person who receives the tobacco smoke. A relationship is built on harmony and trust between the two.

Among the Rotinonshonni, this process of peacebuilding begins with the *ohonto kari wen takwen*, or "the words that come before all else." A representative of the people gives thanks to the earth first. Then, he works his way up the ladder of creation, until, finally, he thanks the creator. These gestures are to ensure that everyone is aware of their equal place in the creative order. It brings a sense of respectfulness in council. They are now considered to be of one mind and can work to find a solution to whatever the issue might be, ensuring a more harmonious outcome. It is believed that if it is understood that we are all an equal part of the social order of creation, we can better see our similarities, rather than our differences.

After this is completed, the representatives of the people may speak. No one is allowed to interrupt. Everyone must wait until the person speaking is finished. This process ensures that everyone is heard without interruption. The next person to speak must then summarize what the previous speaker has said to ensure he has understood everything correctly. This repetition avoids problems of misinterpretation occurring. Only then can he proceed with what he wants to say. To show anger and emotion that might disrupt the conciliatory process taking place shows a lack of respect for the opinion of the previous speaker.

If we look at the position of leadership in Rotinonshonni society, we see it as something that filters from the people at the top to the representatives of the people below. Contrast this then to Euro-Western institutions of government where power resides with individual leaders at the top making decisions for those below. These include decisions that may force individuals to go to war whether they believe in the cause or not, perhaps in spite of their unwillingness to participate in it. In Rotinonshonni society, if one chooses not to fight, a leader or government cannot compel him to do so. Warfare is considered a sign of the failure of its leaders in resolving disputes and keeping the peace. If that happens, leadership is deferred to those chosen by the people to make war, who may then try to compel others to join them. Therefore, it is incumbent upon leaders chosen by the people to do everything to keep the peace. Otherwise, they might forfeit their responsibilities to those less willing to do so.

Among the Rotinonshonni, governance begins locally with the extended clan family. In the case of the *Kenienké haka*, a member nation of the Rotinonshonni, there were three clans: turtle, wolf and bear. During times of necessity, the men and women of the three clans would go into council separately. A male representative would then seek the consensus of the community from the women clan mothers. The three clan leaders would then meet and discuss the issue at a village council with the bears sitting across from the wolves and turtles. If the issue was of national importance, runners were sent to other villages with messages set in wampum strings and remembered by the runners. A Grand Council might be called at Onondaga, the centre of Rotinonshonni territory. At a Grand Council, there were fifty representatives in all. These representatives would speak on behalf of the fifty women who comprised the voice of the people. The women stayed behind because they were the sole proprietors of the land and were depended upon for cultivating much of the produce. Balance had to be maintained between the roles of men and the roles of women.

During the past century that saw two world wars and various smaller conflicts, leaders in Rotinonshonni society have tried to keep their men from joining the militaries of the United States or Canada. Leaders at Onondaga, like Oren Lyons, and at Six Nations, such as Jacob Thomas, have held fast to their conviction in not allowing their young people to go to war. Thomas said many times that his people did not invent the weapons of modern warfare, and therefore they should not use them or participate in global conflicts that have nothing to do with them.[6] Nonetheless, in spite of their efforts, the choice that individuals make for themselves in going to war is accepted as an individual choice and has to be respected even by those making the peace. However, leadership goes beyond keeping the peace among humans. In order for true peacebuilding to take place, it is incumbent on indigenous leaders to build relationships with the natural things in the world that have an effect on their lives.

HOW ARE INDIGENOUS PEACEBUILDERS DEVELOPED?

In today's world, one of the most difficult aspects of indigenous peacebuilding for the dominant Euro-Western society to come to terms with is the holistic worldview that sees all things as being interrelated. These indigenous ways of knowing include social relations with human and non-human beings that indigenous peacebuilders depend on for their people's survival. These leaders must learn proper conduct at a young age so that they are respectful of the other living beings that make up creation. Today, indigenous peacebuilders are continually exposed to aggressive Euro-Western methods of governing at the expense of their own forms of governance. Indigenous leaders understand that they must adapt to a changing world but not at the expense of their own peacebuilding capacities. This adjustment requires innovative methods of learning and integration of the old and the new.

For Rotinonshonni peacebuilders, their education begins as an informal way of understanding the world in which they live. As children brought up in a traditional lifestyle, it is a daily process of learning that involves every facet of their lives. The first relationships developed are with the extended family and the people of the community. This development begins with the clan or in the *Kenienké* (Mohawk) language, *kahwá:tsire*. The Ojibwa refer to it as a *Do:dem*. It is the link within the extended human family, the environment, and non-human family relations, both physical and spiritual. Its importance is that it links all of the above with the individual. The *Kahwá:tsire* may be of an animal or a bird. For other indigenous societies living in the southern hemisphere, it may be a plant. This linking of the three in a relationship is an important part of the holistic outlook of indigenous peoples in their development of relationships toward peacebuilding and in living in harmony with their surroundings.

In Ojibwa cosmology, these three types of relations are regarded to be animate, meaning that they are alive. Ojibwa cosmology is divided between things that are animate, or living, and things that are inanimate, not living. Hence, a sacred pipe or even particular stones and rock formations may be considered to be as animate as a human being in whom a spirit or living energy is encompassed. On the other hand, this group doesn't include a common pipe, stone, or just any rock formation. A process or event is required in order to make them come to life. This animation requires a ceremonial process, such as participating in a vision quest, or may include an event that has taken place among the primordial beings in the beginning of creation that is still remembered by the society. In the rigueur of developing relationships toward peacebuilding, one's character is tested through the vision quest as to whether he or she can be a leader.

The children of the Ojibwa and Cree learned at an early age that they have a responsibility toward all of their relations. Even before they entered the world, the learning process had begun. Mothers started speaking to their unborn babies while the babies were still in the womb. They shared with the unborn child the lessons of life. They described for the child the different animals they might encounter. The Ojibwa felt that the soul of the baby is active and aware even before birth.[7] *Kenienké* mothers still sing to their babies while in the womb. These ideas and practices are presently endorsed by some Euro-Western medical practitioners who acknowledge that infants in the womb are quite aware of their surroundings before birth. Today, it is not uncommon for mothers of all backgrounds to sing to their unborn babies, but this circumstance has not always been the case. Among the Rotinonshonni, special children designated to be leaders are segregated from the rest in order to be trained in peacebuilding. It is referred to as being hidden under the husk of corn.

These indigenous children learn their responsibilities relative to the other beings that are a part of their world. For the Ojibwa and Cree, the vision quest takes place over four days and four nights without food or water. However, in time, some are able to go without for much longer periods. The fasting continues as the child gets older over a period of time, usually in the spring and fall, until the child, by way of the awakened dream state, learns from the non-human world with whom he or she is to have a special relationship for the rest of his or her life. Once the relationship is cemented, the child then honors this non-human being by offering feasts and prayers of thanks. Sometimes, it requires keeping a part of the physical manifestation of this being in a special bundle.

The Ojibwa and Cree believe that in order to be successful as a peacebuilder, they must develop a relationship with each of the animate aspects of creation—the human and non-human. When this is accomplished, it can be said that they are in a state of *Pimadiziwin*. The person is living a 360-degree life cycle to its fullest. Although members of the Ojibwa and Cree still fast, it is usually done today at a much later age. Few modern-day leaders have undergone a fast as part of their training.

Kaokwa:haka and *royan:er* Jacob Thomas mentioned that during his youth, he was taught the proper way to walk and speak. The lessons he received in his youth helped him become a noted orator among his people. Much of what he learned came from his grandmother. Among the Rotinonshonni, the grandmother on the maternal side of the family is an important influence on her grandchildren. Thomas said that when he was in his youth, he went out with a girl from his community. His grandmother, upon hearing who this girl was, told Jacob that she was a cousin on the maternal side of the family. This meant that she was a member of the same *Kahwá: tsire* (clan) as himself. He then had to leave the girl and find another. Unfortunately, he went out with another girl only to learn the same thing about her. Jacob said that the third time he got lucky and married the girl. He said that his grandmother knew all of the relations in an extended family. He also mentioned that it was important to make sure that you don't marry someone closer than a fourth cousin on either the maternal or paternal side of the family, even if they are not of the same clan. Grandmothers are there to remind children of the proper way to conduct themselves in the society.

Humans are not the only beings with whom indigenous people like the Rotinonshonni, Cree, and Ojibwa are required to develop relationships and show proper conduct toward. For instance, there are places that upon entering require particular protocols, such as the sacrifice of tobacco. These places are considered to be animate or alive. When indigenous peoples make offerings in such places, they are showing respect for the generations that walked in these places before them, as well as for those who have passed away and now live in the beyond. These places are known through oral traditions and are believed to have energies that can be tapped into, bringing good fortune or bad fortune depending on the amount of respect shown.[8]

For most indigenous peoples living on Turtle Island in North America, learning is experiential. In the past, indigenous parents were criticized by Euro-Western authorities for not using corporal punishment with children when they got into trouble and allowing them too much freedom. However, freedom was not without social conduct and structure. For example, there was always someone in the extended family who could take care of a child if there was a problem or who could direct a child if a mistake was made. For instance, in *Kenienké* society, it was a mother's brother who disciplined his nephews and not the parents. Likewise, children were taught that if they made mistakes, they alone had to take responsibility for their actions. Therefore, it was essential that they received instruction from all members of the extended family and even the members of the community. A common reprimand in *Kenienké* communities was to blow water in the child's face. This act was a non-abusive form of punishment that allowed the child to know they had done wrong without causing physical harm. In the Rotinonshonni language, the word mother—*ista*—can apply to every woman in the clan. Each woman has a responsibility in the upbringing of the children.

The breakup of the extended family by Euro-Western authorities in favor of the nuclear family has resulted in detrimental consequences for the coherence of indigenous societies where everyone was a part of an extended family of relations. Both politicians and clergy did everything they could to break it up, believing that severe corporal punishment and the undermining of women as parental authority figures was in the best interest of indigenous children. History has shown that they were wrong and indigenous peoples were right, as today women are viewed with more respect by Euro-Western society than in the past, and corporal punishment is disallowed. It was not that long ago, within my generation, that both parents and teachers were given the authority to administer corporal punishment. This corporal punishment became excessive abuse in the residential schools set up for indigenous children, the consequences of which are still felt to this day.

WHO TEACHES THE INDIGENOUS PEACEBUILDERS TO BECOME LEADERS?

Those who are the teachers of the future peacebuilders are also the ones who have the most knowledge. These people are the elders, both men and women, and they play a significant role in the lives of indigenous children. They have wisdom and experience they can pass on. Usually, this knowledge has been passed down through many generations. Sometimes, these elders belong to ancient societies. Two examples of such individuals are the late Dan Pine from Garden River who was a member of the *Wabano* society and my former colleague Jim Dumont who taught Native studies at the University of Sudbury and who is the keeper of the Eastern Door for the *Ojibwa Midewiwin* society. Both Dan and Jim would be considered elders. However, in the past, elders were simply the oldest and wisest in the community, as everyone followed the same tradition.

Traditionally, the elders among the Ojibwa would pass along their most important information during the winter through oral traditions. This season is the time when the spiritual and physical aspects of creation come to rest. These stories are called *Atisokan* and are recounted by the elders to the young. More common historical stories are passed on in *Tabadjimowin* stories.

The Ojibwa had four different ways of passing on their most essential knowledge. These ways are called the *Nanidawi*, the *Wabana*, the *Tcisaki*, and the *Midewiwin*. The last two are still significant to this day. A person belonging to one of these traditions has a particular expertise in an area of Ojibwa knowledge. Professor Grim[9] offers a brief description of what these four societies represent to the Ojibwa. The *Nanidawi* is a person with the ability to find and cure illness. He does this by way of the waking dream. The awakened dream is a state one acquires after many years of fasting. It was known by many indigenous societies and is something we all have the potential to do. As an example, have you ever fallen asleep and found yourself awake in your dream? The common response is a feeling of fear and then waking up. Through fasting, one acquires the ability to put oneself in the dream state and then control the situation within the dream world. It is during this time that the archetypal spirits called *Manito* may enter the doorway between the spirit world and the physical world. Drumming and singing by others can help the person remain in the awakened dream state where he can discover answers to problems that might baffle him.

Persons who have knowledge about the evening celestial bodies to be passed on are known as the *Wabano*. These medical practitioners use a sacred fire to help them in their curing. They are able to handle live coals without burning their hands. This occurrence is familiar to other indigenous healers as well. They use fire to invoke the waking dream state. They are able to help a person by manipulating the energy of heat as part of the healing process. However, the night energies are difficult to control and therefore, need even more scrutiny than the others. The *Kenienké: haka* believe that night energies are too unpredictable and should be left alone. There are also some Ojibwa that feel the same way.

Next is the *Tcisaki*, or those who do what is referred to as the shaking lodge. This recitation is done by the *Tcisaki* entering a small lodge and placing himself in a wakened-dream state. Sometimes, he may be tied up. Once there, the archetypal energies enter after a celestial like tree creates an opening between the earth and the sky worlds. The vortex that is created allows the *Tcisaki* to access the four energy levels above and below depending on his ability. Some of the songs that were learned in this ceremony were written on bark scrolls, many of which had been confiscated and now remain in museums throughout the world. I have been fortunate enough to personally witness this and have been affected by the healing properties of the *Tcisaki*. The Algonguin refer to this as *Kosowpajigan*.

The *Midewiwin* is the most prevalent among the Ojibwa today. It is open to anyone of *Anishnabé* (Ojibwa, Pottowotomie, Odawa and Algonguin) descent. Through learning of stories, songs, and practicing the seven teachings (wisdom, love, respect, bravery, honesty, humility and truth), the initiate becomes an integrated part of the Ojibwa cosmology. Foremost for the *Midewiwin* is knowledge of herbs and medicines. Essential to the rite of passage into this society is the death and rebirth of the initiate. Usually, this involves a transition from a novice level to entry into a new and more sophisticated level of development. Once this occurs, the person proceeds to a lifetime of learning and reaching new levels of the Ojibwa cosmology below and above.

These are the non-human beings that inhabit the eight worlds of the Ojibwa as recorded by William Jones[10] from a birch-bark scroll:

1. *Kiwadin*—north
2. *Shawana*—south
3. *Wabanang*—east
4. *Nigibianang*—west
5. *Nisawagi wabanang kiwade nang*—northeast
6. *Nisawagi shawanak negabiaanak*—southeast

7. *Nisa wagi nigabianang kiwadenung*—northwest: the wind most feared, called also *maskawag nodin*—strong wind, the lines and circles signify much wind
8. *Nisa waga wabanaak shawanaak*—southeast, all of the eight worlds signify that *manitos* are everywhere
9. *Windigo*, called *pabono kya*—ruler of the winter region—He makes the winter
10. *Nigik*—otter
11. *Mons*—moose
12. *Makwa*—bear
13. *Midéwineni*—one of the rallying *manitos* of the *midewiwin*
14. *Madodasanan*—for sweat lodges, which must be entered before entering the *midé* lodge
15. *Adi kamiq*—caribou fish or white fish
16. *Kinonja*—pike (long nose) pickerel
17. *Nama*—sturgeon
18. *Ni'ka*—goose
19. *Namagas*—trout
20. *Kukukuha*—owl
21. *Nincip*—mallard
22. *Pikwakocip*—whistle-duck, arrowhead duck
23. *Kinawaawacip*—long-neck duck (redhead duck)
24. *Adcidcak*—Crane
25. *Wawibiwanga*—teal duck—has red hair, rather long legs, is not a swimmer but stays near the water
26. *Mang*—loon
27. *Migis*—cowry shell
28. *Migis*—wampum
29. *Maskinonga*—muskalonge, a kind of pickerel, large, overgrown
30. *Mangamaque*—speckled trout
31. *Migizi*—bald eagle
32. *Anzik*—fishduck (anziwag)
33. *Wabanzik*—whitefish (dark)
34. *Mbanaba nibanaba*—a kind of fish (larger than a sturgeon, sprouts water and found in Lake Superior) perhaps a giant sturgeon
35. *Shada*—pelican (looks like a seagull, catches fish and holds it under its neck)
37. Kayashk—seagull
38. *Nigibi a nisi*—westerner (fowl)
39. *Shigag*—skunk
40. *Ami'k*—beaver

41. *Piju*—lynx
42. *Wabos*—rabbit
43. *Adik*—caribou
44. Omitted
45–48. Goods, presents
49. *Anishnabé midéwi* = a person performs the *myshi rik*
50. Same as 49
51 and 52. *Midéwagan nagasaq asama gaya*—mystic lodge, wampum beads, tobacco

A rectangle represents the lodge of the *Midéwiwin*. The winding paths about the circles within are the course taken in the medicine dance. It is important to note that in Ojibwa cosmology, these three types of beings—human, non-human and spirit—are part of a natural process that work together. As well, there are many Ojibwa who don't belong to any society or category such as those mentioned above and whom may still have important knowledge to pass on.

Teachers such as these carry knowledge that is extremely important in the peacebuilding process. Like the sacred places where offerings are made, it is a requirement when receiving such knowledge to offer tobacco to the person sharing the knowledge. If all you can afford is a piece of cloth, then that has as much value as a fur coat a rich person might offer. The person who has the knowledge will know if the recipient is sincere or not. The prevalent opinion among these peacebuilders is that a price should not be asked in order to obtain knowledge, but rather an appropriate offering should be made. This gift may include a monetary sum, as elders have to buy their food and pay their rent. In the past, this wouldn't have been necessary.

It is important to understand that when dealing with knowledge concerning energies, a person with bad intentions will receive benefits for only a short time. These energies will eventually rebound against the person using them. In the Ojibwa understanding of life, everything comes full circle. As mentioned, only when a person is living up to his or her potential by practicing the seven teachings (wisdom, respect, honesty, courage, love, humility and truth) can he or she be a practitioner in the knowledge of the society.

Besides these important values to be learned, peacebuilders must also learn practical everyday knowledge, such as how to survive. With the transition away from the holistic traditional life and the inception of modern technology, many of these skills, such as animal tracking, are being lost. To be a good tracker requires a love for nature and the environment and requires many years of practice. One must know the prints that animals make and the different gaits that the animals use when moving. A good tracker can tell a story about a particular animal: where it has been, where it is going, how fast it is moving, and how large it is. Other traditional skills, such as building a fire out of items in the environment, are known today by only a few. In order to be able to survive, one has to know how to find food and water, make fire, and build a shelter. Other important lessons include learning how to hunt, skin, fish, trap, and tan animal hides. One must also show respect for the land and animals.

The Cree people of James Bay have retained some of this knowledge and have amalgamated their traditional knowledge and values in the modern Euro-Western education system. The *nitibaaihtaan*, or tallyman, is responsible for seeing that these things are fulfilled. He sets the beaver quotas so that they can be safely harvested as well as the dates for trapping. He knows that at the end of March, beaver traps have to be removed from the water, due to the fact that the females are pregnant. He also makes sure that the trappers remain within their boundaries. If one of his trappers moves into another's territory and discovers a new beaver lodge, it is up to him to inform the *nitibaaihtaan* of that area. The Cree refer to a person who is a good hunter as *naabaaw*. In chart form,[11] what constitutes a good hunter and a good leader are noted below.

A Good Hunter	*A Good Leader*
does not boast	is a good hunter
never causes others embarrassment	teaches by example
never brags about how he killed an animal	consults others and values their opinions
reveals the information about a hunt slowly and often without words	exercises leadership
shows modesty	obtains consensus among his hunters
shares with others	
when game is scarce, is still able to catch something	

A PERSONAL JOURNEY IN INDIGENOUS PEACEBUILDING

Kaokwa: haka elder Jacob Thomas explained the changes he had seen in the last century with respect to how relational knowledge toward peacebuilding is passed on. He said that when he was a boy, there were no television, radio, automobiles, or even telephones. Elders from other communities would visit his family. They stayed for months at a time because it was difficult to travel. They would sit and tell stories all day long or they would go to the longhouse and practice songs, speeches, and ceremonies. One song, the *hai, hai*, a part of the roll call of the *royaner* (good-minded chief—or trees of equal height) can take over an hour to sing. The children were always welcome to watch and learn. They would then practice what they had heard. There were even times when the elders would call them over and let them practice with them. In itself, the protocols for elevating someone to the level of a *royaner* and becoming a peacebuilder took about ten hours to complete.

Thomas also comments on what he observes today. Because of varied and improved transportation options, people often visit and then leave the next day. Children are preoccupied with new and different activities such as watching television in contrast with practicing ceremonies. The biggest change, however, is in the relationship between the elderly and the young. Today, elders are often relegated to live in old-age homes, while at the same time, the young are put into daycare centers. This way, there is no chance for a true relationship between those who are the most knowledgeable and those who are of the age of learning. As the elders of Jacob Thomas's generation pass away, less and less of traditional knowledge is being passed on.[12]

Without doubt, one of the most dramatic effects on indigenous systems of learning was the residential schools. This system of education, imposed on indigenous peoples, was highly destructive to their ways of knowing. Although the residential school system has been abolished in Canada and the United States, the system still exists in other countries.

I had to wait many years before someone like Jacob Thomas came along and offered this knowledge to those who would attend his nine-day recitals on the Great Law of Peace. Thankfully, with the support of wife Yvonne, we were able to learn. It was one of the reasons I decided to include the story of the Peacemaker in my own traditional dissertation. It was Jacob Thomas who cooked medicines all night, then performed a sweat lodge ceremony, and gave me three beads of wampum before I commenced on a walk following the oral tradition of the Peacemaker. Finally, it would be *Kaokwa:haka* elder Norma General who would ask me to help facilitate journeys with members, elders, and leaders from various Six Nations communities back to the traditional homelands following the Path of the Peacemaker, bringing community, traditional homeland, and oral tradition together.

As we can see, indigenous peoples all over the world have had to face great obstacles in trying to preserve their peacebuilding traditions. The positive aspect of this is that some children are beginning to see the value in learning about their own responsibility within their cultures toward relational peacebuilding. They are the leaders of the future.

BIBLIOGRAPHY

Anonymous. *Cree Trappers Speak.* James Bay: Waskaginish, 1988.

Colden, Callwallader. *The History of the Five Nations depending on the Province of New York in America.* New York: Allerton Book Co., 1972.

Grim, John. *The Shaman: Patterns of Religious Healing Among the Ojibwa Indians.* Norman: University of Oklahoma Press, 1983.

Jenness, Diamond. "The Ojibwa Indians of Parry Island: Their Social and Religious Life." *The Cycle of Life and Death (Chapter IX) Anthropological Series,* vol. 17, no. 78 (Ottawa: National Museum of Canada, 1935), 90–95.

Jones, William. *Ojibwa Texts*, vol. 7., collected by William Jones, edited by Truman Michelson. New York: G.E. Stechert & Co., 1917–1919.

Kineitz, Vernon. *The Indians of the Western Great Lakes 1615–1760.* Dearborn: University of Michigan Press, 1981.

Newell, William B. "Crime and Justice among the Iroquois Nations." *Caughnawaga Historical Society.* Montreal: McGill University Press, 1965.

Thomas, Jacob. "The Great Law of Peace Recital," recited at Grand River, Ontario, June 1994.

NOTES

1. Cadwallader Colden, *The History of the Five Nations depending on the Province of New York in America* (New York: Alberton Book Co., 1972), 2. The history of the five Indian nations of Canada, which are dependent on the Province of New York, are a barrier or bridge between the English and French in that part of the world. In other words, they hold much power. The American botanist and politician Cadwallader Colden (1688–1776), a diverse thinker whose scholarship encompassed nature of the universe, and medicine, was also lieutenant governor of New York.

2. Colden, *History, Five Nations*, 2.

3. Jacob Thomas, "The Great Law of Peace Recital" (Grand River, Ontario, June 1994). It is important to note that Cayuga Chief Jacob Ezra Thomas, Snipe Clan, recited from the Great Laws of Peace—Chief Thomas recited the origin, meaning, and relevance of the Great Law for interested people in early summer, June 1994, over a nine-day period. Chief Jacob Thomas was considered one of the most knowledgeable people from Six Nations regarding the Great Law and the Handsome Lake Code. Chief Thomas was at the forefront of local community efforts to preserve and promote the languages and ceremonies. In 1994, Chief Thomas hosted a reading of the Great Law in English in an effort to pass on the knowledge of this significant historical event to those who no longer speak their language and was the first Aboriginal leader to break "new ground" by conveying the Great Law in English language (1992, 1994). If they took up the weapons of war, they would be breaking the Great Peace. This great white wind was predicted in the Great Law. *Cayuga Hoya:neh* Jacob

Thomas was the deliverer of the message at Six Nations Grand River Territory. He recited it in English as well as in three of the *Hodinohso:ni:* languages. The messages provided within the Great Law had joined six separate nations in unity. As a result of the power of unity and the power of a good mind, the oldest League of Nations was formed. Because European colonists have hacked at the roots of the Great Tree, the message of Peace and Love has not been able to get further than those who have been part of the Six Nations.

4. William B. Newell (*Tai-wah-ron-ha-gail*, Mohawk), "Crime and Justice among the Iroquois Nations" (Montreal: Caughnawaga Historical Society, 1965), 21. Both of his parents were Natives (his mother was an Iroquois woman, Louisa Stump, of Caughnawaga) and he was known as Rolling Thunder II and as a physician. William B. Newell, a very respected professor of anthropology, provides detailed contradictory evidence about the complex social, political, and legal regime developed by Iroquois Nations and refers to a traditional justice system that draws on a traditional spirit of social responsibility and restitution, while adding to it the formal decision-making procedures of the longhouse called the "Longhouse Justice System." In Mohawk Nation, faithkeepers have been included as one possible "first contact" between the people and their system. In reference to Thanksgiving, Newell has been known to say, "Thanksgiving Day was first officially proclaimed by the Governor of the Massachusetts Bay Colony in 1637 to commemorate the massacre of 700 men, women, and children who were celebrating their annual green corn dance—Thanksgiving Day to them—in their own house. . . . Gathered in this place of meeting, they were attacked by mercenaries and Dutch and English. The Indians were ordered from the building and as they came forth they were shot down. The rest were burned alive in the building." Furthermore, Newell said the next one hundred Thanksgivings commemorated the killing of the Indians at what is now Groton, Connecticut [home of a nuclear submarine base], rather than a celebration with them. He said the image of Indians and Pilgrims sitting around a large table to celebrate Thanksgiving Day was "fictitious," although Indians did share food with the first settlers. See also Mitchel Cohen's "Why I Hate Thanksgiving."

5. Newell, *Crime, Justice, Iroquois*, 23.

6. Thomas, "Great Peace."

7. Diamond Jenness, "The Ojibwa Indians of Parry Island: Their Social and Religious Life," *The Cycle of Life and Death (Chapter IX) Anthropological Series,* vol. 17, no. 78 (Ottawa: National Museum of Canada, 1935), 90–95. Jenness portrays North American Indians' culture in motion, such as Cree, Ojibwa, and Algonguin of Northern Ontario, Labrador Naskapi, and dancing societies of the Sarsi Indians. Despite anthropological devotion to their social and religious life, they are no longer punishable by death. However, the Native Americans' right to hunt and fish as part of the Aboriginal spiritual and mystic belief system has been negatively and grossly impacted by European contact.

8. Vernon Kineitz, *The Indians of the Western Great Lakes 1615–1760* (Dearborn: University of Michigan Press, 1981). In order to authenticate Aboriginals' existence in the Great Lakes region of Canada and the United States at about 12,000 years, Kineitz considers an archeological analysis of human remains in the

Great Lake Basin and the possibility of a land bridge that once connected Siberia and Alaska. Furthermore, the Native Americans who settled in the Great Lakes Basin 10,000 years ago consist mainly of three Nations (groups) that shared a common linguistic stock called Algonguin. This circumstance means that the three groups spoke different dialects of the same base language, allowing communication between groups. These three Nations include Ojibwa, Ottawa, and Potawatomi. The Ojibwa nation occupied parts of Canada, Wisconsin and the upper peninsula of Michigan. Also, the Ottawa, to some degree a more nomadic people, occupied the northern 1/3 of Michigan's lower peninsula, and traveled throughout the Great Lakes area further west, past the Mississippi River, trading goods with Western nations. Finally, the Potawatomi nation occupied the southern region of Michigan's Lower Peninsula and parts of Ohio, Illinois, and southern Wisconsin. The three Algonguin Nations lived similar life styles, all depending on wild game, fish, farming and mineral resources for food and shelter. The Ojibwa nation, residing furthest north, experienced poor soils and a short growing season; they could not depend on summer crops because an early frost could wipe out the entire crop stock. They may have depended more heavily on seeds, nuts, and game meat as main staples. Aquatic resources from Lake Superior, such as fish, shellfish, plants and driftwood, would have also been key to survival in the North Country. Ojibwa clans also had access to some of the most productive copper deposits in the northeastern United States, a useful trade item during cold years that brought hardship. Ottawa clans also had a hand in copper distribution and were known for their keen business and travel skills, and acted as a mediator between nations. Experiencing a longer growing season than the Ojibwa nation, the Ottawa Nation made fish, maize, and squash important staples for survival.

9. John Grim. *The Shaman: Patterns of Religious Healing Among the Ojibwa Indians* (Norman: University of Oklahoma Press, 1983). Interestingly, Professor John Grim is currently a senior lecturer and scholar coordinator of the Forum on Religion and Ecology at Yale University. Grim traces the ecology and preparation of Black Elk as a healer and an advisor, or shaman, to his Lakota people. In brief, shamans exemplify the realization of cosmological power—the shamans' skills at activating the therapeutic and inspirational relationships with more-than-human forces such as *Warao* cosmology to negotiate with the powerful spirits show a desire to reconnect with the pre-agricultural "golden age" or the primal root of all creation toward an *entheogenic* experience.

10. William Jones, *Ojibwa Texts*, vol. 7, collected by William Jones, Truman Michelson, ed. (New York: G.E. Stechert & Co., 1917–1919). Jones covers the traditional belief system of the Anishinaabeg peoples, made up of Algonguin/Nipissing, Ojibwa/Chippewa/Saulteaux/Mississaugas, Odawa, Potawatomi, and Oji-cree, located primarily in the Great Lakes region of the United States and Canada, and includes common medicinal plants and their uses.

11. Anonymous, *Cree Trappers Speak* (James Bay: Waskaginish, 1988). High levels of mercury in the Cree population of James Bay, Quebec, between 1988 and 1993/1994, were observed between Eastmain and Whapmagoostui communities as a result of the consumption of contaminated fish from natural lakes and hydroelectric

reservoirs. Delayed walking and speaking in children and serious medical problems in adults were reported, further impacting and inhibiting the Aboriginals' natural freedom to fish and Aboriginal knowledge from being passed down through the generations—thus violating continuation of Aboriginal culture. At the same time, the incident sparked a strong decisive powerful leadership to rise as the Crees of Whapmagoostui and the Inuit of Kuujjuaraapik united to take charge of that project, and subsequent projects thereafter. See also Cree-Naskapi Commission 1996: Report, and the Grand Council of the Crees (Eeyou Istchee).

12. Thomas, "Great Peace."

Chapter 12

War on Earth?

Junctures between Peace and the Environment

Andrea Levy and Jean-Guy Vaillancourt

Since the 1990s when articles began to appear with such titles as "Can Peace Research and Ecology Be Linked?"[1] there has been a steady growth of both scholarly and popular interest in the points of intersection between peace and the environment. But the perception that the two realms are connected in important ways dates back many decades.

One of the first manifestations of popular consciousness of some of the connections between peace and environmental questions emerged in the 1960s and 1970s, when protests against nuclear testing and the nuclear industry brought together the peace movement and environmental groups. It was, of course, the ties between peace and environmental activism that were at the root of the founding of the organization Greenpeace in Vancouver in 1971, when a group of activists, including draft resister Rex Weyler, set out to protest U.S. underground nuclear testing at the island of Amchitka off the west coast of Alaska.[2] Beyond the question of the environmental consequences of the production of nuclear weapons and the potential impact of their use, some attention was also paid by peace activists to the environmental implications of war itself, as in the case of the effects of defoliants such as napalm and Agent Orange used by the United States during the Vietnam War.

But while the relatedness of the pursuit of peace and concern with environmental degradation was perceived on the ground by activists in both the peace and environmental movements in the 1960s and 1970s, the junctures between peace and the environment began to be examined in a systematic way by scholars in the 1980s and 1990s, when the ecology's place in peace studies became established and academics could argue for the emergence of ecological or environmental peace as a distinct intellectual movement.[3]

A variety of analytical frameworks and classificatory schemes have been deployed to elucidate the interrelationship between peace and the environment. In general, there are three main foci:

- the environment as a casualty of war: the myriad ways in which military activities engender environmental degradation as an unintended consequence or deliberate strategy;
- the environment as a cause of war: an interrogation of environmental degradation as an actual or potential trigger of or exacerbating factor in violent conflict;
- environmental sustainability as a condition of peace: an examination of environmental protection as an actual or potential factor in peacemaking.

THE MILITARY ASSAULT ON THE BIOSPHERE

One of the most obvious, yet relatively little studied, intersections of environmental concerns and issues of war and peace is the adverse impact on the environment of preparing for and waging war. Until recently, the military has tended to escape scrutiny in discussions of environmental degradation, in spite of accumulating evidence that, collectively, the world's militaries are the single worst perpetrator of environmental destruction. As the world's largest institutional consumer of energy,[4] the Pentagon alone is responsible for emitting more greenhouse gases than the vast majority of countries; and the world's militaries are the biggest producer of toxic waste on earth, to cite just two such sobering statistics.

It is in the last two decades that the effects of military activity on the environment have begun to be tracked and studied more systematically, confirming that military operations take an incalculable toll on the global environment. This damage encompasses the deliberate destruction of the environment and natural resources as a military strategy as well as the unintended consequences of military preparation, production and warfare. And both forms of assault on the environment have long histories. Intentional environmental disruption and destruction has been a strategy of war from time immemorial, but with the advent in the twentieth century of new and more noxious chemical and biological agents, the potential and actual damage of such actions is vastly more far-reaching and long-lived. The novel concept of "ecocide" gained currency precisely with the deliberate use of chemical agents by the U.S. military during the Vietnam War to cripple the enemy by defoliating forests that served as cover and to destroy crops that provided sustenance.[5] It was this issue in large part that spurred the introduction of the first international legal provisions aimed at prohibiting environmental warfare.[6]

The 1991 Gulf War offers a more recent instance of scorched earth tactics, with the catastrophic Iraqi torching of Kuwaiti oil fields and the dumping of millions of barrels of Kuwaiti oil into the Gulf, as well as the U.S. bombing of Iraqi oil refineries, with predictably but incalculably devastating environmental consequences including massive damage to marine ecosystems, decimation of marine life and birds.[7] Burning continuously for more than a month, the oil fires alone released an estimated five hundred thousand metric tons per day of oil-related pollutants.[8] The Turkish military's burning of forests as part of its counterinsurgency strategy against the Kurdistan Worker's Party in the early 1990s is another very contemporary example of low-tech environmental warfare, as is the Israeli Defence Forces' destruction of hundreds of thousands of fruit-bearing trees and especially olive groves[9]—a form of economic/environmental warfare that dates back far enough in human history to have been the object of a biblical injunction.[10]

Another very current case that sits ambiguously between calculated and unintended environmental damage by armed forces is the use of armor, munitions and missiles manufactured from depleted uranium (DU), a metal made from low-level radioactive waste from nuclear weapons production and nuclear power generation which has a half-life measured in billions of years. DU weapons were used by the U.S. military in the Balkans, Iraq, and Afghanistan, releasing many tons of DU into the environment in the form of large fragments and dust which are chemically and radiologically toxic. Although there is continuing controversy about the precise health and environmental risks of DU, there is evidence that it produces widespread contamination of ground surfaces and groundwater, and it is suspected as a possible cause of cancer and birth defects, prompting wide-ranging calls for a ban based on a precautionary approach.[11]

Although most of the environmental consequences of military activity in war and in peace time are not intended, the devastation is no less real. At its most extreme, as in the case of British testing of anthrax on the Scottish island of Gruinard during World War II and U.S., British, and French nuclear testing in the Pacific in the 1950s and 1960s, entire islands have been obliterated or rendered completely uninhabitable by humans for indefinite time periods, not to mention the inestimable effects on other species. In the realm of "collateral" environmental damage, the production, testing and use of nuclear weapons has been most extensively documented. Here the research dates back decades, with pioneering studies such as *Nuclear Wastelands*,[12] which examined in great detail the health and environmental effects of nuclear weapons programs, ranging from the toxic effects of uranium mining in

Canada to Soviet dumping of hundreds of tons of radioactive waste into the sea of Japan in contravention of a worldwide ban. This type of research, as the authors of this landmark study stressed, is limited by the secrecy and deception in which nuclear weapons programs are invariably shrouded. But again, the environmental implications are staggering. Atmospheric, underground and underwater nuclear-weapons testing alone has released massive amounts of radioactivity into the environment.[13]

From a Canadian vantage point, the most notable recent illustration of the environmental impact of warfare is Afghanistan, a country suffering the consequences of decades of armed conflict, in addition to the current war. Already in 2003, the United Nations Environment Programme (UNEP) reported extensive environmental degradation directly and indirectly related to war and the attendant breakdown of governance: the forest cover has been destroyed, for example, by a combination of illegal timber trading, bombing, and the pressures of millions of displaced persons in need of firewood and building materials; there has been damage to groundwater, desiccation of wetlands, soil erosion, and loss of biodiversity.[14]

Afghanistan is also one of the most heavily land-mined countries in the world. And the innumerable explosives littering former conflict areas constitute yet another environmental scourge spawned by warfare. Beyond maiming and killing some twenty-four thousand people every year, and directly destroying vegetation and wildlife, landmines set in motion a chain of incidents leading to deforestation, soil erosion, pollution of water with heavy metals through decomposition of casings, the accumulation of toxins in blast sites, the destruction of wildlife habitat and the altering of food chains. And there are tens of millions of anti-personnel landmines (estimates range from 45 to 110 million) lurking in some seventy-five countries, not including even harder to estimate quantities of unexploded ordnance. Owing to both their direct and indirect effects, landmines rank as possibly "the most widespread, lethal and long-lasting form of pollution we have yet encountered."[15]

Displacing persons and producing refugees is another indirect form of military-induced environmental damage, as refugee populations have little choice but to encroach on fragile ecosystems. And in general the military is bad news for biodiversity. In addition to the direct annihilation of animal and plant life, it contributes, particularly in times of conflict, but also in peace time, to habitat destruction, the disruption of migratory routes, and the illegal predation of species at risk, among other injuries. Moreover, although never the top priority of most governments to begin with, the environment gets even shorter shrift during armed conflict, when government is often strained and disrupted and focused on more "immediate" problems.[16]

Of course, these are but a few examples of the extensive adverse impact of warfare and military activity on the environment. And in light of the sheer complexity of the web of life in all its subtle interconnectedness, we need to bear in mind the myriad uninvestigated and undocumented effects, especially "sublethal" effects (for example, the disruption of the reproductive cycles of various species of wildlife caused by toxicity from depleted uranium or white phosphorous) many of which will remain unknown. As one review of the state of research in the area of the ecology of warfare concludes, there is a dearth of studies that consider cumulative and/or multiple impacts of warfare on ecosystems.[17]

In addition to insistence on the need for more research to fill in the tremendous gaps in knowledge of the environmental consequences of military activity, a point stressed repeatedly in discussions of military impact on the environment is the inadequacy of international and national legislation designed to protect the environment from the ravages of war as well as from peace-time military operations. In November 2009, UNEP published a report aimed at strengthening the legal framework for environmental protection during armed conflict.[18] But Laurent Hourcle has pointed out that even if there were a robust legal framework for environmental protection in situations of armed conflict, there would have to be adequate mechanisms of enforcement; not only are these currently lacking, but as Hourcle notes, nations are not rushing to develop them.[19]

Finally, there is the oft-repeated point that the scandalously disproportionate consumption of resources—natural (oil, land, minerals) and financial—by the global military represents a lost opportunity to invest in mitigating environmental degradation and engage in environmental protection (an argument that applies with equal force to many other realms chronically neglected throughout much of the world, purportedly for lack of funding, such as health, welfare and education). To amend Eisenhower's famous lines: Every warship launched and every rocket fired signifies also a theft from future generations of humans and from all the other species with whom we share the planet.

With respect to this dimension of the nexus between the environment and issues of war and peace, even this very cursory glance yields little in the way of encouraging signs for either peace or the environment, especially considering the unceasing escalation of global military spending, which increased by some 45 percent in the 10 years between 1998 and 2008, reaching an unprecedented USD1.55 trillion,[20] a figure that is forecast to grow.[21] On a wishful note, Lothar Brock has suggested that unfolding knowledge of the disastrous environmental effects of war may spark international pressure to avoid wars for ecological reasons.[22] Certainly, the innumerable and devastating environmental casualties of military operations constitute yet another pressing argument for peace.

A LOOMING THREAT TO PEACE?

Paradoxically, it is virtually the opposite angle that dominates discussions of the relationship between peace and the environment. Rather than coming to grips with the consequences of armed conflict for environmental degradation, the talk in high places revolves more and more around the consequences of environmental degradation for the likelihood of armed conflict.

Since the end of the Cold War, the environmental crisis has increasingly come to be regarded as a potential source of violent conflict, and the now abounding references in the popular press to "resource wars," "water wars" and "climate wars" reflect a creeping militarization of discourse around the environmental crisis. Warnings by eminent scientists and statesmen in the North that in the coming decades the world will be plunged into a series of violent conflicts owing to the confluence of resource scarcity, climate change and demographic pressure are now commonplace.[23] Images of an invasion of "environmental refugees" are regularly evoked in the media. Rather than partaking of the language proper to ecology, which emphasizes the planetary interdependence of species and ecosystems, such talk is redolent of a Hobbesian war of each against all in casting environmental crisis as the catalyst of desperate competition among human societies culminating in a violent contest for survival.

The now common pronouncements in the press and by dignitaries, scientists and policy planners linking climate change with looming violent conflict elide a protracted debate over the concept of "environmental security" that now spans four decades and figures as the most controversial effort to link questions of war and peace with environmental issues.

Environmental security has been defined in different ways by different people. For some, the concept was simply a reflection of the growing awareness of the gravity of environmental degradation and an attempt to draw attention to the urgency of the crisis by emphasizing the risk to humanity's survival. In the 1980s, scholars such as Arthur Westing, a pioneer in documenting the military's impact on the environment, saw impending ecological catastrophe as warranting a reconsideration of what had traditionally been conceived as a threat to security. As they saw it, the global environmental crisis constituted as much, if not more, of a threat to peace and human survival as nuclear war insofar as a sustainable habitat for human and other life represented the most fundamental condition of peace.

In the same vein, the linkage of the environment and security figured in Chapter 11 of the 1987 Brundtland Report, *Our Common Future*, and in many UN documents, as a handmaiden in the quest for "sustainable development," highlighting first of all the perils of nuclear and other weapons of mass destruction for the environment. As articulated in the Brundtland Report,[24] this approach to the environment as a peace and security issue also invokes environmental stress as a potential thread in the "web of causality" associated with conflict, but affirms that where the environment is concerned, security can never be ensured by military means; it views the nation state, along with the very notion of national sovereignty, as ill-suited to deal with threats to shared ecosystems. The thrust of Chapter 11 is distinctly antimilitarist and the text explicitly calls for a complete rethinking of the concept of security.

In these cases, the reference to environmental security is intended to promote a perception of environmental degradation as a threat to the collective welfare of humanity and, in some readings, a spur to changes in the kinds of practices that produce perilous kinds and degrees of environmental degradation.

In its most publicized form, however, the idea of environmental security centers on the notion that environmental degradation functions as an actual and potential catalyst of violent conflict among and/or within states, and as such poses a threat to national security, as conventionally conceived. The controversy surrounding this question has reheated in recent years in connection with the mounting evidence of the devastating implications of global warming—drought, extreme weather, coastal flooding, degradation of agricultural land and scarcity of fresh water in some areas, and so on—and the attendant warnings about the looming threat of violent conflict, giving rise to a reprise in the new millennium of many of the same disputes over the notion of environmental security that were waged in the 1980s and 1990s.[25]

It was with the conclusion of the Cold War that the concept of environmental conflict first gained popular currency, notably with the publication in the February 1994 issue of *The Atlantic Monthly* of an article by Robert D. Kaplan entitled, *The Coming Anarchy*.[26] In his piece, Kaplan identified the environment as *the* national security question of the twenty-first century, wielding as evidence the work of Canadian scholar Thomas Homer-Dixon, who has been pivotal in the last 20 years in advancing the thesis that environmental degradation, in the form, for example, of water stress and soil erosion, is likely indirectly to trigger or exacerbate violent conflict, primarily in the form of civil war in those (poor) countries most vulnerable and ill-prepared to adapt to environmental shocks, giving rise to a flood of "environmental refugees."

Whereas Homer-Dixon is considered, even by staunch critics, to be scholarly and cautious,[27] Kaplan's piece was sensationalist and alarmist, referring to the environment as "a hostile power" and evincing an attitude of contempt toward the lot of the poor countries of the global South—the anticipated big losers in the environmental wars—delivered irremediably into chaos, violence and totalitarianism. He painted a portrait of the industrialized world with its great reserves of wealth and resources and its cutting-edge technology as equipped to adapt to the challenges of a degraded natural environment and a world of increasingly scare resources. In his vision, world population growth, environmental despoliation, and ethnic and religious tensions are the ingredients of a future resembling dystopian fictions such as *Blade Runner* and *Soylent Green*, and he intimated that the rich countries should hasten to buttress themselves against the threats posed by a global South descending into social and political havoc accelerated by the effects of climate change. In a post–Cold War world, it is a fortress mentality, Kaplan urged, that should define U.S. foreign policy.

Another widely publicized contribution to what is called the "securitization" of the environmental question appeared in 2003 in the form of a Pentagon-commissioned report by CIA consultant Peter Schwartz and Doug Randall.[28] It sought to analyze the implications for U.S. national security of an abrupt climate change scenario that would entail a significant drop in temperature in Europe, North America, and Asia and a rise in temperature in Australia, Africa, and South America, leading, the authors speculated, to aggressive wars over food, water, and energy. Indeed, according to Schwartz and Randall, war will become the defining fact of human existence, and there is likely to be a proliferation of nuclear weapons. They anticipate the building of fortress states by the United States and Australia, as these are the two states with the reserves and resources necessary to attain self-sufficiency. Referring to the United States, they wrote, "Borders will be strengthened around the country to hold back unwanted starving immigrants from the Caribbean islands . . . Mexico, and South America."

Even more recently in April 2007, a report was published by a group of retired high-ranking American officers[29] that considers various grim consequences of climate change—resource wars, climate refugees, the threat of eco-terrorism—and describes climate change as a "threat multiplier," posing risks for international security and a threat to U.S. national interests. The authors recommend integrating policies for combating climate change into national security and defense strategies.

Unlike Kaplan and Schwartz and Randall, they call upon the American government to act to reduce greenhouse gas emissions in order to mitigate the potentially catastrophic effects of climate change and to help the most vulnerable nations improve their capacity to cope with those effects. At the same time, the report alludes to the Cold War and the strategy of containment in a way that conjures up an axis of environmental evil—it is never quite clear from the analogy whether it is climate change that is the object of containment or the poor nations subject to its dire effects.

Alongside concerns about the future conflicts that are liable to arise as a result of environmental degradation, there is also a raft of analyses of current conflicts as precipitated or fuelled by environmental factors; the Darfur conflict is sometimes held up as one of the first "climate wars" in the sense that it is thought by some to be driven by the movement of nomadic herders propelled by desertification, itself partly attributable to climate change, to migrate into farming areas where they began competing with pastoralists for arable land and access to water. Thus, UN Secretary General Ban Ki Moon described Darfur in a *Washington Post* column on June 16, 2007, as "an ecological crisis arising at least in part from climate change."

From its inception in the 1970s and 1980s, this trend toward the securitization of the environmental question has elicited a barrage of criticism from scholars and others who have sought to expose the questionable premises and assumptions on which the environmental conflict thesis, particularly in its more facile forms, rests. Some of the most searching critical perspectives on the concept of environmental security come from the ranks of the peace research community; they tend to be situated in the positive peace research tradition that relates causes of violent conflict to oppressive systems, and they often share much with the ongoing left critique of neo-Malthusian readings of the environmental crisis as misguided in their propensity to naturalize scarcity and demographic pressures, thus obscuring the socio-structural determinants of these problems.[30] In addition, they advance the argument that the frames of reference typical of security discourse are antithetical to what is needed to arrive at a sustainable and just world. The critique is very wide-ranging and space allows for only a brief overview.

It is argued, for instance, that at its narrowest, the concept of environmental security reduces what we understand of the environment to discrete resources—land, water, timber, oil, and various minerals—rather than conceiving it as a series of complex ecosystems; thus already at the outset we are faced with a reductionist and misleading view of what constitutes the environment. As Ken Conca has observed, the very emphasis on scarcity evokes the metaphor of the market, and "we are encouraged to think of the environment as a scarce commodity with market value."[31]

Then there is the matter of scarcity itself. The argument that scarce resources cause or contribute to conflict tends to naturalize the existence of scarcity, making it a quantitative limit rather than a relative and socially determined state. And even granted the existence of ultimate limits to carrying capacity, the question arises: whose scarcity is the target of security concerns? Many critics of environmental security maintain that the problem of conflict over resources lies with the nature of societies and not with nature itself, to borrow a phrase from Lothar Brock,[32] and thus the massive economic disparities that mark the North-South divide are more important as a source of conflict over environmental issues than the relative scarcity of non-renewable resources. Moreover, the focus in much environmental security discourse around resource wars tends to be on potential and actual armed conflict over resources in the global South, rather than on the resource dimension of armed aggression on the part of the hyperdeveloped industrial nations, as in the case of the Gulf wars. Thus, for critics, the fact of inequitable global resource consumption and the question of "whose scarcity" are fundamental to a critical examination of environmental security as traditionally conceived, a point to which we will return.

Similarly, there are problems with the understanding of "security." While the concept is highly contested and there have been many efforts in the last forty years to broaden its compass and redefine it,[33] critics argue that security is still commonly understood from the vantage point of the Realist school of international relations, the Cold War paradigm and a framework of states' interests, all of which are unsuitable to understanding or addressing environmental problems. It is a common objection that because the traditional "referent object" of security (that which is to be secured) is the state and, because the military is viewed as the privileged instrument for protecting the security of the state, environmental security is unavoidably bound up with notions of national sovereignty and militarism. This concern was a central theme of one of the most widely cited critiques of environmental security over the last two decades. In Daniel Deudney's 1990 essay, "The Case Against Linking Environmental Degradation and National Security," he argues that the notion of environmental security rests on eliding the qualitative difference between a military threat (which is mainly external, national in scope, highly intentional and violent) and an environmental threat.[34] Deudney argues further that because security is indelibly associated with nationalism and an us-versus-them mentality, linking the environment and security would likely lead to misrepresenting the environmental threat as a threat from without and even blaming other nations for it, when what is urgently needed is a one-planet mindset, a concerted international response and transnational solutions.[35]

Critics of environmental security tend to agree with Deudney that in the contemporary world and especially in light of ecological interdependence, there is no security to be had at the national level; they argue implicitly or explicitly for a new approach to security, such as that embodied in the concepts of human security[36] and ecological (as opposed to environmental) security,[37] or reject the use of the language of security altogether as inapposite and detrimental in connection with the environmental crisis.

As Conca puts it, rather than stressing planetary interdependence, environmental security "reinforces the notion that societies can and should seek to insulate themselves from the effects of global environmental change."[38] In a very real sense, it is the disturbances to the prevailing global order likely to be wrought by environmental destruction that become the object of concern in environmental security discourse, rather than the fundamental issue of environmental destruction and the practices that engender it. The standard linkage of environment and security also tends to favor the status quo, which is at counterpurposes with the civilizational sea of change that any hope of addressing the environmental crisis must entail. As David Mutimer explains, "Because security aims to protect a referent from threat, it will tend to privilege the present condition of that referent."[39]

Then there is the very thorny and highly contested issue of what role environmental factors do actually play in conflict. It is this question that has generated the most intense and ongoing debate. Critics of the environmental security thesis do not dispute the grim reality of climate change and the environmental devastation that it may hold in store for human civilization, and particularly for the poorest and most vulnerable nations; nor do they typically deny any and all links between environmental degradation and conflict. But they point out that the many research studies have yielded very contradictory results with respect to the effects of resource scarcity on conflict[40] and that despite the intuitive appeal of the hypothesis that environmental degradation may, does, and will issue in violent conflict, the preponderance of evidence thus far suggests that environmental degradation can perhaps exacerbate intrastate (rather than interstate) conflict, but even then only in conjunction with many other precipitating and causal factors.

Moreover, many claims for the environmental conflict thesis are based on studies of places that seem "woefully overdetermined for conflict,"[41] rendering it difficult to isolate the role of environmental drivers. Indeed, one of the principal arguments adduced by environmental security critics concerns the often overly simplistic view of the causal pathways from environmental degradation to violent conflict. They point out that environmental degradation is never an independent variable in the roots of conflict and emphasize how difficult it is to disentangle the social, economic, cultural, and environmental causes, warning against the error of "environmental determinism."[42] In a particularly scathing attack, Rohan d'Souza charges the proponents of "Green War" (including Homer-Dixon and Kaplan) with erasing the manner in which aspects of political economy, histories of exploitation, and structured inequalities influence and shape relationships between power, the environment, and the social production of scarcity, and of seeing wars not as resulting from "specific economic and political dynamics and forms of power but instead from a simple quantitative unsettling between societies and their resources."[43]

Another bone of contention concerns the case studies. The critics argue that the linkage between environmental degradation and armed conflict often rests on a tendentious selection of cases or, as Idean Salehyan frames the objection, a failure to "look at the dogs that do not bark";[44] researchers examine only cases with violent outcomes, so this skews the results toward confirmation of the hypothesis.

Darfur is a case in point. The role of climate change is disputable since the conflict is, of course, immensely complex and overdetermined, and there are other compelling explanations for soil exhaustion and disenfranchisement of local people from their land, such as the introduction of mechanized farming by Northern elites under the impetus of the World Bank.[45] At the same time, there are many places where problems like water scarcity, desertification, and famine have not issued in conflict. "In short, resource scarcity, natural disasters, and long-term climatic shifts are ubiquitous, while armed conflict is rare; therefore environmental conditions by themselves cannot predict violent outbreaks."[46]

Beyond the question of the validity of the causal linkage, there are questions raised about both the ideological functions and the policy implications of the linkage. Although he has since turned his attention to other dimensions of the environmental security debate, in 2001 Jon Barnett published a study that sought to unpack the unproven and politically loaded assumptions underlying mainstream environmental security thinking, arguing that it is often designed to deflect criticism of the overweening privilege of the North and project the environmental crisis as a foreign enemy lurking in the global South.

> "The environment-conflict literature is almost entirely premised on the ethnocentric assumption that people in the South will resort to violence in times of resource scarcity. Rarely, if ever is the same argument applied to people in the industrialized North. The peace and security being referred to is the peace and security of the industrialized states, not the positive peace and security to which the majority of the world's people are entitled. This Northern peace is a negative peace, and its security is resistance to change."[47]

As Geoffrey Dabelko and P. J. Simmons sum up this line of criticism, environmental security discourse "focuses disproportionate attention and blame" for environmental degradation on the global South, creating an us-versus-them perspective and diverting attention away from the responsibility of Northern countries by virtue of their economic practices and consumption habits.[48]

The racist implications emerge clearly in statements such as this by James R. Lee of the American University writing in the *Washington Post* on January 4, 2009:

> "We're used to thinking of climate change as an environmental problem, not a military one, but it's long past time to alter that mindset. Climate change may mean changes in Western lifestyles, but in some parts of the world, it will mean far more. Living in Washington, I may respond to global warming by buying a Prius, planting a tree or lowering my thermostat. But elsewhere, people will respond to climate change by building bomb shelters and buying guns."[49]

And there's not even a hint here that the tree-planting, Prius-driving folks in the North who consume vastly more of the world's energy and other resources than those in the global South may bear a heavy burden of responsibility for the havoc wreaked by climate change,[50] or that, through the IMF, Northern elites have imposed structural adjustment programs on countries in the global South that result in environmentally devastating practices such as large-scale deforestation, which in turn contributes to climate change by eliminating sinks for carbon dioxide emissions. As Simon Dolby, another distinguished critic of the uses and abuses of environmental security, observes, by casting environmental crisis in terms of "external" threats, the dominant discourse on environmental security can easily be enlisted in support of a "global managerialist" agenda on the part of Northern states intended to preserve their unsustainable and inequitable patterns of consumption.[51]

Similarly, the allusions to a possible "invasion" of environmental refugees and the violence to which this mass migration is expected to give rise can betray a fear rooted in Northern privilege. It is also a hypothesis fraught with difficulties. Some critics maintain that little empirical evidence exists to support the linkage of environmental degradation and migration.[52] And again the argument is made that migration is an overdetermined phenomenon, making it difficult to disentangle the possible environmental causes of migration from the social, political, and economic motives. Moreover, environmental problems are typically also political problems stemming from human practices, approaches to resource management, issues of access, and so on.

In a discussion of the predictions in the Stern Review that two hundred million people will be displaced by climate change in the next four decades, Henrik Urdal stresses that while the adverse effects of climate change should not be minimized, the processes of sea-level rise and soil and water degradation are likely to be gradual rather than abrupt, leaving time for mitigation and adaptation, and that in any case the majority of those forced to migrate will not cross international borders,[53] contrary to some of the more paranoid environmental security scenarios.

Looking at a series of recent studies and surveying the state of the debate, Salehyan also underscores the ideological function of claims regarding the causal links between environmental degradation and violent conflict, observing that, too often, the role of political institutions in managing and redistributing resources and managing or failing to manage conflict is overlooked, which enables decision-makers to deflect responsibility for civil wars and human rights violations.[54]

From the inception of the environmental security debate, critics have consistently raised the question of whether the attempt to make the environment a matter of national security does not originate in the desire on the part of the security community, especially in the United States, to assure itself a central role in the post–Cold War world and whether efforts to marry the environment to concerns about security, particularly as that concept has traditionally been understood, represent a bid to build a case for an increased role of the military in the societal quest for solutions to environmental problems. Thus, discussing the 2007 National Security and Climate Change report, Gwynne Dyer writes, "What they are selling is a mission. The next mission of the U.S. Armed Forces is going to be the long struggle to maintain stability as climate change continually undermines it. The 'war on terror' has more or less had its day, and, besides, climate change is a real, full-spectrum challenge that may require everything from special forces to aircraft carriers."[55] And to return to Jon Barnett's critique of environmental security as ideology, the ultimate aim of environmental security discourse is arguably to set the stage for eventual military intervention in "defense" of the overconsumption of global resources by wealthy states.

For some, wedding the issue of environmental degradation to the concept of security is a double-edged sword, to the extent that it can be seen as a strategy to highlight the urgency of environmental problems and place them among the highest priorities of government, as well as paving the way for the possibility of recourse to exceptional measures that would move us beyond current constraints on the capacity to act. For others, the risks outweigh the benefits.

As scholars such as Nils Gleditsch, Daniel Deudney, and Jon Barnett stress, looking at the ecological crisis from the vantage point of security cannot fail to have an impact on the way we go about attempting to remedy the problem and is at odds with understanding it as a common global problem that requires supranational solutions and an unprecedented level of international cooperation since the environment has no national frontiers. While the critics of environmental security tend to agree that the effects of climate change and pollution, as well as dwindling nonrenewable—and now also renewable resources—constitute the most serious challenge on humanity's horizon, they fear that securitizing the environmental crisis, especially in the absence of consensus on a new conception of security unhitched from conventional assumptions about safeguarding national interest by military means, is likely to lead to narrow and unsuitable responses based on seeing the environmental crisis through a missile tube or a gun-sight, to borrow David Mutimer's phrase.[56] As Jon Barnett and W. Neil Adger sum up the implications for policy:

> "If the economically and politically powerful developed countries that also emit large amounts of greenhouse gases primarily understand vulnerability to climate change in developing countries as a risk to their national security through migration or violent conflict, then their responses may be more weighted towards increasing border protection and defence spending, rather than towards the reduction of emissions and efforts to foster adaptation."[57]

What role, if any, the military could or should play in connection with environmental protection is another aspect of the debate around environmental security, especially as, contentious or not, environmental threats are increasingly being incorporated into national security frameworks. In the United States, for instance, climate change now figures as a concern in the Quadrennial Defense Review, where it is cited as a possible source of conflict and as a factor in military operations, "placing a burden to respond on civil institutions and militaries around the world."[58]

In his pathbreaking essay on the place of the environment in peace studies, Ken Conca judged as incoherent the suggestion by a group of international organizations that the military be conscripted to support sustainable development and conservation of biodiversity in the absence of any critical reflection on the nature and function of the military and the interests it represents.[59] Certainly, there are innumerable examples of profound conflicts of interest between military objectives and environmental protection, where the military works actively to defeat environmental aims or evade environmental regulations, from the Brazilian military's attempts to foil efforts to preserve the Amazonian rainforest habitat of the Yanomami indigenous people[60] to the U.S. Navy's sonar testing program that is known to harm whales and other marine mammals.[61] At the same time, even among scholars critical of the dominant approach to environmental security, some allow a possible role for the military, as for Geoffrey Dabelko, who has pointed out that although traditional military tools are mismatched to address environmental problems, the military has other capacities, such as engineering, that do not entail the use of force and that could be deployed in environmental remediation projects, for example, and efforts to reduce vulnerability to climate change.[62]

Australian environmental scholar Robyn Eckersley launched a lively debate a few years back by attempting to make a case for "ecological intervention" and "ecological defence," military intervention to prevent specific types of environmental damage on the models of humanitarian intervention and humanitarian defence.[63] This stance came as a surprise to many, since Eckersley is one of the scholars who, without entirely rejecting the relevance of the security framework in contending with the worldwide environmental crisis, echoes and advances many of the criticisms of the trend toward the securitization of environmental problems: she advises great caution about treating a non-military threat as a military threat, for example, since it fosters a view of the ecological crisis as an external problem and displaces ecological risks onto communities that are ultimately the least responsible for problems such as climate change, the most vulnerable to its effects in the short and medium term, and the least well-equipped to cope with those effects.[64] While maintaining that in most instances military intervention is "a singularly inappropriate means" to address environmental problems and keenly aware of the deep contradictions associated with the theory and practice of humanitarian intervention, she nevertheless advanced the argument that certain types of transboundary environmental emergencies, both in cases where human life is threatened and where it is not, could warrant a military response. The idea of providing justification, even under very strict conditions, for the use of armed force to prevent crimes against nature elicited a spate of objections and questions from scholars skeptical about the validity (on legal, philosophical, political and ethical grounds) and implications of opening the door to military intervention of this kind.[65] But this type of reflection becomes more pressing since the military's involvement in environmental remediation is no longer a matter of theoretical debate, as attested by its mobilization this year to help with the clean-up of the worst oil spill in history, the BP spill in the Gulf of Mexico.

Most of the leading critics of environmental security conclude that in practical terms the securitization of environmental issues has had a negative impact to date. For many years, Jon Barnett warned against the likely colonization of environmental issues by the logic and priorities of national security. More recently, he suggests that this has indeed come to pass—that rather than greening security, the integration of environmental concerns into the security framework has militarized environmental issues; and he makes the crucial observation that environmental security has not advanced the work of the environmental and peace movements insofar as it has not led to a trade-off of military security for environmental security or to the allocation of greater resources for tackling environmental problems. Defense budgets are not shrinking to the advantage of environmental protection.[66]

Although the environmental conflict thesis has been thoroughly challenged by critics, its currency has not diminished; if anything, it appears to be gaining ground—not the first time by any means that a contested claim has become prevailing belief, even among some activists committed both to peace and environmental activism. It is telling that the first environmental activist to win a Nobel Peace Prize, Kenyan Greenbelt Movement founder Wangari Mathathai, echoed the environmental conflict thesis in her speech: "It is evident that many wars are fought over resources which are now becoming increasingly scarce. If we conserved our resources better, fighting over war would not then occur."[67]

GREENER PASTURES FOR PEACE?

One major criticism of environmental security as a concept and a subdiscipline is that it tends to focus on environmental degradation as an actual or potential trigger of or exacerbating factor in violent conflict without attending adequately to the possibility that environmental problems could, on the contrary, serve to promote cooperation and thereby contribute to peacebuilding. In fact, some scholars maintain that the threat and reality of ecological degradation can just as easily act as a precipitating factor in cooperation as conflict, and that therefore the exclusive focus on conflict in many analyses of environmental security is misguided and misleading.[68] Similarly, from the perspective of peacebuilding, it is arguable that even in those instances where environmental degradation could prove a catalyst of conflict the appropriate response would be to minimize the likelihood of violence by ensuring that mechanisms exist for nonviolent conflict resolution.[69]

Ken Conca is a scholar who has pursued this line of argument. His 1994 essay, "In the Name of Sustainability: Peace Studies and Environmental Discourse," to which we referred earlier, was one of the seminal scholarly reflections on the impact of the theory and practice of environmentalism on the discipline of peace studies. Although he identified some tensions between the underlying assumptions of peace studies and one authoritarian strain of mainstream environmentalism informed by neo-Malthusian thinking, Conca saw promise, for example, in the emphasis on interdependency by both ecology and peace studies and on the need to build forms of community that transcend national borders. More recently, he has made the case for the potential of environmental degradation as a catalyst for cooperation rather than conflict.[70] Calling for a research agenda devoted to environmental peacemaking as an alternative to the contentious and counterproductive environmental security framework,[71] he seeks to reframe the fundamental question such that, instead of asking whether and how environmental degradation leads to conflict, scholars would seek to discover whether environmental cooperation can contribute to peace in the sense of "rendering violent conflict less likely or less imaginable."[72]

Conca is one of several scholars who believe the environment can create opportunities for peacebuilding. Lothar Brock is another. He maintains, for instance, that by encouraging states to communicate and cooperate on a regular basis, environmental problems may render the use of force less acceptable in international conflict resolution.[73] This theoretical twinning of peacebuilding and environmental cooperation finds practical expression in the growing practice of integrating environmental issues into conflict resolution processes, as well as in the phenomenon of "peace parks," a special form of transboundary protected area, which can be loosely defined as "any conservation zone that, by virtue of multiple jurisdictions could either help resolve a conflict or maintain peace."[74]

In their 2002 book, Conca and Dabelko assembled a series of case studies, many of which involved water-sharing arrangements, as a preliminary inquiry into the environmental peacebuilding hypothesis. On that basis, the editors drew some mixed conclusions concerning the capacity of environmental cooperation to create a climate of trust, a recognition of mutual benefit among governments, along with transnational ties, all of which may be conducive to peace.

This hypothesis is being tested by the United Nations Environment Programme. UNEP's Expert Advisory Group on Environment, Conflict and Peacebuilding, established in 2008, issued a report discussing the connections between natural resource disputes and intrastate conflicts and calling for a stronger focus on environmental issues (by which it primarily means resource management) in post-conflict planning, on the grounds that conflicts involving natural resources are far more likely to relapse in the first five years following a settlement.[75]

Seeing conservation as a practical tool in settling conflicts or maintaining peace in instances where environmental issues may not even be implicated in a conflict is seen to go a step further in the direction of environmental peacebuilding, as in the case of "peace parks," which seek to use conservation as a means of conflict mitigation. The first such peace park was established in the Cordillera del Condor region between Ecuador and Peru. After decades of territorial conflict, the two nations signed a peace treaty overseen by four guarantor nations, which included the creation of a conservation zone at the newly established border.

Supporters of the peace park strategy agree that establishing transboundary conservation areas are never sufficient to bring about peace between adversaries, but they maintain that environmental issues can help to open up dialogue between adversaries and surmount deadlocks by appealing to a common interest—avoiding ecological degradation—and a shared economic opportunity, typically in the form of ecotourism.

Naturally, peace parks are not without contradictions, as many scholars in the field hasten to point out, especially as conservation zones can and do spawn conflict.[76] They have been the object of bitter controversies on the ground, as the involvement of large international conservation groups and outside experts has sparked resentment from local interests. The parks are also sometimes seen to contribute to marginalizing indigenous communities, denying access to resources and even leading to forced relocation. They also come in for criticism on various counts from scholars of varying political perspectives. Rosaleen Duffy offers some especially trenchant objections. While confirming the need for international cooperation in environmental management, she argues that, far from politically neutral schemes for conservation and conflict mitigation, peace parks are enmeshed in market-oriented approaches to environmental management (especially the promotion of ecotourism) and neoliberal forms of global governance.[77] Such critical perspectives confute Nelson Mandela's oft-cited remarks about the complete consensus around the peace parks concept.[78] But defenders of peace parks see promise, provided certain conditions are met, including building in provisions for sustainable livelihoods.

NO PLANET, NO PEACE!

The importance of including environmental issues in peacemaking ultimately brings together both detractors and proponents of the linkage of environment and conflict. The former stress the possibility that environmental problems can, under certain circumstances, contribute to cooperation, confidence-building and conflict resolution; the latter see efforts to foster cooperation on environmental issues as vital to avoiding future conflict; a "precautionary peace policy,"[79] in Klaus Toepfer's phrase.

There is little doubt among scholars and policy planners that, in one form or another, the environment will loom ever larger in matters of war and peace, as states, species and individuals contend with climate change and all it entails, with desertification and the accumulation of vast amounts of hazardous waste, with habitat destruction (human and other) and the rapid erosion of biodiversity, and with all the other environmental ills which humankind is failing, tragically, to remedy.

BIBLIOGRAPHY

Ali, Saleem H., ed. *Peace Parks: Conservation and Conflict Resolution*. Cambridge, MA: MIT Press, 2007.

"Anarchy." *The Atlantic*. February 1994, www.theatlantic.com/doc/199402/anarchy.

Barnett, Jon. *The Meaning of Environmental Security*. London: Zed Books, 2001.

Barnett, Jon, and W. Neil Adger. "Climate Change, Human Security and Violent Conflict." *Political Geography,* vol. 26 (2007): 639–655.

BBC News. "Global Crisis 'to Strike by 2030.'" March 19, 2009, http://news.bbc.co.uk/1/hi/uk/7951838.stm.

Bearden, David M. "Exemptions from Environmental Law for the Department of Defense: Background and Issues for Congress, Congressional Research Service Report to Congress." May 15, 2007, http://www.fas.org/sgp/crs/natsec/RS22149.pdf.

Brown, Oli, Alec Crawford, and Christine Campeau. "Environmental Change and the New Security Agenda." Paper for the International Institute for Sustainable Development, June 2008.

Buckland, Ben. "A Climate of War? Stopping the Securitisation of Global Climate Change." Paper written for the International Peace Bureau, Geneva, June 2007.

CNA. "National Security and the Threat of Climate Change." Alexandria, USA: The CNA Corporation, 2007, http://securityandclimate.cna.org/.

Collins, Alan, ed. *Contemporary Security Studies*. Oxford: Oxford University Press, 2007.

Conca, Ken. "In the Name of Sustainability: Peace Studies and Environmental Discourse." *Peace & Change,* vol. 19, no. 2 (April 1994): 91–113.

Conca, Ken, and Geoffrey Dabelko, eds. *Environmental Peacemaking*. Washington, DC: Woodrow Wilson Center Press, 2002.

Dabelko, Geoffrey D. "Planning for Climate Change: The Security Community's Precautionary Principle." *Climatic Change,* vol. 96 (2009): 13–21.

Dalby, Simon. *Environmental Security*. Minneapolis: University of Minnesota Press, 2002.

Dalby, Simon, Mark Woods, Matthew Humphrey, et al. "Online Symposium on Ecological Intervention," http://www.cceia.org/resources/journal/21_3/feature_and_symposium/001.html.

Department of Defense. "An Abrupt Climate Change Scenario and Its Implications for United States National Security." Report prepared by Global Business Network (GBN), October 2003, www.gbn.org/ArticleDisplayServlet.srv?aid=26231.

Deudney, Daniel. "The Case Against Linking Environmental Degradation and National Security." *Millennium,* vol. 19, no. 3 (1990): 461–476.

Deudney, Daniel, and Richard Matthew, eds. *Contested Grounds*. Albany: State University of New York 1999.

Deweerdt, Sarah. "War and the Environment," *World Watch Magazine,* vol. 21, no. 1 (January/February 2008) http://www.worldwatch.org/node/5520.

Dodds, Felix, and Tim Pippard, eds. *Human and Environmental Security*. London: Earthscan, 2005.

D'Souza, Rohan. "'Benign Capitalism by Another Name,' Review of *Collapse*, by Jared Diamond." *Conservation and Society,* vol. 3, no. 1 (2005): 238–247.

Diehl, Paul F., and Nils Petter Gleditsch, eds. *Environmental Conflict*. Boulder, CO: Westview Press, 2001.

Dyer, Gwynne. *Climate Wars*. Toronto: Random House, 2008.

Eckersley, Robyn. "Ecological Intervention: Prospects and Limits." *Ethics & International Affairs*, vol. 21, no. 3 (Fall 2007): 275–96, http://www3.interscience.wiley.com/cgi-bin/fulltext/117999035/PDFSTART.

———. "Environmental Security, Climate Change, and Globalizing Terrorism," in *Rethinking Insecurity, War and Violence: Beyond Savage Globalization?*, Damian Grenfeld and Paul James, eds. New York: Routledge, 2009, 90–91.

Finger, Mathias. Paper presented to the Thirteenth General Conference of the International Peace Research Association, Groningen, July 3–7, 1990.

Flintan, Fiona. "Environmental Refugees—A Misnomer or a Reality." A Contribution to the Wilton Park Conference Report on Environmental Security and Conflict Prevention, March 1–3, 2001, http://www.ucc.ie/famine/GCD/Paper%20for%20Wilton%20Park.doc.

Homer-Dixon, Thomas. "Terror in the Weather Forecast." Op-ed piece, *New York Times*, April 24, 2007.

Homer-Dixon, Thomas, and Jessica Blitt. "Key Findings," in *EcoViolence: Links Among Environment, Population, and Security*, Thomas Homer-Dixon and Jessica Blitt, eds. Lanham, MD: Rowman and Littlefield, 1998, 223–228.

Hulme, Karen. *War Torn Environment.* Leiden, The Netherlands: Martinus Nijhoff, 2004.

International Institute for Strategic Studies. "Global Military Spending Unaffected By Recession," http://www.iiss.org/whats-new/iiss-in-the-press/february-2010/global-military-spending-unaffected-by-recession/.

International Physicians for the Prevention of Nuclear War and the Institute for Energy and Environmental Research. *Radioactive Heaven and Earth: The Health and Environmental Effects of Nuclear Weapons Testing In, On, and Above the Earth.* New York: Apex Press, 1991.

Johnson, Larry. "Iraqi Cancers, Birth Defects Blamed on U.S. Depleted Uranium." *Seattle Post-Intelligencer*, November 12, 2002.

Kegley, Charles, Jr. "Placing Global Ecopolitics in Peace Studies." *Peace Review,* vol. 9, no. 3 (1997): 425–430, http://www.informaworld.com/smpp/ftinterface~content=a787824215~fulltext=713240930.

Klare, Michael T. "The Pentagon vs. Peak Oil." *Alternet*, June 15, 2007, http://www.alternet.org/environment/54195/.

Lee, James R. *Washington Post*, January 4, 2009.

Machlis, Gary, and Thor Hanson. "Warfare Ecology." *BioScience,* vol. 58, no. 8 (September 2008): 729–736.

MSNBC.com. "Warming as Dangerous as War, U.N. Chief Says." March 1, 2007, http://www.msnbc.msn.com/id/17401890/.

Makhijani, Arjun, Howard Hu, and Katherine Yih, eds. *Nuclear Wastelands: A Global Guide to Nuclear Weapons Production and Its Health and Environmental Effects*. Cambridge, MA: MIT Press, 1995.

McNeely, Jeffrey A. "The Effects of War on Biodiversity in Tropical Forests." Paper presented to Conference on Extreme Conflicts in Tropical Forests, Osaka, Japan, November 4–7, 2001, http://www.envirosecurity.org/ges/EffectsWarOnBiodivTropForests2001.pdf.

Nordås, Ragnhild, and Nils Petter Gleditsch. "Climate Conflict: Common Sense or Nonsense?" Paper presented at the International Workshop on Human Security and Climate Change, Oslo, June 2005, www.graduateinstitute.ch/ . . . /Environmental-Security-Article-Nordas-Gleditsch.pdf.

Osler Hampson, Fen, et. al. *Madness in the Multitude: Human Security and World Disorder*. New York: Oxford University Press, 2002.

Raleigh, Clionadh, and Henrik Urdal. "Climate Change, Environmental Degradation and Armed Conflict." *Political Geography,* vol. 26 (2007): 674–694.

Ratner, Jonathan. "Global Military and Defence Sector Set to Grow." nationalpost.com, February 11, 2010, http://network.nationalpost.com/np/blogs/tradingdesk/archive/2010/02/11/military-and-defence-sector-set-to-grow.aspx#ixzz0fRy2sZwh.

Revkin, Andrew C. "Growing Pentagon Focus on Energy and Climate." *Dot Earth,* New York Times.com, February 1, 2010, http://dotearth.blogs.nytimes.com2010/02/01/growing-pentagon-focus- on-energy-and-climate.

Renner, Michael. *Fighting For Survival: Environmental Decline, Social Conflict, and the New Age of Insecurity*. New York: W.W. Norton, 1996.

Sarafa, Rami. "Roots of Conflict: Felling Palestine's Olive Trees." *Harvard International Review,* vol. 26 (2004): 24.

Salehyan, Idean. "'From Climate Change to Conflict?' No Consensus Yet." *Journal of Peace Research,* vol. 45, no. 3 (2008): 315–326.

Snyder, Craig, ed. *Contemporary Security Studies,* 2nd ed. London: Palgrave, 2008.

Toepfer, Klaus. "Putting Poverty to the Sword." From a 2005 message to the International Conference on the Conservation of Korea's Demilitarized Zone, http://www.dmzforum.org/Reference/Mandela-Turner%202005%20DMZ%20Forum%20Conference%20Address.pdf.

Torres Nachón, Claudio. "The Environmental Impacts of Landmines," in *Landmines and Human Security,* Richard A. Matthew, Bryan McDonald, and Keith R. Rutherford, eds. New York: SUNY Press, 2006.

UN. "Peace, Security Development, and the Environment," in *Our Common Future,* Report of the World Commission on Environment and Development, 1987, http://www.un-documents.net/ocf-11.htm.

UNEP. *Desk Study on the Environment in Iraq*. Geneva: UNEP, 2003.

———. *Afghanistan: Post-Conflict Environmental Assessment*. Geneva, 2003, http://postconflict.unep.ch/publications/afghanistanpcajanuary2003.pdf.

———. *From Conflict to Peacebuilding: the Role of Natural Resources and the Environment*. Geneva, 2009, http://www.unep.org/pdf/pcdmb_policy_01.pdf.

———. *Protecting the Environment during Armed Conflict*. November 2009, postconflict.unep.ch/publications/int_law.pdf.

Urdal, Henrik. "Demographic Aspects of Climate Change, Environmental Degradation and Armed Conflict." Paper for the United Nations Expert Group Meeting on Population, Distribution, Urbanization, Internal Migration and Development, New York, January 21–23, 2008.

Vanasselt, Wendy. "Armed Conflict, Refugees and the Environment," in *World Resources 2002–2004—Decisions for the Earth, Balance, Voice and Power*. Washington, DC: World Resources Institute, 2003, http://earthtrends.wri.org/text/environmental-governance/feature-43.html.

Weyler, Rex."Waves of Compassion: The Founding of Greenpeace." *UTNE Reader*, October 15, 2008, http://www.utne.com/archives/WavesofCompassion.aspx.

NOTES

1. The title of a 1990 paper by Mathias Finger presented to the Thirteenth General Conference of the International Peace Research Association, Groningen, July 3–7.

2. Rex Weyler relates the story in "Waves of Compassion: The Founding of Greenpeace," *UTNE Reader*, October 15, 2008, http://www.utne.com/archives/WavesofCompassion.aspx.

3. See Charles Kegley Jr., "Placing Global Ecopolitics in Peace Studies," *Peace Review*, vol. 9, no. 3 (1997): 425–430, http://www.informaworld.com/smpp/ftinterface~content=a787824215~fulltext=713240930.

4. Michael T. Klare, "The Pentagon vs. Peak Oil," *Alternet*, June 15, 2007, http://www.alternet.org/environment/54195/.

5. Sarah Deweerdt, "War and the Environment," *World Watch Magazine*, vol. 21, no. 1 (January/February 2008), http://www.worldwatch.org/node/5520.

6. Karen Hulme, *War Torn Environment* (Leiden, The Netherlands: Martinus Nijhoff, 2004), 9.

7. UNEP, *Desk Study on the Environment in Iraq* (Geneva: UNEP, 2003), 68.

8. Hulme, *War Torn*, 65.

9. Rami Sarafa, "Roots of Conflict: Felling Palestine's Olive Trees," *Harvard International Review*, vol. 26 (2004): 24.

10. Deuteronomy 20:19.

11. For an overview of the question, see Larry Johnson, "Iraqi Cancers, Birth Defects Blamed on U.S. Depleted Uranium," *Seattle Post-Intelligencer*, November 12, 2002.

12. Arjun Makhijani, Howard Hu, and Katherine Yih, eds. *Nuclear Wastelands: A Global Guide to Nuclear Weapons Production and Its Health and Environmental Effects* (Cambridge, MA: MIT Press, 1995).

13. On the effects of nuclear testing see International Physicians for the Prevention of Nuclear War and the Institute for Energy and Environmental Research, *Radioactive Heaven and Earth: The Health and Environmental Effects of Nuclear Weapons Testing In, On, and Above the Earth* (New York: Apex Press, 1991).

14. UNEP, *Afghanistan: Post-Conflict Environmental Assessment* (Geneva, Switzerland: UNEP, 2003), http://postconflict.unep.ch/publications/afghanistan pcajanuary2003.pdf.

15. From a 1994 Statement of the United Nations Secretary-General cited in Claudio Torres Nachón, "The Environmental Impacts of Landmines," in *Landmines and Human Security,* Richard A. Matthew, Bryan McDonald, and Keith R. Rutherford, eds. (New York: SUNY Press, 2006), 191.

16. This point is made forcefully by Wendy Vanasselt, "Armed Conflict, Refugees and the Environment," in *World Resources 2002–2004—Decisions for the Earth, Balance, Voice and Power* (Washington, DC: World Resources Institute, 2003), http://earthtrends.wri.org/text/environmental-governance/feature-43.html.

17. Gary Machlis and Thor Hanson, "Warfare Ecology," *BioScience,* vol. 58, no. 8 (September 2008): 732.

18. UNEP, *Protecting the Environment during Armed Conflict*, November 2009, postconflict.unep.ch/publications/int_law.pdf.

19. Hourcle, "Environmental Law of War," 687.

20. International Institute for Strategic Studies, "Global Military Spending Unaffected By Recession," http://www.iiss.org/whats-new/iiss-in-the-press/february-2010/global-military-spending-unaffected-by-recession/.

21. Jonathan Ratner, "Global Military and Defence Sector Set to Grow," nationalpost.com, February 11, 2010, http://network.nationalpost.com/np/blogs/tradingdesk/archive/2010/02/11/military-and-defence-sector-set-to-grow.aspx#ixzz0fRy2sZwh.

22. Brock, "Peace through Parks," 411.

23. For example, in his first speech about global warming on March 1, 2007, UN Secretary General Ban Ki Moon said that the climate crisis is likely to become a major driver of war and conflict ("Warming as Dangerous as War, U.N. Chief Says," msnbc.com, March 1, 2007, http://www.msnbc.msn.com/id/17401890/), while John Beddington, Britain's chief scientist, made headlines with his alarming statements about the violence in store for the world as a result of environmental crisis ("Global Crisis 'to Strike by 2030,'" BBC News, March 19, 2009, http://news.bbc.co.uk/1/hi/uk/7951838.stm).

24. "Peace, Security Development, and the Environment," in *Our Common Future,* Report of the World Commission on Environment and Development, 1987, http://www.un-documents.net/ocf-11.htm.

25. To cite just a few references, see the special issue of the journal *Political Geography,* vol. 26 (2007), devoted to the question of climate change and conflict; Idean Salehyan, "From Climate Change to Conflict? No Consensus Yet," *Journal of Peace*

Research, vol. 45, no. 3 (2008): 315–326; Ben Buckland, "A Climate of War? Stopping the Securitisation of Global Climate Change," paper written for the International Peace Bureau (Geneva, June 2007); and Ragnhild Nordås and Nils Petter Gleditsch, "Climate Conflict: Common Sense or Nonsense?" paper presented at the International Workshop on Human Security and Climate Change (Oslo, June 2005), www.graduateinstitute.ch/ . . . /Environmental-Security-Article-Nordas-Gleditsch.pdf.

26. http://www.theatlantic.com/doc/199402/anarchy.

27. For an example of Homer-Dixon's fairly circumspect conclusions, see Thomas Homer-Dixon and Jessica Blitt, "Key Findings" in Thomas Homer-Dixon and Jessica Blitt, eds., *EcoViolence: Links Among Environment, Population, and Security* (Lanham, MD: Rowman and Littlefield, 1998), 223–228. However, in popularizing his ideas, Homer-Dixon also glosses over many of the nuances that mitigate the claims. See his op-ed piece in the April 24, 2007, *New York Times* where he maintains, "Climate stress may well represent a challenge to international security just as dangerous—and more intractable—than the arms race between the United States and the Soviet Union during the cold war or the proliferation of nuclear weapons among rogue states today."

28. "An Abrupt Climate Change Scenario and Its Implications for United States National Security," report prepared by Global Business Network (GBN) for the Department of Defense (October 2003), www.gbn.org/ArticleDisplayServlet.srv?aid=26231.

29. CNA, "National Security and the Threat of Climate Change," Alexandria, USA: The CNA Corporation, 2007, http://securityandclimate.cna.org/.

30. See, for example, Simon Dalby's discussion of the "Malthusian spectre" in chapter two of his *Environmental Security* (Minneapolis: University of Minnesota Press, 2002).

31. Ken Conca, "In the Name of Sustainability: Peace Studies and Environmental Discourse," *Peace & Change*, vol. 19, no. 2 (April 1994): 104.

32. Brock, "Peace through Parks," 410.

33. Again, the literature on the subject is vast. For a brief overview, see, for example, David Mutimer, "Beyond Strategy: Critical Thinking in the New Security Studies" in *Contemporary Security Studies*, 2nd ed., Craig Snyder, ed. (London: Palgrave, 2008), 34–58.

34. Daniel Deudney, "The Case Against Linking Environmental Degradation and National Security," *Millennium*, vol. 19, no. 3 (1990): 461–476.

35. Deudney has reiterated and elaborated on his objections in subsequent essays; see, for example, "Environmental Security: A Critique," in *Contested Grounds*, Daniel Deudney and Richard Matthew, eds. (Albany: State University of New York, 1999), 187–219.

36. On human security, see Fen Osler Hampson, et. al., *Madness in the Multitude: Human Security and World Disorder* (New York: Oxford University Press, 2002). See also Felix Dodds and Tim Pippard, eds., *Human and Environmental Security* (London: Earthscan, 2005).

37. See Jon Barnett's development of the concept of ecological security in *The Meaning of Environmental Security* (London: Zed Books, 2001), 109–121.

38. Conca, "In the Name of Sustainability," 105.

39. Mutimer, "Beyond Strategy," 45.

40. See the summary in Clionadh Raleigh and Henrik Urdal, "Climate Change, Environmental Degradation and Armed Conflict," *Political Geography,* vol. 26 (2007): 674–694. Based on their own quantitative study, these authors conclude that environmental variables have only a moderate effect on the risk of civil conflict.

41. Ken Conca "The Case for Environmental Peacemaking," in *Environmental Peacemaking,* Ken Conca and Geoffrey Dabelko, eds. (Washington, DC: Woodrow Wilson Center Press, 2002), 6.

42. The term is used by Idean Salehyan in "From Climate Change to Conflict?" 318.

43. Rohan D'Souza, "Benign Capitalism by Another Name," review of *Collapse*, by Jared Diamond, *Conservation and Society,* vol. 3, no. 1 (2005): 242. In Homer-Dixon's case the accusation may be overstated: Henrik Urdal, himself a detractor of any facile linkage between environmental conditions and conflict, defends Homer-Dixon from similar charges levelled by other critics, pointing out that he does attend to the issue of resource distribution in several of his analyses. See "Demographic Aspects of Climate Change, Environmental Degradation and Armed Conflict," paper for the United Nations Expert Group Meeting on Population, Distribution, Urbanization, Internal Migration and Development (New York, January 21–23, 2008), 9.

44. Salehyan, "From Climate Change to Conflict?" 318.

45. This point is discussed by Michael Renner, who happens also to be a proponent of the linkage between climate change and the potential for armed conflict in *Fighting For Survival: Environmental Decline, Social Conflict, and the New Age of Insecurity* (New York: W.W. Norton, 1996), 68–72.

46. Salehyan, "From Climate Change to Conflict?" 319.

47. Barnett, *The Meaning of Environmental Security*, 53.

48. Dabelko and Simmons, "Environment and Security," 132.

49. James R. Lee, *Washington Post,* January 4, 2009.

50. For example, Africa, the continent on which Robert Kaplan fixated his fears in "The Coming Anarchy," produces negligible amounts of CO_2 (3.6 percent) by comparison with OECD countries.

51. Simon Dalby, "Threats from the South?" in *Contested Ground,* Daniel Deudney and Richard Matthew, eds. (Albany: State University of New York 1999), 160–163.

52. See, for example, Fiona Flintan, "Environmental Refugees—A Misnomer or a Reality," A Contribution to the Wilton Park Conference Report on Environmental Security and Conflict Prevention, March 1–3, 2001, http://www.ucc.ie/famine/GCD/Paper%20for%20Wilton%20Park.doc.

53. Urdal, "Demographic Aspects," 5.

54. Salehyan, "From Climate Change to Conflict?" 317.

55. Gwynne Dyer, *Climate Wars* (Toronto: Random House, 2008), 10.

56. Mutimer, "Beyond Strategy," 36.

57. Jon Barnett and W. Neil Adger, "Climate Change, Human Security and Violent Conflict," *Political Geography,* vol. 26 (2007): 649.

58. Cited by Andrew C. Revkin in "Growing Pentagon Focus on Energy and Climate," Dot Earth, NewYorkTimes.com, http://dotearth.blogs.nytimes.com2010/02/01/growing-pentagon-focus- on-energy-and-climate.

59. Conca, "In the Name of Sustainability," 107.

60. Jeffrey A. McNeely, "The Effects of War on Biodiversity in Tropical Forests," paper presented to Conference on Extreme Conflicts in Tropical Forests, Osaka, Japan, November 4–7, 2001, http://www.envirosecurity.org/ges/EffectsWarOnBiodiv TropForests2001.pdf.

61. David M. Bearden, "Exemptions from Environmental Law for the Department of Defense: Background and Issues for Congress," Congressional Research Service Report to Congress, May 15, 2007, 4–5, http://www.fas.org/sgp/crs/natsec/RS22149 .pdf.

62. Geoffrey D. Dabelko, "Planning for Climate Change: the Security Community's Precautionary Principle," *Climatic Change,* vol. 96 (2009): 18.

63. Robyn Eckersley, "Ecological Intervention: Prospects and Limits," *Ethics & International Affairs*, vol. 21, no. 3 (Fall 2007): 275–96, http://www3.interscience .wiley.com/cgi-bin/fulltext/117999035/PDFSTART.

64. Robyn Eckersley, "Environmental Security, Climate Change, and Globalizing Terrorism," in *Rethinking Insecurity, War and Violence: Beyond Savage Globalization?* Damian Grenfeld and Paul James, eds. (New York: Routledge, 2009), 90–91.

65. See the contributions by Simon Dalby, Mark Woods, Matthew Humphrey, and others to the online symposium on ecological intervention, http://www.cceia.org/resources/journal/21_3/feature_and_symposium/001.html.

66. Jon Barnett, "Environmental Security," in *Contemporary Security Studies,* Alan Collins, ed. (Oxford: Oxford University Press, 2007), 199. Nevertheless, he also sees the concept of environmental security as retaining some value for certain ends, such as drawing attention to environmental dimensions of social vulnerability and communicating the urgent character of the impact of climate change impacts on atoll countries.

67. Cited in Oli Brown, Alec Crawford, and Christine Campeau, "Environmental Change and the New Security Agenda," paper for the International Institute for Sustainable Development, June 2008, 6.

68. Paul F. Diehl and Nils Petter Gleditsch, "Controversies and Questions," in *Environmental Conflict,* Paul Diehl and Nils Petter Gleditsch, eds. (Boulder, CO: Westview Press, 2001), 4.

69. Buckland, "A Climate of War?" 11.

70. See, for example, Conca, "The Case for Environmental Peacemaking," 1–21. Conca uses the term "ecological security" interchangeably with environmental security, while other scholars counterpose them and define them in fundamentally incompatible ways, as in the case of Jon Barnett.

71. Conca, "The Case for Environmental Peacemaking," 4.

72. Conca, "The Case for Environmental Peacemaking," 9.

73. Brock, "Peace through Parks," 421.

74. This is the definition proposed by Saleem H. Ali in "A Natural Connection between Ecology and Peace," in *Peace Parks: Conservation and Conflict Resolution,* Saleem H. Ali, ed. (Cambridge, MA: MIT Press, 2007), 2.

75. UNEP, *From Conflict to Peacebuilding: the Role of Natural Resources and the Environment,* Geneva, 2009, http://www.unep.org/pdf/pcdmb_policy_01.pdf.

76. See the discussion in Anne Hammill and Charles Besançon, "Measuring Peace Park Performance," in Ali, *Peace Parks*, 25–29.

77. Rosaleen Duffy, "Peace Parks and Global Politics," in Ali, *Peace Parks*, 55–68.

78. "I know of no political movement, no philosophy, no ideology, which does not agree with the peace parks concept as we see it going into fruition today. It is a concept that can be embraced by all." From a 2005 message to the International Conference on the Conservation of Korea's Demilitarized Zone, http://www.dmzforum.org/Reference/Mandela-Turner%202005%20DMZ%20Forum%20Conference%20Address.pdf.

79. Klaus Toepfer, "Putting Poverty to the Sword."

Chapter 13

Indigenous Processes of Conflict Resolution

Neglected Methods of Peacemaking by the New Field of Conflict Resolution[1]

Hamdesa Tuso

Almost three decades have passed since Western scholars, practitioners, and to some extent policy makers, embraced conflict resolution as a legitimate area for scholarly endeavor and a useful tool within the realm of professional practice. The new field of research and practice came to be known as Alternative Dispute Resolution (ADR). Within this relatively brief span of time, the field has expanded exponentially, both in theory and in practice. Curriculums have been organized by degree-offering institutions of higher learning in North America, Europe, and Australia. Some universities in developing societies have also begun offering degrees in this field.[2] Some basic concepts have become a part of the language of discourse in local communities and international relations. Already, there are some feverish activities to consolidate the accumulated knowledge in the form of conflict resolution handbooks.[3] Also, some efforts have been focused on snatching the last words from the mouths of the retired pioneers, so that a complete history relative to the evolution of this newly created profession can be accurately recorded and preserved for future generations.

In my view, Western scholars and practitioners have every right to be proud of the remarkable accomplishments attained within a relatively short period of time. This achievement has been possible, in part due to modern technology, the literate tradition on which Western civilization has been anchored, the availability of skills regarding research, the existing capacity to organize ideas and practical projects, and the availability of resources to enable theorists and practitioners to embark on a new profession of such status. Also, and more significantly, is the fact that Western intellectuals have been able to create a new paradigm that rejected absolute power as a preeminent tool to settle disputes.

This structure is in striking contrast to the paradigm which led Europe to two world wars, which ravaged Europe, led to the Cold War, and which debilitated many regions in developing societies. Notwithstanding these significant achievements, it is fairly safe to state that the field of conflict resolution still remains a Euro-centric model in all aspects of its functions (e.g., degree curriculum, theoretical frame, research orientation, and practice). More serious is the fact that conflict resolution as conceived and practiced in the West has been elevated to occupy a much more visible and domineering space in the world of ideas and practice. Conversely, many other indigenous practices which have been modeled for many centuries by indigenous communities around the world remain largely ignored.

There have been those who have argued that conflict is a culturally constructed social phenomenon and that its resolution must take into account the cultural context in which it takes place. Specifically, the works of Witty,[4] Avurch and Black,[5] Avurch,[6] Abu-Nimer,[7] Lederach,[8] Augsburger,[9] Sponsel and Gregor,[10] Fry and Bjokqvist,[11] and Davidheiser[12] stand out in this regard. Also, more recently a number of textbooks in the field of conflict analysis and resolution have added some specific references to the propositions that culture does play a significant role in the dynamics which influence conflict formation, escalation, and resolution. Examples of the theorists who have moved to this direction include Pruitt and Kim[13] and Folger et al.[14]

In this critical essay, I will attempt to point out how the newly Western-based field of conflict analysis and resolution has largely neglected indigenous processes of conflict resolution practices, which have engendered a longer history of successful *functions* than in "traditional" societies. The essay will have five major themes. In the first theme, I will attempt to show the extent to which a comparative approach to the field has been neglected. In the second theme, I will discuss the negative consequences of such neglect by the literate world regarding the nature and the value of indigenous systems of conflict resolution. The third theme will focus on the common features found in indigenous systems of conflict resolution (this will be based on a preliminary examination of the available cases). The fourth theme will discuss the negative consequences of neglect regarding indigenous processes of peacemaking by the literature of ADR. The fifth theme will explore the potential of indigenous systems of conflict resolution, and how to expand the new field by developing a comparative approach. Also, under this section, some major challenges facing scholars in the area of indigenous forms of conflict resolution will be explored.

Before embarking on the substance of this work, it is critical to define a number of terms. Perhaps more significantly the term *indigenous* needs special attention. Scholars use the term indigenous in two broad applications regarding culturally related practices. In the first sense, it is used in reference to the broad range of cultural practices and products, which are found outside the Western world. Stating it differently, it refers to anything created outside the scope of Western influence. In the second sense, the term indigenous refers to communities that are not independent states, and are encapsulated into modern states as marginalized and subordinate populations. Additionally, they are generally characterized as communities which place high value on coexistence with nature, as opposed to its exploitation and abuse; they have their own economic systems, which do not correspond with the conventional capitalistic economy.[15] In the context of the current work, the term indigenous refers to the former category as described above. More specifically, it refers to the broad range of peacemaking traditions, which have been developed by non-traditional societies.

One issue is the extent of the absence of literature regarding the views from indigenous systems of conflict resolution. In any field of knowledge basic concepts are written in a core body of literature. Early volumes are used as reference books or textbooks. They are known as classic books in the particular field. In keeping with tradition, scholars within the field of conflict resolution have also produced what can also be considered classic books. For the purpose of establishing the presence or the absence of ideas and practices, which have been developed by indigenous communities, I examined a number of prominent books (altogether, sixteen of them) in the field of conflict resolution.[16] Upon examination of the content of these classic works, one can easily reach a conclusion that there is a distinct absence of the vast array of peacemaking processes invented and practiced by indigenous communities around the world.

WHY HAVE INDIGENOUS SYSTEMS OF CONFLICT RESOLUTION BEEN NEGLECTED?

In my view, understanding the historical roots which have contributed to this level of neglect, relative to the oldest and widely used practices of peacemaking forms will help us to view this issue in a proper perspective. Thus, I will briefly discuss seven basic reasons, which have contributed to the neglect of indigenous processes of peacemaking.

THE HISTORIC BIAS TOWARD THE PRACTICES IN THE TRADITIONAL CULTURES

The European bias toward the traditional cultures commenced with the civilizing mission, which began in 1500 when Portugal and Spain received an endorsement, at their request, from the pope to conquer and colonize any territory which was not occupied by Christians. The actual motives can be categorized into two broad areas. The first is rooted in the history of European expansion, which eventually led to the European domination of the world, which reached its zenith in 1914. A chief motivation for this new thrust was that by the beginning of the fifteenth century, Europe was entering the industrialization phase of its development, and securing new material sources for an intense new enterprise which was very critical.[17] The second was psychological, the pride that was gained from dominating peoples of other cultures. As scholars have observed, any form of domination necessitates a rationale (justification) for controlling its victims.[18] It was during this period and the ensuing centuries that the projection of the non-Western cultures as savage, and unworthy of recognition by the "civilized world," became very popular in Western thought and perception. It was during this period that places like Africa were condemned as the "Dark Continent," only to be viewed as a natural place for partition, colonization, and a source for importing slaves.[19] To be sure, the damnation of African culture and its peoples predates European colonization; the prejudice toward African culture was rooted in Semitic religions. Believers were taught that blacks were the descendants of Ham, the son of Noah, and since he was cursed by his father, blacks were also cursed. It was based on this thesis that slavery was justified.[20] Later on, another layer of powerful negative thesis was developed by European scientists regarding African peoples, which posited that the Africans, as a category, belonged to the last leg of human evolution; therefore they were closer to the ape family and were racially inferior. The third level of negative thesis emerged when Western historians declared that Africa had no history.[21] During the same period, similar types of prejudice were manifested against other societies in Asia, the Americas, the Middle East, and Australia. After the 1940s, the decolonization movement went forward with considerable speed.

THE REINFORCED BIAS AGAINST TRADITIONAL CULTURES DURING THE COLD WAR

The Cold War emerged as decolonization went forward with considerable speed. In due course, remaining under colonial rule became a politically, socially, and psychologically unacceptable status in the eyes of many nationalists in developing societies. In addition, maintaining and managing colonial territories became politically and economically difficult for colonial powers. It also became a morally unacceptable proposition to the citizens of the European imperial powers. The Cold War emerged, in part, due to this sudden transformation in developing societies. The Soviet Union saw a new opportunity to compete against and challenge the Western dominance of the world, which had emerged during the previous five centuries. The United States saw the emergence of the Soviet Union as a new competitor, and a dangerous one, to its national economic and security interests and those of its Western allies. It was in this context that, during the period of the late 1950s and early 1960s, two dominant economic models emerged regarding development strategies for the newly decolonized developing societies. The United States proposed and promoted a new paradigm known as the modernization school[22] and the Soviet Union promoted a revolutionary political/economic model.

The key tenets contained in the modernization school were as follows: (1) there are two economic sectors in developing societies—the traditional and the modern; (2) the traditional system was backward and incompatible with modernity; (3) special development centers should be developed, which would transform these societies from backwardness (traditional) to modern; and (4) these modern centers should be managed by the Western-educated and pro-democracy cadre of professionals.[23]

The basic elements promoted in the revolutionary model were as follows: (1) every society goes through five development stages—peasantry, feudalism, capitalism, socialism, and communism; (2) the developing societies are backward due to traditional cultures; (3) the developing societies need state controlled economic development plans, which will accelerate the rate of development so that they can catch up with the developed economic systems; (4) in order to achieve such goals, the economic development has to be centralized; (5) the governments have to be run by the revolutionary elements—the polite race in the societies; and (6) any element that opposes this revolutionary approach has to be eliminated through a revolutionary process. This process included extremely negative propaganda, terrorizing any local leaders who showed sympathy for the cultural past, and physically liquidating those opposed to the revolutionary movement.[24]

These two models were promoted by the two super powers, who had claimed to have been persuaded by these two diametrically opposite ideologies regarding social change and the future of developing societies. Yet both of them possessed strikingly similar views regarding the cultures of developing societies: (1) both models castigated the traditional cultures of the developing societies as backward and a hindrance to the project of development and modernization; (2) both models focused on the urban elite, who by their own disposition had benefited from supporting external projects; (3) both models, in a variety of ways, supported the militarization of the centers of powers; (4) both models increased the dependence of the urban elite who ruled the states in those societies based on external rewards, and as a result neglected the development of traditional cultures of their respective societies; (5) both models promoted the application of power as a method of resolving conflicts; and (6) both models elevated the cause of state integration, usually at the expense of local autonomy and cultural identities. The status of indigenous systems of conflict resolution and the integral parts of the traditional cultures also suffered as a result of the policies promoted by the two models.

THE BIAS OF THE URBAN ELITE IN DEVELOPING SOCIETIES TOWARD THE TRADITIONAL CULTURES

Urban elites in developing societies inherited the newly independent states when their colonial masters departed. These newly independent states also inherited the Western legal system as a frame of reference to resolve conflicts in their respective societies. However, the Western legal system remained a tool to be used in matters relating to the state such as land, insurgency against the state, taxation, and so on. At the same time, indigenous systems of conflict resolution remained in effect in most communities around the world. This situation led to a dual system of conflict resolution in those societies, the Western legal-based approach, and the one based on indigenous processes of conflict resolution. However, the urban elite depended on the indigenous systems when it came to matters of great importance, such as marriage, homicide, intra- and inter-community conflicts, and so forth. While the indigenous systems survived in this manner, it still remains a marginalized and neglected affair. For example, most African students and scholars I have spoken with over the last two decades or so refer to indigenous systems of conflict in their respective societies as "informal" or "traditional." The relevant point here is that there was no investment by new state systems in the study of indigenous systems of conflict resolution and therefore such knowledge and practice remained unattended to by the "literate" world. While the Western-based legal system was taught in modern universities, where the newly educated elite acquired their skills and legitimacy to embark on their professional lives, the knowledge of indigenous systems of conflict resolution was excluded due to the fact that it was perceived unworthy to be included in the modern university curriculum. Therefore this critical knowledge remained marginal; the sole mission of passing such knowledge and practices of these processes of peacemaking to the next generations was relegated to oral forms of communication at family and local village levels.

ADR WAS CREATED TO ADDRESS THE NEEDS OF THE WESTERN, INDUSTRIALIZED SOCIETIES

Prior to the birth of Alternative Dispute Resolution, which was consolidated during the 1970s in United States, there was the legal mechanism, which was ostensibly created to resolve conflicts between the states, and the same tool was used in dealing with domestic disputes.[25] The very name of the new field, "Alternative Dispute Resolution," signifies that it is a new profession that was created to address needs in the industrialized West. It is obvious that all these activities were based on the Western experience regarding social changes which took place in the 1960s and 1970s. Yet these changes had little connection, if any, with daily experiences in the traditional societies around the world.

The Limitation of the Pioneers Regarding the Cultural Traditions of the Traditional Societies

Pioneers of the new ADR field were scholars who had specialized in a particular area within their respective discipline. It is well known that most social science disciplines were mostly based on the experiences of Western societies (with the exception of the field of anthropology). Some scholars who pioneered the new field of conflict resolution launched into a new area of inquiry and practice because they were generally dissatisfied with theoretical orientation and practices, which were anchored in their own disciplines. The classic case relative to this type of dissatisfaction is represented by the experience of John Burton, who was trained in the area of international relations, and subsequently became a practitioner in international diplomacy and conflict resolution. Essentially, his writings, which he completed after he had left an Australian government position, were intended to provide an alternative vision and create new models in dealing with social conflict, in particular deep-rooted conflicts. Others, such as Lewis Coser (sociology) and Christopher Mitchell (international relations), expanded their search from their original discipline.

Lack of Representation in Terms of Experience from Traditional Societies

Historically, in general, there has been a disproportionate representation of persons with urban backgrounds in higher education, where new areas of knowledge were proposed, refined, and published for the larger community. Therefore, the direct benefits of modern universities never reached persons from rural areas of the world communities, which, for the most part, is where groups practice indigenous systems of conflict resolution. This problem is particularly acute in developing societies with a special level of severity among indigenous peoples in the Americas, Australia, Europe, and the former Soviet Union. More relevant to the current situation is that institutions where the new profession is being developed are primarily located in Australia, North America and Europe. Unfortunately, they have not been able to break down those historic barriers against people of developing societies, particularly those communities in rural areas. This situation is compounded by two related factors, which continue to plague institutions of higher learning. The first problem relates to the social phenomenon of cultural reproduction in the academic world. This social phenomenon takes two forms. The first form illustrates that universities, through their established procedures, tend to hire new faculty members who share similar values and beliefs to personnel in respective departments and administration. In my observation, this is the reason that minorities remain marginal groups in academic departments in North America and other continents. The second issue is that academicians tend to support graduates who pursue lines of research established by their faculty. While this approach is totally legitimate, at least in my view, the problems stem from the fact that the field of conflict resolution, as it currently exists, is based on information which had been collected from a very limited human universe in the first place.

The Mission and Promise of the Modern State

When colonial European powers departed from their respective territories, there were explicitly and implicitly stated expectations from all newly independent states in developing societies. The new leadership of these newly decolonized states promised national integration, modernization, equality, and social justice "for all citizens." The premise of the new development/modernization movement was predicated on the notion that old traditions had to be removed and modern ideas and practices had to be embraced.

THE BIAS OF ANTHROPOLOGISTS

Anthropology, as a field, has been dedicated to the study of cultures from a comparative perspective. Indeed, Western anthropologists have spent an inordinate amount of resources (funds, energy, and time) to explore cultures in non-Western societies. However, as the products of Western culture themselves, they carried the Euro-centric worldview to the study of other cultures. Also, it seems that the basic mission of the field was to explore the nature of other cultures for the purpose of transferring knowledge-based benefits to their own societies. As a result, a particular focus was to accumulate information from "uncivilized" societies and assist them in reconstructing their patterns of human evolution. Thus, anthropologists tended to look for cultural groups that they considered the "most savage" and the most violent. Based on these attitudinal orientations and strategic goals for research, they looked more for violent activities in such societies at the expense of peacemaking activities. Sponsel and Gregor, in their reflective work wrote the following regarding this subject:

> "In anthropology, until recently, conflict, aggression, and violence have claimed most of our attention; peace, both interpersonal and inter-group, has received relatively short shrift. For example, Brain Ferguson's recent (1988) bibliography on the anthropology of conflict all 366 pages of reference; of these, only four pages are devoted to peace and conflict resolution. . . . On the face of it, a disproportionate interest in warfare by anthropologists is strange. For human society to persist, even the most violent of them, there must be order, sociability, reciprocity, cooperation, and empathy,—perhaps, even compassion and love. In even the most warlike societies, the vast preponderance of time is spent in the pursuit of ordinary, peaceful activities that embody these qualities."[26]

THE CONSEQUENCES OF THE NEGLIGENCE OF INDIGENOUS SYSTEMS OF CONFLICT RESOLUTION

In this section, I will argue that there have been negative consequences as a result of the negligence and marginalization of indigenous systems of peacemaking. More specifically, I will discuss five general areas (categories) of negative consequences as a result of the marginalization of indigenous systems of peacemaking.

There is a disconnect between modern legal systems and the cultures of indigenous populations. The modern legal system, for the most part, is the invention of European civilization and in many respects does not correspond with the cultural values of traditional societies. Some critical features of the legal systems are as follows: (a) the central focus to establish sufficient evidence accompanied by well developed technical arguments; this approach inherently favors the party that has resources to hire the most skilled lawyers (e.g., the O. J. Simpson case); (b) this approach does not take into account the future relationships between the parties—in most traditional societies repairing the damaged relationship is the chief goal of peacemaking; (c) for the most part, it focuses on the individual grievances—it does not recognize the interconnections between the individual, family, and community; (d) the legal approach to conflict resolution depends totally on the coercive power of the state; (e) it has no room for the spiritual dimension of peacemaking; and (f) the main goal in the legal approach is to win over the opponent, not to repair the damaged relations as a result of the conflict. Naturally, when the source of the conflict, which stems from dysfunctional relationships between parties, is not addressed, the conflict may continue at an attitudinal level.

To illustrate the nature and quality of the disconnect between indigenous peoples and the state legal system, I wish to cite a vignette. In 1996, while I was still teaching at the Institute for Conflict Analysis and Resolution, George Mason University, Fairfax, Virginia, my graduate assistant was recruited by the Organization of the American States (OAS) to work in Guatemala. As most readers may know, the state of Guatemala has a bloody history regarding its treatment of the indigenous population who happened to be the majority. The OAS ostensibly recruited her to help the government of Guatemala to improve its record in the area of human rights violations. After a few months, she reported to her contact faculty members, in writing, indicating that the indigenous peoples in Guatemala did not trust the legal system and did not use it at all; the reasons are obvious—the Spanish dominant minority had used its legal system to marginalize and control the indigenous population in Guatemala.

I can report a similar view among the Oromos in the Ethiopian empire state, where the state legal system was used to strip them of their basic rights in all critical aspects of life. Ethiopia has had three radically different regimes during the last seventy years—the government of Emperor Haile Sellassie (1932–1974), the regime of the Dergue (the military junta) (1974–1991), and the government of the Tigray Liberation Front (TPLF) (1991–present). Each of these regimes had its own constitution, and each regime used its constitution to marginalize the indigenous majority population in the periphery, where the Oromos constitute the majority of the population. As a result, the Oromos by and large do not trust the Abyssinian legal system.

Indigenous systems of conflict resolution should occupy a major space in the cultural landscape of the populations in developing societies. This aspect of their culture remained vulnerable to the abuse of power by the urban ruling class, who control the state apparatus. The Somali experience under Siad Barre illustrates this point. The Somalis possessed two indigenous traditions, the clan system and the eldership system, which survived colonial administration, Islam, and the modern state. The clan system ensured the survival of each member in a very austere material environment, where the competition for daily survival becomes an imperative function of the clans system, while the indigenous system of conflict built bridges between the clans to create and sustain relatively harmonious relationships. However, both of these indigenous systems were undermined by the regime of Siad Barre; he pitted clans against clans, and elders against elders. When his regime collapsed in 1991–1992, the intensive and destructive cycle of contentious conflict between General Mohamed Adeed and Mohammed Hamidi ensued, leading to the total collapse of the societies' basic social and psychological infrastructures, and the Somali society looked like a bottomless pit, so to speak. The national nightmare, which was experienced and is still being experienced by the Somali society during that period and up to the present, can justifiably be explained by Chinua Achebe's imagination in his highly acclaimed novel, *Things Fall Apart.*[27]

The Western systems of conflict resolution, while rich in theories of social sciences and practical models, have not developed the concepts and practices, which adequately meet the spiritual dimension of peacemaking which involves rituals. In 1996, I was confronted by a Liberian journalist—a Liberian American. At the time, she lived in Baltimore, Maryland, and was running radio talk shows about events in Africa. She invited me to join her for lunch in Washington, DC. During our conversation, I told her that some experts in conflict resolution from George Mason University and other organizations in North America had visited Ghana to meet with community leaders from Liberia. At the time, ethnic conflict in Liberia was still going on. As soon as I uttered those words, she became agitated and spoke with a loud voice.

> "What do these, so called, experts from North America know about the conflict in Liberia; they do not know our culture and they do not understand our fears. They come and tell us that we should forgive and forget. In my case, the other group wiped out my entire family members, and we lost all our properties. How do I forget and how do I know that these acts of violence would not be repeated again?"

As she continued with expressions of concern and frustration, it was evident that she had much deeper fears and anguish over the loss of her family members, and her dissatisfaction with the Western-based model of conflict resolution, as applied in dealing with the conflict in her country.

> "In our culture when blood is shed as a result of such conflicts, there are rituals to be performed. The members of the community of the aggressors come out

> and be accountable and participate in such rituals; it is such activities, which would assure the victims of violent conflicts that such hostile acts against them would not be repeated; then, forgiveness and healing would be much easier."

There is a lack of adequate preparation on the part of indigenous communities to deal with modern state based bureaucracy. As indicated previously, historically the educated elite in developing societies relegated the indigenous processes of conflict resolution to the status of backwardness and irrelevance to the functions of the modern sector, while in the rural areas, the masses continued practicing the traditional ways of resolving conflicts. For example, there has not been much research conducted to establish the critical features of indigenous processes of peacemaking, which have common threads or are radically different from the state based legal system. Neither is there credible research nor are there suitable models that have been developed to reconcile concepts and practices of the two systems. The problem is becoming more acute regarding this issue as a result of more recent movement by the indigenous peoples around the world, asserting their rights to use their own indigenous methods of conflict resolution. In my view, this movement has evolved as a result of the fact the West has embraced conflict resolution (ADR). Consequently, it is natural for such groups to take a more proactive position with respect to their processes of peacemaking, including in dealing with conflicts which take place within modern sectors.

The recent political event in Bolivia illustrates this point. Evo Morales, an indigenous political leader, was elected president, the first in the history of that state. Once elected, he elevated members of the indigenous population to high positions of government as one of his priorities. Also, it seems that he and his supporters wanted to inject the cultural values of the indigenous population in Bolivia into the affairs of government. For example, the minister of justice was an indigenous woman who had not been trained as a lawyer. This situation presents contradictions at two levels. First, by definition, when someone is appointed as the minister of justice in a modern state system, that individual automatically becomes the chief law officer for that particular state. That appointment, ipso facto, assumes that person knows the legal system. That kind of knowledge usually comes from formal training in the legal system. Second, the bureaucracy of the department of justice is based on the modern legal system and is usually staffed with trained lawyers. The relevant issue in this case stems from the fact that there was no adequate preparation to bridge the gap between the indigenous systems and the justice system which was based on the state legal system. The lack of the necessary preparation in dealing with two fundamentally different approaches relative to the cause of justice was revealed in the answer the new justice minister gave to a reporter. The reporter asked the new justice minister to explain how she could be the minister of justice, when, in fact, she was not trained as a lawyer. In her response to the question of the reporter, she referred to the fact that the indigenous people view justice in a different light. This statement is fundamentally true. However, she did not explain how she and her associates bridged the gap between the two fundamentally different systems. The gap becomes self-evident, as she has the responsibility of running a modern state bureaucracy, which has been staffed by lawyers trained in the Euro-centered legal tradition.[28]

The state/international legal based system has proven to be inadequate in dealing with inter-communal violent conflicts. This point refers to inter-communal conflicts that have taken place within a larger collectivist societal system. The inadequacy of legal approaches stems from two major factors. First, collectivist societies generally have culturally crafted systems rich with rituals for dealing with inter-communal conflicts. In recent years, such conflicts have been handled through the power approach; power which either uses physical violence to alter power relations in the conflict or state, or an internationally sanctioned legal approach to punish the aggressor party. These two approaches do not adequately deal with the emotional trauma as a result of the conflict.

Nor do they address the future relations of the communities, which have engaged in violent conflicts. To illustrate this point, I will cite three internationally known inter-communal conflicts during recent years, where such patterns of action have taken place. The first was the conflict in Lebanon. Lebanon experienced a violent inter-communal conflict between 1975 and 1990, which resulted in the destruction of the infrastructure of the state system. After two decades of destructive civil war, the situation became calm, essentially as a result of intervention by Syria. However, the psychological, emotional, and spiritual dimension of the conflict was even more serious.[29] As is the case in most of the societies in the Arab world, there are indigenous processes of conflict resolution, known as *sulha,* which are commonly practiced in the villages in Lebanon.[30] In contrast to most other Arab states, where *sulha* is not recognized by the state legal system, in Lebanon this form of peacemaking has been recognized as a legitimate process of peacemaking. As is quite common in many indigenous processes of conflict resolution, the strength of *sulha* lies in its features, which emphasize forgiveness, reconciliation, and healing, and is facilitated by elders and reinforced by a rich set of rituals. As had happened in so many other communities, the indigenous practices had been relegated to the back room, so to speak. Several years later, after the violence had stopped, Lebanese who had been affected by violent conflict during the prolonged civil war turned to *sulha* in a haphazard way, in search of reconciliation and healing.

Rwanda is another such state where inter-communal conflict has caused much death and destruction, both physically and emotionally. Within a hundred days, between 800,000 and 1,000,000 Tutsi ethnic members and moderate Hutus were killed by an organized Hutu militia. The killings of so many unarmed civilians were declared genocide by the international community. Such a declaration, ipso facto, led to the establishment of UN Criminal Tribunal. Thousands of Hutu suspects were placed in crowded jails for several years, waiting for their turns to face the investigation by the newly established tribunal. With limited resources and given the high number of suspects to be investigated regarding the crime, the government in Kwagale determined that, if they were to continue on this path, it would take some hundred years before they completed the trials. Therefore, the government made a fundamental decision regarding the entire matter—it went back to *Gacaca*, a community based indigenous process of peacemaking. The basic elements of the *Gacaca* process, as specified in dealing with crime committed during the genocide, was that an individual who had participated in the genocide would confess to the community where the crime took place, and ask the community for forgiveness, and the concerned community would forgive him/her.[31] While one can argue that the *Gacaca* approach was not a perfect solution in dealing with those who committed crimes during Rwandan genocide, it was a culturally codified method of conflict resolution, which gave much deeper meaning to the populace. In my view, this process would have been much cleaner and enriching if it had been conducted by local elders. Instead, it was organized at the order of government officials, most probably Tutsi bureaucrats, who were the victors in the conflict. This instance is another case in which the well-developed indigenous process of conflict resolution, in the evolution of the ethnic communities in Rwanda, had been neglected as a result of the emergence of the legal system during the colonial era. It was subsequently adopted by the leadership of independent Rwanda. Indeed, *Gacaca* was implemented in a haphazard manner; it was something that was thought of at the last minute.

The third case is the role that indigenous processes of conflict resolution played during the violent conflict in Somalia, which ensued after the collapse of the regime of Siad Barre. The indigenous forms of peacemaking in Somalia survived many social forces (colonialism, Islam, the state system, and the Cold War). It is the most enduring, most trusted cultural practice in the Somali society.[32] It will be recalled that the Somali society plunged into social strife of an epic proportion after the regime of Siad Barre collapsed in 1991, as a result of a power struggle between two ambitious individuals—namely, General Mohammed Adeed and Ali Mahadi—which eventually led to the collapse of the state infrastructure and the catastrophic civil war that ensued. Several international and regional organizations such as the UN, the Arab League, and the Organization of African Unity (OAU) attempted to intervene to make peace among various Somali factions. In relative terms, it was the Somali indigenous form of peacemaking, which was more successful in making peace in Somalia than any other mechanism of peacemaking.[33] Once again, the Somali experience illustrates that an indigenous system of conflict resolution is the mechanism which the populace relate to and trust the most. It deals with different dimensions of the conflict. However, it had been neglected by the state system, the ruling class, and academic institutions.

INDIGENOUS PROCESSES OF CONFLICT RESOLUTION—A COMPARATIVE APPROACH

Thus far, our knowledge of indigenous processes of conflict resolution is primarily based on personal experience, for those who grew up in societies where the communities practiced this form of peacemaking, or by reading case studies. Little research has been done from the angle of comparative studies. From the outset, it should be admitted that since indigenous communities around the world live in vastly different material and social ecology, the task of producing comparative studies is difficult. However, in my view, attempts have to be made. By examining case studies in a comparative way, one can gain insight regarding the basic characteristics found in indigenous forms of peacemaking. In the following paragraphs, I wish to share with the readers some preliminary observations regarding the common features, which I found in the cases studies, which were selected from North America, Africa, the Middle East, and the South Pacific. Based on content analysis of these cases, the following common features were established: (1) The goal of peacemaking is to establish the truth regarding the cause of conflict by collecting evidence from the parties and witnesses. This theme suggests that there will be no peace and reconciliation between the conflicting parties unless the cause of the conflict is established and the party responsible for the cause is held accountable. (2) In these communities, once a conflict takes place, it does not remain the responsibility of the individual who caused the conflict only; the family and the community take the responsibility in assisting to establish the facts and in resolving the conflict. This is in contrast to the modern legal system, where the focal point for resolving the conflict is placed solely on the individual. (3) The elders are key players in resolving conflict. (4) Spirituality plays a key role in peacemaking. (5) Stories or parables are important forms of discourse in mediation. (6) During peacemaking, connections are made between the individual, family, community, nature and the supernatural. (7) Conflict resolution is used to focus on the need for unity and in keeping the tradition of the family and the community. (8) Conflict resolution is not an option, it is mandatory. (9) The goal of conflict resolution is not based on class and power, it is based on the worth the community places on the individual irrespective of power and the social status of the parties. (10) The main goal of conflict resolution is to repair damaged relations and not to exact punishment, although punishments are involved where damage has been done as the result of the conflict. (11) Forgiveness is critical to achieving the goal of repairing the damaged relationships as a result of conflicts. (12) The rituals play a key role in the process of peacemaking.[34]

HOW DO THESE COMMON FEATURES FOUND IN INDIGENOUS PROCESSES OF PEACEMAKING COMPARE WITH BASIC ASSUMPTIONS AND PATTERNS OF PRACTICES OF ADR?

In the next section, I will briefly describe how ADR differs from indigenous processes of peacemaking. In examining the key literature regarding the current status of mediation as conceived, taught, and practiced in Western societies, I was able to establish the following features: (1) There is an assumption that conflict can be settled and managed through rational planning. (2) The needs, desires, and interests of the individual are the overarching goals of conflict resolution. (3) Material resources are often the codes which Western parties and mediators use to describe or establish a process of conflict resolution. (4) Issues for regarding negotiation are often materially based.[35] (5) There are no provisions made to address the spiritual dimension of conflict. (6) Participation in the conflict resolution process is based on the parties' willingness to participate; it is not mandatory. (7) The individual party in conflict has the sole responsibility to resolve the conflict. (8) The concerns of the larger community in which the conflict takes place are not expressed explicitly during the mediation process. (9) Rituals are not included in mediation. (10) The mediator is expected to be neutral and an outsider. (11) Professional training is the source of legitimacy; personal reputation in the community and trust are not considered as important. (12) Confession and forgiveness do not play any significant role in mediation.[36]

In my view, the existence of such a gap between the central themes and functions which are found in indigenous processes of conflict resolution and those found in the ADR has profound implications with respect to the curriculum for the degree programs in the field of conflict analysis and resolution. Should we assume that all the students who would be graduating from the conflict studies programs in Western societies will practice in individualist societies?

THE OPPORTUNITIES AND THE CHALLENGES ASSOCIATED WITH PURSUING THE STUDIES OF INDIGENOUS PROCESSES OF CONFLICT RESOLUTION

Thus far in this essay, my discussion has focused on five general areas: (1) how traditional methods of conflict resolution had been neglected; (2) the factors which have contributed to the marginalization of this form of peacemaking; (3) the consequences of the marginalization of this form of peacemaking; (4) some preliminary observations regarding the basic features commonly found in indigenous methods of conflict resolution; and (5) ADR and its distinct features, which are different from indigenous processes of conflict resolution. In the last section, I wish to explore, though briefly, the opportunities and challenges relative to the studies of indigenous systems of conflict resolution.

THE OPPORTUNITIES

Why should we study indigenous processes of conflict resolution? I commence this discussion with the assertion that as long as indigenous processes remain marginalized and neglected, the field of conflict resolution will remain incomplete and indeed impoverished. In my view, there are several strong reasons why the scholars in the field of conflict resolution should study indigenous processes of conflict resolution.

As discussed previously, the European colonization of the world created a wall of prejudice against non-Western cultures; it depicted non-Western cultures as backward and unworthy to invest resources (time, energy and funds) in studying. After decolonization, the rulers of new states manifested ambivalence toward their own cultures at best; they viewed indigenous processes of peacemaking in the same manner as their colonial masters. The pro-West group was taught to get rid of traditional systems, which were considered backward, and also to reject pro–Soviet Union views, where the revolution should cleanse the traditional systems, which, according to their point of view, was backward and irrelevant. This level of sustained attack over some five centuries has made indigenous peoples (particularly the educated elite) think that, somehow, their cultures are inferior and backward. Thus, they have nothing to offer to the modernity project. In my view, systematic studies of indigenous process of conflict resolution will contribute greatly toward the restoration of honor and dignity to the cultures of the non-Western peoples of the world. Specifically, they would have more confidence in their own systems of conflict resolution.

Much more solid and robust research and publication in this area will help the field of conflict resolution to develop and enhance a cross-cultural perspective and will make the field of conflict resolution more comparative as a field of learning and practice. Currently, dramatic changes are taking place in many traditional societies, with significant impacts on interpersonal and inter-group relationships. For example, stratification is emerging in such communities with the result of an imbalance of power in inter-relationships at all social levels. Such changes are altering the social context in which indigenous forms of peacemaking take place. In my view, introducing social science research regarding the practices of indigenous forms of peacemaking will help to identify such changes and the negative impact on indigenous forms of peacemaking—with such knowledge, potential remedies could be considered. John Burton, in his important work entitled *Conflict Resolution as a Political System*,[37] wrote a critique, arguing that Western approaches to governance has been based on power rather than the consideration of human needs. He passionately recommended that conflict resolution should be incorporated into the political system. He proposed this approach as an alternative to the Western legal-based approach in dealing with human basic needs. I believe pursuing research and publication in the area of indigenous mechanisms of conflict resolution will assist and enhance our understanding of how conflict resolution can be incorporated into the political system. Such endeavors, as discussed in this section, have the potential to encourage the elites, particularly the academic community, to re-enter, so to speak, the cultural arena of the majority in the rural area, at least at the intellectual level, from which they had distanced themselves, because *traditional* cultures were viewed as backward and irrelevant to contemporary social issues.

The Challenges

There are several major challenges, which the field of conflict studies has to face in pursuing this line of research and practice. In the following paragraphs, I will briefly discuss them. Currently, it is estimated that there are about five thousand ethnic groups in the world. A critical question arises relative to the required resources (funds, expertise, time, and energy) to do credible research regarding the peacemaking process of each group. In other words, the question emerges, how will we ever be able to study all of these systems of peacemaking with professional efficiency and equity? If we have to select some of these for focus, what criteria will be used? Will it even be ethical to make such selections?

The rise of modern elites in developing societies has created unique complexities regarding the status of indigenous cultures—when the utilization of indigenous cultures suits their political interests, including indigenous processes of conflict resolution, they embrace and use traditional culture. However, if respecting the basic tenets of indigenous cultures does not support their immediate political needs, they are totally capable of and willing to abuse these cultures. The best example relative to this type of political phenomenon is the case of President Siad Barre, who ruled Somalia for some twenty years with an iron fist. In Somalia there were two major African traditions—the clan system and the eldership—which survived Islam and colonialism. In environmentally hostile conditions, which are prevalent in Somalia, the clan system was created to ensure the survival of the individual, and at times the clans clashed over resources (e.g., land, water, etc.) for the survival of their clan members, and the eldership system managed conflicts between the clans. When oppositions rose from various clans to challenge his autocratic rule, in order to stay in power, he (Siad) pitted clans against clans, and elders against elders. Thus, the catastrophic inter-clan strife, which took place in Somalia after the collapse of his regime, ensured that the Somali society behaved as though it was a bottomless pit.[38]

Another pattern of misuse of the indigenous processes of conflict resolution is also emerging in developing societies. Since ADR emerged in the West, conflict resolution as a field has become more attractive to the elite in developing societies; it has become a new fad, so to speak. As a result, some elites are claiming to be experts in indigenous forms of peacemaking when they are not, and they are using their relative power in the society, their education and name recognition, to present themselves as peacemakers in modern elite-powered conflict. The case of the Peace Committee in Ethiopia (PCE), mostly comprised of academics, which was created after the fall of the *Dergue* (military junta) in 1991, presumably to ameliorate the ensuing ethnic schisms between the Tigrean led government and members of other ethnic communities, illustrates this point. The relevant point for our discussion here is the mischievous process which the PCE undertook after the fraudulent elections of 2005, where the opposition challenged the outcome of the disputed elections and violence ensued, briefly, when Meles Zenawi's security forces opened fire against the members of the opposition party, killing and wounding several hundred people.

In addition, the regime imprisoned the leadership of the opposition party. The PCE negotiated with Meles Zenawi, the prime minister, to release the political prisoners, on the conditions that they accepted wrongdoing against the government, and write individual letters of apology. Then, the chairman of PCE made claims to the media that the PCE used traditional methods of conflict resolution in facilitating the agreement.[39] As indicated in this work previously, such a tactic is contrary to the indigenous forms of peacemaking in indigenous communities. In this context, the critical question becomes, who represents the real experience and practice of indigenous forms of peacemaking? In my view, the prevailing bias against anything *traditional* in the context of contemporary global systems makes it very difficult for this area of inquiry and practice to be more attractive for funding for research and practice. Also, such prevailing bias could discourage potentially academically strong students from pursuing graduate studies in this area. In the context of contemporary notions of ideals of justice and equality between all segments of human society, some aspects of practices in indigenous systems of peacemaking may be problematic. For example, most practices of peacemaking by indigenous communities are done by elders, which, ipso facto, favors older males. Women around the world are becoming dissatisfied with male hegemony in societal daily lives, as they are increasingly having more access to modern education, and becoming more empowered. Equipped with modern education, can the younger persons participate in peacemaking? Will that be acceptable to such cultures?

Critics of indigenous processes of peacemaking have argued that it vests too much in keeping harmony in the community and, thus, those who have more power in the community ultimately control the process, using it to maintain their status of privilege and power in the community.[40]

CONCLUSION

In this essay, I have argued that the indigenous processes of conflict resolution, which, by far, have a much longer history, and successful functioning in traditional societies have been neglected by the theorists and practitioners of ADR, a profession that is only about three decades old. The level and nature of the neglect is manifested in the absence of textbooks relative to indigenous systems of conflict resolution, the lack of courses in the curriculums of the degree programs offered in Western universities, the lack of examples reflecting everyday social realities from traditional societies, and the absence of the spiritual dimensions, usually shown through rituals, which are commonly present in indigenous processes of conflict resolution. What is even more significant is the fact that ADR has been promoted as the new paradigm on the block to the world community, as though it is universal in all its forms and dimensions, and relevant to all cultures and social realities. Therefore, it is not surprising that the reactions from non-Western societies toward ADR have been lukewarm at best, and at times, there is outright rejection of the new model.[41]

In my view, in order for the field of conflict resolution to take indigenous processes of conflict resolution more seriously, as suggested in this essay, we need to understand the historical and cultural background in which the Western and the traditional cultures have interacted during the last five centuries. Also, I have suggested that the negligence of indigenous processes of conflict resolution by the literate world in the past, and, more recently, by the theorists and practitioners of ADR, has had negative consequences for the peoples of traditional societies, which have experienced considerable levels of group humiliation, ambivalence toward their own culture, division, and disorientation. Curiously, more recently, some communities, which had experienced violent conflicts, have turned to indigenous processes of peacemaking in the hope of finding more appropriate mechanism of healing and reconciliation. These episodes have also revealed that individuals and communities turn to the traditional techniques of peacemaking more in some haphazard manners due to the fact that their culturally based methods of peacemaking have been neglected for so long. As the same time, there are no well-trained experts in the tradition of the social sciences, who can provide leadership in such endeavors. As a matter of fact, some members of the elite sector, as discussed in the chapter, tend to become involved, when actually they know very little, and their knowledge about the processes of indigenous systems of conflict resolution is based only on conventional wisdom, or on some vague memories.

In my view, the indigenous processes of conflict resolution should be the new frontier for the profession of conflict resolution. It both presents real promise and has the potential to broaden our horizon regarding human capacity to invest more in peaceful coexistence. It also presents real challenges. In particular, those institutions which offer graduate degrees in the field of conflict resolution have an unparalleled opportunity to guide their graduate students to do ethnographic studies, focusing on peacemaking activities in major cultures in different parts of the world. The next phase of such study should include comparing the main features commonly found in different processes of conflict resolution, the interactions between the state-based legal system and indigenous systems of peacemaking, the evolution of the hybrid types of peacemaking, and the application of indigenous processes of peacemaking in dealing with inter-ethnic conflicts.

BIBLIOGRAPHY

Abu Numier, Mohammed. "Conflict Resolution Approaches: Western and Middle Eastern, Lessons and Possibilities." *American Journal Economics & Sociology,* vol. 55, no. 1 (1996): 1–20.

———. *Nonviolence and Peace Building in Islam: Theory and Practice*. Tallahassee: University of Florida Press, 2003.

Achebe, Chinua. *Things Fall Apart*. Johannesburg: Heinemann Publishers, 1996.

Augsburger, David W. *Conflict Mediation Across Cultures*. Louisville: Westminister John Knox Press, 1992.

Avruch, Kevin. *Culture and Conflict Resolution.* Washington, DC: United States Institute of Peace, 1998.

Avruch, Kevin, P.W. Black, and J.A. Scimecca, eds. *Conflict Resolution: Cross-Cultural Perspectives.* New York: Praeger, 1991.

Azar, Ed, and John Burton, eds. *International Conflict Resolution: Theory and Practice.* Boulder, CO: Lynne Rienner Publishers, 1986.

Burton, John W. "Conflict Resolution as a Political System, Working Paper I." *The International Journal of Peace Studies,* vol. 6, no. 1 (1993): 1–33.

———. *Resolving Deep Rooted Conflict*. Lanham, MD: University Press of America, 1987.

Coser, Lewis. *Functions of Social Conflict*. New York: The Free Press, 1956.

Curle, Adam. *Making Peace*. London: Tavistock, 1971.

Davidheiser, Mark. *The Role of Culture in Conflict Mediation: Toubabs and Dambians Cannot be the Same*. PhD diss., University of Florida, 2004.

Deutsch, M. *Resolution of Conflict*. New Haven, CT: Yale University Press, 1985.

Deutsch, Morton, et al., eds. *The Hand Book of Conflict Resolution: Theory and Practice*. San Francisco: Jossey-Bass, 2006.

Farah, Yusfu. *Roots of Reconciliation: Local Level Peace Processes in Somaliland.* http://www.mbali.info/doc29.htm.

Fisher, Roger, and William Fisher. *Getting to Yes*. New York: Penguin, 1991.

Folger, Joe, et al. *Working with Conflicts: Strategies for Relationships, Groups, and Organizations*, 4th ed. Boston: Pearson, 2009.

Forster, S., et al. *Bismarck, Europe: The Berlin Conference 1884–1885 and the Onset of Partition.* London: Oxford University Press, 1996.

Fry, Douglass, and Kay Bjorkqvist, eds. *Cultural Variation in Conflict Resolution: Alternatives to Violence.* Mahwah, NJ: Psychology Press, 2009.

Godenberg, David. *The Curse of Ham: Race and Slavery in Early Judaism, Christianity and Islam (Jews, Christians and Muslims, from the Ancient to the Modern)*. Princeton, NJ: Princeton University Press, 2003.

Guillermoprieto, Alma. "The New Boliva: Part II." *The New York Review of Books*, September 21, 2006.

Halpern, Orly. "In Ethiopia, Elders Dissolve a Crisis the Traditional Way." *The Christian Science Monitor*, http://www.csmonitor.com/2007/2009/p01-woaf.html.

Hume, David, and Mark Turner. *Sociology and Development: Theories, Policies and Practices*. New York: St. Martin's Press, 1990.

Kaplan, Seth. "The Remarkable Story of Somaliland." *Journal of Democracy*, vol. 19, no. 3 (July 2008): 1–13.

Kemp, Graham and Douglas Fry, eds. *Keeping the Peace*. New York: Routledge, 2004.

King, Laurie E. "Rituals of Reconciliation and Processes of Empowerment in Post-war Lebanon," in *Traditional Cure for Modern Conflict: African Conflict Medicine*, I. William Zartman, ed. Boulder, CO: Lynne Rienner Publishers, 2000, 25–50.

Kriesberg, Louis. *Constructive Conflicts: From Escalation to Resolution*. Lanham, MD: Rowman & Littlefield, 1998.

———. "The Conflict Resolution Field: Origins, Growth, and Differentiation," in *Peacemaking in International Conflict: Methods, Techniques*, I. William Zartman, ed. Washington, DC: USIP Press, 2007, 25–60.

Lederach, John Paul. *Preparing for Peace: Conflict Transformation Across Cultures*. Syracuse, NY: Syracuse University Press, 1995.

Makinda, Samuel. *Seeking Peace from Chaos: Humanitarian Intervention in Somalia*. Boulder, CO: Lynne Rienner Publishers, 1993.

Meffitt, Michael. *Dispute Resolution Handbook*. San Francisco: Jossey-Bass, 2005.

Memmi, Albert. *The Colonizer and the Colonized*. Boston: Beacon Press, 1965.

Menkhaus, Ken. "Traditional Conflict Management in Contemporary Somalia," in *Traditional Cures for Modern Conflicts: African Conflict Medicine*, I. William Zartman, ed. Boulder, CO: Lynne Rienner Publishers, 1999, 142–167.

Mitchell, C.R. *The Structure of International Conflict*. New York: St. Martin's Press, 1989.

Moore, C.R. *The Mediation Process: Practical Strategies for Resolving Conflict*, 2nd ed. San Francisco: Jossey-Bass, 1996.

Nader, Laura. *Harmony Ideology: Justice and Control in a Zapotec Mountain Village*. Stanford, CA: Stanford University Press, 1990.

Pinto, Jean Marie. *Original Dispute Resolution: An Analysis of the Peacemaker System of the Navajo Nation*. M.S. Thesis, Nova Southeastern University, 1998.

Pruitt, Dean. *Social Conflict: Escalation, Stalemate, and Settlement*, 3rd ed. Boston: McGraw-Hill, 2004.

Pruitt, Dean, and Sung Hee Kim. *Social Conflict*. Lanham, MD: Rowman & Littlefield, 1998.

Sahnoun, Mohamed. *Somalia: The Missed Opportunities*. Washington, DC: USIP Press, 1994.

Sandole, Dennis, Sean Byrne, Ingrid Sandole-Staroste, and Jessica Senehi, eds. *Handbook of Conflict Analysis & Resolution*. New York: Routledge, 2008.

So, Alvin Y., *Social Change and Development: Modernization, Dependency, and World-System Theories*. New Bury Park, CA: Sage, 1990.

Sponsel, Leslie E., and Thomas Gregor. *The Anthropology of Peace and Nonviolence*. Boulder, CO: Lynne Rienner Publishers, 1994.

Stavariannos, L.S. *The World Since 1500: A Global History,* 6th ed. Englewood Cliff, NJ: Prentice Hall, 1991.

Tiemessen, Alana. "After Arusha: Gacaca Justice in Post-Genocide Rwanda." *African Studies Quarterly,* vol. 8, no. 1 (2004): 1–16.

Wehr, Paul. *Conflict Regulation.* Boulder, CO: Westview, 1979.

Wesseling, H.L. *Divide and Rule: The Partition of Africa.* London: Praeger, 1996.

Williams, Sir Eric. "Speech during the Occasion of receiving an Honorary Degree at Andrews University." Berrien Springs, Michigan, 1974.

Wilmer, Franke. *The Indigenous Voice in World Politics: Since Time Immemorial (Violence, Cooperation, Peace).* Thousand Oaks, CA: Sage, 1993.

Witty, Cathy. *Mediation and Society: Conflict Management in Lebanon.* London: Academic Press, 1981.

NOTES

1. Howard Johnson, my graduate assistant, worked on most of references for this work. He also the read the paper and made constructive suggestions. I am grateful for his valuable contribution toward the completion of this paper.

2. Louis Kriesberg, "The Conflict Resolution Field: Origins, Growth, and Differentiation," in *Peacemaking in International Conflict: Methods, Techniques*, I. William Zartman, ed. (Washington, DC: USIP Press, 2007), 25–60.

3. For example, currently, there are three handbooks on the subject of conflict analysis and resolution. See Dennis Sandole, et al., eds. *Handbook of Conflict Analysis & Resolution* (New York: Routledge, 2008); Michael Meffitt, *Dispute Resolution Handbook* (San Francisco: Jossey-Bass, 2005); Morton Deutsch, et al., (eds.), *The Hand Book of Conflict Resolution: Theory and Practice* (San Francisco: Jossey-Bass, 2006).

4. Cathy Witty, *Mediation and Society: Conflict Management in Lebanon* (London: Academic Press, 1981).

5. Kevin Avruch, P.W. Black, J.A. Scimecca, eds. *Conflict Resolution: Cross-Cultural Perspectives* (New York: Praeger, 1991).

6. Kevin Avruch, *Culture and Conflict Resolution* (Washington, DC: United States Institute, 1998).

7. Mohamamed Abu-Namier, *Nonvioence and Peace Building in Islam: Theory and Practice* (Tallahassee: University of Florida Press, 2003).

8. John Paul Lederach, *Preparing for Peace: Conflict Transformation Across Cultures* (New York: Syracuse University Press, 1995).

9. David W. Augsburger, *Conflict Mediation Across Cultures* (Louisville: Westminister John Knox Press, 1992).

10. Leslie E. Sponsel and Thomas Gregor, *The Anthropology of Peace and Nonviolenc*e (Boulder, CO: Lynne Rienner Publishers, 1994).

11. *Cultural Variation in Conflict Resolution: Alternatives to Violence,* Douglass Fry and Kaj Bjorkqvist, eds. (Mahwah, NJ: Psychology Press, 2009).

12. Mark Davidheiser, *The Role of Culture in Conflict Mediation: Toubabs and Dambians Cannot be the Same*, PhD diss., University of Florida, 2004.

13. Dean Pruitt and Sung Hee Kim, *Social Conflict: Escalation, Stalemate, and Settlement,* 3rd ed. (Boston: McGraw Hill, 2004).

14. Joe Folger, et al., *Working with Conflicts: Strategies for Relationships, Groups, and Organizations,* 4th ed. (Boston: Pearson, 2009).

15. Franke Wilmer, *The Indigenous Voice in World Politics: Since Time Immemorial (Violence, Cooperation, Peace)* (Thousand Oaks, CA: Sage, 1993).

16. The list of the reviewed sources is as follows: Lewis Coser, *Functions of Social Conflict* (New York: The Free Press, 1956); Adam Curle, *Making Peace* (London: Tavistock, 1971); John Burton, *Resolving Deep Rooted Conflict* (Lanham, MD: University Press of America, 1987); Ed Azar and John Burton, ed., *International Conflict Resolution: Theory and Practice* (Boulder, CO: Lynne Rienner, 1986); Paul Wehr, *Conflict Regulation* (Boulder, CO: Westview, 1979); C.R. Mitchell, *The Structure of International Conflict* (New York: St. Martin's Press, 1989); M. Deutch, *Resolution of Conflict* (New Haven, CT: Yale University Press, 1985); D. Pruitt and S. Kim, *Social Conflict* (Lanham, MD: Rowman & Littlefield, 1998); C. Moore, *Mediation Process: Practical Strategies for Resolving Conflict,* 2nd ed. (San Francisco: Jossey-Bass, 1996); Roger Fisher and William Fisher, *Getting to Yes* (New York: Penguin, 1991); Louis Kriesberg, *Constructive Conflicts: From Escalation to Resolution* (Lanham, MD: Rowman & Littlefield, 1998); C.R. Moore, *The Mediation Process: Practical Strategies for Resoling Conflict,* 2nd ed. (San Francisco: Jossey-Bass, 1996).

17. L.S. Stavariannos, *The World Since 1500: A Global History,* 6th ed. (Englewood Cliff, NJ: Pentice Hall, 1991).

18. Albert Memmi, *The Colonizer and the Colonized* (Boston: Beacon Press, 1965).

19. S. Forster, et al., B*ismarck, Europe: The Berlin Conference 1884–1885 and the Onset of Partition* (London: Oxford University Press, 1996); H.L. Wesseling, *Divide and Rule: The Partition of Africa* (London: Praeger, 1996).

20. David Godenberg, *The Curse of Ham: Race and Slavery in Early Judaism, Christianity and Islam (Jews, Christians and Muslims, from the Ancient to the Modern)* (Princeton, NJ: Princeton University Press, 2003).

21. Sir Eric Williams, a Speech during the Occasion of receiving an Honorary Degree at Andrews University, Berrien Springs, Michigan (1974).

22. Alvin Y. So, *Social Change and Development: Modernization, Dependency, and World-System Theories* (Newbury Park, CA: Sage, 1990); David Hume and Mark Turner, *Sociology and Development: Theories, Policies and Practices* (New York: St. Martin's Press, 1990).

23. So, *Social*; Hume and Turner, *Sociology*.

24. See *The History of Marxist/Leninst Theory*, http://www.friessian.com/mar .htm. The "revolutionary" regimes, which were supported by the Soviet Union used these tactics in dealing with their opponents, including those who argued for maintaining traditional values. The case of Cuba, the regime in Afghanistan during the Soviet Union invasion, and the *Dergue* (military junta) in Ethiopia (1974–1991) illustrate this point.

25. Augsburger, *Conflict*, 192.

26. Sponsel and Gregor, *The Anthropology of Peace*, 199.

27. Chinua Achebe, *Things Fall Apart* (Johannesburg: Heinemann Publishers, 1996).

28. Alma Guillermoprieto, "The New Boliva: Part II," *The New York Review of Books*, September 21, 2006.

29. Laurie E. King, "Rituals of Reconciliation and Processes of Empowerment in Post-war Lebanon," in *Traditional Cure for Modern Conflict: African Conflict Medicine*, I. William Zartman, ed. (Boulder, CO: Lynne Rienner Publishers, 1999), 25–50.

30. Witty, *Mediation*.

31. Alana Tiemessen, "After Arusha: Gacaca Justice in Post-Genocide Rwanda," *African Studies Quarterly*, vol. 8, no. 1 (2004): 1–16.

32. Ken Menkhaus, "Traditional Conflict Management in Contemporary Somalia," in *Traditional Cures for Modern Conflicts: African Conflict Medicine*, I. William Zartman, ed. (Boulder, CO: Lynne Rienner Publishers, 1999), 142–167.

33. Yusfu Farah, *Roots of Reconciliation: Local Level Peace Processes in Somaliland*, http://www.mbali.info/doc29.htm; Seth Kaplan, "The Remarkable Story of Somaliland," *Journal of Democracy*, vol. 19, no. 3 (July 2008): 1–13.

34. Kemp and Fry, in their review of ten case studies of "peaceful" societies, established similar patterns of handling conflicts by those communities. Of course, their work focused on peaceful societies, whereas my studies included both communities who are peaceful and those who use violence. See Graham Kemp and Douglas Fry, eds., *Keeping the Peace* (New York: Routledge, 2004).

35. The first four of these points have been identified by Abu Numier, "Conflict Resolution Approaches: Western and Middle Eastern, Lessons and Possibilities," *American Journal Economics & Sociology*, vol. 55, no. 1 (1996): 1–20.

36. See the list of sources as presented in note 15.

37. Burton, John W., "Conflict Resolution as a Political System, Working Paper I," *The International Journal of Peace Studies*, vol. 6, no. 1 (1993): 1–33.

38. Mohamed Sahnoun, *Somalia: The Missed Opportunities* (Washington, DC: USIP Press, 1994); Samuel Makinda, *Seeking Peace from Chaos: Humanitarian Intervention in Somalia* (Boulder, CO: Lynne Rienner Publishers, 1993).

39. Orly Halpern, "In Ethiopia, Elders Dissolve a Crisis the Traditional Way," *The Christian Science Monitor*, http://www.csmonitor.com/2007/2009/p01-woaf.html. However, there was sustained critique of the PCE regarding this case, which appeared for several months on http.//www.Ethiomedia.com.

40. Anthropologist Laura Nader is among the many critics of indigenous processes of conflict resolution. See her seminal work, *Harmony Ideology: Justice and Control in a Zapotec Mountain Village* (Stanford, CA: Stanford University Press, 1990).

41. Jean Marie Pinto, *Original Dispute Resolution: An Analysis of the Peacemaker System of the Navajo Nation*, MS thesis, Nova Southeastern University, 1998.

Chapter 14

"The Problem from Hell"

Examining the Role of Peace and Conflict Studies for Genocide Intervention and Prevention[1]

Paul Cormier, Peter Karari, Alka Kumar, Robin Neustaeter, Jodi Read, and Jessica Senehi

The "crime without a name," as Winston Churchill put it in an August 1941 BBC radio broadcast,[2] was labeled "genocide" by Raphael Lemkin, and was adopted into international law in Geneva, in 1948. In her book, *"A Problem from Hell": America and the Age of Genocide*, Samantha Power discusses the brutal murder of millions of people in Armenia (1915–1917), Cambodia (1975–1979), Iraq (1988), Bosnia (1992–1993), Rwanda (1994), Srebrenica (1995), and Kosovo (1998–1999).[3] Through detailed reporting based on documents and interviews, Power demystifies behind-the-scenes thoughts, decisions, and responses by individuals, leaders, and the U.S. government. Typically, a myriad of factors culminated in what Power calls a lack of will to respond. Power also describes a different response—individuals who made a commitment to advocate for the rights of the vulnerable, the marginalized, the jeopardized, and the powerless. Power calls for an engaged citizenry to take an activist stance and hold their governments accountable, and demand effective and timely measures to stop genocide.

We found that the book resonated powerfully and fundamentally with our commitment to peace and social justice, and also raised questions along the fault lines of the peace and conflict studies (PACS) field: (a) Power focuses on decision-making to intervene militarily, and PACS examines effective nonviolent measures for achieving social justice; (b) these genocides are very direct and visible, but there is also structural violence and indirect, invisible oppression—another face of genocide—within our own societies; (c) the language of human rights focuses on name-blame-shame type approaches toward perpetrators of the crime of genocide, whereas PACS methodologies emphasize mutual respect toward all parties and separating the people from the problem; and, finally, (d) in the face of the kind of brutality and victimization of whole groups of people that has occurred in the past centuries and continues to take place, how can we maintain the hope, optimism, and belief in human agency that is such a part of the PACS field, and is it realistic to do so?

We address these questions in the theoretical background of this paper. A general conclusion is that by fracturing the problem, we can perhaps find footholds and handholds for scaling this precipice. We do this in two ways: First, we address in turn, the factors that (a) facilitate genocide itself; (b) facilitate responses characterized by inaction; and (c) facilitate responses characterized by effective intervention and prevention. We further develop this analysis with a consideration of the intervener's location either within the region of conflict or external to it. This analysis is a beginning sketch, and should be further developed and tested. This process is significant for facing up to some of the cloudier areas in our field, and critically interrogating what this field can offer in situations that manifest extreme conflict and violence.

DILEMMAS FOR THE FIELD

Again, examining genocide in terms of our field and our reading of Power's book raised some dilemmas for the PACS field—especially in the North American construction of the field—that are typically avoided. Here, we raise these issues and discuss them briefly, but each one is worthy of a full-length article in itself. Further, we review some of the theoretical perspectives from PACS to the examination of this topic.

Commitment to Nonviolence

As A. J. Muste was famously quoted in the *New York Times* in 1967, "there is no way to peace, peace is the way," that is, process and outcome are inextricable.[4] At the heart of the PACS field is a commitment to nonviolence: its moral authority,[5] its transformative potential,[6] and its strategic possibilities.[7] While Power exposes how genocide is a tool of political maneuvering that hinders an effective response to people's suffering and how genocide often occurs under the cover of war, she consistently affirms military or armed intervention to stop genocide. A concern is that the use of violence to stop violence increases harm to people, does not get to the root of the issues, and locates power in weapons rather than people.

In the PACS field, this gap between nonviolence and military intervention is rarely, if at all, bridged, nor discussed in length. Nonviolence typically encompasses the issues of war resistance, peace activism, and conscientious objection, as well as compelling critiques of militarization.[8] While, recently, critiques of war are often accompanied by affirmation of the commitment and sacrifice of service men and women, in North America, there is also an emotional history to this issue that has not been fully or publicly aired. For example, U.S. soldiers, often traumatized, returning from the U.S.-Vietnam war were called "baby killers." And young war resisters were labeled "unpatriotic," "disloyal," "cowardly," and often left their life in the United States behind to settle in Canada or abroad.

A fuller discussion and examination of these issues is important for the PACS field. Meanwhile, Power offers many nonviolent approaches for the populace and government to consider. The analysis below only includes nonviolent interventions. There is a breadth of nonviolent interventions that can take place that may eliminate or mitigate the need for military intervention. It has often been observed that many important nonviolent responses to the Holocaust were not taken, for example, the admission of more Jewish refugees to Canada and the United States, or the acceptance, in 1939, rather than the turning away of the passenger ship the *St. Louis*, which carried nine hundred German Jewish refugees.[9]

North American Genocide and Structural Violence

Another concern is how to distinguish between the direct violence of genocidal wars of the past century with the settlement of Canada by colonial powers and the current violence many Aboriginal people face in North America. For example, colonial laws like the Indian Act in Canada were designed to destroy a racial group. Masked as assimilation and presented as the "glorious settlement" of Canada, the well-documented results have been: the indigenous population disenfranchised from their homes and forced from their lands, children taken from their families and placed with non-Aboriginal people, entire populations wiped out, forced marches/relocations, a legacy of abuse from residential schools, and documented forced infection with deadly disease.[10] Even as people stood in disbelief as acts of genocide unfolded before their eyes around the word, aboriginal people in North America fought, and continue to fight, for their existence.

Using the word genocide to describe Aboriginal–non-Aboriginal relations in Canada and the United States can be unsettling. This issue is a difficult conversation that even the tireless activist Raphael Lemkin avoided.[11] However, the damage of an unacknowledged loss—what Kenneth Hardy calls a "dehumanized loss"[12]—leads to rage, sadness, sorrow, and despair that leads to violence toward self and others. Such denial blocks, impedes, and constrains potential resolution, restitution, and restoration of dignity, respect, value, community, and health.

Therefore, it is our responsibility, in fact an immense weight, to address these issues. Perhaps a detailed and rich analysis of how to understand the intervention of genocide can lead to a cultural mind shift—even a global civic culture of peace as Boulding envisioned[13]—and can help promote the capacity for both recognizing and changing destructive and dehumanizing power relations, structural inequalities, social and cultural devaluation, and ethnocide even when it is in our own society. Because it is typically harder and more risky to raise local human rights issues, perhaps considering the factor of location (within the conflict region or external to it) is an important consideration in identifying options and strategies of response.

"Name-Shame-Blame" Versus "Win-Win" Approaches

In the PACS field, there is recognition that conflict is a part of social life and can be handled constructively, whereas violence is seen as something to be avoided. Typically, in the field of conflict resolution, identity-based conflict is addressed by creating a space of equal safety and neutrality.[14] This step is required to keep the trust of the parties. When does that effort at balance belie justice or serve the purposes of the identity-group in power at the expense of the less powerful group? How, and at what point, do we address issues of power? Is "name-blame-and-shame" an alternative tool of conflict resolution or antithetical to conflict resolution approaches? Advocacy for justice and a balance of power has always been part of the peace and conflict studies field (for example, see Laue, 1982), but how does that fit in with the majority of work that emphasizes a "win-win" approach?

While the dilemma of whether peace serves the interests of or undermines justice is fairly well known[15] and while the PACS field has always had social justice as a central aim, it is important to remember how subtle and enervating this dilemma might be. How does practice for peace and conflict resolution change, or need to change, when power differentials are steep and violence is happening? In the context of violent conflict, those who attempt to build peace or reach out to the "enemy" may be seen as sentimental at best or dangerously naive at worst.

It is not always clear when escalating layers of conflict gradually escalate to genocidal violence. Genocide is often perpetrated in the name of one identity group against a minority group, and not everyone in the dominant group can necessarily be seen as a perpetrator. Within the "bystander" populace, individuals and networks have worked in various ways to resist, sabotage, or overturn genocidal processes in their societies. Within the targeted group, there are varying ideas, strategies, and choices about how to resist. The identification of numerous means and points of intervention in intergroup and identity-based conflicts allows choices and creates possibilities for intervention of intergroup divisions, hatred, and tolerance that helps individuals, groups, and policymakers position themselves to be of influence.

Despair Versus Agency

A significant insight that comes from both reading about genocide and Power's analysis is the incredible sense of loss that genocide generates. Even the secondary trauma from reading about genocide or working with victims may be overwhelming. Direct trauma affects millions of survivors, including the many refugees who have settled in North America from other parts of the world. Most people in North American have been affected by genocide, political violence, or war—if not in their generation, then in their parents' or grandparents' family. For this reason as well, studying genocide may trigger deep feelings of personal loss or loss of community. Power quotes the words of observers: "infuriating," "maddening,"[16] "frustrated,"[17] "appalled," "livid,"[18] "grief-stricken,"[19] "pain and anguish,"[20] "obviously a man in pain."[21]

Stepping into this emotional terrain is risky. How do we keep ourselves safe, resilient, and effective as peace workers in the face of even vicarious trauma? It is difficult to raise these issues, because they can be so disturbing and because we may become agents of vicarious trauma when we discuss them. Discussing these issues may be re-traumatizing for those who are affected by these issues, and, at the least, we need to consider how to respond to profound emotions that emerge when these issues are discussed. Clearly, peace and human rights education is important, but what information at what age is appropriate to share? How do we process our own feelings around these issues so that our own buttons do not get triggered in our work? For the peacemaker whose work is based on the belief that it is possible for people to create peace, such a sense of loss could potentially lead to despair and burn-out.

At the same time, we can see where people have acted successfully to find inspiration, courage, and hope. One of the most moving aspects of Power's work is the focus on personal narratives that bear testimony to the faith, courage, and perseverance of individuals to act for the collective good even in the face of state power, and speak to human agency and possibility—often relying on naming the problem. Raphael Lemkin devoted his life to the scholarly articulation and international legislation of genocide. U.S. Senator William

Proxmire was a leader in persuading the U.S. Senate to ratify the Convention and for 19 years, beginning in 1967, he gave more than 3,211 speeches on this topic, no two the same. Canadian Major General Romeo Dallaire, whose appeals to the United Nations for reinforcements in Rwanda were unheeded, became a spokesperson who spoke and wrote about his painful experience in order that people become more aware of the pain of genocide and the responsibility to protect. In 1998, African American prosecutor Pierre Prosper argued in the first case before an international criminal tribunal, that in the context of Rwanda, sexual violence against women carried intent of genocide, that is, to "destroy the very foundation of a group."[22] Fragmenting this monolithic problem into smaller components—for example, recognizing the things that have been accomplished—creates more possibilities to see how action, including our own, can be effective.

Framework

Theorists have often preferred "elegant" theories and "Occam's razor" where the simplest and most obvious explanations are the most likely to be true. But in the complex network of social problems, a multiplicity of factors interconnect in complex, and, often, unpredictable ways. This complexity makes social problems harder to understand and resistant to change as systems have a way of absorbing shock and returning to a kind of homeostasis. This complexity also opens up possibilities for myriad points of entry and myriad roles for interveners as agents of problem-solving, healing, and change. Ultimately, resolution of broad social conflicts and social problems requires social movement and social change, which can be seen as a long-term process of social healing. Perhaps all interventions make an impact though they are hard to see when looking at the big picture until eventually a tipping point is reached, and the momentum for change becomes more powerful than the pull of history.

PACS approaches embrace conflicts' complexity, and provide a consideration of many factors. The intensity and development stage of a conflict impacts how it is approached.[23] External guarantors, allies, and other external parties can have a critical role in the escalation or de-escalation of conflicts and political violence.[24] There are different types of mediators who bring varying degrees of power to leverage sources or credibility, for example, high-profile "primary mediators," such as U.S. Presidents, and low-profile, "secondary mediators," such as religiously-based mediators, often Quakers or Mennonites.[25] Conflicts are understood to be driven by a complexity of material as well as intangible interests.[26] Further, a multitude of social dimensions can drive conflict: demographic, economic, political, historical, linguistic, and psychocultural. Conflicts further play themselves out and are driven by dynamics at multiple levels of analysis: for example, elites, middle-tier elites, and the grassroots.[27] That is, the personal is political.[28] Global dynamics also affect domestic relations.[29] This structure means that conflict resolution can take place at these different levels and everyone can and should be involved. Age is a consideration, and while high proportions of youth in a society can be associated with revolution, young people can also be peacemakers and drive positive social change.[30] Conflict mitigation can and should occur in different social arenas, or tracks, including government; professional conflict resolution; business; private citizens; research, training, and education; religious approaches; funding; and public opinion and communication.[31]

Taking into account conflict complexity, this analysis sketches a framework that examines the situational, interest-based, ideological, and emotional factors that (a) shape human action to initiate and escalate genocide; (b) inhibit, constrain, or deter human action to intervene in genocide; and (c) promote human action to not engage in or to intervene against genocide. The notion that there are situational, interest-based, ideological, or emotional factors is an analytical categorization, only as these types of factors influence each other in complex and significant ways. The term "ideological" is used to refer to cognitive factors, keeping in mind that knowledge is socially constructed. In any particular case, not all of these factors may be in play, and not all the factors in play are equally salient. The goal of this analysis is to identify as many factors as possible in order to clarify different avenues for intervention and thereby to promote the agency of individuals, groups, and policymakers at various stages of violence escalation and de-escalation: early intervention, post-genocide work, and prevention of future genocides.

ESCALATION OF GENOCIDE

Within the Conflict Zone

Situational. Situational factors that might facilitate genocide include autocratic political systems and economic conditions, as well as a prostrate populace.[32] War itself can serve as a cover for genocide. Law can serve the interests of genocide. For example, numerous laws were developed by the Nazi regime to control and segregate Jews during the Holocaust. By legal act, governments have restricted, relocated, and defined the identity of indigenous peoples.[33] Momentum toward genocide builds with the escalation of dehumanizing practices: for example, in Armenia—disarmament of the population, the rounding up and killing of 250 intellectuals, Armenian notables killed in every province, Armenian workers no longer used, churches desecrated, schools closed, teachers who refused to convert were killed, deportation of civilians to Syria, lack of facilities contributing to death, and property seized.[34] Genocide is progressive violence.

Interests. The political and economic interests of the perpetrators may drive the genocide of a group. Removing populations may be driven by elites' greed, mistrust, and expansionism, as a strategy for securing power and ownership of a territory. The victims of genocide are seen as obstacles to the agenda of the perpetrators.

Ideology. Nationalism at the exclusion of minority groups may fuel genocidal violence characterized as "ethnic cleansing." While history may be situational, interpretations and the use of history may be manipulated to motivate genocide. Folklore and cultural narratives may demonize minority groups.[35] Propaganda and media may justify or mask what is happening within a country. For four years leading up to the Serbian army's invasion of Bosnia, Serbian president Slobodan Milosevic waged a disinformation campaign, including staged films of Bosnian men raping Serbian women, to infuriate Serbian soldiers against Bosnian Muslims.[36]

Emotional. Ethnic hatred, and a destructive re-channeling of a society's fears, humiliation, unresolved shame, and sense of devaluation can fuel the intense emotions required for genocide. Love of country and countrymen can be manipulated with propaganda that inflames these negative emotions. During the break-up of the former Yugoslavia, in the early 1990s, Serbian president Slobodan Milosovic and Bosnian leader Radovan Karadzic used the historic Battle of Kosovo and the death of Prince Lazar in the fourteenth century, among other propaganda, to rally Serbs to the process of so-called ethnic cleansing of Muslims in Bosnia to the point of creating a sense of "time collapse."[37] Fear of being seen as an outsider may motivate people to be active perpetrators to prove their loyalty in order to save themselves.[38]

External to the Conflict Zone

Situational. External states may have historical ties to regional parties and act as their "external ethno-guarantors."[39] Many observers feared that the regional wars that were the break-up of the former Yugoslavia could lead to a devastating global war if Russia became involved to support the Serbs, Turkey became involved to support the Bosnian Muslims, and Germany or Western Europe came to the aid of the Croats.

Interests. Greed and economic desire may motivate other state actors in the global community to provide weapons.[40] For example, Germany provided the chemicals that were used by Saddam Hussein against the Kurds. Small states such as land-locked Switzerland are vulnerable and may claim neutrality. In

World War II, by providing a banking center to Nazi Germany, Switzerland may arguably have facilitated genocide, while creating a disincentive for the Allies to bomb or invade their nation.

Ideology. Belief in the balance of power may motivate external actors to support a country that is perpetrating genocide in order not to disrupt what is seen as a global balance of power. For example, Pol Pot's Khmer Rouge in Cambodia received the tacit support of China and the Soviet Union. In Rwanda, radio had a critical role in the planned genocide in Rwanda when Radio-Télévision Libre des Milles Collines (RTLM) disseminated propaganda portraying Tutsis as "cockroaches," a threat, and outsiders, along with popular music and scripted programming that was purported to be the real conversations of Rwandans.[41]

Emotional. Emotions of ethnic hatred or devaluation as well as indifference to human suffering may deter intervention.

LACK OF INTERVENTION AGAINST GENOCIDE

Within the Conflict Zone

This section refers to constraints to intervention of both victims and those not directly targeted in the conflict zone. It may not always be clear who is in which group, and both groups make choices at early stages in the escalation to genocide regarding their responses to the situation.

Situational. The reality of power makes action difficult. Ineffective human rights laws fail to protect people. Separation, segregation, control of movement, and control of means of communication seriously constrain or prevent people's ability to gather, strategize, or even understand what is going on.

Interests. Those who may not have directly instigated genocide may still be willing to benefit economically, socially, or politically as a result of it. People at the grassroots level may seize the opportunity of genocide to increase their possessions. In the Polish town of Jedwabne, where 1,600 Jews were murdered by their neighbors, some of the worst perpetrators seized the property of the victims for themselves.[42] During the Rwandan genocide, hungry landless impoverished young people seized the opportunity of the chaos to kill land-owning men, usually older than fifty, and seize their farms.[43]

Ideology. Media and propaganda may convince those not targeted that nothing is wrong. There may be a belief that the victims have brought the situation on themselves, and it is the responsibility of the victims to correct the situation. Victims and those not directly targeted may believe there is nothing they can do. When Lemkin tried to bring his family to the United States in advance of the Holocaust, they were complacent and felt the escalating violence was simply the price of martyrdom and their fate.[44] A sense of defeatism pervades the situation.

Emotional. Both victims and those not directly targeted may feel paralyzing and realistic fear in the face of the violence.[45] Those who are not targeted may harbor ethnic hatreds themselves, be indifferent to the pain of others, or experience passivity.

External to the Conflict Zone

Situational. Problems of such magnitude and complexity are really quite challenging. Outside governments weigh the financial and human costs of intervention. The outcome of intervention is unpredictable and raises concerns about unintended consequences.

Interests. For governments, intervention may entail political, security, and economic risks, and can seriously jeopardize strategic economic interests. Even intervention such as economic sanctions might be resisted if it affects business sectors in the sanctioning country. When arguing for the passage of the UN Convention on Genocide, Sen. Proxmire argued that lawmakers were more responsive to constituent pressure and profit than human dignity, as there were more than a hundred treaties and conventions on economic issues—such as the Tuna Convention with Costa Rica, a Halibut Convention with Canada, and a Road Traffic Convention, allowing licensed American drivers to drive on European highways, among others.[46]

Ideology. The notion of "gentleman's bias"[47] demands that ambassadors refrain from critiquing or undermining the governments where they are stationed. There may be a lack of knowledge or agreement about what to do, and a sense of futility and defeatism. Or there may be serious concerns about the financial, time, and human cost of intervention, as well as unintended consequences of such intervention.

Often outsiders do not believe stories about the escalating atrocities when they hear them. They dismiss reports as "propaganda," "exaggerated," "hoaxes," "unbelievable," and "unsupported with evidence."[48] Outsiders may be relatively complacent about the violence because they believe that there are atrocities on both sides, and that brutality is part of war. Devaluation or dehumanization of the victim leads to inaction and may be combined with a sense that the region of conflict is characterized by primitiveness and tribalism and has a natural propensity for violence.[49] Outsiders may believe that it is happening on both sides and not recognize the acts of murder that are taking place. Disbelief in the possibility for evil actions and that things could get so much worse than they are at a given point inhibits intervention. There may be a sense that the problem belongs to the victim and there is no responsibility to protect or intervene. In general, while knowledge of the violence might be getting out to government, the general public may be largely ignorant of what is going on, or not understand it. Denial of the problem may set in as a defense mechanism.

The media may play a critical role in how conflict and intervention is understood by the public.[50] In the current age of Google, Yahoo!, Twitter, CNN, and 24/7 news feeds, the public is constantly exposed to information on both extraordinary and frivolous world events. Everyone becomes a spectator to everything that is going on in the world. How do persons interpret, respond to, or make sense of issues that are happening across the world or next door? The amount of information can overwhelm one's ability to process and understand, to make sense of, and to act on this information.

Emotional. Thinly masked ethnic hatred, prejudice, or devaluation of the other may contribute to inaction. Outsiders who fail to act may be accused of indifference to pain. Counterintuitively, increased news coverage and awareness of a multiplicity of horrific social issues throughout the world can engender issue fatigue, even hopelessness and despair, or the desire for isolationism.

GENOCIDE INTERVENTION

Within the Conflict Zone

This section refers to those factors which facilitate genocide prevention and intervention by both victims and those not directly targeted in the conflict zone.

Situational. A vibrant civil society and thriving business sector and economy make a society resilient to genocide.[51] Good leaders are able to work constructively for peace. Getting people together to discuss issues and create networks and crosscutting ties provide communication links. Effective and enforceable laws are a deterrent to political misconduct, corruption, and abuse.

Interests. Thriving trade and interdependent economic and social relations may provide a disincentive for war. Business is an important track of diplomacy and aspect of civil society.[52]

Ideology. Nonviolent protest challenges prevailing ideas about violence and initiates, sustains, and gives form to a social process of making meaning. To be in a position to influence, it is important to demonstrate the case for, and to educate for, peace and tolerance. It is important to get out the story of what is happening and the atrocities that are occurring, and to name what is happening. The media has a role in getting this information to the public. For oppressed groups, the homeplace can be a site of resistance, where grandmothers, grandfathers, mothers, fathers, aunts, and uncles provide socialization that maintains a group's culture, identity, and history (often encoded in folklore), and strategies for survival, as well as comfort and re-humanization.[53]

Emotional. Impatience with the status quo drives people to resist and take action. Sometimes people call up the strength to resist when there is no way. Power describes a busload of Kurdish men who resisted after lengthy rides in inhumane conditions to their would-be mass graves in Iraq. In the tumult that arose as a result, only one man, Ozer, was able to survive undetected under a mound of bodies when they were shot in retribution, and eventually crawl out and find refuge. Ozer's story and what happened to all of those men is now told in Power's book. During the genocide in Rwanda, when the girls from a Catholic school were taken to a field and shot, one girl was able to persuade one of the men to save her, and was the sole survivor.[54]

Situational. Power refers to the International Criminal Court as "a giant without arms."[55] Restructuring and empowering the UN is a possibility that needs to be seriously investigated. Early warning systems can facilitate international mediation before conflict escalates further. Power emphasizes that many perpetrators weigh daily how far they can go, and therefore it is essential for the United States and others states to immediately and forcefully condemn racially based violence when it erupts. Naming and condemning the reprehensible action and the individuals responsible for it are important steps. Getting experts together—including academics from the PACS field—for consultations during a crisis is critical.

Interests. It is important to name the interests in the region, and to seek clarification of U.S. national interests in particular nations. Public dialogue can be a process of interrogating, lobbying, and reshaping arguments to clarify how stopping genocide is a U.S. interest.

Ideology. Lobbying and advocacy is perhaps one of the most important interventions. Education can promote widespread understanding of genocide and ways to address it. Peace education can build a culture of human rights that is resilient to genocide and prepared to respond. Education about current affairs can also provide early warning and alert governments and people to what may need to be addressed. Stories about current and past genocides need to be told. Credible sources and eyewitnesses who report atrocities are important for building awareness and compassion. When journalists or government officials are dispersed or murdered, civilians fleeing the massacres tell their stories. They must be heard. Again, the media has a role in this. Nonviolent action and protest is part of a public discourse that can affect policy, raise consciousness of the issues and build solidarity at local and international levels. Constructive narratives can chart pathways to peace. The decision

Table 14.1. Factors that Contribute to Genocide, Lack of Intervention, and Intervention

		Situational	*Interests*	*Knowledge*	*Emotional*
Escalation of Genocide	Within the Conflict Zone	Autocratic political systems, economic conditions, prostrate populace. War is a cover-up. Laws legitimize genocide. Momentum of dehumanization.	Political and economic interests can drive genocide, greed, mistrust, and expansionism.	Folklore, cultural narratives and history manipulated to motivate genocide.	Ethnic hatred, fear mongering, humiliation, unresolved shame. Propaganda stirs emotions. Destructive othering.
	External to the Conflict Zone	Historical ties to regional parties build ethno-alliances.	Greed and economic interests motivate business partnerships.	Strategic global balance of power (Cold War).	Indifference, othering, and ethnic hatred.
Lack of Intervention against Genocide	Within the Conflict Zone	Ineffective human rights laws. Separation, segregation, control of movement and communication hamper resistance.	Economic, social and political benefits of genocide trump intervention.	Media and propaganda hide the genocide. Victims brought it on themselves.	Paralyzed by the violence and fear of violence.
	External to the Conflict Zone	Challenge of magnitude and complexity. Outcome is unpredictable. Direct and indirect financial and human risks and costs unknown.	Political, security and economic risks can jeopardize interests.	Gentleman's bias diplomacy. Unbelievable evil. Believe atrocities on both sides. Victims' problem. Disbelief.	Indifference, overwhelmed by horror and evil, issue fatigue, prejudice, othering, hopelessness, despair.
Genocide Intervention	Within the Conflict Zone	Vibrant civil society and economy. Leaders build peace and cooperation. Effective and enforceable laws.	Thriving democracy, trade and business build diplomacy and civil society.	Culture of nonviolence, peace, tolerance, and humanization.	Resistance. Impatience with status quo.
	External to the Conflict Zone	Strengthen the International Criminal Court, restructure United Nations. Early warning system. Responsibility to protect practices. Foreign states and bodies immediately act and follow-through with threats. Name and shame.	Clarify interests in particular nations. Understand how preventing genocide is in nation's interest.	Education, lobbying, advocacy, activism. Peace, human rights and current affairs education. Tell stories of past genocides. Build public discourse. Use media.	Build capacity to believe the unbelievable, impatience and courage.

to make the prevention of genocide a priority can build the momentum for change; this decision requires international condemnation when massacres, political violence, and genocide occur. It is important for outsiders to listen for what victims and those attempting to intervene on the ground are requesting when making policy decisions.

Emotional. A broader conception of sacrifice may be needed to address global problems, and global inequality that fuels political greed and violence. It is painful to absorb survivors' stories of horror, and there must be the capacity to believe the unbelievable. We must also recognize the emotions of the perpetrator and not always expect rational actors. Impatience and courage are critical for working for social justice and peace.

CONCLUSION

The study of genocide must be central to the PACS field. Alternatives to violence have defined the PACS field, and more work needs to be done to examine and evaluate nonviolent alternatives to genocide by different types of actors and at every stage of the escalating violence, the de-escalation of violence and so called "post-conflict" phases, as well as prevention. Social justice and civil rights have been central to the development of the field, and this work also needs to be further developed in order to address the many faces of genocide, including the forms of the cultural devaluation and murder that devastates whole groups of peoples, including indigenous peoples throughout the world, violence against women (femicide), violence against children (infanticide), and all people who face extraordinary material deprivation (modern slavery, extreme poverty). While anger, rage, and hatred might be an understandable and normal response to genocide and violence—what Kenneth Hardy calls de-humanized loss[56]—it remains critical to explore a breadth of strategies and possibilities to re-channel this anger, make sense of the past, and use past experience to create better societies.

The PACS field is distinguished by its commitment to both theory and practice, and their interconnection. Praxis, as Paulo Friere put it, is "reflection and action upon the world in order to transform it."[57] It is not enough to critically analyze, but to also chart paths and break paths toward peace. This analysis seeks to provide a framework that might promote action and de-facilitate the bystander position by providing insight and options. An important variable is location relative to the conflict and violence.

There is also a group of people that move between the conflict zone and locations distant to it. These are often diplomats (such as Hans Morgenthau in Armenia); journalists (such as Samantha Power herself); military personnel (such as Romeo Dallaire in Rwanda); refugee survivors; and scholars who through research, or because they are from a conflict zone, travel internationally. Raphael Lemkin was such a scholar. He was also a refugee. While growing up in the Bialystock region of Poland, during the World War I period, when Germany and Russia were battling in Poland, his family fled their farm to hide in the neighboring forests. In September 1939, six days after the Wehrmacht's invasion of Poland, he fled, at first on foot, and eventually made his way to the United States, where, with the help of a professor for whom he had translated the Polish criminal code, he obtained a position at Duke University. Such cultural go-betweens are in a unique, if often bedeviled position, as mediators between knowledge systems, who may be able to be effective advocates for victims of political violence and genocide.

While people far from the violence might easily not act nor intervene for numerous reasons, including lack of awareness, as outsiders they may also have more security and capacity to speak out, bring resources, and provide refuge during crises. The great thinkers and peacemakers who, over the past five decades, have inspired the field of peace and conflict studies, have been leaders in addressing power relations, social injustice, and violence. But there is much more work that needs to be done, and, as Power argues, it means involving civil society. This includes finding inspiration—sometimes even in the forms of songs and stories—to sustain us on the journey, which is really the journey of humanity, to a world with peace and justice for everybody.

BIBLIOGRAPHY

Boulding, E. *Building a Global Civic Culture: Education for an Interdependent World.* Syracuse, NY: Syracuse University Press, 1988.

Byrne, S. "Mired in Intractability: The Roles of External Ethno-guarantors and Primary Mediators in Cyprus and Northern Ireland." *Conflict Resolution Quarterly,* vol. 24, no. 2 (2007): 149–172.

Byrne, S., and N. Carter. "Social Cubism: Six Social Forces of Ethno-territorial Conflict in Northern Ireland and Quebec." *Journal of Peace and Conflict Studies,* vol. 3, no. 2 (1996): 52–71.

Byrne, S., and L. Keashly. "Working with Ethno-Political Conflict: A Multi-Modal and Multi-Level Approach to Conflict Intervention." *International Peacekeeping,* vol. 7, no. 2 (2000): 97–120.

Churchill, W. *A Little Matter of Genocide: Holocaust and Denial in the Americas 1942–present.* San Francisco, CA: City Lights Book, 1997.

Diamond, J. *Collapse: How Societies Choose to Fail or Succeed.* New York: Penguin, 2005.

Diamond, L., and J.W. McDonald. *Multi-Track Diplomacy: A Systems Approach to Peace.* Bloomfield, CT: Kumarian Press, 1996.

Enloe, C. *Bananas, Beaches and Bases: Making Feminist Sense of International Politics.* Berkeley: University of California Press, 2000.

Freire, P. *Pedagogy of the Oppressed.* New York: Continuum, 1986.

Gandhi, M. *The Essential Gandhi: An Anthology.* Louis Fischer, ed. New York: Random House, 1962.

Goldstein, J.S. *War and Gender: How Gender Shapes the War System and Vice Versa.* Cambridge: Cambridge University Press, 2001.

Gross, J.T. *Neighbors: The Destruction of the Jewish Community in Jedwabne, Poland.* Princeton, NJ: Princeton University Press, 2001.

Hardy, K., and T. Laszloffy. *Teens Who Hurt, Clinical Interventions to Break the Cycle of Violence.* New York: Guilford Press, 2005.

Hedges. C. *War Is a Force that Gives Us Meaning.* New York: Anchor Books, 2003.

hooks, bell. *Yearning: Race, Gender, and Cultural Politics.* Boston: South End Press, 1990.

Kayitesi, Berte. Public lecture, Winnipeg International Storytelling Festival, Winnipeg, Manitoba, May 9, 2008.

King, M.L., Jr. *I have a Dream: Writings and Speeches that Changed the World.* J.M. Washington, ed. San Francisco: Harper, 1992.

Laue, J. "Ethical Considerations in Choosing Intervention Roles," *Peace and Change,* vol. 8 (1982): 29–42.

Lederach, J.P. *Preparing for Peace: Conflict Transformation across Cultures.* Syracuse, NY: Syracuse University Press, 1995.

———. *Building Peace: Sustainable Reconciliation in Divided Societies.* Washington, DC: U.S. Institute of Peace. 1997.

Mac Ginty, R., and A. Williams. *Conflict and Development.* London: Routledge, 2009.

McEvoy-Levy, S., ed. *Troublemakers or Peacemakers? Youth and Post-Accord Peace Building.* South Bend, IN: University of Notre Dame Press, 2006.

Millet, K. *Sexual Politics.* New York: Doubleday, 1970.

Morse, A. *While Six Million Died: A Chronicle of American Apathy.* New York: Random House, 1968.

Pearson, F.S., and J. Sislin. *Arms and Ethnic Conflict.* Lanham, MD: Rowman & Littlefield, 2001.

Power, S. *"A Problem from Hell": America and the Age of Genocide.* New York: Perennial, 2003.

Princen, T. *Intermediaries in International Conflict.* Princeton, NJ: Princeton University Press, 1992.

Ross, M.H., ed. *Culture and Belonging in Divided Societies: Contestation and Symbolic Landscapes.* Philadelphia: University of Pennsylvania Press, 2009.

Ross, M.H. *The Management of Conflict: Interpretations and Interests in Comparative Perspective.* New Haven, CT: Yale University Press, 1993.

Rothman, J. *Resolving Identity-Based Conflicts in Nations, Organizations, and Communities.* San Francisco: Jossey-Bass, 1979.

Sharp, G. *Waging Nonviolent Struggle: 20th Century Practice and 21st Century Potential.* Boston: Extending Horizons Books, 2005.

Strobel, W.P. *Late-breaking Foreign Policy: The New Media's Influence on Peace Operations*. Washington, DC: U.S. Institute of Peace, 1997.

Snyder, L. *Roots of German Nationalism*. Bloomington: Indiana University Press, 1978.

Tifft, L., and L. Markham. "Battering Women and Battering Central Americans," in *Criminology as Peacemaking*, H. Pepinsky and R. Quinney, eds. Bloomington: Indiana University Press, 1991.

van Tongeren, P., M. Brenk, M. Hallema, and J. Verhoeven, eds. *People Building Peace II: Successful Stories of Civil Society*. Boulder, CO: Lynne Rienner, 2005.

Volkan, V. *Bloodlines: From Ethnic Price to Ethnic Hatred*. New York: Farrar, Strauss, and Giroux, 1997.

Wolff, Stefan. *Ethnic Conflict: A Global Perspective*. Oxford: Oxford University Press, 2006.

NOTES

1. This chapter originally appeared under the same title in the Spring 2010 issue of *Peace and Conflict Studies*, vol. 17, no. 1, pages 43–70.

2. Cited by S. Power, *"A Problem from Hell": America and the Age of Genocide* (New York: Perennial, 2003), 29.

3. Power, *"Problem from Hell."*

4. J.P. Lederach, *Preparing for Peace: Conflict Transformation across Cultures* (Syracuse, NY: Syracuse University Press, 1995).

5. M.L. King, Jr., in *I Have a Dream: Writings and Speeches that Changed the World*, J. M. Washington, ed. (San Francisco: Harper, 1992).

6. M. Gandhi, in *The Essential Gandhi: An Anthology*, Louis Fischer, ed. (New York: Random House, 1962).

7. G. Sharp, *Waging Nonviolent Struggle: 20th Century Practice and 21st Century Potential* (Boston: Extending Horizons Books, 2005).

8. For example, C. Enloe, *Bananas, Beaches and Bases: Making Feminist Sense of International Politics* (Berkeley: University of California Press, 2000); J.S. Goldstein, *War and Gender: How Gender Shapes the War System and Vice Versa* (Cambridge: Cambridge University Press, 2001).

9. A. Morse, *While Six Million Died: A Chronicle of American Apathy* (New York: Random House, 1968).

10. For example, W. Churchill, *A Little Matter of Genocide: Holocaust and Denial in the Americas 1942–present* (San Francisco, CA: City Lights Book, 1997).

11. S. Power, *"Problem from Hell."*

12. Kenneth Hardy and T. Laszloffy, *Teens Who Hurt, Clinical Interventions to Break the Cycle of Violence* (New York: Guilford Press, 2005).

13. E. Boulding, *Building a Global Civic Culture: Education for an Interdependent World* (Syracuse, NY: Syracuse University Press, 1988).

14. For example, J. Rothman, *Resolving Identity-Based Conflicts in Nations, Organizations, and Communities* (San Francisco: Jossey-Bass, 1997).

15. Lederach, *Preparing for Peace*; J.P. Lederach, *Building Peace: Sustainable Reconciliation in Divided Societies* (Washington, DC: U.S. Institute of Peace, 1997).

16. Henry Morganthau Sr. in Power, *Problem from Hell*, 7.

17. An Associated Press correspondent in Power, *Problem from Hell*, 10.

18. Lemkin in Power, *Problem from Hell,* 19.

19. Szmul Zygielbojm, who committed suicide, in Power, *Problem from Hell*, 31.

20. Arthur Goldberg, U.S. intelligence, in Power, *Problem from Hell*, 36.

21. Lawyer's description of Raphael Lemkin in Power, *Problem from Hell*, 49.

22. Pierre-Richard Prosper, "Declaration of Pierre-Richard Prosper," Department of Defense (March 8, 2005) http://www.state.gov/documents/organization/55821.pdf, 8.

23. S. Byrne and L. Keashly, "Working with Ethno-Political Conflict: A Multi-Modal and Multi-Level Approach to Conflict Intervention," *International Peacekeeping,* vol. 7, no. 2 (2000): 97–120.

24. S. Byrne, "Mired in Intractability: The Roles of External Ethno-guarantors and Primary Mediators in Cyprus and Northern Ireland," *Conflict Resolution Quarterly,* vol. 24, no. 2 (2007): 149–172.

25. Byrne, "Mired in Intractability."

26. M.H. Ross, *The Management of Conflict: Interpretations and Interests in Comparative Perspective* (New Haven, CT: Yale University Press, 1993).

27. Lederach, *Building Peace.*

28. K. Millet, *Sexual Politics* (New York: Doubleday, 1970).

29. L. Tifft and L. Markham, "Battering Women and Battering Central Americans," in *Criminology as Peacemaking,* H. Pepinsky and R. Quinney, eds. (Bloomington: Indiana University Press, 1991).

30. S. McEvoy-Levy, ed., *Troublemakers or Peacemakers? Youth and Post-Accord Peace Building* (South Bend, IN: University of Notre Dame Press, 2006).

31. L. Diamond and J.W. McDonald, *Multi-Track Diplomacy: A Systems Approach to Peace* (Bloomfield, CT: Kumarian Press, 1996).

32. For example, R. Mac Ginty and A. Williams, *Conflict and Development* (London: Routledge, 2009).

33. For example, W. Churchill, *A Little Matter.*

34. For example, Power, *Problem from Hell.*

35. For example, L. Snyder, *Roots of German Nationalism* (Bloomington: Indiana University Press, 1978); L. Tifft and L. Markham, "Battering Women and Battering Central Americans," in *Criminology as Peacemaking,* H. Pepinsky and R. Quinney, eds. (Bloomington: Indiana University Press, 1991).

36. C. Hedges, *War Is a Force that Gives Us Meaning (*New York: Anchor Books, 2003).

37. V. Volkan, *Bloodlines: From Ethnic Price to Ethnic Hatred (*New York: Farrar, Strauss, and Giroux, 1997).

38. For example, J.T. Gross, *Neighbors: The Destruction of the Jewish Community in Jedwabne, Poland* (Princeton, NJ: Princeton University Press, 2001).

39. Byrne, "Mired in Intractability."
40. F.S. Pearson and J. Sislin, *Arms and Ethnic Conflict* (Lanham, MD: Rowman & Littlefield, 2001).
41. W.P. Strobel, *Late-breaking Foreign Policy: The New Media's Influence on Peace Operations* (Washington, DC: U.S. Institute of Peace, 1997).
42. Gross, *Neighbors.*
43. J. Diamond, *Collapse: How Societies Choose to Fail or Succeed* (New York: Penguin, 2005).
44. Power, *Problem from Hell.*
45. Mac Ginty and Williams, *Conflict and Development.*
46. Power, *Problem from Hell.*
47. Power, *Problem from Hell*, 260.
48. Power, *Problem from Hell*, 8–9.
49. S. Wolff, *Ethnic Conflict: A Global Perspective* (Oxford: Oxford University Press, 2006).
50. Strobel, *Late-breaking Foreign Policy.*
51. P. van Tongeren, M. Brenk, M. Hallema, and J. Verhoeven, eds., *People Building Peace II: Successful Stories of Civil Society* (Boulder, CO: Lynne Rienner, 2005).
52. Diamond and McDonald, *Multi-Track Diplomacy.*
53. bell hooks, *Yearning: Race, Gender, and Cultural Politics* (Boston: South End Press, 1990).
54. B. Kayitesi, public lecture, Winnipeg International Storytelling Festival, Winnipeg, Manitoba, May 9, 2008.
55. Power, *Problem from Hell*, 491.
56. Hardy and Laszloffy, *Teens Who Hurt.*
57. Paulo Freire, *Pedagogy of the Oppressed* (New York: Continuum, 1986).

Part Three

Pedagogy

Chapter 15

Peace and Conflict Studies

Reclaiming Our Roots and Designing Our Way Forward

Thomas Matyók

Peace and conflict studies is a transformative leadership field, interdisciplinary in nature and poised to provide a range of nonviolent actions to address complex social issues faced by current and future generations. Whether conflict work is at the micro, meso, macro, or mega levels of analysis, it is about creating positive social change and establishing just peace. Some may not agree with my use of the term peace and conflict studies to incorporate all aspects of the academic study and practice of conflict analysis and resolution. I use the term in the same way that other academic disciplines define their study, incorporating sub-disciplines as their fields mature. It is vitally important that all conflict workers, regardless of the level at which they study and practice, identify with the larger definition of the field. As peace and conflict studies is still emerging, and we work to better draw the lines that define our field of study and practice, I suggest the following model: conflict analysis and resolution as the philosophical foundation of the field,[1] peace and conflict studies as the academic field of study, and conflict resolution as the practice component of the field.

A field of study is not a jumble of skills. Conflict resolution practices are important competencies for peace and conflict workers, but they should not define the field, nor who we are. Confusing conflict resolution skills development with peace and conflict studies is not helpful. Within the academy, however, peace and conflict studies curricula have often lacked focus, and quickly moved from their core purpose of social change. Peace and conflict studies promised much: a reliable guide to conflict amelioration and lasting agreement. But conflict resolution—as the applied component of the field—quickly came to define the field and abandoned this transformational role. Chaotic and lacking definition, it deserted its humanist heritage for a more salable product, teaching students trade-like skills.

It is time to discuss the discipline's future, its distinction and validity, and, most importantly, how best to prepare tomorrow's scholars and practitioners in the field of peace and conflict studies. My purpose is to initiate a dialogue about the evolving and appropriate role of pedagogy in preparing peace and conflict scholars and practitioners. Although some even ask whether the field will survive in the academy, as a profession, peace and conflict studies is a legitimate leadership field providing significant scholarship and practice in the creation of social change and the establishment of positive peace.

Most current research, unfortunately, focuses on the present state of professional training. The construction of peace is a deliberate activity requiring skilled professionals. As strong as individual programs in peace and conflict studies are, it is time to identify how we will progress as a profession and reclaim direction. This chapter formulates future directions, and provides a conceptual framework for curricular development.

Throughout this chapter, I use the term peace and conflict studies. Peace and conflict studies are transnational, transdisciplinary, and bridge theory and practice.[2] Conflict analysis and resolution is the philosophical foundation, and peace and conflict studies is the academic discipline and professional field. Using the term *conflict resolution* to define the field misleads. Conflict resolution encompasses the skills required for success by conflict workers, but it is not the academic field of study. Continued use of the term conflict resolution to establish our field's parameters contributes to its marginalization by keeping the field skills-based and narrowly focused. And conflict resolution presumes resolution as the preferred conclusion. The interdisciplinary character of peace and conflict studies is both strength and dilemma. A transdisciplinary, collaborative approach to the study of peace and conflict provides a solid foundation for understanding complex issues, yet it can, if ill planned or uncoordinated, produce a poorly focused and fractured curriculum.[3] Peace and conflict studies programs are often located in schools of interdisciplinary studies, employing instructors drafted from various university departments. Petty cross-disciplinary rivalries, however, may inhibit cooperation and block development of coherent programs.[4] Yet university and college curricula may also approach too narrowly the study of conflict, following parochial interests and ignoring conflict's complexity, depth, and nuance. Unformed in theory or practice, degrees are cobbled together.[5] Despite some increase in undergraduate programs, most peace and conflict studies—as well as conflict resolution—syllabi are post-graduate. And only a handful of institutions in the United States grant doctorates.[6]

Conflict resolution is relatively new in the roster of university disciplines. In the half-century of systematic, academic study of peace and conflict, two paths emerged: one—legalistic—emphasized a quasi-judicial process to mediate and contain conflict, the other—humanistic—sought transformation of enmity into amity by holistically studying the phenomenon of human conflict. Though still debated, reconciling the two may not be possible. I advocate for a humanistic curricular platform and suggest we are at a *tipping point.* It is time to decide which path governs how we prepare conflict workers.

Future academic preparation of peace and conflict scholars and conflict workers grounded in the humanities requires novel thinking. Traditional education models are inadequate to prepare scholars and practitioners for conflict work's complexity. I suggest an *engaged scholarship* model of undergraduate and graduate curricula. The model assumes humanistic definitions of the field and convergence on knowledge supporting the positive and peaceful transformation of conflict. Transformative, positive peace seeking and humanistic conflict resolution practices will restore the field's progressive qualities. It will distinguish graduates as something more than *lawyers writ small.*

THE FIELD'S DEVELOPMENT

It seems that conflict resolution is as old as humankind.[7] For ninety-nine percent of human history, cooperation among humans has been the norm,[8] suggesting the importance of conflict resolution as an important part of humankind's social evolution. However, the documented history of formal peace and conflict practices begins with the Kingdom of Mari (Modern Day Syria) in 1800 B.C.E. where its kings used arbitration and mediation to resolve disputes among themselves and between vassals. The history and practice of conflict resolution is well documented;[9] yet formal study of conflict is recent. Anchored to centuries of thought,[10] the conflict resolution movement only began to define itself as a distinct field of study following World War II.[11] It emerged as an academic discipline in the late 1960s and early 1970s.[12]

Four waves frame the study and practice of conflict analysis and resolution and introduce the field's developmental narrative.[13] The first wave was the social change begun in the 1960s with the *power to the people* movement. People's trust in social institutions began to erode throughout the 1960s. The Viet Nam War and Watergate changed the direction of American society. Through political engagement, people began to take back power from elites. Forms of alternative dispute resolution showed up on the social scene first. The second wave pursued professionalization in the 1970s, the third focused on the structural nature of conflict and human needs, and wave four moved the field toward a transformation focus under the umbrella of peace studies. We now find ourselves riding a fifth wave that provides an opportunity for the field to design its way forward and emerge as a theory-based discipline with a defensible place in the academy. In reclaiming our transformative roots, a humanistic frame informs curriculum development. Within this framework, conflict resolution skills development is one component of professional training.

The evolution of the field as a form of study has been a messy one. The field incorporates every form of conflict resolution from interpersonal negotiation to the extra-legal (war), and currently there is an ongoing competition regarding the practices that should define the discipline. The field lacks focus and is more a collection of conflict resolution skills and techniques than a disciplined field of study.[14]

Currently, graduates and practitioners of conflict resolution programs, lacking defined knowledge and skill competencies, are adrift in the professional marketplace and hard pressed to articulate their unique qualifications.[15] Fuzzy definition of knowledge and skill competencies is exacerbated by conflict resolution's response-driven nature.[16] It addresses extant conflict rather than *provention* or transformation. Many students of conflict resolution enter practice too early, poorly prepared, and potentially doing as much harm as good.[17] Too often, graduates of conflict resolution programs find themselves unable to market their skills; unable to demonstrate convincingly useful skills, they request letters of recommendation to apply to second, alternate graduate degree programs. The professional employment market is all too often limited in its demand for conflict workers. And graduates of conflict resolution programs may not carry appropriate skills into the marketplace. It is time to strengthen the profession through a curriculum grounded in core competencies.

Required is a competency-based platform for teaching conflict resolution within the defined field of peace and conflict studies, one that is action-oriented and combines theory with mentored practice. If a profession, it is essential we have unified educational strategies for teaching peace and conflict transformation.[18]

ENTRENCHED IN THE ACADEMY

Peace and conflict studies, as an academic newcomer, struggles for acceptance and legitimacy. Roughly 450 academic programs exist in the United States, covering conflict resolution subjects at various levels.[19] The number and variety of programs seems irrelevant if one has no qualitative criteria to judge; any port serves when all ports are equally unmapped. This instability describes the current conflict resolution field. It is a jumble of curricular approaches trying to teach skills uncoupled from a comprehensive grasp of social complexity. The field is and remains a poorly defined set of practices that may or may not be specific to a distinct discipline.[20] A review of conflict resolution programs shows classes are found in the curricula of many institutions that are taught by unspecialized faculty with little direct training in the field or those whose chief interests are not peace and conflict studies. Thus, conflict resolution has an unscholarly reputation. Lacking core knowledge and skill competencies for conflict workers,[21] graduates may or may not be competent to do what they say they are able to do, transform or resolve conflict.

Professionalization results from deliberate study built upon a common body of knowledge and honed by supervised practice. As in medicine or law or any genuine professional field, the preparation of the graduate cannot be random. Conflict resolution's increasing randomization and the virtual absence of mentored application of theory makes a professional identity iffy, at best, impossible at worst.[22] Absent clearly established core knowledge and skill competencies, grounded in theory and research, it is doubtful that conflict resolution practitioners can claim true professional status. Certainly, those consulting conflict resolution professionals rightfully expect practitioners to possess minimum qualifications. And, characterization as a professional requires vastly more than a rambling hodgepodge of skills.

The current field of conflict resolution pays small attention to the academic preparation of conflict workers. A review of the literature reveals precious little research on pedagogic or curricular issues. Training conflict workers follows two alternatives: the technical or the transformative.[23] A technical educational framework, of course, aims at the cessation of conflict and implies a post-conflict state that may only achieve a *negative peace*, the absence of direct violence. Technical proficiency may result in the resolution of conflict, but it does not necessarily lead to just and equitable outcomes. Technical conflict resolution may lead to maintaining unjust social conditions rather than changing them.[24]

In the relatively new discipline of peace and conflict studies, how do its students differ from those who study conflict from the vantage of political science, sociology, psychology or a host of other perspectives? As in medicine, so in the social sciences, increasing knowledge reveals greater complexity and tends toward specialization. The multiplication of academic disciplines in the modern university reflects this phenomenon. Conflict resolution, lacking clarity and rigor, is at the academic margins. It is an ill-defined and loosely structured field in which peace research and conflict resolution are trivialized. The field is marginalized because we have not defined our center.

Current emphasis on preparing professionals in the field is freighted by technique and accumulating knowledge of ill-defined value. Analysis of conflict and its transformation receives a perfunctory nod in *academe's* groves. A narrow, practice-centered approach leads to solutions chasing problems rather than developing context-specific intervention methods.[25] The answer, I believe, rests on the use of varied analytical systems synthesized—brought to bear—on the dynamic structure of conflict itself and driven by the goal of purposeful and effective change.

AN ALTERNATIVE CURRICULAR APPROACH

In contrast, transformation works to end conflict while simultaneously addressing the structure that produced conflict, replacing it with something healthier, and, as a result, moving toward a *positive peace*, the absence of direct and structural violence and the presence of justice. Social justice and issues of fairness are important aspects of conflict resolution practices.[26] A social justice centered curricula becomes the defining characteristic of the academic preparation of conflict workers. We require a discipline recognizing our humanity with all its complexity, a discipline that acknowledges the existential quality of conflict. This thinking reflects three beliefs: cooperation is a *normal* condition of humankind,[27] when conflict occurs it can be creatively and peacefully transformed[28] and, finally, analysis alters conditions.[29] Conflict analysis and resolution requires simultaneous, parallel activities designed to modify personal and social behaviors and even cultural perspectives. It looks forward, asking antagonists to create a future in which both discover satisfaction. We cannot be lured into the comfortable trap of mechanistic procedures. Our purpose in educating professionals is for more than mere perfection of technique. Technique must be informed by analysis and explore peaceful transformation and reconciliation. This result is accomplished by multidisciplinary practices. Multidisciplinary practices ensure all dimensions of conflict are analyzed and addressed. But, few conflict professionals have been trained that way.[30]

WE MAKE THE PATH BY WALKING

Peace and conflict studies is informed by a range of other, essentially humanistic, disciplines and borrows methods and skills suited to particular situations and circumstances. It recognizes that the range of human experience is a tapestry whose warp and woof is the sum of all culture and experience. Its goal is community and positive peace. This goal sets it apart as a stand-alone profession. One practicing humanistic conflict transformation assumes a broad, *renaissance* approach to the study and reshaping of contention. Renaissance-style practitioners join wide-ranging academic interests with specific conflict transformation skills. He or she seeks to understand the peculiar structure and dimension of a situation. Indeed, practitioners internalize the concept that the process of resolution is, itself, loaded with assorted baggage. Virtually all disciplines offer some useful tools for understanding the character and components of conflict.

Peace and conflict studies provides the purpose for humanistic conflict resolution practice. Peace and conflict studies generates a context empowering people to act. It is progressive and forward looking. Positive peace is a deliberate, not unintended, outcome. The humanistic approach to conflict creates new, future-centered narratives. While the politicalization of conflict resolution fragments a common humanity with the introduction of power, peace-centered transformation seeks to restore a *tribal,* or community, context to conflict resolution.

Since conflict is seldom simple, imposed rationalization creates a facade of order where none exists in reality. It removes individual conflict from the broad interests of the community. Without a communal context, conflict resolution is likely to be unstable and does little to transform the origin of the conflict. A peace-centered transformative type of conflict resolution requires practitioners who are *generalists* in the best sense of the word, individuals who are comfortable with complexity

A CURRICULUM LOOKING FORWARD

The strength of the peace and conflict studies field rests upon a *renaissance* approach to learning, one not tethered to disciplinary thinking, and an emphasis on altering behaviors. An interdisciplinary methodology, however, must not become a license for shallow or shoddy learning. Validity demands academic rigor. And, such rigor is best formed within a curricular framework flexible enough to accommodate cross-disciplinary collaboration but rigid enough to be defined as unique within the academy.

Professional Identity

Professional identity derives from programs in higher education. In many ways, development of identity in the field of peace and conflict studies mirrors some of the frustrations experienced by teachers in creating a coherent

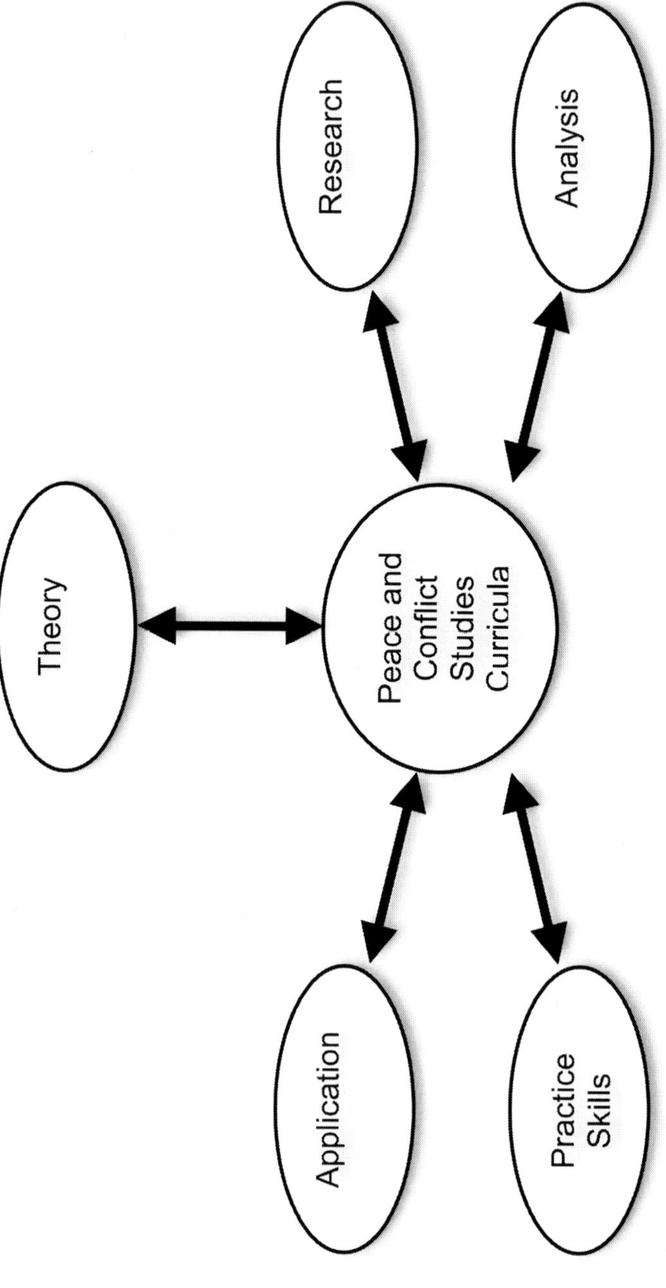

Figure 15.1. A Curricular Model

and unified sense of self.[31] Mastery of rigorous curricula contributes to a feeling of professional identity and enhances graduates' ability to present themselves as experts in conflict.

I propose a curricular model (Figure 15.1) that integrates academics and practice. Introduced is an overarching macro framework for peace and conflict studies curriculum development. This conceptual model of curriculum development is a tool by which scholars and practitioners can stretch their thinking to new levels. The model can be easily modified for use at undergraduate and graduate levels of study. Core and elective classes can be divided among the theory, research, and analysis dimensions of study, ensuring a solid foundation for practice is established.

Future peace and conflict workers are mentored and receive immediate feedback on their performance. Students will have an opportunity to observe conflicts and intervention methodologies *in situ*. Mentoring and coaching by practicing professionals will be an important aspect of fieldwork. Extensive fieldwork will set the foundation for a career defined by reflective practice. The model is flexible enough to allow for contextual differences while ensuring a degree of unity among programs with core competencies anchoring individual program development. The model is informed by other professional fields such as social work and education. The practice skills and application dimensions ensure graduates of conflict resolution programs have had the benefit of extensive fieldwork under the supervision or practicing professionals.

Core Competencies and Learning Goals

I propose that peace and conflict studies be anchored in core competencies and threaded across curricula. To move the ball forward, programs can be built that ensure the following competencies are achieved. Learning goals can be used in developing courses and course learning objectives.

Theoretical background of the field. Conflict analysis and resolution is the philosophical background of the field of peace and conflict studies.[32] Graduates will be grounded in a common body of conflict analysis and resolution theory.

Global competence. Graduates will be able to operate in a global environment. Curricula are internationalized.

Collaboration. Graduates are competent in working with state and nonstate actors as well as governmental and nongovernmental organizations in the field.

Cultural competency. Graduates are able to live and work in multiple cultures, simultaneously. Graduates are able to employ de-colonized research and analysis methodologies.

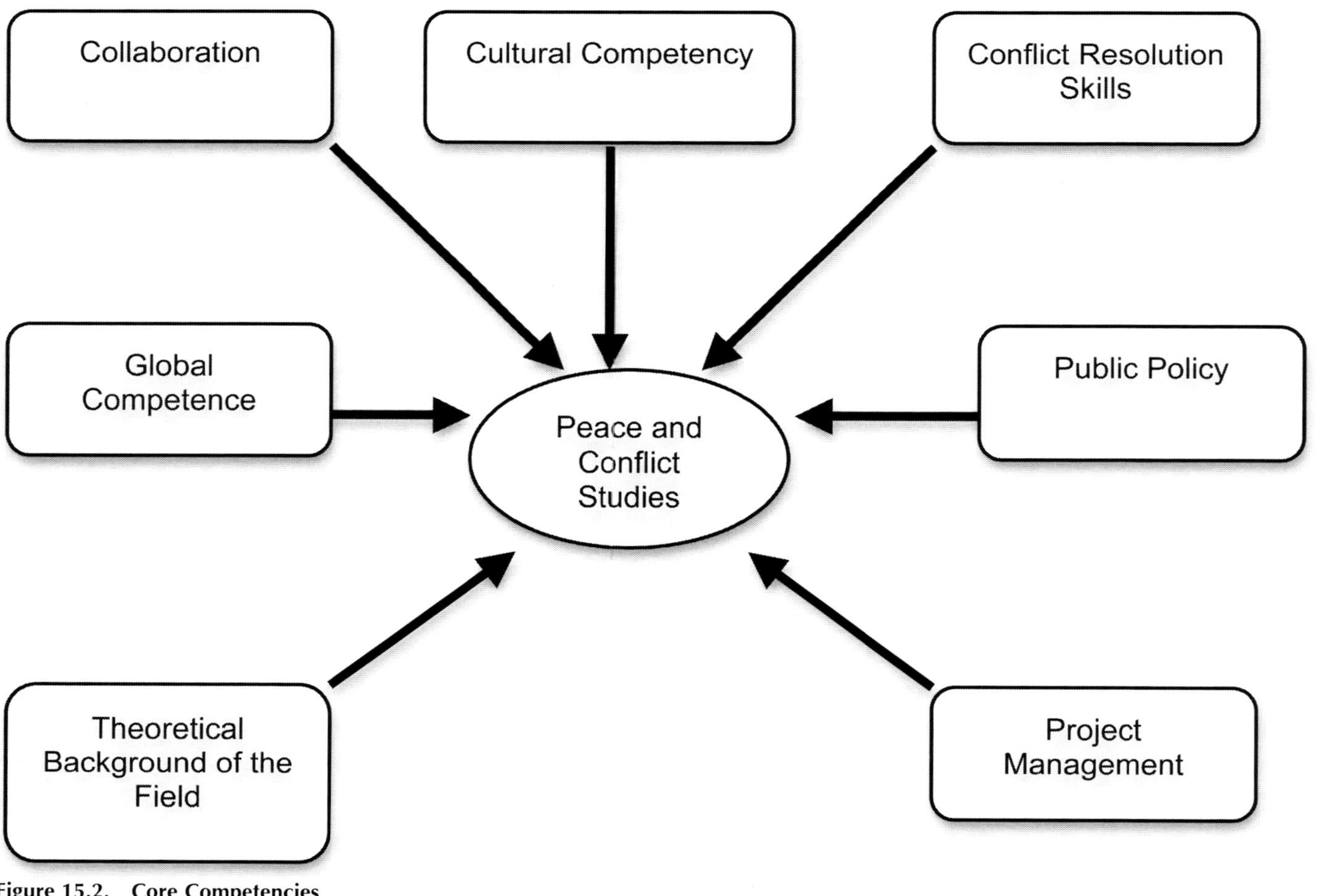

Figure 15.2. Core Competencies

Conflict resolution skills. Graduates have mastered basic conflict resolution skills; interpersonal negotiation, mediation, facilitation, group problem solving, etc.

Public Policy. Graduates are able to understand how public policy development influences conflict and conflict transformation. And, how to use field experiences to frame policy development.

Project management. Graduates are able to design and implement conflict intervention programs.

UNDERGRADUATE PROGRAMS

Core courses focus on providing peace and conflict studies students with a strong theoretical background in peace and conflict. The goal is to provide common and basic elements in the field of peace and conflict studies. A common language is created.

Undergraduate programs should provide common and basic elements in conflict resolution. And, as skills develop, there should be ample opportunity for practice in which academic study informs practice and practice reinforces academic skills. Core courses in the peace and conflict studies major should emphasize three crucial bodies of knowledge:

1. an understanding of the historical evolution of peace and conflict studies and the literature reflecting such development;
2. knowledge of the specialized terms employed in the discipline; and
3. mastery of common methodologies in the field.

There must be a strong liberal arts electives component to peace and conflict studies programs. Micro program tracks should be avoided in favor of classes categorized by discipline and content increasing students' understanding of complexity, nuance, and narrative in conflict.

Among elective courses in a conflict resolution major, there is need for classes developing students' cultural literacy. Graduates in the discipline are strengthened through a strong interdisciplinary grounding with courses such as cultural anthropology and global social work. Globalization—political, economic and social—broadens the range of disputes and anyone concerned with their peaceful transformation must recognize diversity and be prepared to act in a realm of many cultures and world views.

Required literature courses are a must. A literature component should be a part of any conflict resolution program adding richness and depth of understanding. Literature is narrative, and introducing students to its analysis contributes to an understanding of people and conflict—people in conflict. A study of literature, especially the literature of other cultures, often reveals people and their social context in ways and in depths unavailable in other disciplines.

Incorporating anthropology and global social work into conflict resolution programs not only develops insight into other cultures but, even more importantly, exposes students to an essential decolonized methodology. A participant-observer approach is essential to understand the culture of conflict and resolution processes. It is invaluable when students engage in fieldwork.

The scope and depth of undergraduate conflict resolution programs can be enhanced with the introduction of fifteen credit-hour capstone semesters including a senior thesis (the senior thesis is, in a sense, an interdisciplinary examination and might take the form of a case study centering on the culture of conflict analysis and resolution drawing on the student's field experience as a participant-observer). The final semester of off-campus fieldwork can be augmented with weekly seminars analyzing the week's experience and linking it to theory (the model of mentored student-teaching and social work field instruction programs is worth considering).

A field experience such as that described is unique in conflict studies programs. Combining academic rigor, scholarship, and practice, it is an innovative approach to an undergraduate major in peace and conflict resolution and a sound foundation for graduate studies.

GRADUATE PROGRAMS

Graduate programs should be heavily grounded in theory and critical analysis with a strong practice component supported through integrated fieldwork. Classes focusing on conflict theory will inform students' later analysis in the field. This approach is twofold: first, it provides graduates of peace and conflict studies undergraduate programs with a higher level of knowledge vis-a-vis theory, and second, it provides non–conflict studies undergraduates with a strong theoretical foundation that may be missing. My experience is that many students who enter graduate programs in conflict resolution lack the theoretical underpinning in conflict that is necessary for success in the field as a humanistic practitioner. A juridical approach to conflict resolution is technique oriented and does not necessarily require the understanding and application of conflict theory.

The second element of a graduate education should be extensive fieldwork.[33] As an applied social science, there should be ample opportunity for students to engage as practitioners in conflicts of all types; community becomes laboratory and text. Future conflict workers need to gain practical experience under the guidance of conflict workers and the mentorship of peace and conflict studies faculty. I am thinking here of the practice teaching model used in schools of education, and the fieldwork evaluation model employed in social work programs. Only through the application of theory in the field are students able to fully understand how theory and practice inform each other, and how new knowledge in the field is developed. Sixty-six percent of conflict resolution programs offer field experiences and thirty-nine percent require a practicum.[34] I suggest a much more aggressive approach, possibly incorporating fieldwork throughout the program, as a centerpiece of the curriculum, not an afterthought, but public scholarship.

Peace and conflict studies programs can benefit from the use of portfolios. Portfolios provide students with an opportunity to focus their graduate education across the curriculum. Rather than a jumble of disjointed classes, students weave classes together to create a whole that acts as the centerpiece of their capstone thesis and integrated seminar. The program is treated holistically.

Graduate peace and conflict studies programs should rely heavily on case studies. The case study format will help prepare graduate students in developing skills they will use in their fieldwork; a foundation is set. The case study approach incorporates the three major components of any curriculum: theory, research, and practice. An important aspect of case study work is that it moves learning away from the acquisition of knowledge and engages students as creators of new knowledge. Students become active learners modeling the skills they will take into the field.

Research methodology classes should be an important part of any curriculum. Research classes will help breach the divide that can develop between theory and practice.[35] Partnerships are an essential aspect of any curriculum. Supervised field experiences with partners will contribute to the development of professionalization in the field. Partners can become advocates for graduates in our field. Partners, too, can provide essential feedback regarding the knowledge, skills, and abilities they are looking for in program graduates. Individual work in peace and conflict studies classes should be kept to a minimum. Conflict work is collaborative work. Students should engage in group work throughout the curriculum. The development of collaborative skills is vital to future success in the field.

CONCLUSION

In an attempt to define conflict resolution as a genuine academic discipline, a critical analysis of programs in the United States argues for a rich body of core classes and electives, made richer still by focusing on a common body of knowledge and skills.[36] This is not reflective of the current state of conflict resolution programs. They are all over the map. Academic programs are insular with little significant collaboration across the field, there is no agreement on core competencies.[37] Curriculum development is *ab ignitio* at individual institutions dictated by institutional requirements, not student needs.[38] A field reacting to institutional stresses is not designing itself into the future. After fifty years of wandering the academic landscape, let us finally agree on who we are and what we should teach to acquire that identity.

Designing our way forward as a field will involve reflection and expanded vision. Resources and commitment are required. The field of peace and conflict studies should be defined by its humanistic characteristics and approach to the peaceful transformation of conflict.

Once defined as a field in the humanities, undergraduate and graduate programs in peace and conflict studies should develop a core of subjects providing scholars and practitioners a shared body of knowledge. Next, programs at undergraduate and graduate levels should develop curricula integrating scholarship and practice akin to teacher education and social work models. Supervised fieldwork is the centerpiece of such programs. In the fieldwork phase, peace and conflict studies faculty act as coaches, mentors, and facilitators linking students, fieldwork supervisors, and the university. Scholarship and practice inform each other in creating knowledge.

BIBLIOGRAPHY

Barrett, J. *A History of Alternative Dispute Resolution: The Story of a Political, Cultural, and Social Movement.* San Francisco: Jossey-Bass, 2004.

Botes, J. "Graduate Peace and Conflict Studies: Reconsidering Their Problems and Prospects." *Conflct Management in Higher Education,* vol. 5, no. 1 (2004).

Byrne, S., and J. Senehi. *Handbook of Conflict Analysis and Resolution.* London: Routledge, 2008.

Cochran-Smith, M. "Learning to Teach Against the (New) Grain." *Journal of Teacher Education,* vol. 52, no. 1 (2001): 3–4.

Fast, L. "Frayed Edges: Exploring the Boundaries of Conflict Resolution." *Peace & Change,* vol. 27, no. 4 (2001): 528–545.

Feiman-Nemser, Sharon. "From Preparation to Practice: Designing a Continuum to Strengthen and Sustain Teaching." *Teachers College Record,* vol. 103, no. 6 (2001): 1013–1055.

Feiman-Nemser, Sharon, and H. Featherstone. *Exploring Teaching: Reinventing an Introductory Course.* New York: Teachers College Press, 1992.

Fitzduff, M. "Core Competencies for Graduate Programs in Coexistence and Conflict Work—Can We Agree?" in *Leadership Notes, Series 1.* Washington, DC: Woodrow Wilson Center, September 2006.

Galtung, J. *Peace by Peaceful Means: Peace and Conflict, Development and Civilization.* London: SAGE Publications, 1996.

———. "Peace Education is Only Meaningful if It Leads to Action." *UNESCO Courier,* vol. 50, no. 1 (1997): 4–8.

———. *Transcend & Transform: An Introduction to Conflict Work.* Boulder, CO: Paradigm Publishers, 2004.

Harty, M., and J. Modell. "The First Conflict Resolution Movement, 1956–1971: An Attempt to Institutionalize Applied Interdisciplinary Social Science. *Journal of Conflict Resolution*, vol. 35, no. 4 (1991): 720–758.

Katz, N. "Report on Graduate and Undergraduate Programs in Conflict Resolution." *Peace & Change*, vol. 11, no. 2 (1986): 81–95.

Kriesberg, L. "Contemporary Conflict Resolution Applications," in *Leashing the Dogs of War: Conflict Management in a Divided World*, Chester A. Crocker, Fen Osler Hampson, and Pamela Aall, eds. Washington, DC: United States Institute of Peace Press, 2007, 455–476

———. "The Development of the Conflict Resolution Field," in *International Conflict: Methods and Techniques*, I. William Zartman and J. Lewis Rasmussen, eds. Washington, DC: United States Institute of Peace Press, 1997, 51–77

Lederach, J.P. *Building Peace: Sustainable Reconciliation in Divided Societies.* Washington, DC: United States Institute of Peace, 1997.

Mayer, B. *Beyond Neutrality: Confronting the Crisis in Conflict Resolution.* San Francisco: Jossey-Bass, 2004.

Polkinghorn, B., H. La Chance, and R. La Chance, "Constructing a Baseline Understanding of Developmental Trends in Graduate Conflict Resolution Programs in the United States," in *Pushing the Boundaries: New Frontiers in Conflict Resolution and Collaboration*, R. Fleishman, C. Gerard, and R. O'Leary, eds. Bingley, UK: JAI Press, 2008, 233–265.

Ramsbotham, O., T. Woodhouse, and H. Miall. *Contemporary Conflict Resolution.* Cambridge: Polity Press, 2005.

Sandole, D. "Traditional 'Realism' versus the 'New' Realism: John W. Burton, *Conflict Prevention*, and the Elusive 'Paradigm Shift.'" *Global Society*, vol. 20, no. 4 (2006): 543–562.

Schellenberg, J. *Conflict resolution: Theory, Research, and Practice.* Albany: State University of New York Press, 1996.

Smith, D. "A Map of Peace and Conflict Studies in U.S. Undergraduate Colleges and Universities." *Conflict Resolution Quarterly*, vol. 25, no. 1 (2007): 145–151 (retrieved from Academic Search Premier).

———. "Peace and Conflict Resolution Programs at the Undergraduate Level: Fostering the Next Generation of Peacemakers." *ACResolution*, vol. 6, no. 3 (2007): 20–21.

Ury, W. *Must We Fight?* San Francisico: Jossey-Bass, 2000.

Warfiled, W. "Some Minor Reflections on Conflict Resolution: The State of the Field as a Moving Target." *Negotiation Journal* (October 2002): 381–384.

Windmueller, J., E.K. Wayne, and J. Botes. "Core Competencies: The Challenge for Graduate Peace and Conflict Studies Education." *International Review of Education*, vol. 55 (2009): 285–301.

Zelizer, C., and L. Johnston. *Skills, Networks & Knowledge: Developing a Career in International Peace and Conflict Resolution*. Alexandria, VA: Alliance for Conflict Transformation, Inc., 2005.

NOTES

1. D. Sandole, "Traditional 'Realism' versus the 'New' Realism: John W. Burton, *Conflict Prevention*, and the Elusive 'Paradigm Shift,'" *Global Society*, vol. 20, no. 4 (2006): 543–562.
2. J. Galtung, May 2010.
3. L. Kriesberg, "Contemporary Conflict Resolution Applications," in *Leashing the Dogs of War: Conflict Management in a Divided World*, Chester A. Crocker, Fen Osler Hampson, and Pamela Aall, eds. (Washington, DC: United States Institute of Peace Press, 2007), 455; J. Windmueller, E.K. Wayne, and J. Botes, "Core Competencies: The Challenge for Graduate Peace and Conflict Studies Education," *International Review of Education*, vol. 55 (2009): 285.
4. M. Fitzduff, "Core Competencies for Graduate Programs in Coexistence and Conflict Work—Can We Agree?" Leadership Note Series, Washington, DC, September, 2006; Windmueller, "Core Competencies."
5. B. Polkinghorn, H. La Chance, and R. La Chance, "Constructing A Baseline Understanding of Developmental Trends in Graduate Conflict Resolution Programs in the United States," in *Pushing the Boundaries: New Frontiers in Conflict Resolution and Collaboration*, R. Fleishman, C. Gerard, and R. O'Leary, eds. (Bingley, UK: JAI Press, 2008), 233–265; Windmueller, "Core Competencies."
6. D. Smith, "A Map of Peace and Conflict Studies in U.S. Undergraduate Colleges and Universities," *Conflict Resolution Quarterly*, vol. 25 (2007): 145.
7. N. Katz, "Report on Graduate and Undergraduate Programs in Conflict Resolution," *Peace & Change*, vol. 11 (1986): 81.
8. W. Ury, *Must We Fight?* (San Francisico: Jossey-Bass, 2000).
9. J. Barret, *A History of Alternative Dispute Resolution: The Story of a Political, Cultural, and Social Movement.* (San Francisco: Jossey-Bass, 2004).
10. Kriesberg, "Contemporary."
11. M. Harty and J. Modell, "The First Conflict Resolution Movement, 1956–1971: An Attempt To Institutionalize Applied Interdisciplinary Social Science," *Journal of Conflict Resolution*, vol. 35 (1991): 720; J. Schellenberg, *Conflict Resolution: Theory, Research, and Practice* (Albany: State University of New York Press, 1996); Smith, "Map."
12. J. Galtung, "Peace Education Is Only Meaningful If It Leads To Action," *UNESCO Courier*, vol. 50 (1997): 4; N. Katz, "Report," 81; O. Ramsbotham, T. Woodhouse, and H. Miall, *Contemporary Conflict Resolution* (Cambridge: Polity Press, 2005).
13. S. Byrne and J. Senehi, *Handbook of Conflict Analysis and Resolution* (London: Routledge, 2008).

14. B. Mayer, *Beyond Neutrality: Confronting The Crisis In Conflict Resolution* (San Francisco: Jossey-Bass, 2004); W. Warfiled, "Some Minor Reflections on Conflict Resolution: The State of the Field as a Moving Target," *Negotiation Journal* (2002): 38; J. Windmueller, E.K. Wayne, and J. Botes, "Core Competencies: The Challenge for Graduate Peace and Conflict Studies Education," *International Review of Education*, vol. 55 (2009): 285.

15. Mayer, *Beyond Neutrality*; D. Sandole, "Traditional 'Realism'"; Windmueller, "Core Competences"; C. Zelizer and L. Johnston, *Skills, Networks & Knowledge: Developing a Career in International Peace and Conflict Resolution* (Alexandria, VA: Alliance for Conflict Transformation, 2005).

16. Warfield, "Minor Reflections."

17. Galtung, "Peace Education"; N. Carstarphen, C. Zelizer, R. Harris, and D. Smith, "Graduate Education and Professional Practice in International Peace and Conflict," United States Institute of Peace Special Report 246 (Washington, DC: USIP, 2010).

18. Smith, "A Map."

19. Smith, "A Map."

20. L. Fast, "Frayed Edges: Exploring The Boundaries of Conflict Resolution," *Peace & Change*, vol. 27 (2002): 528; J. Galtung, 2008.

21. J. Botes, "Graduate Peace and Conflict Studies: Reconsidering Their Problems and Prospects," *Conflict Management in Higher Education,* vol. 5 (2004); Fitzduff, "Core Competencies"; Windmueller, "Core Competencies."

22. Mayer, *Beyond Neutrality*; Warfiled, "Minor Reflections."

23. Windmueller, "Core Competencies."

24. J. Galtung, *Peace.*

25. Lederach, *Building Peace.*

26. Katz, "Report."

27. Ury, *Must We.*

28. Galtung, *Peace*; Galtung, *Transcend & Transform.*

29. Ury, *Must We.*

30. Sandole, "Traditional 'Realism.'"

31. S. Feiman-Nemser, "From Preparation to Practice: Designing a Continuum to Strengthen and Sustain Teaching," *Teachers College Record,* vol. 103, no. 6 (2001): 1013–1055.

32. Sandole, "Traditional 'Realism.'"

33. S. Feiman-Nemser and H. Featherstone, *Exploring Teaching: Reinventing an Introductory Course* (New York: Teachers College Press, 1992), 1024.

34. Polkinghorn, "Constructing."

35. Windmueller, "Core Competencies."

36. Polkinghorn, "Constructing."

37. Windmueller, "Core Competencies," 288.

38. Windmueller, "Core Competencies."

Chapter 16

Narrative in the Teaching and Practice of Conflict Analysis, Transformation, and Peacebuilding

Peter M. Kellett

> "We must develop the capacity of compassionate attentiveness to the words of others."[1] "Narrative learning . . . is not solely learning from the narrative; it is also the learning that goes on in the act of narration."[2]

Conflict, conflict transformation, and peacebuilding are inherently narrative enterprises. Specifically, if we accept the notion of *Homo narrans*—that humans are fundamentally storytelling animals[3]—and if we take Shapiro's call to heart, our job as educators is to help students to compassionately and attentively understand the narrative dynamics by which people create, express, maintain, and potentially transform oppositional differences—conflicts.[4] In matching narrative technique and methodology to the narrative reality of how people do conflict, a narrative approach to teaching and practicing conflict analysis, transformation, and peacebuilding may be uniquely positioned to build the capacity of students, practitioners, and teachers to learn to engage with the lived reality of conflict and its transformation.

This chapter brings together current ideas in the theory of narrative teaching and learning[5] and conflict management and transformation[6] to ask the central question: *How are conflict narratives and their narration valuable in facilitating the learning of students and the technique of practitioners?* Rather than review techniques that integrate narrative, of which there are many available across several disciplines and varied applications,[7] this chapter is organized around the typical questions that students wrestle with as they engage with narrative as the basis of their study of conflict and offers some key best practices, challenges, and guidelines for using personal narratives in teaching conflict transformation and peacebuilding. This format provides insight into the mechanics of how students learn from, with, and through narratives as they develop the compassionate attentiveness to their own and others' words.

THE LEARNING CYCLE OF CONFLICT NARRATIVES

I teach conflict communication and peacebuilding practices through the use of an interpretively based and cyclical narrative process known as the Learning Cycle of Conflict Narratives.[8] Specifically, the simple step research process and related analytical questions constitute a methodology for recollecting/collecting real personal conflict narratives grounded in interpretive theory and research techniques.[9] This method is, I believe, preferable to the fictional conflict "case studies" prevalent in many conflict and peace textbooks. For the sake of brevity, I have collapsed the seven-step model into three main phases: collecting conflict narratives, understanding conflicts through narratives, and questioning and change.

The second key assumption underlying this learning cycle model is that interpretive analysis of narratives can lead to understanding and deeper critique that can result in changes (where realistic and desired) that ultimately lead to the person living and having different stories to tell in similar circumstances in the future. Hence, the cyclical process begins and ends with narrative practices—with students *learning* to makes sense of and respond to conflicts differently where needed.[10] Of course, practitioners and teachers of conflict may not necessarily use this specific methodology, but at least I hope to capture the ins and outs of learning from a narrative approach more generally as I describe this learning cycle method, the assumptions entailed by it, and the guidelines I typically share with students as they work with conflict narratives.

COLLECTING CONFLICT NARRATIVES BEGINNING WITH THE STORY SO FAR

Those of us teachers and practitioners who have our students learn from conflict narratives—especially ones they collect and narrate for the class, will likely encounter questions that students will bring to the process. These questions—detailed below—are important in and of themselves as part of a discussion and learning. Typical student questions include the following.

Is the Story I Am Thinking of a Conflict?

Students who ask this question are typically wrestling with the criteria you are using to classify an event, experience, or process as a conflict and/or peace-building opportunity. Students often need to clarify the boundary between related types of events, such as a traumatic event or difficult/tumultuous period in their lives that may have the turbulent energy commonly associated with a conflict, or the struggle associated with its transformation or peace-building, but may not actually be a conflict, per se. It is important to provide some necessary conditions for a story to constitute an account of a conflict. There will be little learning if students are not writing about conflicts. I provide students with five simple criteria that they ought to use to make sure they are working with an actual conflict. The story should include *conflicted interaction*, that is the opposition between the people involved manifests to some extent and in some important ways in actual talk and behavior between and around them (i.e., with others they talk to about the conflict). The story should have a *relational dispute* at its core. Students ought to be able to identify what is oppositional between the people involved in the story. Of course, the meaning of a dispute may well be disguised, multilayered, and multifaceted, but without some opposition between the people, the story is not a conflict. The various people in the story ought to engage in *characterization* of themselves and of each other. Simply, conflicts necessarily engage narrative processes and tactics of portraying or representing self and other, and the motives of those involved in the conflict in relation to the dispute between them. Typically, for example, someone is a villain and someone is a victim, hero/shero, or fool. Often these relational representations become double binds that speak of the entrenchment of a conflict. At least they speak of both the narrative means by which people characterize themselves and each other and may provide a useful means of critique and openings for peacebuilding (discussed in more detail below). The story should evoke the *patterns* underlying the conflict and the relational dynamics between the people involved. Simply, a conflict is typically an event that has a systemic relationship to other events and dynamics and the student researcher ought to evoke this as it is a crucial part of learning and transformative practices. Is conflict, for example, partly a repeating pattern from a previous generation, past relationships, or early childhood? A conflict will also itself have a pattern of how it manifests—some are slow smoldering and muted, some are dramatic and volatile. Students need to become aware of how and why conflicts have various energy and behavioral dynamics and contours. Finally, a conflict should have a *deeper meaning*. Not necessarily something dark and despicable (many student conflicts revolve around cheating and relational betrayal), but something beyond itself worth investigating. Learning to ask what's beyond and beneath a conflict is important as the conflict is collected as this helps students put the story in context and makes sense of it *as a conflict*.

Some students also ask whether a conflict needs to be something that actually came out into the open in a relationship, or if it can be something that may have remained unspoken, even predominantly intrapersonal. Does a conflict, in fact, have to be expressed in behavior/communication or can it be one that a person wrestles with in the inner dialogue of their own mind? Teachers and practitioners will naturally come at a question like this from their own disciplinary standpoint to some extent. My discipline is communication studies, so I prefer to work with conflicts that are expressed through actual talk between people, and I assume transformation and peacebuilding involve processes managed through actual talk, but this is not necessarily everyone's preference.

Why Can I Not Find or Recall a Conflict to Write About?

When the assignment is to recollect a conflict story from personal experience, almost always one or two students will claim that they are either too "positive" to have conflicts, or that they just don't have conflicts with people that are worth writing about. Typically underlying these statements is a need to feel permission to dig into their lives in a different way and simply explore. Part of this need for permission is also sometimes a cultural bias against both acknowledging that conflict occurs in their lives, and that this does not mean the relationship being talked about is necessarily weak or threatened. Part of it may involve students learning how the way they live and narrate their lives might preclude conflicts that may be valuable—the classic avoiders. The best technique I have found to deal with this question is to have students begin by journaling more than one story until one becomes the primary one they want to work with.

What Makes a Good Conflict Story?

In a student context, this question is often partly driven by grade concerns around what the instructor thinks is a good story. Partly it is a more profound question about data quality and learning, in that narrative quality is linked to quality of learning.[11] They want to learn something valuable and realize that a good story is essential. I advise students to make sure a story contains and represents as much as the audience (instructor and the class) for the story needs to have to provide a working understanding of what happened, why, and with what effects. A good story should also invite and engage the audience by communicating the thoughts, feelings, experiences, motives and desires of the participants. I believe this should be done by reconstructing (and where possible, recording) the actual talk between people where much of the process of doing conflict and its transformation take place. Even a few representative moments of conversation can provide much for the analysis of the conflict, particularly when the conversational moments make sense as representative of a bigger discursive context such as political discourse, relational archetypes, or gender differences, and where the talk helps provide insight into the energy and meaning of the conflict. I also make sure they understand the principles of narrative data collection in terms of related research techniques in ethnography and ethics.[12] Related questions under this topic include the following:

How long should a story be? I usually tell students to aim for three or so pages and that the rest can be background. At first they will often express concern that they will not get three pages out of a story, but typically end up going over three pages. If a story is much less than three pages, then perhaps the story isn't significant.

Does the conflict have to be a dramatic event? Students need to recognize the different energy and dynamics profiles of conflicts and that not all conflicts are volatile arguments and that some linger, pop up, and can even be displaced into other areas of a relationship. The question hints at a more profound issue of how we think about conflicts. Specifically, is a conflict a distinct event, or are they better characterized as processes, episodes, or discursive formations? Or are they combinations of events and processes? It is important to work from a common understanding of what is the unit of analysis being worked with, and enable students to learn how to depict both the process and event qualities/phases of conflicts.

Whose perspectives do I need to make the story complete? Do I need both sides for it to be a "good" story? Students often get frustrated when you are having them discuss a case that is incomplete in that all of the participants in the conflict have their perspective represented in the story. There are also often facts missing that they wish they would know, as it would help them make sense of what happened in the case being discussed. I do encourage them where possible to collect all sides of the story, but this is also sometimes not possible. Nor is it always possible to engage all concerned in a transformation process. It is important for students to understand that the notion of having the "whole story" is largely mythical, and that it is more important to think in terms of what of the story is it possible and realistic to collect and work from there. It also stimulates students' imaginations to have them creatively fill in the other voices in a story. I have found this to be a very useful technique and is best done ahead of a discussion where students sign up to develop what might be the other peoples' voices in the conflict. Performing these other voices enables much valuable learning in terms of embodying the characters, reading between the voices for commonalities and oppositions, and engaging with the conflict bodily. These are all useful learning techniques grounded in narrative performance theory concepts.

Does the conflict need to be one that is peacefully resolved, from the past, or ongoing (unfinished) now? Students often believe that a complete story and one that was peacefully resolved is somehow a better story, a better piece of data. I am clear with students that they need to work with the story that they are most drawn to exploring. Working with the one they are most drawn to, even if it means they prefer not to share it with the class, or it is incomplete, usually ensures they will learn the most from its analysis. This story could be one they are right in the middle of, affording them the learning potential of figuring out the way forward from their analysis. It could be one from their distant past that may or may not be peacefully concluded. It could be one that is part of understanding a deeper mystery of dynamics in their family.

Where Does the Conflict Begin and the Background End?

Where the conflict begins and ends is always an interesting question. Often students want to include a background section to preview the story so that the reader understands the basis of what is happening in the specific conflict event being described in the narrative. I advise them to make the background brief and only include information that would be awkward or unnatural to include in the story text itself. The question also hints at a more profound question beyond the practicalities of writing a paper: where are the boundaries of a conflict story and, therefore, a conflict event? This question can be an interesting discussion. Students engage with both the practicalities and theoretical issues associated with drawing a line, however arbitrary and tentative, between the conflict being described and the lives of the people in the story, and even their biographical and social histories. Conflicts are embedded in lives as expressions of broader and deeper dynamics, and bracketing the story from that context is not easy. Reflection on the choices made around this question is useful.

How Do I Pick and Choose What to Include and How to Portray Things in the Conflict Narrative?

With this question, students as well as practitioners who use narratives to impact a conflict are expressing their engagement—sometimes confrontation—with the politics of narrative research and practice. There are valuable lessons to be learned around this question, as students wrestle with the following issues: Whose story/stories do we collect to account for a conflict? Who do I believe or empathize with more and how does this affect my writing of the story and analysis of the conflict the story represents? If it is my story I am telling, what and why do I include and exclude specific facts when writing the story? What are the alternative stories to mine or the peoples' I have collected? How do the seemingly small choices of representation (particularly in terms of motives, characterization and character, plot and story moral/meaning) affect the account that the story provides? Wrestling with these issues is at the heart of understanding the narrative reality of conflict and the effective use of narrative in analyzing and impacting conflicts.

Learning to identify and collect/recollect and tell a "good" conflict story is the first phase of learning through narratives and brings the benefit of working with the complexity and organic nature of stories as a mirror for how people use narratives in their lives more generally. Understanding life stories brings similar challenges and opportunities as studying conflict stories.

UNDERSTANDING CONFLICTS THROUGH NARRATIVES

This step entails analyzing the narrative data collected and creating an interpretive account—an understanding of the conflict. This account bridges between the raw data collected and the recommendations for change that follow next, so it is important to emphasize the need for their analysis to be a deep, thoughtful, systemic account of the conflict that is designed to bring to the surface why the conflict happened through a careful description of what happened. Of course, the interpretive account will reflect particulars of the theoretical material of a course. At the same time, students tend to wrestle with two key questions that will be expanded upon below.

HOW DO I CREATE A "BIG PICTURE" ACCOUNT OF THE CONFLICT FROM THE PARTS OF THE CONFLICT I WAS ABLE TO COLLECT?

With this question, students are wrestling with issues at the heart of interpretive methodology. These have to do with the processes and ethics of interpretation, as well as the desire to be able to *read* stories for what they do contain, and for what they don't contain that provide clues to the meaning of a conflict. If students do not clearly understand how to do interpretive analysis then they will often resort to applying a linear list of questions to the story without much of a sense of how all of the factors and variables intersect in a conflict. This systemic thinking is crucial and often difficult because students often find themselves paralyzed as they try to create an account of how many things come together as a system that underlies a conflict. Students stuck in this moment will say things like "Where do I begin because everything connects to everything else?" The simple answer is to begin anywhere. If everything connects together, then it should not matter much where the analysis begins.

To enable students to get started in a way that is manageable and results in an interpretation that uses the fine details of the story, I have them use a three-part process of *description*, *reduction* and *interpretation*.[13] Students begin by describing everything in the story that indicates a conflict and how the people seem to create it and respond to it. They describe the behavior, the actual talk between the people and its intensity, the way the people appear to be thinking through what they are doing, and the way that the conflict embodies the five definitional criteria of a conflict. If both sides are available, then they look for ways that those accounts differ and ways that they are consistent in the experience and meaning of the conflict. Students also pinpoint clues to the meaning of the conflict. Beginning with careful description it is crucial in students' learning to work with narratives like careful researchers. They also learn not to jump right to recommendations, something that circumvents and limits learning. Students then carefully reduce that description to its essential structure as a set of interconnected dynamics and issues. Simply put, they boil the description down to the bones of the conflict. From this point, they interpret, which means to create an account that connects what they have described on the surface of the conflict (description) to its structure (reduction) in a way that makes the conflict make sense in light of course concepts. This exercise trains students, on the one hand, to work with the fine details of a story much like a specimen, and, on the other hand, to link what they have seen together as a whole and to course concepts.

HOW DO I KNOW THAT MY INTERPRETATION IS TRUE?

The other main question students wrestle with in this step has to do with accuracy of interpretation and what it means to create an account that is essentially interpretive by definition. Students often bring with them assumptions that are grounded in myths of truth and accuracy in (social) science. They often feel uncomfortable with the idea that their interpretation of a conflict is based on opinion, not scientific fact. This thinking is an important mythology to get through. It is important to give students some background on interpretive social science and the way that their experiences are part of a broader debate. It is also important to enable students to free themselves up to interpret, as long as they are rigorous, fair, and balanced in their interpretations. One technique I have found that embodies these research values is to have them develop as part of their interpretation, a "plausible scenario."[14] This project involves creating a short summary of the conflict that embodies as many of the facts and interpretations as possible and is therefore as accurate as possible based on what is known. Through this, students learn to think in terms of what is *plausible* as an account versus what is necessarily *demonstrably true*. Once students learn how to explicate a story for the meaning and dynamics of a conflict, and once they recognize that this story is necessarily interpretive and therefore plausible rather than necessarily true they free themselves to begin to think of recommendations for the people in the conflict with the proviso that these recommendations are also inherently interpretive.

QUESTIONING AND CHANGE: DISCOVERING NEW MEANINGS AND POSSIBILITIES FOR NARRATIVES

Beginning with the assumption that if relational reality is in part negotiated into being, it may be possible to renegotiate that reality; students will be oriented in this phase from the mechanics of conflict analysis to the imaginative and practical techniques of conflict transformation and peacebuilding. This section explicates some of the key questions and learning experiences/goals that students work through as they develop transformative capacities.

WHAT DOES IT MEAN TO CHANGE CONFLICT PRACTICES (BEHAVIOR, THOUGHTS, AND COMMUNICATION), AND HOW DOES THIS ACTUALLY HAPPEN?

Asking students or clients based on a conflict analysis to discuss changes that need to occur within the behaviors, thought processes/habits, and communications of a conflicted relationship is a crucial step in teaching and/or facilitating conflict transformation. Learning how to bridge analysis and change is challenging for many students, because they are not necessarily trained in understanding how and why changes are brought about and implemented. Change is rarely a simple and unproblematic process of ending one dysfunctional pattern or of adopting more effective communication habits, although this is often the mindset with which people come to the process. Changes are more often complex, and work within personal, relational and socio-cultural frameworks. The dangers of not exploring this bridging between analysis and transformation are that students view change simplistically—for example, in terms of "stop doing something, start doing something else, and things will improve." This way can work, but rarely is conflict transformation so simple and linear. Another danger is that they resort to telling you what they think you would like to hear, but often in thinly understood terms. I have heard the phrase along the lines of "this couple/this family/these coworkers need to improve their dialogue practices" many times in class and in papers. This does little in terms of evidencing valuable student learning because it stops at *what* needs to be done and does not expand into the *how* or *why* issues.

Drawing on the work of narrative practitioners like Winslade and Monk (2001),[15] I have found it most useful to teach the bridging of analysis and transformation with the notion of developing conversational scripts for the participants of the conflict. Specifically, I have found it useful to have students create good questions and topics for each participant to explore, and topics/questions they might explore together as the basis of a collaborative exploration and early stages of narrating their movement beyond this conflict. For example, one student recently told me of an experience of working through a difficult intimate relational break-up. They remained close friends after the conflicted break-up, but the long-distance nature of the relationship put a great deal of pressure on the time they were together to the point that things were magnified and exacerbated and conflicts started to be prevalent when they were together. They were, I believe, unconsciously using conflict to tell themselves and each other that the relationship needed to be redefined (from intimate to friends), but they did not have the conversational scripts or awareness of how to do this. Or they may have been waiting for the other to lead the change. Instead, he would get angry as she texted someone while they were together. She would get angry when he had other plans besides being with her when he was home. The conversational scripts that I had him work on pertained to exploring how to be better at interpreting and understanding the meaning of such seemingly petty conflicts in a relationship, and how to better communicate about and balance relational pressures, common relational goals, and (where appropriate) decline, ending, and so on. He developed an effective list of twenty or so questions—some for him, some for her, and some they might have explored and discussed together that tapped into both the meaning of the conflict they lived through and the desire to learn from it and change/improve in such a context in future. He had a bridge between the conflict and what might be done differently to work from.

The questions and topics outlined as possible *conversational scripts* provide a useful bridge between the analysis and the change processes when the questions/topics draw directly from a fusion of the specifics of the analysis and the theoretical material of the course. That is, the conversational scripts developed should be theoretically informed and directly related to a high quality analysis of the conflict. Problems arise when students simply develop generic questions like "How might you as the participants of the conflict improve your conflict communication through dialogue?" A better question here would be "How might you both improve specific active listening skills and valuing of the other's perspective when you are discussing a core difference between you?" In this way, students learn to effectively integrate course concepts as the building blocks of the bridge between analysis and transformation.

When teaching students about transformation and change, there are several issues that they will need to learn to think through. The issue of what changes are realistic and desirable is important. What type of change is recommended (are they improving something, eliminating something, interpreting and responding to something differently)? How changes would actually be implemented (how will the change come about through talk, behavior and thought patterns)? What might those different behaviors, thoughts and patterns of communication look like (how might a conversational sequence look different based on the changes recommended)? These are some of the important finer-level nuances of learning that are useful to focus on when talking about transformation and change.

HOW DO CHANGES IN PRACTICES RESULT IN CHANGES TO RELATIONAL REALITY?

One of the key steps in most conflict analysis processes has to do with the participants imagining and systemic mapping of how changes might impact their relationship and how these changes might impact the conflict patterns they experience. This question is quite often difficult for students because they are trained in causal thinking and working with evidence, but the systemic intelligence that comes with being able to imagine complex changes and their impact is a skill they wrestle with. Students will often also resort to causal clichés like "we need to communicate more effectively and thereby avoid this type of conflict in future." They recognize that change in thought, behavior, and communication might result in positive change, but understanding specifically *how* this happens is, I believe, a crucial learning goal. Students ought to be able to imagine how changes in patterns of behavior might impact changes in other patterns of behavior—that is, as systemic effects within and around relationships. Students ought also to be trained in imagining desired relationships and mapping the changes necessary to reach their goals. I have actually begun using drawing as a way of mapping effects, patterns, and changes and this can be a useful way for more visual learners to understand these dynamics.[16]

Referring to the same student above, upon analyzing his "break-up" conflict story, I asked him about what he learned from the experience in terms of what he needs to change and where he would begin. He told me that what he would like to work on most is his language use both in the everyday reality of the relationship and particularly in conflict. Of course, he realized that language is intimately connected with self, with the dynamics of how he connects with the other, and with contextual dynamics, but the notion that he might change the language (including use of silences) he chooses (and related thoughts and behaviors) gave him a place to begin rethinking his conflict communication and behavior. Specifically, his desire was to question and change his use of language that is linked to habitual narrative patterns of portraying self as the victim and his partner as the "bad guy." Digging beneath this layer, he realized that his deeper desire, coming from a broader place in his life, was to be *understood* and when he felt that he wasn't being understood he would resort to passive-aggressive narrative tactics that polarized himself and his girlfriend into victim (himself) and villain (her). This behavior then set in motion a pattern of communication that became typical for them, in which quite immature tactics would spiral the conflict into polarities. Examining the intersection of her communicative style (for example, texting an ex-boyfriend while sitting with him) and reaction to his tactics (giving her the silent treatment to punish her and to show her that they had a problem) and expounding this through remembering the actual talk sequences of a conflict (passive-aggressive tactics of his lead to an equivalent one from her resulting in a frustrating miscommunication) provided further insight into the dynamics that characterized their relationship and, in some part, why it ultimately failed.

His lesson from narrating his conflict—bringing it back to life—was that of the importance of examining the dynamics of actual talk/behavior/thought, and that his "voice" habits and practices of talk can be a valuable starting point for questioning and possibly changing deeper patterns of thought and behavior in conflict.[17] He began to imagine how adopting specific changes (avoiding passive aggressive tactics, portrayals of self as victim) could bring changes to the lived reality of everyday life (maturing communication/behavior/thought leads to more fulfilling relationships). Going back to the header quote of the chapter, recognize that when the student narrated his conflict and his learning and opened it up to the audience for discussion, it was an enormously important part of the learning process. Other students probed his motives, his identity as a communicator and a boyfriend, and how he handled the situation. This discussion added much to his reflection on the conflict.

It is important here to recognize the key word of "specific"—that is, it is important to get students to think in terms of specific changes and how they might change or modify undesired patterns or create new more desirable ones. Staying on the level of specifics, while at the same time getting students to imagine broader effects of these changes will help them avoid resorting to clichés like "improving our communication will mean we have less conflict in the future." It is also important to have students reflect and imagine with a view to what is realistic and practical in terms of changing the behavior of both/all of the participants. Students need to imagine changes when one side is willing to change, when both sides are willing to change, and so on, to develop the understanding of how things typically proceed in the real world of their lives. It is also useful to bring timeline discussions into the reality of the imagination. Specifically, having students pinpoint how long particular changes might realistically take to have specific effects is a useful way to ground them in the realities of how difficult relationship change can be, especially one that is marked by complex conflict. Similarly, participants in a bad break-up are unlikely to stop and deconstruct the system of interconnections by which they both "negotiated" that bad break-up into reality. Rather, in real life they will more than likely move forward, try to find someone less like the person they most likely blame for their negative experience, and so it goes. So in teaching this imaginative part of conflict transformation, it is important to have students balance this desire by articulating what they think would be realistic and desirable for the partners to deconstruct and change as these changes pertain to the various people in the conflict. Students learn best when imagination and realism are fused in the learning process.

HOW DOES CHANGE RESULT IN MOVING TOWARD A NEW STORY, AND HOW DOES THIS NEW REALITY CHANGE FUTURE CONFLICT STORIES?

In my experience, this is the most difficult part of the transformation/change part of the learning process for students. Partly, they are working imaginatively with skills and techniques that are new to them and that are complex to implement, especially if, for example, a mediation is performed as part of class discussion. Using skills, such as encouraging externalizing conversations and getting the participants to map the effects of the conflict, are extremely valuable, but not easy in the moment.[18] Partly they have the challenge of imagining a different relational reality and how it might mean the people in the conflict will live different conflict processes and therefore have stories to tell that are different than the one being analyzed. This possibility is in some ways an interpretive measure of change—how would next time be different from last time in terms of the conflict and the story told that reflects it? Focusing on how and why narrative realities can change and therefore actually be different in future is a key narrative imagination competence that I believe students of conflict and peace ought to develop. Balanced with this is, of course, a realistic sense of what can change and what factors (social, psychological, communicative, and structural) impact those possibilities for the desired story that is being imagined. Students need to recognize that there is always uncertainty in terms of what will happen in reality.[19] Again, balancing imagination (possible) and realism (probable), students develop what might be termed a critical imagination. They expand upon possibilities and reflect on what is realistic, desired, and possible given real circumstances and dynamics and create a concrete account of what could be that is different from what was. These learning processes, we hope, will be captured in their account of how the story resulting from a similar future conflict might be different based on their learning.

Engaging the creative and imaginative functions of conflict narratives, exploring what was, and what could be, brings a great deal of learning quality to the study of conflict. Students learn that (most) stories can be opened up, questioned, changed, and that changes to dynamics captured in stories can result in changes to lived reality that those stories represent and of which they are expressions. Hence, narratives enable students to experience not just *what* needs to change but *how* conflicted relationships can be changed narratively. It is this "narrative capital" and "repertoire" of possibilities that we hope to develop for students.[20]

CONCLUSION

Conflict narratives and their collection, analysis, telling and sharing provide an invitational, personal, real-life, creative, engaging, and challenging form of data by which students and practitioners can develop interpretive, analytical and synthetic skills necessary for deeper levels of learning about conflict. This connection is particularly true in terms of students learning the specifics of collection, analysis, change and transformation. Deeper lessons can also be drawn about the relation between narrative/narration and life through the narrative study of conflict. Narratives, especially ones shared by other students and practitioners from their lives, provide a unique means by which students are challenged to recognize patterns across, within and around stories, see beyond and beneath the story that is told, imagine possibilities that might change the dynamics and flow of a conflict, compare and contrast the stories told by different conflict participants, and develop a keen sense of the ethics and challenges of collecting, working with, interpreting, and making recommendations based on what is almost always an incomplete and politically nuanced (narrative) account of a conflict experience. Further work on the relationship between narrative/narration and conflict is encouraged, particularly work that illuminates how life stories, culture, identity, conflict, and learning are interconnected.

BIBLIOGRAPHY

Bar-on, D., ed. *Bridging the Gap: Storytelling as a Way to Work through Political and Collective Hostilities*. Hamburg: Korber-Stiflung, 2000.

Bathmaker, A.M., and P. Harnett. *Exploring Learning, Identity and Power through Life-history and Narrative Research*. Oxon: Routledge, 2010.

Benhabib, S., and F. Dallmyer. *The Communicative Ethics*. Cambridge, MA: MIT Press, 1990.

Bochner, A.P., and E. Eisenberg. "Perspectives on Inquiry: II. Theories and Stories." Pp. 21–41 in *Handbook of Interpersonal Communication,* 2nd ed., M. Knapp and G. Miller, eds. Thousand Oaks, CA: Sage, 1994.

Bruner, J. *Acts of Meaning*. Cambridge, MA: Harvard University Press, 1990.

Cobb, S. "Empowerment and Mediation: A Narrative Perspective." *Negotiation Journal*, vol. 9, no. 3 (1993): 245–255.

———. "A Narrative Perspective on Mediation: Toward the Materialization of the Storytelling Metaphor," in *New Directions in Mediation: Communication Research and Perspectives*, J.P. Folger and T.S. Jones, eds. Thousand Oaks, CA: Sage, 1994.

———. "Theories of Responsibility: The Social Construction of Intentions in Mediation." *Discourse Processes*, vol. 18, no. 2 (1994): 165–186.

———. "The Social Construction and Transformation of Conflict." Notes from lectures at the Fielding Institute, Santa Barbara, 1996.

———. "Fostering Coexistence in Identity-based Conflicts: Towards a Narrative Approach," in *Imagine Coexistence*, A. Chayes and M. Minow, eds. San Francisco: Jossey-Bass, 2004, 294–310.

Collins, R., and P.J. Cooper. *The Power of Story: Teaching Through Storytelling*. Scottsdale, AZ: Gorsuch Scarisbrick, 1997.

Fisher, W. R. *Human Communication as Narration: Toward a Philosophy or Reason, Value, and Action*. Columbia: University of South Carolina Press, 1987.

Goodson, I., G.J.J. Biesta, M. Tedder, and N. Adair. *Narrative Learning*. London: Routledge, 2010.

Holbrook, J. "Transforming Conflict Narratives into Dialogue in Performative Negotiation." Lecture presented at the City Law School Applied Storytelling Conference, London, 2007.

Jensen, J.V. *Ethical Issues in the Communication Process*. Mahwah, NJ: Lawrence Erlbaum, 1997.

Johannesen, R.L. *Ethics in Human Communication*. Prospect Heights, IL: Waveland, 1981.

McIntosh, P. *Action Research and Reflection Practices: Creative and Visual Methods to Facilitate Reflective Learning*. London/New York: Routledge, 2010.

Kellett, P.M. *Conflict Dialogue: Working with Layers of Meaning for Productive Relationships*. Thousand Oaks, CA: Sage, 2007.

Kellett, P.M., and D.G. Dalton. *Managing Conflict in a Negotiated World: A Narrative Approach to Conflict*. Thousand Oaks, CA: Sage, 2001.

———. *Managing Conflict in a Negotiated World: A Narrative Approach to Conflict*. Thousand Oaks, CA: Sage, 2001.

Langellier, K.M. "Personal Narratives: Perspectives on Theory and Research," *Text and Performance Quarterly*, vol. 9 (1989): 243–276.

McAdams, D.P. *The Stories We Live By: Personal Myths and the Making of the Self*. New York: The Guilford Press, 1993.

Shapiro, H.S. *Losing Heart: The Moral and Spiritual Miseducation of America's Children*. Mahwah, NJ: Lawrence Earlbaum, 2006.

Steinberg, S., and D. Bar-on. "An Analysis of the Group Processes in Encounters Between Jews and Palestinians Using a Typology for Discourse Classification." *International Journal of Intercultural Relations*, vol. 26 (2002): 199–214.

Van Maanen, J., ed. *Representation in Ethnography*. Thousand Oaks, CA: Sage. 1995.

Winslade, J., and G. Monk. *Narrative Counseling in Schools: Powerful and Brief*, 2nd ed. Thousand Oaks, CA: Corwin Press Inc., 2007.

———. *Narrative Mediation: A New Approach to Conflict Resolution*. San Francisco: Jossey-Bass, 2001.

NOTES

1. H.S. Shapiro, *Losing Heart: The Moral and Spiritual Miseducation of America's Children* (Mahwah, NJ: Lawrence Earlbaum, 2006).

2. I. Goodson, G.J.J. Biesta, M. Tedder, and N. Adair, *Narrative Learning* (London: Routledge, 2010).

3. See J. Bruner, *Acts of Meaning* (Cambridge, MA: Harvard University Press, 1990); W.R. Fisher, *Human Communication as Narration: Toward a Philosophy or Reason, Value, and Action* (Columbia: University of South Carolina Press, 1987). D.P. McAdams, *The Stories We Live by: Personal Myths and the Making of the Self* (New York: The Guilford Press, 1993).

4. P.M. Kellett and D.G. Dalton, *Managing Conflict in a Negotiated World: A Narrative Approach to Conflict* (Thousand Oaks, CA: Sage, 2001); P.M. Kellett, *Conflict Dialogue: Working with Layers of Meaning for Productive Relationships* (Thousand Oaks, CA: Sage, 2007).

5. A.M. Bathmaker and P. Harnett, *Exploring Learning, Identity and Power through Life-history and Narrative Research* (Oxon: Routledge, 2010); R. Collins and P.J. Cooper, *The Power of Story: Teaching through Storytelling* (Scottsdale, AZ: Gorsuch Scarisbrick, 1997); I. Goodson, et al., *Narrative Learning*.

6. D. Bar-on, ed., *Bridging the Gap: Storytelling as a Way to Work through Political and Collective Hostilities* (Hamburg: Korber-Stiflung, 2000); S. Cobb, "Empowerment and Mediation: A Narrative Perspective," *Negotiation Journal,* vol. 9, no. 3 (1993): 245–255; Cobb, "A Narrative Perspective on Mediation: Toward the Materialization of the Storytelling Metaphor," in *New Directions in Mediation: Communication Research and Perspectives*, J.P. Folger and T.S. Jones, eds. (Thousand Oaks, CA: Sage, 1994); Cobb, "Theories of Responsibility: The Social Construction of Intentions in Mediation," *Discourse Processes*, vol. 18, no. 2 (1994): 165–186; Cobb, "The Social Construction and Transformation of Conflict," notes from lectures at the Fielding Institute, Santa Barbara, 1996; Cobb, "Fostering Coexistence in Identity-based Conflicts: Towards a Narrative Approach," in *Imagine Coexistence*, A. Chayes and M. Minow, eds. (San Francisco: Jossey-Bass, 2004), 294–310; S. Steinberg and D. Bar-on, "An Analysis of the Group Processes in Encounters between Jews and Palestinians Using a Typology for Discourse Classification," *International Journal of Intercultural Relations*, vol. 26 (2002): 199–214; J. Winslade and G. Monk, *Narrative Mediation: A New Approach to Conflict Resolution* (San Francisco: Jossey-Bass, 2001); Winslade and Monk, *Narrative Counseling in Schools: Powerful and Brief,* 2nd ed. (Thousand Oaks, CA: Corwin Press Inc., 2007).

7. See, for example, the work of Winslade and Monk 2001 in counseling applications; Holbrook 2007 in legal mediation (J. Holbroook, "Transforming Conflict Narratives into Dialogue in Performative Negotiation," The City Law School Applied Storytelling Conference, London, 2007) and Bar-on 2000 and Steinberg 2002 for applications to interethnic conflicts and peacebuilding; see also the work of TRT [To Reflect and Trust] and PRIME [Peace Research Institute in the Middle East] for related NGO work on Israeli-Palestinian conflicts.

8. In particular, see Kellett and Dalton, *Managing Conflict*; Kellett, *Conflict Dialogue*.

9. A.P. Bochner and E. Eisenberg, "Perspectives on Inquiry: II. Theories and Stories," in *Handbook of Interpersonal Communication*, M. Knapp and G. Miller, eds. (Thousand Oaks, CA: Sage, 1994), 21–41; P. Harnett, "Life History and Narrative Research Revisited," in Bathmaker and Harnett, *Exploring*, 159–170; K.M. Langellier, "Personal Narratives: Perspectives on Theory and Research," *Text and Performance Quarterly*, vol. 9 (1989): 243–276; J. Van Maanen, ed., *Representation in Ethnography* (Thousand Oaks, CA: Sage, 1995).

10. See Kellett, *Conflict Dialogue,* 6–7.

11. See Goodson, et al., *Narrative Learning*.

12. See S. Benhabib and F. Dallmyer, *The Communicative Ethics* (Cambridge, MA: MIT Press, 1990); J.V. Jensen, *Ethical Issues in the Communication Process* (Mahwah, NJ: Lawrence Erlbaum, 1997); R.L. Johannesen, *Ethics in Human Communication* (Prospect Heights, IL: Waveland, 1981); P. Sikes, "The Ethics of Writing

Life Histories and Narratives in Educational Research," in Bathmaker and Harnett, *Exploring*, 11–25.

13. See Kellett, *Conflict Dialogue*, 42–45.

14. See Kellett, *Conflict Dialogue*, 50–51.

15. See Winslade and Monk, *Narrative Mediation.*

16. P. McIntosh, *Action Research and Reflection Practices: Creative and Visual Methods to Facilitate Reflective Learning* (London/New York: Routledge, 2010).

17. E. Love, "Bringing a Story to Life: Story Dramatization with Listeners," in *The Power of Story: Teaching through Storytelling*, R. Collins and P.J. Cooper, eds. (Scottsdale, AZ: Gorsuch Scarisbrick, 1997), 81–88; B. Weeks, "The Story Is in the Telling: Finding Your Own Voice," in Collins and Cooper, *The Power of Story*, 63–78.

18. See Winslade and Monk, *Narrative Mediation.*

19. J.H. Rolling, "This Do in Remembrance of Me: Narrative Uncertainty and the Frothing of Contentious Identity," in Bathmaker and Harnett, *Exploring*, 130–144.

20. Goodson, et al., *Narrative Learning.*

Chapter 17

Community Engagement in Peace and Conflict Studies

Connecting and Advancing Pedagogy, Research, and Practice

Sherrill Hayes

This chapter examines the role of community engagement and the application of engaged scholarship for integrating and sharing the knowledge of practitioners, scholars, and students in peace and conflict studies. The core issues in PACS of social change, prevention of war and violence, and community impact[1] are so inextricably linked together in scholarship, practice, and pedagogy that any attempt to divide them would be divisive to the development of the field. Whether one's area of expertise is international disarmament, land-use disputes, community violence, family conflict, or peace education, all PACS professionals engage with communities of individuals, bodies of scholarly and practice-based knowledge, and new generations looking to progress and develop as professionals. It is the position of this chapter that the only way the field will survive and develop is through recognizing the interdependence of scholarship, practice, and pedagogy and developing a holistic approach to the knowledge created out of that relationship. To ensure that PACS survives and thrives, all peace and conflict professionals should use the integrated knowledge to educate the next generation, whether they are scholars, practitioners, or a combination of both.

This chapter begins with a general discussion of some of the most common methods of community engagement and some examples of community engagement specific to PACS. The next section discusses the possibilities of community engaged learning for framing PACS. The chapter continues by providing a framework for community engaged scholarship and pedagogy, building on engaged scholarship, action research, community-based research, and other related models,[2] and proposing this as an overarching framework for community engagement for PACS. The author will next provide an example of using this engaged scholarship framework as a tool for teaching a graduate-level Dispute System Design (DSD) course and demonstrate the opportunities for students, faculty, and practitioners, as community partners, to better understand applied research and develop theoretical and professional models and strengthen partnerships. The chapter concludes with some thought on engagement and PACS scholarship and pedagogy.

COMMUNITY ENGAGEMENT IN PEDAGOGY AND SCHOLARSHIP

Beginning with work of Ernest Boyer[3] on the *scholarship of application* and later the *scholarship of engagement*, individual scholars and degree programs have worked tirelessly to make their work both more relevant to users and theoretically grounded.[4] Academic programs have focused, or in some cases refocused, their missions of scholarship, pedagogy, and service on engaging with communities.[5] The motivation underlying many of these developments has been to fulfill higher education's civic mission and redefine the roles of faculty, student, and community partner in the educational process.[6] Service-learning, community-based research, engaged scholarship, and community engagement are all activities that include community partners as integral members of the learning and knowledge creation processes.[7] The key pedagogical feature of this effort has been to recognize that combining classroom and community experience is a valid form of learning in higher education.

Service-learning remains the principal form of community engagement in higher education. Service learning is defined as

> a credit-bearing, educational experience in which students participate in organized service activity that meets identified community needs and reflects on the service activity in such a way as to gain further understanding of course content, a broader appreciation of the discipline, and an enhanced sense of civic responsibility.[8]

For practitioners, scholars, and students of PACS, this type of thinking is not groundbreaking and the relationship between the two areas has been noted,

> Peace studies is all about the analysis of social problems and conflict, theories and strategies for social change, skills and techniques of empowerment and conflict resolution, and histories of successful nonviolent struggle (including education). Its substantive goals are identical to, or in close proximity to, some of the pedagogical goals of service learning.[9]

Although service learning began as an overarching term for most forms of community engagement, the use of this term has changed and in some cases been replaced with community-based learning.[10] Most scholars now refer to the range of interactions between "town and gown" with an umbrella term like "community engagement," about which there remains debate, but most agree that fulfilling a civic mission, reflecting on experience, and developing professional skills are critical parts of any form of community engagement.[11]

Many scholars have also seen beyond the pedagogical applications of engagement and used it to make important contributions to knowledge creation and theory development in a field through community-based, feminist, and action research.[12] Some scholarly applications of engagement include conducting evaluations of community-based programs, studying the processes of service learning, program development, and developing effective community partnerships.[13] Many PACS scholars frame their work under the umbrella of community-based research (CBR) or action research, since they collect data from communities in which they may participate as practitioners and/or emphasize the importance of social justice and social change.[14] Although many PACS scholars research and teach in communities, the longer-term relationship with these communities is not always clear, but clarifying and developing those longer-term relationships are key aspects of community engagement frameworks.

Scholars often view collaborations involving students and practitioners as primarily beneficial *for practice* rather than seeing the partnership as a co-educational process or as fertile ground for quality scholarship. Evidence suggests that the principal reason community partners engage with universities is to view themselves as co-educators and co-creators of knowledge.[15] Van de Ven recognized this and defined "engagement" as "a relationship that involves negotiation and collaboration between researchers and practitioners in a learning community; such a community produces knowledge that can both advance the scientific enterprise and enlighten the community of practitioners."[16] Research and pedagogy that engages with communities and explicitly seeks to both validate practice knowledge and co-create new knowledge is called "engaged scholarship." It will be argued later in the chapter that the engaged model is appropriate for PACS in terms of pedagogy, scholarship, and service since it is reciprocal in nature more so than a unidirectional "scholar as expert" model.

FRAMING A PEACE AND CONFLICT DISCIPLINE

This mission of connecting community, classroom, and scholarship through engagement has been especially appealing in interdisciplinary applied social science and professional programs, like PACS, because of the potential to expose students to and conduct research directly on issues relating to social justice, grassroots social change, and the political, economic, cultural, and interpersonal contexts in which professionals practice.[17] Although PACS programs have primarily seen their pedagogical and scholarly missions interrelated with social change, empowerment, professional skill development, and community impact, literature on community engagement in PACS through service-learning, community-based research, and other forms has been sparse.[18] PACS scholars have noted that the service-learning process offers students' insights into theoretical perspectives and concepts like feminist theory, "nonviolentists," "negative peace," and reflective practice.[19] The most frequently cited outcomes of community engagement experiences for students and faculty are increased awareness of complex realities of conflicts, revelation of personal perspectives biases (usually based on age, gender, ethnicity, etc), linking classroom knowledge and experiential reflection through use of critical thinking (i.e., using debriefing), and positive evaluations of the community-engagement experience.[20]

Despite many positive examples of community engagement projects in PACS and social justice programs from universities in Canada, the United States, and around the world,[21] little is known about the direct and longer impact of these programs on the students, faculty, and community partners who engage in them. It is simply presumed that "engagement happens" and, thus far, little has been done to consider or assess the subsequent development of pedagogy, scholarship, and best practice models for PACS as a discipline and/or profession. Faculty understand that providing students with relevant "real-life" experience better prepares them for their future professional work, but have little understanding of how and why those experiences develop professionals in the field.

In practitioner-oriented PACS programs, the curricula typically focus on applying specific knowledge and practicing technical skills rather than on developing a professional mindset and situating it within a larger discipline. As professional programs have focused on skills development and used experiences like service learning to develop those skills, a growing body of literature has demonstrated that many professionals fail to stay up to date and adopt current research findings into their practice. This skill focus has led to a widening "theory-practice gap."[22] In addition to the "theory-practice gap," academics have their own problems with "knowledge production." Although researchers are generating more scholarship, fewer scholars cite each other, build on related work, and develop the discipline. A number of studies demonstrate greater understanding and perceived impact of research results when scholars and practitioners work together to transfer, interpret, and implement the findings of the research. This research points to the necessary interconnections between scholars and practitioners at all stages in the research process.[23]

The pages of the most prominent PACS journals are principally populated with research from scholars from the more traditional "parent" academic disciplines (e.g., political science, sociology, psychology, law) rather than from scholars in the hundreds of PACS undergraduate and graduate programs in North America and around the world. Although PACS programs are generally considered interdisciplinary, scholars and scholar-practitioners typically come from one of the parent disciplines and their work tends to be influenced by or grounded in that discipline or practice. Since many PACS scholars must keep themselves grounded in both PACS and their parent discipline, few have attempted explicitly to incorporate their work into a body of distinctively identifiable peace and conflict scholarship. This tendency leaves one to wonder if there is a peace and conflict scholarship beyond that developed by and within other disciplines. This situation can leave students and practitioners either frustrated by trying to remain current in several different disciplines or resigned to specializing to the detriment of a broader view.

Peace and conflict studies have not been alone in this apparent void. Many academic programs, especially interdisciplinary professional ones, suffer from a lack of a specific core scholarship.[24] Difficulties seem to abound in "professionalizing" fields with multi-disciplinary knowledge bases.[25] Several authors have provided an important recounting of the history of the early years of social work as it moved from a primarily disjointed band of volunteers doing "good work" to a paid profession with standards of practice.[26] A key turning point in social work's struggle was an explicit discussion in the academic literature of whether or not the field contained the characteristics identified in sociological literature to define itself as a "profession." Once a professional field has been established, debates over evidence-based, best practices may be expected to continue for decades, bouncing back and forth between scholars and practitioners, but this difficult dialogue between these different ways of knowing created something new—a profession and academic discipline of social work.[27] Because of its parallels, the social work experience seems to demonstrate important lessons for PACS. While it is clear that the preparation of PACS practitioners has been disjointed and unfocused across different programs, it seems to have been a reflection of the field, since the students who come to PACS programs are as multidisciplinary as the academics and professionals in the field. Without a core literature or a need to develop a core literature, all parties' interests have remained in their fields of origin.

FRAMING THE PACS DISCIPLINE USING COMMUNITY ENGAGED PEDAGOGY

An engaged professional is one who is not only technically competent, but also one who is ethically and socially cognizant, one who considers the contributions of the community as co-producers of knowledge, and one who forecasts and considers the consequences of their actions and product. Adopting a professional mindset should be an important part of the educational mission of PACS programs and this requires concentrated effort to create a profession, rather than allowing one to emerge organically.[28]

Although the apparent division between scholars and practitioners has made PACS and other applied, interdisciplinary fields appear disjointed, it is a matter of reframing. It is the interdisciplinary, applied nature of the field that is the field's greatest asset, because it makes PACS distinctive from its parent disciplines. The key is not changing the core of the field to better cater to one group, but providing a framework to integrate successfully the needs of practitioners, scholars, and students.

The engine of this process most logically occurs in existing areas where scholars, professionals, and students intersect, such as community-engaged courses in PACS programs. These courses offer opportunities to combine scholarly and professional knowledge through the mechanism of student, faculty, and community partner interaction. This combination of elements is important because not only is it a normative part of professional development, but research also demonstrates an important "buy-in" from all three of these stakeholder groups into these interactions.[29] Community engaged research courses, in which students create and carry out a research project, bring together classroom and community and offer clear linkages among pedagogy, scholarship, and service,[30] more than simple service-learning opportunities, offer students opportunities to engage the true expertise of both faculty (research) and community partners (real-world problem solving). While both scholars and community partners have noted the significant challenges of short-term community research courses, combining these practices facilitates essential learning outcomes that include fostering broad knowledge of human cultures and the natural world, strengthening intellectual and practical skills, deepening personal and social responsibility, and practicing integrative and applied learning.

In addition to student learning, applied research courses provide significant opportunities for scholarship and longer-term community relationships, especially if faculty adopt a less proscriptive approach to students' involvement. Faculty often take a proscriptive approach to simplify the process for students. However, when students collect data without being involved in crucial aspects of the research process, they lack understanding of equally essential professional skills, such as the development of the ethical, community, and professional contexts in which research takes place. In addition, limiting students' roles also limits the roles of community partners. Since faculty develop the questions, methods, and reporting structures for students, this typically rules out community partner involvement as well. This division propagates a nineteenth-century model of scholarship, which assumes that "expert" knowledge is based in scholarship, not practice, and treats community partners as "data collection sites" rather than collaborators or co-creators of knowledge. If the purpose of professional education is to prepare students for their future roles, teaching courses in a traditional way does not prepare students for the professional world of the twenty-first century, which will require, at minimum, a better understanding of the value of high quality program evaluation and a greater emphasis on civic engagement and university-community partnerships.[31]

In order for community engagement to begin framing the discipline of PACS, leadership must first come from higher education faculty teaching these courses. Much of the initial work in re-empowering students and community partners will be incumbent upon faculty, because of the role they have taken in creating the current situation. Ultimately, faculty, students, and community partners must all begin to understand their role in knowledge creation, validation, and professional education. As a potential starting point in this process, the author proposes a model based on the work of scholars who explore engagement, action research, community-based research, and service learning and offers an application of how this model has been applied in a graduate course in Dispute System Design.

COMMUNITY ENGAGEMENT FRAMEWORK FOR PACS

The need for a model that frames PACS in the thinking of community engagement, which can be applied to pedagogy and scholarship, led to the development of the model for community engagement in peace and conflict studies in Figure 17.1. Although projects may begin at any point, the discussion below begins with formal discussions among principal stakeholders, as this would be the likely starting point for most teaching, research, and service projects. The descriptions below attempt to address the major points of the model most relevant to the work of PACS professionals and scholars. However, there are many potential subtleties and applications, which this brief review will be unable to address. Readers are encouraged to see this as a framework for developing engagement, not a proscriptive "how-to" model.

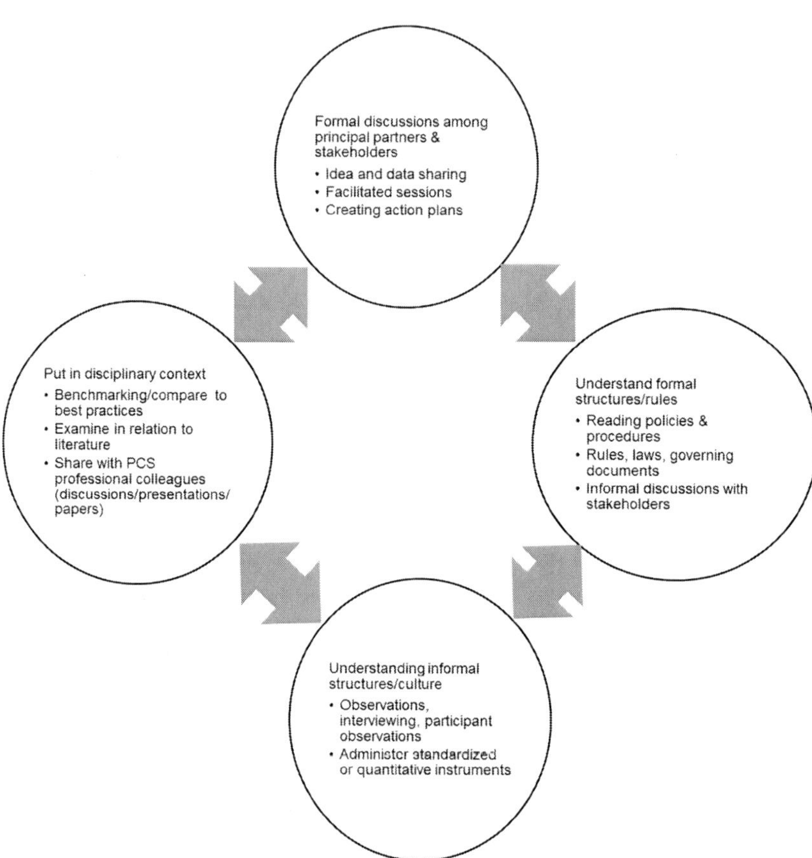

Figure 17.1. Model for Community Engagement in Peace and Conflict Studies

FORMAL DISCUSSIONS AMONG PRINCIPAL PARTNERS/ STAKEHOLDERS

Discussion is important in community engagement, since it helps stakeholders build a rapport, determine the potential for a working relationship, identify strengths and needs, and determine the problems that will be addressed. Problem formulation, in particular, is often rushed or taken for granted, since most people tend to be "solution-minded, rather than problem-minded."[32] Frequently, this initial stage is rushed or parties assume that informal conversations and "coffee shop" talk is enough to start a partnership, but some level of formality is essential. Consequences of rushing this initial process often mean that stakeholders find out much later that there was a "misunderstanding" about project goals or expectations causing outcomes to suffer for all parties. Research questions may lack critical depth, methods may be inappropriate, applicability to related practices or community needs suffer, and students end up filing documents when they thought they would be interviewing clients. Almost all of these misunderstandings are avoidable by approaching any partnership with the same seriousness as one would enter any other significant negotiation. In addition, although requirements (if it is a formal course) may dictate some of a student's role, it is important that students understand the negotiable and non-negotiable expectations and be able to have a certain level of flexibility, if demanded by the interactions with the community partner. These expectations include having a clear syllabus and discussion of course requirements early in the semester. The phrase "But my professor said . . ." will only work so many times for a student working with a community partner.

All parties should have some part in the discussion of developing an action plan, which not only includes issues, such as research design, work plans, timelines, and access, but assuming that the team completes the project and comes "full circle," this point is when issues like sustainability and continuing the partnership will take place. It is likely to be the student who will continue to be involved with the partner or have the greatest insight into the potential for sustaining an ongoing relationship, so including them in these conversations, even if the semester is over and they see the project as finished, is important.

Since PACS professionals are accustomed to working closely with stakeholders to indentify the issues, rather than just potential solutions, this stage in the engagement process should be both familiar and comfortable for those involved. While the word "formal" may be off-putting to some, especially where distance or cultural issues may interfere, this process can be conducted through e-mail, telephone, and a handshake, but for the sake of all involved, it must be clear to everyone that an agreement to begin a relationship is being struck.

If PACS scholars or educators find themselves coming to this stage later in the research process, possibly after some initial research or indirect involvement that sparked an interest in more direct engagement, it may be important to explain to the potential partner the work that has already been done. Being upfront reduces the likelihood of unpleasant surprises later—for example, discovering a stinging critique of an organization, government, or practice, which could jeopardize the relationship, students, or researchers working with the partner.

UNDERSTANDING FORMAL STRUCTURES/RULES

Developing an understanding of the formal structures or "rules" under which one is working is essential. While gathering this information typically begins with informal or formal discussions with partners, individuals embedded in a system cannot always be completely aware of the types of constraints under which they operate on a daily basis, nor do they know what may interest others. One should have already built enough rapport to gain access to official documents that may not be publicly available or published, such as employee handbooks, procedural manuals, government reports, large datasets, or other written documentation. If not, this may require additional conversations with contacts. Likewise, students and researchers need to explain the formal structures and rules under which they are working to community partners. Partners may not be aware of the requirements or timelines of assignments faculty have set for students or the need for researchers to submit documentation of procedures and ethics to institutional review boards or timelines for providing results of research to funders. Developing a mutual understanding of the issues over which individuals have little control helps to clarify better behaviors being researched and the conditions under which teaching, research, and service projects take place. For PACS scholars and students interested in macro-context and structural conflict, this aspect of any project may be the most interesting, but for partners unfamiliar with this type of thinking, it may be the most mystifying.

UNDERSTANDING INFORMAL STRUCTURES/CULTURE

This element of any engaged project is the one most familiar to social and behavioral science researchers as "data collection" and to practitioners as "the process" or "intervention." This part is where most define that "the work" takes place. In this model, however, everything up to this point, whether a research-, teaching-, or service-related project, is also important "work." Researchers may apply the terms "formative" and "summative" research to these different elements of the process and practitioners may call this "prework" or "intake," but in an engaged process, these two processes are ongoing, necessarily inform each other, and ultimately will all have a place in any products produced.

The information gathered during this stage of the process about these informal structures or cultural aspects will probably play a prominent role in products, discussions, and action plans, since they are generally accepted as what the "experts" (e.g., researchers/students under guidance of faculty/mediators) do to "help" the "others" (agency, business, government). This point is not to minimize the importance of these processes, since they are crucial, but to demonstrate the relatively brief amount of time they occur in the broader process and amount of work that comes before and will take place after data is collected or an intervention is completed. The methods used, from ethnographic to standardized psychological instruments, will vary depending on the demands of the project, expertise of the researchers/students, and the agreement of the partners.

PUT IN DISCIPLINARY CONTEXT

This stage of the research process includes the grounding, communication, and interpretation of the findings of the research within the PACS community. A number of studies point to the limited impact of research on practice and other disciplinary scholarship and research, which has more impact when transferred, interpreted, and implemented collaboratively by scholars and practitioners.[33] Researchers should engage in discussions with colleagues, produce written reports and working papers, and direct presentations to scholarly audiences of their ongoing research, not just finished products, to allow opportunities for different interpretations, alternate meanings, and pragmatic and political negotiations about results to reconcile conflicting interests. This process will ensure a scholarly rigor, but also provide a broader contextualization of the research. Ultimately, the application of knowledge to solve problems is most useful to the community and practitioners; however, the application leads to further problem formulation and restarts the cycle of engaged scholarship.

In this spirit, the engagement process proposed in this chapter will seem familiar to many PACS scholars and professionals. Important advances in both scholarship and practice, such as dispute systems design, restorative justice, and "Muppet Diplomacy,"[34] were developed as the result of this kind of process. The critical difference between the ones that are known and those that are not appears to be documenting the process and getting it into publication.

Logically, then, this process turns back on itself to the beginning, where the results of this research are presented to a formal group of the partners and stakeholders. This group will then determine what these results mean to that group and appropriate action plans will be formed to determine how best to consider what, if anything, these results mean for the formal structures, informal structures, and discipline.

AN EXAMPLE OF COMMUNITY ENGAGEMENT THROUGH PEDAGOGY: DISPUTE SYSTEM DESIGN

As discussed above, student-led research courses in PACS programs are uniquely situated to help facilitate engagement between scholars, students, and community partners working on issues of peace and conflict. Using a model like the one presented above can provide a framework to guide this process, which should ultimately provide benefits to all parties involved.

The example presented below came from a graduate level course in dispute system design (DSD), an applied research methodology intended to assist organizations in identifying the existing strengths and growth areas related to resolving disputes within their organization. The information presented about the course came from three primary sources: written policies from course syllabi, lecture notes from the courses, and the author's experience of having taught the course multiple times within the last five years. The course was chosen for several reasons: it is a required course for all students; research projects occur with community partners; the majority of the students select their own sites rather than being placed by faculty; on-site supervisors are chosen for their experience in a field of expertise; and the nature of the partnership agreements are less formal than internships or funded research. The discussion below breaks the issues in the course down into the *process* and *products* of the course, both of which are essential to the class and the engagement model.

THE PROCESS

The course is a fifteen-week graduate seminar with readings, discussion and intensive student participation in organizational research. Grading in the course is based on student performance, class participation, and improvement on three sequential, cumulative written assignments, including an initial structural, cultural, and systems analysis of the organization; an altered or reconstructed design of the organizational dispute systems; and a final paper that serves as a final report to the organization.

Students select and conduct an analysis of a private, public organization, or NGO to use throughout the course. Students are provided with a letter explaining the purposes and role of the student "consultant" in the course and organization, which is sufficient to begin the conversation for students in most cases. The professor has some initial direct contact with organizations if there are questions about the project or the student's role. Faculty spend the early weeks of the course providing students with sufficient background material to engage the organization (e.g., provide letters for initial contact, agreements for access) and begin the "formative" research process. In the first few weeks, students also divide themselves into working groups of approximately four people and class time each week is devoted to small group discussion of their experiences on site and in the research process. Distance education technologies, such as e-mail and class postings through the Blackboard course management system, augment class discussions and provide additional opportunities for students to seek advice and feedback on emerging issues and ideas.

Once students have secured permission, they begin to work with their principal contact and/or a senior member of the organization to determine the scope of work, which may include determining the sources and intensity of conflicts in the organization, developing a plan and timeline of research, and deciding on the most appropriate research methods. Direct involvement with members of the organization and consideration of the research process and products is required, since the methods and processes are not predetermined. Although no methods are prescribed to students, they discuss their options and make decisions in consultation with faculty and peers. Students generally choose some combination of document analysis, observation, interview, and survey methods. Much of the remainder of the course involves discussions of data collection, saturation, appropriate analyses, recommendations, and peer editing. The potentially sensitive nature of the conflict issues being discussed in class require that all students keep class discussions confidential or, if the organization is seriously concerned about confidentiality, students give the organization a pseudonym. Students learn the importance of acting as on-going consultants and coaches to the organization throughout the process and the implications of continuing if the organization adopts final recommendations.

THE RESEARCH PRODUCT

In the first assignment, using the model by Ury and colleagues or Costantino and Merchant,[35] students analyze the basic structure, systems, and practices responsible for conflicts. The data may include results of all informal and formal data collection methods used, although most students rely primarily on formal data (analyses of documents, interviews, surveys, observations) for the majority of their analyses. The structural and cultural information in this paper provides the foundation for the design work done later in the course. The information in this paper is typically as formative as it is summative, as feedback from peers and faculty will usually result in additional data being collected and new analyses of existing data continuing until the final paper is submitted.

The main goal of the second paper is to create a set of recommendations designed to address organizational conflict that directly follow the evidence collected in the first paper. The paper must include information gathered for the first paper, as well as knowledge and insights gained from course reading, class discussions, and continuing consultation with the organization. The intention is not to produce an ideal state for the organization, but one that is based on the data collected to reflect the realities and possibilities of the organization. Students are encouraged to have open discussions with their organizations to "reality test" the practicalities of these proposed changes before committing them to writing.

The final paper includes an introduction, literature review, description of the case study, the methodology, and the organizational analysis (first paper), followed by a section with recommendations (second paper) and references. In conjunction with the final paper, students prepare a ten- to fifteen-minute presentation for the class and the professor. This exercise is intended as preparation for presenting the project to the organization. Therefore, students are evaluated on the professional manner in which they conduct the presentation and are provided formal feedback by peers and the professor.

DSD AND COMMUNITY ENGAGEMENT

Feedback from students and community partners over the last few years has demonstrated that the course is having the intended educational and practical impact. Students often use this project as a starting point for their capstone practicum projects, which come the following semester. This longer-term engagement means that even if these organizations did not invest in the outcomes of the research, they became invested in the individual student. Several organizations have further engaged with students and faculty in additional research and service projects, at least three projects have resulted in funded and published research, and two projects notably resulted in students obtaining work. As the course has developed, students have actually begun to recognize that one semester is inadequate to conduct a full process of engagement and have suggested lengthening the course to two semesters, rather than scaling back the project. Although not all students are as enthusiastic about the research, they all seem to gain valuable skills in seeing themselves as conflict professionals and working with organizations in that capacity.

WHAT COMMUNITY ENGAGEMENT MEANS FOR THE FUTURE OF PACS

Academic courses such as the one described above demonstrate an important intersection of scholarship, practice, and professional development. Students obtain hands-on experience in developing professional skills like consultancy, research design, data analysis, report writing, and program evaluation that cannot be replicated in the classroom alone. In return, they develop and strengthen university-community partnerships by providing professional consultancy and evaluations that many organizations may not be able to afford and faculty may not have time (or incentive) to provide, given the focus on publishing and grant writing. Faculty benefit by making contact with a range of community and professional partners with whom they may never otherwise have connected, creating possibilities for grant writing and publishable research, for which there is incentive. Faculty members who wish to enhance their pedagogy and scholarship through community engaged practices should consider including students and community partners in research and curriculum development.

The application of an engaged scholarship model as an explicit part of academic preparation in PACS programs would appear to assist in the development from a group of disjointed, interdisciplinary programs and professionals into a cohesive, collaborative academic discipline and recognized profession. The explicit integration of scholars, students, and community professionals can provide a better informed and more nuanced field with a knowledge base grounded in real experiences of those who are closest to the population, phenomenon, or issue, which honors the role of professionals as a co-educators and co-generators of knowledge. In the longer term, explicit engagement should provide specific opportunities to discuss the intersections and disparities of scholarly and practical knowledge and allow PACS professionals to develop a discipline literature grounded in practice and rooted in theory.

BIBLIOGRAPHY

Abbott, Pamela, and Liz Meerabeau. *The Sociology of the Caring Professions.* London: Routledge, 1998.

Banerjee, M., and C. Hausafus. "Faculty Use of Service-Learning: Perceptions, Motivations, and Impediments for the Human Sciences." *Michigan Journal of Community Service Learning,* vol. 14, no. 1 (2008): 32–45.

Basinger, N., and K. Bartholomew. "Service-Learning in Nonprofit Organizations: Motivations, Expectations, and Outcomes." *Michigan Journal of Community Service Learning,* vol. 12, no. 2 (2006): 15–26.

Baxter, Jorge. "Muppet Diplomacy: Sesame Workshop's Approach to Promoting Peace Around the World." *Conflict Resolution Education Connection,* March 26, 2010, http://www.creducation.org/cre/homebase/content_presentations/muppet_diplomacy/ (July 29, 2010).

Boulding, Eloise. "Preface," in *Teaching for Justice: Concepts and Models for Service-learning in Peace Studies*, Kathleen Weigert and Robin Crews, eds. Washington, DC: American Association for Higher Education, 1999, ix–xi

Boyer, Ernest. "The Scholarship of Engagement." *Bulletin of the American Academy of Arts and Sciences,* vol. 49, no. 7 (1996): 18–33.

Bringle, R., and J. Hatcher. "Implementing Service Learning in Higher Education." *Journal of Higher Education,* vol. 67, no. 2 (1996): 222.

Carnegie Foundation for the Advancement for Teaching and Learning. "Community Engagement Classification," January 2010, http://classification.carnegiefoundation.org/descriptions/community_engagement.php (22 July 2010).

Costantino, C.A., and C.S. Merchant. *Designing Conflict Management Systems: A Guide to Creating Productive and Healthy Organizations.* San Francisco: Jossey-Bass, 1996.

Crews, Robin. "Peace Studies, Pedagogy, and Social Change," in *Teaching for Justice: Concepts and Models for Service-Learning in Peace Studies*, K.M. Weigert and R.J. Crews, eds. Washington, DC: American Association for Higher Education, 1999, 24.

Elliott, P. *The Sociology of Professions.* London: The Macmillan Press, 1972.

Gardner, Howard, Mihaly Csikszentmihalyi, and William Damon. *Good Work: When Excellence and Ethics Meet.* New York: Basic Books, 2001.

Golde, C.M. *Applying Lessons From Professional Education to the Preparation of the Professoriate,* in Volume 113, C.L. Colbeck, K.A. O'Meara, and A.E. Austin, eds. San Francisco: Jossey-Bass, 2008, 17–26.

Hansen, T. "The History of the Professionalization of Social Work: Lesson for the Field of Conflict Resolution." *Peace and Conflict Studies,* vol. 14, no. 2 (2007): 1–26.

Hugman, Richard. "Social Work and De-Professionalization," in *The Sociology of the Caring Professions*, Pamela Abbott and Liz Meerabeau, eds. London: Routledge, 1998, 178–198

Fischer, Joel. *Toward Evidence-Based Practice: Variations on a Theme.* Chicago: Lyceum Books, 2009.

Janke, Emily. "The Promise of Public Scholarship for Undergraduate Research: Developing Students' Civic and Academic Scholarship Skills." *Higher Education in Review,* vol. 3 (2006): 51–68.

Kecskes, Kevin, ed. *Engaging Departments: Moving Faculty Culture from Private to Public: From Individual to Collective, Focus for the Common Good.* San Francisco: Jossey-Bass, 2006.

Kenworthy-U'Ren, Amy. "Service-Learning and Negotiation: Engaging Students in Real-World Projects that Make a Difference." *Negotiation Journal* (2003): 51–63.

Kosic, Ankica, and Sean Byrne. "Community Relations Work with Young People in Vukovar, Croatia: An Exploratory Study in Coexistence Building." *Peace and Conflict Studies* (2009): 62–80.

Kuh, G.E. *High-Impact Educational Practices: What They Are, Who Has Access to Them, and Why They Matter.* Washington, DC: Association of American Colleges and Universities, 2008.

Marullo, Sam, Kathleen Maas Weigert, and Joseph Palacios. "Fostering Engagement for Social Justice: The Social Justice Analysis Concentration at Georgetown University," in *Engaging Departments: Moving Faculty Culture from Private to*

Public, Individual to Collective Focus for the Common Good, Kevin Kecskes, ed. San Francisco: Jossey-Bass, 2006, 172–191.

O'Meara, K. *Graduate Education and Community Engagement,* Volume 113, in *New Directions for Teaching and Learning*, C.L. Colbeck, K. O'Meara, and A.E. Austin, eds. San Francisco: Jossey-Bass, 2008, 27–42.

Saltmarsh, John. "Changing Pedagogies," in *Handbook of Engaged Scholarship: The Contemporary Landscape, Vol. 1*, H.E. Fitzgerald, C. Burack, and S. Seifer, eds. East Lansing: Michigan State University Press, in press, chapter 24.

Saltmarsh, John, and Sherril Gelmon. "Characteristics of an Engaged Department: Design and Assessment," in *Engaging Departments: Moving Faculty Culture from Private to Public, Individual to Focus for the Common Good*, Kevin Kecskes, ed. San Francisco: Jossey-Bass, 2006, 24–44.

Stocking, V.B., and N. Cutforth. "Managing the Challenges of Teaching Community-Based Research Courses: Insights From Two Instructors." *Michigan Journal of Community Service Learning,* vol. 13, no. 1 (2006): 56–66.

Strand, K., S. Marulla, N. Cutforth, R. Stoecker, and P. Donohue. *Community-based Research and Higher Education: Principles and Practices*. San Francisco: Jossey-Bass, 2003.

Stringer, Ernest. *Action Research.* Thousand Oaks, CA: Sage, 2007.

Tennet, P., J. Senehi, M. Ross Fowler, and S. Byrne. "The Six University Consortium Student Mobility Project: Promoting Conflict Resolution in the North American Context." *Peace and Conflict Studies* (2009): 15–37.

Tryon, E., R. Stoecker, A. Martin, K. Seblonka, A. Hilgendorf, and M. Nellis. "The Challenge of Short-term Service Learning." *Michigan Journal of Community Service Learning,* vol. 14, no. 2 (2008): 16–26.

Umbreit, M., B. Vos, R. Coates, and K.A. Brown. *Facing Violence: The Path of Restorative Justice and Dialogue.* Monsey, NY: Criminal Justice Press, 2003.

Ury, W., J. Brett, and S. Goldberg. *Getting Disputes Resolved: Designing Systems to Cut the Costs of Conflict.* San Francisco: Jossey-Bass, 1988.

Van de Ven, Andrew H. *Engaged Scholarship: A Guide for Organizational and Social Research.* Oxford: Oxford University Press, 2007.

Weigert, Kathleen, and Robin Crews. *Teaching for Justice: Concepts and Models for Service-Learning in Peace Studies.* Washington, DC: American Association for Higher Education, 1999.

Worrall, L. "Asking the Community: A Case Study of Community Partner Perspectives." *Michigan Journal of Community Service Learning,* vol. 14, no. 1 (2007): 5–17.

NOTES

1. Kathleen Weigert and Robin Crews, "Introduction," in *Teaching for Justice: Concepts and Models for Service Learning in Peace Studies*, Kathleen Weigert and Robin Crews, ed. (Washington, DC: American Association for Higher Education, 1999), 1–7.

2. Jorge Baxter, "Muppet Diplomacy: Sesame Workshop's Approach to Promoting Peace Around the World," *Conflict Resolution Education Connection,* March 26, 2010. http://www.creducation.org/cre/homebase/content_presentations/muppet_diplomacy/ (July 29, 2010); K. Strand, S. Marulla, N. Cutforth, R. Stoecker, and P. Donohue, *Community-based Research and Higher Education: Principles and Practices* (San Francisco: Jossey-Bass, 2003).

Ernest Stringer, *Action Research* (Thousand Oaks, CA: Sage, 2007); William Ury, J.M. Brett, and S.B. Goldberg. *Getting Disputes Resolved: Designing Systems to Cut the Costs of Conflict* (San Francisco: Jossey-Bass, 1988); Andrew H. Van de Ven, *Engaged Scholarship: A Guide for Organizational and Social Research* (Oxford: Oxford University Press, 2007).

3. Ernest Boyer, "The Scholarship of Engagement," *Bulletin of the American Academy of Arts and Sciences,* vol. 49, no. 7 (1996): 18–33.

4. Kevin Kecskes ed., *Engaging Departments: Moving Faculty Culture from Private to Public: From Individual to Collective, Focus for the Common Good* (San Francisco: Jossey-Bass, 2006); John Saltmarsh and Sherril Gelmon. "Characteristics of an Engaged Department: Design and Assessment," in *Engaging Departments: Moving Faculty Culture from Private to Public, Individual to Focus for the Common Good,* Kevin Kecskes, ed. (San Francisco: Jossey-Bass, 2006), 27–44; Van de Ven, *Engaged Scholarship.*

5. Eloise Boulding, "Preface," in *Teaching for Justice: Concepts and Models for Service-learning in Peace Studies*, Kathleen Weigert and Robin Crews, eds. (Washington, DC: American Association for Higher Education, 1999), ix–xi.

6. John Saltmarsh, "Changing Pedagogies," in *Handbook of Engaged Scholarship: The Contemporary Landscape, Vol. 1*, H. E. Fitzgerald, C. Burack and S. Seifer, eds. (East Lansing: Michigan State University Press, in press), chapter 24.

7. For definitions of these, see the following: Carnegie Foundation for the Advancement for Teaching and Learning, "Community Engagement Classification." (January 2010) http://classification.carnegiefoundation.org/descriptions/community_engagement.php (July 22, 2010); Strand, et al., *Community-based Research*; Van de Ven, *Engaged Scholarship.*

8. R. Bringle and J. Hatcher, "Implementing Service Learning in Higher Education," *Journal of Higher Education,* vol. 67, no. 2 (1996): 222.

9. Robin Crews, "Peace Studies, Pedagogy, and Social Change," in *Teaching for Justice: Concepts and Models for Service-Learning in Peace Studies*, K.M. Weigert and R.J. Crews, eds. (Washington, DC: American Association for Higher Education, 1999), 24.

10. Kathleen Weigert, "Moral Dimensions of Peace Studies: A Case for Service-learning," in *Teaching for Justice: Concepts and Models for Service-Learning in Peace Studies*, K.M. Weigert and R.J. Crews, eds. (Washington, DC: American Association for Higher Education, 1999), 23–32.

11. Saltmarsh and Gelmon, "Characteristics of an Engaged Department," 32–33.

12. Van de Ven, *Engaged Scholarship*; Stringer, *Action Research.*

13. M. Banerjee and C. Hausafus, "Faculty Use of Service-Learning: Perceptions, Motivations, and Impediments for the Human Sciences," *Michigan Journal of Com-*

munity Service Learning, vol. 14, no. 1 (2008): 32–45; V.B. Stocking and N. Cutforth, "Managing the Challenges of Teaching Community-based Research Courses: Insights from Two Instructors," *Michigan Journal of Community Service Learning,* vol. 13, no. 1 (2006): 56–66; P. Tennet, J. Senehi, M. Ross Fowler, and S. Byrne, "The Six University Consortium Student Mobility Project: Promoting Conflict Resolution in the North American Context," *Peace and Conflict Studies* (2009): 15–37; Kathleen Weigert and Robin Crews, *Teaching for Justice: Concepts and Models for Service-Learning in Peace Studies* (Washington, DC: American Association for Higher Education, 1999); L. Worrall, "Asking the Community: A Case Study of Community Partner Perspectives," *Michigan Journal of Community Service Learning,* vol. 14, no. 1 (2007): 5–17.

14. Sam Marullo, Kathleen Maas Weigert, and Joseph Palacios, "Fostering Engagement for Social Justice: The Social Justice Analysis Concentration at Georgetown University," in *Engaging Departments: Moving Faculty Culture from Private to Public, Individual to Collective Focus for the Common Good,* Kevin Kecskes, ed. (San Francisco: Jossey-Bass, 2006), 172–191; Kathleen Weigert and Robin Crews, *Teaching for Justice.*

15. N. Basinger and K. Bartholomew, "Service-Learning in Nonprofit Organizations: Motivations, Expectations, and Outcomes," *Michigan Journal of Community Service Learning,* vol. 12, no. 2 (2006): 15–26; Worrall, "Asking the Community."

16. Van de Ven, *Engaged Scholarship,* 7.

17. Weigert and Crews, "Introduction."

18. Amy Kenworthy-U'Ren, "Service-Learning and Negotiation: Engaging Students in Real-World Projects that Make a Difference," *Negotiation Journal* (2003): 51–63; Ankica Kosic and Sean Byrne, "Community Relations Work with Young People in Vukovar, Croatia: An Exploratory Study in Coexistence Building," *Peace and Conflict Studies* (2009): 62–80; Tennet, et al. "Student Mobility Project"; Weigert and Crews, "Introduction."

19. Weigert, *Moral Dimensions.*

20. Weigert and Crews, *Introduction.*

21. Kenworthy-U'Ren, "Service-Learning and Negotiation"; Tennet, et al., *Six University*; Weigert and Crews, *Introduction.*

22. Van de Ven, *Engaged Scholarship*, 3.

23. Van de Ven, *Engaged Scholarship*, 3–6.

24. Pamela Abbott and Liz Meerabeau, *The Sociology of the Caring Professions.* (London: Routledge, 1998).

25. P. Elliott, *The Sociology of Professions.* (London: The Macmillan Press, 1972).

26. T. Hansen, "The History of the Professionalization of Social Work: Lesson for the Field of Conflict Resolution," *Peace and Conflict Studies,* vol. 14, no. 2 (2007): 1–26; Richard Hugman, "Social Work and De-Professionalization," in *The Sociology of the Caring Professions*, Pamela Abbott and Liz Meerabeau, eds. (London: Routledge, 1998), 178–198.

27. Abbott and Meerabeau, *The Sociology of the Caring Professions*; Joel Fischer, *Toward Evidence-Based Practice: Variations on a Theme* (Chicago: Lyceum Books, 2009).

28. Howard Gardner, Mihaly Csikszentmihalyi, and William Damon, *Good Work: When Excellence and Ethics Meet* (New York: Basic Books, 2001).

29. Banerjee and Hausafus, "Faculty Use of Service-Learning; Basinger and Bartholomew," *Service-Learning in Nonprofit Organizations*; Bringle and Hatcher, "Implementing Service Learning"; G.E. Kuh, *High-Impact Educational Practices: What They Are, Who Has Access to Them, and Why They Matter* (Washington, DC: Association of American Colleges and Universities, 2008); K. O'Meara, *Graduate Education and Community Engagement,* Volume 113, in *New Directions for Teaching and Learning*, C.L. Colbeck, K. O'Meara, and A.E. Austin, eds. (San Francisco: Jossey-Bass, 2008), 27–42; V.B. Stocking and N. Cutforth, "Managing the Challenges of Teaching Community-Based Research Courses: Insights From Two Instructors," *Michigan Journal of Community Service Learning,* vol. 13, no. 1 (2006): 56–66; E. Tryon, R. Stoecker, A. Martin, K. Seblonka, A. Hilgendorf, and M. Nellis, "The Challenge of Short-term Service Learning," *Michigan Journal of Community Service Learning,* vol. 14, no. 2 (2008): 16–26; L. Worrall, "Asking the Community: A Case Study of Community Partner Perspectives," *Michigan Journal of Community Service Learning,* vol. 14, no. 1 (2007): 5–17.

30. Emily Janke, "The Promise of Public Scholarship for Undergraduate Research: Developing Students' Civic and Academic Scholarship Skills," *Higher Education in Review,* vol. 3 (2006): 51–68.

31. C.M. Golde, *Applying Lessons From Professional Education to the Preparation of the Professoriate,* Vol. 113, C.L. Colbeck, K.A. O'Meara, and A.E. Austin, eds. (San Francisco: Jossey-Bass, 2008), 17–26.

32. Van de Ven, *Engaged Scholarship*, 17.

33. Van de Ven, *Engaged Scholarship,* 234–236.

34. Jorge Baxter, *Muppet Diplomacy*; M. Umbreit, B. Vos, R. Coates, and K.A. Brown, *Facing Violence: The Path of Restorative Justice and Dialogue* (Monsey, NY: Criminal Justice Press, 2003); Ury, et al., *Getting Disputes Resolved.*

35. Ury, et al., *Getting Disputes Resolved*; C.A. Costantino and C.S. Merchant, *Designing Conflict Management Systems: A Guide to Creating Productive and Healthy Organizations* (San Francisco: Jossey-Bass, 1996).

Chapter 18

Religion and Peace and Conflict Studies

Nathan C. Funk and Christina J. Woolner

In recent years, the field of religion and peacebuilding has gained increasing vitality and dynamism. As a result of shifting trends in the global political landscape as well as multi-faceted developments in the Peace and Conflict Studies (PACS) field, scholars have attended to ways in which religion can both propagate violence and foster peace. On the one hand, shifts in the ideological content of intra- and inter-state conflict since the Cold War, and the rise of so-called "identity" conflicts have placed pressure on scholars to identify ways in which religious identities, interpretations, and institutions can become implicated in destructive human behavior.[1] On the other hand, movements within the field to pay greater attention to cultural diversity, worldview differences, and indigenous peacemaking resources have also led scholars to attend to distinctively religious resources for peace and to the potential benefits of tailoring conflict resolution capacity development efforts to specific religious contexts.[2] Taken together, the contributions of a growing cohort of scholars have led to the emergence of a distinct PACS sub-field that is largely premised on the recognition that religion has "two faces" in its relationship to peace. Religion, they argue, can be both a barrier between groups and a bridge to coexistence; it is both a source of conflict and a resource for reconciliation.[3] In the words of Scott Appleby, religion is "ambivalent" in its relationship to peace.[4]

As a relatively new sub-field within PACS, the study of religion and peacebuilding faces both challenges and opportunities. Developing a coherent approach to a domain of inquiry that is and always has been contested—religion—is no easy task. The field continues to be challenged by secularist biases against engaging religion in an affirmative manner, as well as by religious reservations about active collaboration with secular and religiously diverse partners. Overcoming these attitudes and assumptions will take time and patience. Nonetheless, significant advances have been made in the development of theoretical frameworks and practical methods. Greater clarity has been achieved not just about the role religion plays in contemporary conflicts, but also about ways in which religiously motivated actors and institutions can contribute to peacebuilding.

To advance an understanding of both the challenges and opportunities of the field at this juncture, this chapter begins by situating the contemporary discussion of religion and peacebuilding within a larger context of cultural and intellectual history. We examine two antagonistic, historically formed perspectives on religion and peace, perspectives that are not easily reconciled—a religious stance that sees religion as the only way to peace, and a "hard secularist" stance that regards religion as inherently conflictual—and propose that the emergent PACS approach to studying religion straddles and in some sense attempts to harmonize this longstanding religious-secular divide. The second part of the chapter reviews trends in the theory and practice of the "religion and peacebuilding" field, and outlines distinctive characteristics of this developing PACS approach to religion, peace, and conflict. The chapter's third section provides a brief discussion of challenges and rewards associated with bringing religion into the peace and conflict studies curriculum, and offers reflections on matters of pedagogy. The fourth and final section concludes by engaging several common critiques of religious peacebuilding scholarship and practice, acknowledging potentially valid lines of criticism while also underscoring the continuing relevance and promise of the field.

RELIGION, CONFLICT AND PEACE: OPENING SPACE FOR DIALOGUE

Although the field of religion and peacebuilding is relatively recent, scholars of various disciplines, as well as politicians, practitioners and lay members of religious communities have long been interested in the relationship between religion, conflict, and peace. Historically, two divergent and antagonistic perspectives on the relationship between religion and peace life have emerged, perspectives which continue to find expression both in academic theorizing and in widespread public attitudes. Together, these competing views have shaped the context within which an increasingly structured PACS approach to religion has developed, presenting scholars and practitioners with the challenge of formulating an approach to religion, conflict, and peace that refuses to participate in longstanding "religion versus secularism" polemics, and instead fosters dialogue between secular and religious worldviews—both to ameliorate a significant source of conflict in the contemporary world, and to enlarge the scope for constructive religious peacemaking activity.

TRADITIONAL THINKING: PEACE THROUGH RELIGION ALONE

For centuries, the prevailing wisdom about religion and peace could be summarized by the phrase, "peace through religion alone." In a remarkably broad range of distinctive cultural and religious milieus, there was a pervasive belief that true peace, whether in this world or the next, could only be found through religious beliefs and practices. Often, but not always, there was a corollary to this belief: the premise that authentic peace can only be found through following the teachings of one particular religion, sect, or sub-community. This was frequently associated with the notion that "If everyone embraced our beliefs and practices, there would be peace in the world." In other words, peace is possible but it must be done "our way," in relation to a particular creed, code, cult of worship, and system of communal solidarity.[5]

In the modern secular academy, scholars have found it easy to become sanctimonious when confronted with such convictions, yet a serious PACS approach to religious peacemaking cannot afford to simply dismiss this genre of traditional thinking. An empathetic encounter with the "peace through religion alone" perspective has potential to deepen PACS scholarship and practice, through recognition of ubiquitous themes in the peace wisdom of most premodern societies. First, premodern peace concepts tend to understand peace holistically, characterizing a peaceful state as much more than a simple absence of war or violence. In a wide variety of cultural and religious traditions, peace evokes motifs associated with wholeness, harmony, or completion, and efforts to move in the direction of peace require much more than changes in legislation or reform of the status quo.[6] Second, traditional wisdom about peace frames the absence of peace in human societies existentially and not merely in relation to social structures and institutional constructs. In most religious systems, a "peace deficit" is understood to be a recurrent feature of the human condition: on a day-to-day basis, typical human beings are not fully at peace, with themselves or with others. While vocabulary and specific meanings vary in non-trivial ways, there is nonetheless a measure of consistency in religious characterizations of a human predicament in which something fundamental is lacking, leading to brokenness, suffering, duality, or fragmentation. Third, peacemaking requires transformation, healing, and acceptance of moral guidance and direction—deep changes within individuals and societies, and not merely a shift in social policies or an improvement in negotiation skills. There is scope within most traditional religious worldviews to conceive of peacemaking as sacred activity based on inspired teachings; this approach calls for community and fellowship, and envisions not only an end to fighting but also radical changes in feeling, relationships, and character.

While the "peace through religion alone" perspective has much potential to add spiritual and existential depth to discussions of peace, conflict, and peacemaking, the attitude associated with this perspective nonetheless imposes constraints on conflict analysis and has engendered strong intellectual countercurrents. With respect to conflict analysis, the "peace through religion alone" approach tends to essentialize religious belief systems and pit normative prescription against empirical analysis. Although intellectualism associated with this position can provide a basis for differentiating between authentic manifestations of a given religion and actions which abuse and manipulate religious forms—a valuable distinction within a context of conflict—the approach is at times inarticulate with respect to misdeeds perpetrated in the name of religion, and frequently undervalues contributions to human betterment from non-religious sources or from religious belief systems that are not accorded legitimacy. Hesitancy with respect to empiricism can impede thoroughgoing discussion of the contested nature of religious beliefs, the political entanglements of religious institutions, and the complex interplay of ethno-national, cultural, and religious identities.

HARD SECULARISM: PEACE WITHOUT RELIGION

Historically, perceived excesses of the "peace through religion alone" perspective were a major impetus for the birth of another orientation, "peace without religion." This perspective owes much to the European Renaissance and Enlightenment, and began to exert a strong impact on politics with the Peace of Westphalia in 1648. The Peace of Westphalia ended the sectarian turmoil of the Thirty Years War and began the shift toward a more explicitly secular model of international relations, within which national interest was increasingly regarded as a safer and more appropriate guide to statecraft than religious conviction. This shift toward secular politics was accelerated by the French Revolution's direct attack on religious institutions and celebration of human reason, and reached its apogee in the Russian and Chinese Revolutions, which drew on Marx's view of religion as false consciousness—an opiate intoxicating the oppressed with visions of an ethereal and ultimately unreal peace, and thereby distracting them from the real, ongoing violence of class conflict. While most states today are neither as staunchly secular as France nor as anti-religious as the Soviet Union or Communist China, core tenets of the "peace without religion" perspective retain considerable vitality in the Western academy, and continue to inform much discussion concerning the appropriate place of religion in public affairs.

The "peace without religion" perspective has various formulations, but the general argument is that public religion constitutes a threat to peace. Religion is seen as divisive and predisposed to intolerance or even violence, unless safely confined to the private sphere. This perspective points to historical abuses of religion as a power tool—as a means of exclusion or oppression—and calls for the inculcation of secular ethical principles that do not discriminate between "us" and "them," and that enjoin individuals to care for this world rather than strive for access to another. Aspects of this view are present within contemporary secular orderings of political space, and there is a great deal of academic and popular literature on religion and conflict that highlights its central themes, such as the negative possibilities of absolutism, authoritarianism, intolerance, divisiveness, and irrationality.

By challenging abuses of religion and exclusive reliance on religious epistemology, spokespersons for the "peace without religion" perspective have mounted a potentially constructive critique of many problematic practices, and have highlighted destructive ways in which religious institutions, interpretations, and identities can become entangled in conflict. While institutions are undeniably necessary for the preservation of religious tradition over time, the actual performance of religious institutions can easily mirror that of non-religious institutions, with comparable imperfections. Religion can also raise the stakes of conflict in significant ways, giving added significance to seemingly more mundane rivalries and disputes, while also providing overzealous or unscrupulous political leaders with an enriched rhetorical basis for dehumanizing adversaries and justifying imperial ventures. In many instances of protracted conflict, religion serves as yet another marker between communities struggling for material gain, position, and security, and "peace without religion" does much to unmask such behavior.

Despite the validity of such critiques, the "peace without religion" perspective nonetheless has a number of profound limitations. First, many advocates of the approach tend to scapegoat religion as the primary cause of social and political conflicts[7]—a posture which results in simplistic and often erroneous understandings of complex conflict dynamics, and unwarranted stereotyping of religious teachings, institutions and individuals. Second, in scapegoating religion, advocates of the approach frequently overlook ways in which secular identities and ideologies can also take on fanatical and destructive forms. Just as fundamentalist[8] interpretations of religion may lead to divisiveness and conflict, any ideological system—including secularism—can be used as a basis for asserting hegemony over others or mobilizing a population against resented "outsiders." Indeed, while a remarkable range of autocratic governments in virtually every world region have sought to use religion as a primary justifying ideology, some of the most destructive regimes in history—such as Stalin's USSR and Nazi Germany—were profoundly *irreligious*, even anti-religious.

This tendency to overlook the potential violence of secular belief systems has particularly problematic consequences in the present world historical context. As William Cavanaugh argues, much scholarly treatment of religious violence overlooks the potential for "crusading" in the name of a secular or modernist belief system, and now has the function of underscoring the "otherness" of non-Western peoples whose cultures tend to have a strong religious component.[9] The result is a tendency to view *their* violence as inherently irrational, while allowing Western thinkers to frame violence emanating from their own countries' policies as a civilizing force—as a force for peace. In Cavanaugh's view this constitutes a harmful double standard, and contributes to a sanitized view of contemporary Western political systems (which attempt to minimize the role of religion in state affairs and place checks on public religion) and their interactions with the larger world.

Beyond these shortcomings, one of the greatest flaws of the "peace without religion" perspective is that by focusing exclusively on the conflict potential of religion, an injustice is done to religion's peace potential, and to the many ways in which religion can and does serve as a powerful resource for peacemaking. Religions have both strengths and weaknesses with respect to peace and conflict issues, but these strengths and weaknesses are not unique, and are shared by many other communal, institutional, and ideological forms of association. If we accept Huston Smith's characterization of religion as "institutionalized spirituality,"[10] one-sided antagonism toward religion risks throwing the baby out with the bathwater, while substituting new absolutes for old ones. Furthermore, while some scholars had previously predicted a global decline in religiosity, religion, in various forms, is decidedly here to stay. What is needed, then, is a more nuanced approach to studying religion and its relationship to peace and conflict, an approach that better accounts for the complexities of an era of globalization, democracy, humanism, and multiple modernities (Western and otherwise).

A FLEXIBLE APPROACH: PEACE WITH RELIGION

In many quarters, the "peace through religion alone" and "peace without religion" dichotomy is giving way to new ways of thinking about the role of religion in the public sphere, and about potential contributions of religion to peacemaking. These new ways of thinking are at the core of the emerging PACS approach to religion, which seeks to transcend limitations inherent in religious or secular exclusivism, while recognizing and affirming valid religious and secular claims. A defining characteristic of this PACS approach is its open recognition of the paradox that religion both unites *and* divides: religion evokes universally resonant ideals such as peace, even as it underscores the importance of the *particular*, of irreducibly distinctive truth claims and symbols. It can provide virtually unrivalled motivation for peacemaking activity, but can also be interpreted in ways that are deeply problematic for those who aspire toward human solidarity.

One need not be religious to recognize that religion has tremendous potential for peace. At their best, the world's religions have much to say on the subject, and much to offer. Multiple religious traditions have provided exemplars of peacebuilding who transcend sectarian boundaries and inspire respect both for their moral courage and for their uncommon humanity. These committed religious peacebuilders have done a great deal to foster public spirituality—spreading inspiration far beyond the circle of coreligionists—and have often been at the forefront of efforts to address pressing social concerns. In a broader sense, religious visions and vocabularies have contributed greatly to the theory and practice of reconciliation, and socially engaged religious intellectuals are often among the most perceptive challengers of new orthodoxies and subtle "idolatries" in the modern world, from the often ambiguous "national interest" of power politics to the "invisible hand" of economics. At an institutional level, religious decisions to devote resources and leadership capacity to peace and justice advocacy are highly consequential, and have the potential to catalyze broad-based mobilizations as well as sustained grassroots efforts. In these and many other ways, religion can and does serve as a vital source of inspiration and support for peace. To get the best out of religion, however, we need new ways of thinking in secular and religious quarters alike; we need to think beyond the traditional "peace through religion alone" and "peace without religion" dichotomies. We need a third perspective: "peace with religion."

What does a "peace with religion" approach look like? In short, this approach is premised on open recognition of religion's ambivalent relationship to conflict and peace, tempered by a strong appreciation for the spiritual resources that religion brings to peacemaking. This approach therefore embraces positive contributions of "peace through religion alone" thinking, while remaining mindful of the negative possibilities highlighted by the "peace without religion" approach, and recognizing the need for balance between secular claims to inclusive public space and the religious need to express particularity. Thus, PACS scholars and practitioners who explicitly or implicitly take this approach remain attentive to the conflict potential inherent in religion, while actively endeavoring to identify and foster the religion's peace potential. To this end, they investigate the ways in which beliefs, values, rituals, and practices from a wide range of traditions may contribute to peacebuilding, and seek to clarify the constructive roles that religious individuals and institutions can play in transforming conflict.

KEY THEMES IN THEORY AND PRACTICE

Accepting the "ambivalence" of religion, and endeavoring to better understand what a "peace with religion" approach may mean, PACS scholars have begun to pay far greater analytical attention to the relationship between religion and peacebuilding. Drawing on previously existing PACS frameworks and insights from various disciplines, scholars have begun to develop a richer understanding of what religions may have to offer. They have formulated detailed arguments concerning when and how religious institutions and individuals can be involved in peace processes, while also attending to specific dynamics inherent in religious activism and transformative modes of engagement. While some of this work has advocated efforts to harness the energy of religious activism by using pre-existing strategic templates, much of the new attention paid to religion's peace potential has been conceptually innovative, leading to the development of new ways of thinking about peacebuilding. In what follows, we highlight a number of key themes and contributions of PACS scholarship, which has shaped and continues to shape visions of how "peace with religion" might be sought.

RELIGION AS A SOURCE OF WISDOM AND MOTIVATION FOR PEACE

A starting point for many PACS scholars who focus on religion is to identify religious teachings, values, beliefs, and practices that may contribute to building and sustaining peace. While it is commonly presumed that religious ideals are more consonant than dissonant, researchers have demonstrated awareness that each religion has its own particular understanding of what peace means, in spiritual, theological, and conceptual as well as ritual, practical, and relational terms. There is an assumption that knowledge of how peace is understood within different traditions can provide a meaningful bridge to interreligious understanding, while also clarifying the sources of inspiration that are available for building peace in different political and cultural contexts around the globe. Definitions of peace that are present within a given tradition can provide valuable insight into "keynote" themes of that religion, themes which often resonate with major accents of other traditions, while maintaining their own unique character, "overtones," and correlations with various sets of positive values (e.g., inwardness, justice, wholeness, harmony, community).[11] The three principal Abrahamic faiths, for instance, share an emphasis on the importance of justice and mercy, and relate these concepts to the advancement of peace. For Muslims, the theme of peace evokes not just the presence of a deep sense of safety and well-being, but also the need for constant striving toward just and compassionate relationships with others.[12] For Christians, the teachings of the Bible emphasize the importance of justice, forgiveness and reconciliation as well as nonviolent sacrifice and a search for nonviolent solutions to conflict.[13] Eastern religious traditions also offer rich teachings on peace and on the manner to realize it. *Ahimsa* (nonviolence), *kshama* (forgiveness), and *shanti* (peace) are recurrent themes in sacred Hindu texts;[14] Buddhism's core teaching of interdependence gives strong impetus to social compassion, and in recent years a new movement of "engaged" Buddhism has sought to connect the pursuit of inner peace through meditation and mindfulness to contemporary social justice concerns.[15]

Given the depth and breadth of peace teachings in different religious traditions, PACS scholars need not look far to find examples of ways in which religious teachings and applied spiritual practices have inspired individuals and communities throughout history and around the world to work for peace as well as for social and environmental justice. The best known examples have attained almost iconic status in peace history: Gandhi's nonviolent *satyagraha* struggle against colonial rule in India, Martin Luther King Jr.'s use of New Testament social justice teachings in the civil rights movement, and the Dalai Lama's campaign for Tibetan rights of Tibet. Lesser known examples such as Abdul Ghaffar Khan's nonviolent Muslim peace force[16] and the low-profile, long-term work of the Mennonite Central Committee[17] have similar instructive power with respect to the potential impact of religious values and motivations. While a creative interplay between religious and non-religious sources of inspiration has shaped the trajectory of many notable peace initiatives, ignoring the role of religion in mobilizing and inspiring individuals around the globe to work for peace would be a grave oversight.

RELIGIOUS SOLUTIONS TO RELIGIOUS PROBLEMS

Although various religious traditions contain rich peacemaking resources, the peace teachings of religions have quite obviously not precluded religious individuals and identities from becoming deeply entangled in conflict. However, while hard secularists often maintain that the divisive nature of religion and the destructive involvement of religious actors in conflict is reason enough to dispense with religion altogether, scholars who take a "peace with religion" approach instead argue that if religion and religious actors are involved in conflict, then they should also be engaged in building peace. If indeed religious beliefs, identities, leaders, or institutions are contributing to conflict, then divorcing religion from peacebuilding efforts will only serve to make peace more difficult, as those who abuse or co-opt sacred forms will have been granted a monopoly on religious voice, and marginalized communities will perceive a lack of religious legitimacy in the peace process.[18] Furthermore, a strictly secular approach in a setting where religion is a key fact of life can lead to not only overlooking potential religious resources, but also to a misinformed understanding of what a given conflict is about and how it may best be transformed.

Recognizing that conflicts with a religious dimension require, at least in part, religious solutions, another body of work within the field is largely dedicated to analyzing when and how religious institutions and individuals can be involved in peace processes, and identifying appropriate roles and spaces for religious involvement. Building on the idea of "multi-track diplomacy,"[19] scholars have thus suggested that religious peacebuilding or faith-based diplomacy can and should occur simultaneously with elite political negotiations and secular peacebuilding initiatives.[20] By creating space for religious leaders and institutions to become involved in peacebuilding work, as well as encouraging religious communities to engage one another and work together for peace, a "religious peacebuilding track" has the potential to go a long way in transforming conflict and combating religious extremism. It can help not only to support and lend legitimacy to official processes, but also to shed new light on causes of conflict and resources for peace—resources that emerge from the very traditions militants claim to be defending.[21] Grassroots religious peacebuilding processes can offer alternatives to religious extremism, while also creating spaces for the development of new narratives of coexistence.[22]

INTRINSIC VALUE OF A RELIGIOUS PEACEBUILDING TRACK

While a religious peacebuilding track is certainly an important component of responding to conflicts that have a religious dimension, a religious track has value that goes far beyond merely countering religious extremism and supporting official processes. As outlined earlier, different religious traditions offer a myriad of teachings and practices that can inspire and contribute to building peace. Religious peace teachings can add a sense of moral, ethical, and spiritual significance to the work that individuals and communities undertake, sustaining people through difficult situations and resonating with individuals on a deeper level than strictly "secular" approaches. Engaging religious traditions and making space for religious peacebuilding is also a source of dynamism and constructive challenge, and has helped to expand the peacebuilding "toolbox" in exciting ways.[23] Scholars and practitioners alike have come to recognize that religious teachings, practices, and actors have not only added new meaning and motivation to existing "secular" approaches to peace but also led to innovations in how scholars and practitioners conceive of both the content and processes of peacebuilding.

Engaging religious actors and communities has undoubtedly served to widen the opportunities for people to become engaged in peacebuilding work, to link otherwise disconnected parties, and to recognize different kinds of peacebuilding endeavors and roles. Not only do religious communities have both grassroots support and (in some settings) political clout, but religious institutions are also often the best-positioned mid-level actors that are able to serve as "hubs" in the peacebuilding web, providing a conduit between grassroots communities and elite political processes.[24] Scholars have identified a remarkably diverse range of roles that religious actors and institutions have played in situations of conflict, ranging from mediators, educators, and reconcilers to direct participants in political negotiations or monitors of sensitive human rights situations.[25] Unlike many external third parties and international nongovernmental organizations, faith-based actors tend to have a well-rooted presence in conflict settings, and are often advantageously situated to seek international support for local work.

RELIGIOUS PEACEBUILDING AS A MODE OF CULTURAL EMPOWERMENT

An additional current within the PACS field that has contributed to the potential for "peace with religion" is the growing recognition that peace needs roots in the values and traditions of a given locale if it is to be viable and sustainable. Guided by Lederach's "elicitive" approach to conflict transformation[26] as well as by a growing literature on cross-cultural conflict resolution, scholars have come to pay increasing attention to the ways in which peacebuilding theory and practice must be adapted to different cultural milieus. Respect for peacemaking traditions that fall outside traditional Western rational and cognitive frameworks has also increased, together with recognition that the worldviews and values of most of the global population—especially outside the "secular West"—continue to be profoundly shaped by religion. These new sensitivities have increased the willingness of PACS scholars and practitioners to engage the religious dimension of peacemaking, by affirming the relevance of the knowledge and practices possessed by people in diverse cultural settings, and encouraging empowerment as well as capacity development through sustainable utilization and adaptation of local peace resources.[27]

Conflict resolution practitioners would do well to envision culture as *soil*—that is, as something comparable to the substance in which all organic life takes root.[28] Culture, then, is the base in which all social relations are rooted, and from which all forms of human expression grow. For people whose culture is indelibly defined by religious beliefs and practices, religion is not merely a supplementary "tool" in the peacebuilding process; rather, it is the language through which their community makes sense of itself, its past, and its future. Within highly religious cultural contexts, "peace with religion" provides far more adaptive and culturally appropriate responses than a purely secular approach to peacebuilding, while also providing scope for experimentation and cross-cultural exchange—to the potential benefit of Western-based practitioners. Post-Apartheid South Africa's theological adaptation of the cultural concept of *ubuntu* to energize a truth and reconciliation process provides an apt illustration of this principle.[29]

PEDAGOGY

Bringing religion into peace and conflict studies opens up fresh possibilities not just for theory, research, and practice, but also for pedagogy. Although teaching about the role of religion in conflict as well as in applied peacemaking efforts is in many respects similar to teaching in other substantive areas, PACS courses on religion inevitably bring distinctive new opportunities and challenges, all of which deserve careful consideration.

Some of the principal challenges associated with bringing religion into the PACS classroom are inherent in the breadth, depth, and complexity of the subject matter. Given that most undergraduate and graduate students in

PACS programs are not deeply versed in the tenets of multiple religious traditions, the instructor inevitably faces difficult choices: How much class time should be devoted to exploring specific aspects (beliefs, worldviews, texts, practices, history, internal diversity, peace traditions, perspectives on conflict and violence, etc.) of major world religions? Which religious traditions will have to be left out in the interest of presenting overarching theoretical frameworks, case studies, and peacebuilding methods? How much attention should be given to the lives and works of leading religious peace and justice advocates, or to religious debates concerning interpretation and hermeneutics? How much time should be devoted to the literature on religion as a source of conflict, relative to material exploring ways in which religion can become a resource for peace? How many guest speakers can be invited, given the at times competing needs to give voice to diversity and to cover important material? Such questions are not easily resolved, and most instructors are likely to experience a series of difficult compromises.

Broader philosophical issues concerning the study of religion are also worthy of serious reflection, particularly debates concerning "insider" and "outsider" perspectives. While there are many who would argue that ultimately the instructor must choose between one perspective or the other, assuming either a declared theological positionality or the stance of an objective observer who aspires toward complete, distanced neutrality, it is the authors' conviction that hybrid approaches are possible and hold considerable promise, particularly in institutions with diverse student populations. Ideally, acknowledging positionality and limits to personal knowledge and experience can help to build trust and rapport in the classroom, provided that there is a concomitant and clear effort to signal desire for magnanimous, fair, and open exploration of diverse traditions and positions. The benefits of toggling back and forth between "insider" and "outsider" perspectives on the peace resources of various religious traditions can also be emphasized, encouraging students to use empathy as a tool of analysis and develop a feel for varying "keynote" themes within the peace concepts of world religions (e.g., Christianity and forgiveness, Islam and justice, Buddhism and inner serenity), while also acquiring an analytical understanding of the wide range of potential peace positions (absolute pacifism, relative pacifism, just war pacifism, just war, righteous war, and so forth) within most established religious systems. Inviting guest speakers from various traditions provides a useful counterpoint to textbooks and lectures, while also enriching classroom dialogue and providing students with a firsthand experience of interreligious engagement. Field trips to religious institutions or to the offices of faith-based organizations can further enrich the experiential dimension of a course; offering students a service learning option as a substitute for the standard term paper can enable them to investigate faith-based approaches to social betterment in yet another way.

Care must also be taken to demonstrate awareness of diverse starting points among students in the classroom, which are likely to range from strongly particularistic religious attachment to secular curiosity. Students who are deeply rooted in a particular tradition may or may not be aware of that tradition's internal diversity, and may or may not have been prepared for comfortable discussions of religious plurality. More secular students bring a different set of sensitivities and concerns to the classroom, such as a high level of concern about the shadow side of religion, or intense interest in inclusive spirituality. Whatever their starting points, students can be encouraged to use one another as resources for understanding, and to recognize new opportunities to reflect on their personal relationship to religion and spirituality.

Studying religion from a PACS perspective creates a number of unique opportunities. Many students are likely to complete the course with a greater appreciation for the diversity of approaches to and understandings of peace, and with expanded knowledge of religious peacebuilding activities in many parts of the world. Some are likely to leave with new questions about interpretation and religious pluralism, or with a heightened sense of humility. A few may find themselves unsettled to realize that there is no completely "pure" religious tradition whose followers have never violated or contested essential precepts. Ideally, however, all will have been presented with opportunities to reflect deeply not only on the nature of peace and examples of coexistence in a shrinking world, but also on matters of personal vocation and purpose—that is, on the prospect of a deeply *personal* peace process.

CHALLENGES FOR THE FIELD, AND OPPORTUNITIES

While the field of religion and PACS has become increasingly nuanced and wide-ranging,[30] scholars and practitioners specializing in this area will inevitably encounter criticisms as well as affirmations. Given the field's applied interest in increasing the scope for peaceable expressions of religion and spirituality within political contexts, critiques are to be expected from multiple quarters—from those who fear the imposition of external agendas on religious communities as well as from defenders of secular public space and from fellow social scientists with methodological or empirical concerns. These and other challenges should be anticipated as the field continues to advance, and embraced as means of identifying weaknesses and developing new strengths.

For some critics, especially but not exclusively those who operate within a "peace through religion" alone framework, much of the current literature concerning religion, conflict, and peace offers insufficient attention to the great diversity and incommensurability of religious belief systems and practices. In an attempt to generate broad analytical schemas and explore "religion" as a singular phenomenon, analysts have produced an unsatisfying, "generic" approach that fails to do justice to the particularity and distinctiveness of different religious systems.[31] The result, they claim, is an unsatisfying, "thin" approach to the subject matter that downplays differences, in an ultimately secularizing effort to reduce religious values to common denominators that are largely the same as those held by non-religious social activists. Thus does religious advocacy come to be regarded as one option among many, valued instrumentally, rather than intrinsically.[32]

It is well worth noting that approaches which emphasize the "ambivalence" of religion bring liabilities as well as benefits, particularly for those whose work is on the applied side of the religious peacebuilding field. In the eyes of many this notion may appear inauthentic or even disrespectful, particularly if religion and indeed the sacred are conceived in entirely benign and peaceful terms, and if those who wish to engage religion's peace potential appear interested only in obtaining religious support for preconceived ends. For many religious individuals, treating religion as an additional "tool" in the "toolbox" is problematic, as religion is seen to be something far greater than a tool: a way of life and a means of understanding the world.

Other critics have quite different concerns. For staunch secularists, the idea of engaging religion to advance the cause of peace may well appear to be a deeply misguided notion, a compromise that exchanges marginal, short-term benefits for long-term problems inherent in religious epistemology, traditional values, patriarchal culture, intercommunal rivalry, and so forth. From this standpoint, the entire notion of religious peacebuilding could be dismissed as a misguided effort to elevate the role of religion in public life and policy, to the detriment of a social order based on the privatization of religious conviction. Even where religion is undeniably part of a conflict dynamic, the partisan of "peace without religion" may well argue that involving religion in a peace process will only serve to accentuate social cleavages, reinforce perceptions of irreconcilable values, impede rational dialogue about structural and institutional problems, and thwart pragmatic compromise. In other words, focusing on religion produces inappropriate frameworks for conflict analysis, and prescriptions that take society backward rather than forward. While such arguments appear quite alarmist and distant from most experiences of on-the-ground religious peacebuilding, future scholars and practitioners will no doubt need to prepare solid, evidence-based arguments, not only to make the case that religious peacebuilding fails to conform to stereotypical expectations, but also to document situations in which engaging religious frameworks of meaning proved essential for meaningful dialogue on issues such as human rights and gender equity.

Yet another line of critique emerges from those whose concerns are first and foremost empirical rather than theological or ideological. For analysts concerned above all with aggregate tendencies in religious politics and with patterns of religiously justified violence or discrimination, case studies and anecdotal reports of successful religious peacebuilding can nonetheless be questioned with respect to their representativeness and statistical significance. In protracted conflicts where religious differences are a source of communal identity for rival parties, an outside observer of interreligious dialogue and peacebuilding activities might legitimately question the scalability and efficacy of micro-level processes. Unless religious peacebuilding can overcome its status as a niche activity of committed activists, with what confidence can one expect measurable, macro-level impacts?[33]

All of these criticisms merit serious answers, and can spur improvements in theory, research, and practice. With respect to theological critiques, for example, proponents of a PACS approach can readily concede that comparative analysis and generic frameworks can never fully capture the internal richness, variation, specificity, and depth of a particular religious tradition. At the same time, the anthropological distinction between *etic* and *emic* approaches to analysis can be invoked; neither approach is an adequate substitute for the other, and both approaches enhance understanding. Furthermore, recognition of religion's value as a basis for peacemaking within the context of social science inquiry need not lead to a narrow, exclusively instrumental concern with religion. Putting religion on the peacemaking map and, by extension, in a larger conversation with agencies of governance and civil society activists, is arguably a good thing for religion and peace alike.

Critiques from secularists and fellow social scientists also demand a response. While critiques which emanate from what we have termed a "hard secularist" position are best answered with concrete examples of peaceable religion and perhaps also with discussion of religion's interpretive, flexible qualities, at least one major concession may be necessary. It may well be true that social science is never completely neutral and that in focusing on religious peacebuilding PACS scholars are, in a sense, promoting peaceable religion. That said, it need not follow that a normative position in favor of religious peacebuilding precludes intellectual rigor and concern for evidence. The fact that religious peacebuilding is most often a minority phenomenon does not mean it cannot have a profound effect on a given social ecology, and the existence of compelling case studies suggests, at a minimum, the need for thoroughgoing study and further experimentation.

The advent of religion as a topic of significant interest in the PACS field opens tremendous new opportunities not only to make peace and conflict studies more relevant within contemporary intercommunal conflicts, but also to make religious perspectives on peace more accessible to scholars, students, and peacebuilding practitioners. Given the existence of longstanding public debates on the subject of religion, politics, and peace, efforts to develop the field further will often require a delicate balancing act, so as to better speak with people who do not share the same assumptions about religious faith, social science methodology, or the most proper means of advancing peace. Nonetheless, an inviting new horizon for peace research has now opened, with commensurate opportunities to extend the range of peacebuilding practice.

BIBLIOGRAPHY

Alger, Chadwick. "Religion as a Peace Tool." *The Global Review of Ethnopolitics,* vol. 1, no. 4 (June 2002): 94–109.

Appleby, Scott. *The Ambivalence of the Sacred: Religion, Violence and Reconciliation.* Lanham, MD: Rowman & Littlefield Publishers, 2000.

Cavanaugh, William T. *The Myth of Religious Violence.* New York: Oxford University Press, 2009.

Coward, Harold, and Gordon S. Smith, eds. *Religion and Peacebuilding.* Albany: State University of New York Press, 2004.

Diamond, Louise, and John McDonald. *Multi-Track Diplomacy: A Systems Approach to Peace,* 3rd ed. West Hartford, CT: Kumarian Press, 1996.

Fox, Jonathan. International Studies Association's 47th Annual Convention, San Diego, California, March 2006.

Funk, Nathan C., and Abdul Aziz Said. *Islam and Peacemaking in the Middle East.* Boulder, CO: Lynne Reinner Publishers, 2009.

———. "Localizing Peace: An Agenda for Sustainable Peacebuilding." *Peace and Conflict Studies,* vol. 17, no. 1 (Spring 2010): 101–143.

Gopin, Marc. *Between Eden and Armageddon: The Future of World Religions, Violence and Peacemaking.* New York: Oxford University Press, 2000.

———. *Holy War, Holy Peace: How Religion Can Bring Peace to the Middle East.* New York: Oxford University Press, 2002.

Harris, Sam. *The End of Faith: Religion, Terror and the Future of Reason.* New York: W.W. Norton & Company, 2004.

Heft, James L., ed. *Beyond Violence: Religious Sources of Social Transformation in Judaism, Christianity, and Islam.* New York: Fordham University Press, 2004.

Hertog, Katrien. *The Complex Reality of Religious Peacebuilding: Conceptual Contributions and Critical Analysis.* Lanham, MD: Lexington Books, 2010.

Hitchens, Christopher. *God Is Not Great: How Religion Poisons Everything.* New York: Twelve, 2007.

Johansen, Robert C. "Radical Islam and Nonviolence: A Case Study of Religious Empowerment and Constraint among Pashtuns." *Journal of Peace Research,* vol. 34, no. 1 (February 1997): 53–71.

Johnston, Douglas, ed. *Faith-Based Diplomacy: Trumping Realpolitik.* Toronto: Oxford University Press, 2003.

Johnston, Douglas, and Cynthia Sampson, eds. *Religion, the Missing Dimension of Statecraft.* Toronto: Oxford University Press, 1994.

Juergensmeyer, Mark. *The New Cold War? Religious Nationalism Confronts the Secular State.* Berkeley: University of California Press, 1993.

Landau, Yehezkel. *Healing the Holy Land: Interreligious Peacebuilding in Israel/ Palestine.* Washington, DC: United States Institute of Peace, 2003. http://www .usip.org/pubs/peaceworks/pwks51.html

Lederach, John Paul. *Preparing for Peace: Conflict Transformation across Cultures.* Syracuse, NY: Syracuse University Press, 1995.

Lederach, John Paul. *The Moral Imagination: The Art and Soul of Building Peace.* New York: Oxford University Press, 2005.

Liechty, Joseph. "Mitigation in Northern Ireland: A Strategy for Living in Peace When Truth Claims Clash," in *Interfaith Dialogue and Peacebuilding*, David Smock, ed. Washington, DC: United States Institute of Peace, 2002, 89–101.

Maalouf, Amin. *In the Name of Identity: Violence and the Need to Belong.* New York: Arcade Publishing, 2000.

Panikkar, Raimon. *Cultural Disarmament: The Way to Peace.* Louisville, KY: Westminster John Knox Press, 1995.

Sampson, Cynthia. "Religion and Peacebuilding," in *Peacemaking in International Conflict*, I. William Zartman and J. Lewis Rasmussen, eds. Washington, DC: United States Institute of Peace, 1997, 273–316.

Sampson, Cynthia and John Paul Lederach, eds. *From the Ground Up: Mennonite Contributions to International Peacebuilding.* New York: Oxford University Press, 2000.

Smith, David Whitten, and Elizabeth Geraldine Burr. *Understanding World Religions: A Road Map for Justice and Peace.* Toronto: Rowman & Littlefield Publishers, 2007.

Smith-Christopher, Daniel L., ed. *Subverting Hatred: The Challenge of Nonviolence in Religious Traditions.* Cambridge: The Boston Research Center for the Twenty-first Century, 1998.

Snell, Marilyn. "The World of Religion According to Huston Smith." *Mother Jones,* vol. 22, no. 6 (November/December 1997), http://motherjones.com/ politics/1997/11/world-religion-according-huston-smith (October 28, 2010).

Swartley, William M. *Covenant of Peace: The Missing Peace in New Testament Theology and Ethics.* Grand Rapids, MI: W.B. Eerdmans Publishing Company, 2006.

ter Haar, Gerrie. "Religion: Source of Conflict or Resource for Peace?" in *Bridge or Barrier: Religion, Violence and Visions for Peace*, Gerrie ter Haar and James J. Busuttil, eds. Leiden, The Netherlands: Brill, 2005, 3–34.

Tutu, Desmond Mpilo. *No Future Without Forgiveness.* New York: Random House, 1999.

Williams, Raymond. *Keywords: A Vocabulary of Culture and Society.* New York: Oxford University Press, 1983.

NOTES

1. See, for example, Mark Juergensmeyer, *The New Cold War? Religious Nationalism Confronts the Secular State* (Berkeley: University of California Press, 1993); or Amin Maalouf, *In the Name of Identity: Violence and the Need to Belong* (New York: Arcade Publishing, 2000).

2. See, for example, Harold Coward and Gordon S. Smith, eds., *Religion and Peacebuilding* (Albany: State University of New York Press, 2004); Nathan C. Funk and Abdul Aziz Said, "Localizing Peace: An Agenda for Sustainable Peacebuilding," *Peace and Conflict Studies,* vol. 17, no. 1 (Spring 2010): 101–143.

3. Some pivotal and influential texts that are premised on the "two faces" of religion include Scott Appleby, *The Ambivalence of the Sacred: Religion, Violence and Reconciliation* (Lanham, MD: Rowman & Littlefield Publishers, 2000); and Marc Gopin, *Between Eden and Armageddon: The Future of World Religions, Violence and Peacemaking* (New York: Oxford University Press, 2000). See also Gerrie ter Haar, "Religion: Source of Conflict or Resource for Peace?" in *Bridge or Barrier: Religion, Violence and Visions for Peace*, Gerrie ter Haar and James J. Busuttil, eds. (Leiden, The Netherlands: Brill, 2005), 3–34.

4. Appleby, *The Ambivalence of the Sacred.*

5. While definitions of religion are highly contested within the field of religious studies, we have found Leonard Swidler's definition useful as a basis for PACS-related forms of analysis. According to Swidler, a religion is "an explanation of the *ultimate* meaning of life, and how to live accordingly, based on some notion of the Transcendent, with the four C's: Creed, Code of Ethics, Cult of Worship, Community-Structure." See James L. Heft, ed., *Beyond Violence: Religious Sources of Social Transformation in Judaism, Christianity, and Islam* (New York: Fordham University Press, 2004), ix.

6. Raimon Panikkar, *Cultural Disarmament: The Way to Peace* (Louisville, KY: Westminster John Knox Press, 1995).

7. A range of "new atheist" literature perhaps best exemplifies this attitude. See, for example, Sam Harris, *The End of Faith: Religion, Terror and the Future of Reason* (New York: W.W. Norton & Company, 2004); and Christopher Hitchens, *God Is Not Great: How Religion Poisons Everything* (New York: Twelve, 2007).

8. R. Scott Appleby explains fundamentalism as "a religious response to the marginalization of religion and an accompanying pattern of religious activism with certain specifiable characteristics." He differentiates this mode of assertive religion from ethnoreligious extremism and religious nationalism. See Appleby, *Ambivalence of the Sacred*, 101, 107–108.

9. William T. Cavanaugh, *The Myth of Religious Violence* (New York: Oxford University Press, 2009).

10. Marilyn Snell, "The World of Religion According to Huston Smith," *Mother Jones,* vol. 22, no. 6 (November/December 1997), http://motherjones.com/politics/1997/11/world-religion-according-huston-smith (October 18, 2010).

11. For a good overview of the peace resources in various world religions, see David Whitten Smith and Elizabeth Geraldine Burr, *Understanding World Religions: A Road Map for Justice and Peace* (Toronto: Rowman & Littlefield Publishers, 2007); See also Daniel L. Smith-Christopher, ed., *Subverting Hatred: The Challenge of Nonviolence in Religious Traditions* (Cambridge: The Boston Research Center for the Twenty-first Century, 1998).

12. For discussion of peace and peace resources in Islam, see Nathan C. Funk and Abdul Aziz Said, *Islam and Peacemaking in the Middle East* (Boulder, CO: Lynne Reinner Publishers, 2009), 47–69; Frederick M. Denny, "Islam and Peacebuilding: Continuities and Transitions," in Coward and Smith, eds., *Religion and Peacebuilding*, 129–146.

13. William M. Swartley, *Covenant of Peace: The Missing Peace in New Testament Theology and Ethics* (Grand Rapids, MI: W.B. Eerdmans Publishing Company, 2006); Andrea Bartoli, "Christianity and Peacebuilding," in Coward and Smith, eds., *Religion and Peacebuilding*, 147–166.

14. Rajmohan Gandhi, "Hinduism and Peacebuilding," in Coward and Smith, eds., *Religion and Peacbuilding*, 45–68.

15. Christopher S. Queen, "The Peace Wheel: Nonviolent Activism in the Buddhist Tradition," in Smith-Christopher, ed., *Subverting Hatred*, 25–47.

16. Robert C. Johansen, "Radical Islam and Nonviolence: A Case Study of Religious Empowerment and Constraint among Pashtuns," *Journal of Peace Research*, vol. 34, no. 1 (February 1997): 53–71.

17. Cynthia Sampson and John Paul Lederach, eds., *From the Ground Up: Mennonite Contributions to International Peacebuilding* (New York: Oxford University Press, 2000).

18. Marc Gopin, *Holy War, Holy Peace: How Religion Can Bring Peace to the Middle East* (New York: Oxford University Press, 2002).

19. Louise Diamond and John McDonald, *Multi-Track Diplomacy: A Systems Approach to Peace*, 3rd ed. (West Hartford, CT: Kumarian Press, 1996).

20. See, for example, Douglas Johnston, ed., *Faith-Based Diplomacy: Trumping Realpolitik* (Toronto: Oxford University Press, 2003); Douglas Johnston and Cynthia Sampson, eds., *Religion, the Missing Dimension of Statecraft* (Toronto: Oxford University Press, 1994).

21. Joseph Liechty, "Mitigation in Northern Ireland: A Strategy for Living in Peace When Truth Claims Clash," in *Interfaith Dialogue and Peacebuilding*, David Smock, ed. (Washington, DC: United States Institute of Peace, 2002), 89–101.

22. See Marc Gopin, *Holy War, Holy Peace*; Yehezkel Landau, *Healing the Holy Land: Interreligious Peacebuilding in Israel/Palestine* (Washington, DC: United States Institute of Peace, 2003), available online at www.usip.org/pubs/peaceworks/pwks51.html.

23. Chadwick Alger, "Religion as a Peace Tool," *The Global Review of Ethnopolitics*, vol. 1, no. 4 (June 2002): 94–109; Liechty, "Mitigation."

24. See John Paul Lederach, *The Moral Imagination: The Art and Soul of Building Peace* (New York: Oxford University Press, 2005), 75–86.

25. Cynthia Sampson, "Religion and Peacebuilding," in *Peacemaking in International Conflict*, I. William Zartman and J. Lewis Rasmussen, eds. (Washington, DC: United States Institute of Peace, 1997), 273–316.

26. John Paul Lederach, *Preparing for Peace: Conflict Transformation across Cultures* (Syracuse, NY: Syracuse University Press, 1995).

27. Funk and Said, "Localizing Peace."

28. This metaphor is attributed to Kevin Avruch via a personal correspondence with Larissa Fast, March 23, 2010. This soil metaphor comes from a discussion of culture in Raymond Williams, *Keywords: A Vocabulary of Culture and Society* (New York: Oxford University Press, 1983), 87–93.

29. Desmond Mpilo Tutu, *No Future Without Forgiveness* (New York: Random House, 1999).

30. See, for example, Katrien Hertog, *The Complex Reality of Religious Peacebuilding: Conceptual Contributions and Critical Analysis* (Lanham, MD: Lexington Books, 2010).

31. The authors have encountered this concern in informal conversations with various colleagues specializing in religious and theological studies.

32. See, for example, Alger, "Religion as a Peace Tool." Though the article provides a highly substantive overview of significant works in the field, the title implies an attitude with which some religion specialists are legitimately concerned.

33. Jonathan Fox, personal communication at the International Studies Association's 47th Annual Convention in San Diego, California, March 2006. Fox is author of *Ethnoreligious Conflict in the Late Twentieth Century: A General Theory* (Lanham, MD: Lexington Books, 2002).

Chapter 19

Milestones on a Journey in Peace and Conflict Studies

Neil Katz

This chapter will focus on milestones in my intellectual, academic, and practice journey through my 38 years in peace and conflict studies, and highlight some of the critical "influencers" in my work as a scholar, educator, and active consultant. It begins by describing how I first got interested in the field of peace and conflict studies through involvement in the civil rights and anti–Vietnam War movement, reformulated some of my interests during my dissertation stage at the University of Maryland, and then recast those interests several times through my thirty-seven years at Syracuse University, and this past year as chair of the largest graduate program in the field at Nova Southeastern University. Throughout the article I will pinpoint and highlight major "influencers," including key mentors, organizations, continuing education opportunities, and scholarly works in the field. I will conclude with a summary of my most significant insights or lessons. The hope is that this article might inspire others to reflect on their own personal journey and lessons learned.

BACKGROUND AND THE DEVELOPMENT OF SOCIAL CONSCIOUSNESS

In the beginning, there was baseball. Growing up in a pleasant suburb of St. Louis, most of my memories were of playing baseball with my twin brother and friends, collecting baseball cards, and paying an almost obsessive attention to the fate of Stan Musial and the St. Louis Cardinals. World events and social causes seemed only a temporary distraction but for two events:

(1) a fascination with the trial of Nazi commandant Adolf Eichmann, on whom I did a report in junior high school and suffered nightmares over due to the atrocities I was reading about, and (2) an annual picnic with "Negroes," when my dad would invite his grocery store employees and their families over to our house for a picnic and baseball every summer. Otherwise, there is little in my childhood I can point to as a formative event that would shape my career path. In fact, my world was mostly a safe, predictable, homogenous enclave made up of mostly middle-class, two-parent Jewish families in a town with good schools called University City (also known as "Jew City" to kids outside the neighborhood).

It really wasn't until my late high school years and college that I began to undergo a social conscious awakening. John F. Kennedy's clarion call for a "Peace Corps," supported by his domestic call for social action to "ask not what the country can do for you, but what you can do for your country," challenged me and my classmates to look beyond our immediate horizons. The burgeoning civil rights movement began to intrude on our peaceful existence as I read about nonviolent direct actions in the American South or in Champaign/Urbana, Illinois, my college hometown. I do remember joining civil rights actions in both Rockford and Chicago and considering joining college-age kids going to Mississippi to register Negro voters in what would come to be called the "Mississippi Freedom Summer."

For young males of my generation, the Vietnam War was the watershed event that shaped our social consciousness. Before I left with a group of American college students for a semester abroad in Copenhagen, Denmark in the spring of 1965, I remember attending "education sessions" led by USIA officials. The USIA officials articulated a compelling case to our student group about how the United States was courageously taking up the challenge of the "Free World" by stopping the expansion of insidious Communism in Vietnam, thereby halting a catastrophic "domino effect" which would lead to the triumph of Communism throughout much of the world. Once in Europe, this indoctrination was seriously challenged, and as I listened to arguments denouncing America's growing involvement in Vietnam from European students, professors, and leaders, I began to pay more attention to international events like the Tet offensive, and read reports from progressive journalists such as Bernard Fall, Marcus Raskin, and Richard Barnet.

By the late 1960s, I had undergone a radical shift in my social consciousness and my attentiveness to peace and justice concerns. I had switched my academic focus from contemporary Jewish American fiction writers for my master's thesis to full-time academic concentration on historical and contemporary anti-war and social movements, including extended research on the American labor movement, the student anti-war movements of the 1920s and 1930s, the American civil rights movement of the 1950s and 1960s, and, of course, the anti–Vietnam War movement. While living and studying in Washington, DC, and at the University of Maryland in the late 1960s, I joined several anti-war groups, participated in various anti-war demonstrations and other activities, and subscribed to radical newsletters and journals like *Liberation*, I.F. Stone's *Weekly*, and reports of the Institute for Policy Studies. I then began my dissertation research on a radical pacifist group, the Committee for Nonviolent Action, a group affiliated with the national War Resisters League, who specialized in nonviolent direct action to further their peace and justice concerns. I spent some of the time working with draft resistance colleagues on legal rulings that would help us be successful in applying for and/or receiving conscientious objector status or other military or non-combatant exempt status. It was also at this time that I made a firm decision that my chosen career path would be to best serve causes of peace and justice by becoming a college professor with an activist bent on topics having to do with nonviolence and social change, since that was more in line with my principles and my disposition than other methods of social activism.

My dissertation research topic focused my academic interest and expertise squarely on peace and nonviolence studies. I happened to be in the right academic subject area, at the right time (1970–1972), when several universities became interested in peace and nonviolent studies in reaction to the tragedies at Kent State and Jackson State and to the turmoil on many other college campuses. Even though I had not yet finished my dissertation, my academic work in nonviolence helped me to get hired as the second director of the Nonviolence Studies Program at Syracuse University in August 1972. I continued in this role of director of the undergraduate Program in Nonviolent Conflict and Change or PNCC (the program's name changed from Nonviolence Studies to PNCC in 1975) for the next 25 years.

Four other significant developments occurred during my time at Syracuse University and beyond. The first one began in the late 1970s and early 1980s with the growing interest in conflict resolution, which complemented my earlier interest in nonviolent social change. Interventions such as facilitation, negotiation, and mediation had moved far beyond business and labor-management arenas into numerous areas of workplace and personal life. My interest in exploring the relationship between mobilizing and exercising power to "get to the table," and acquiring high level knowledge and skills to "do well at the table," further developed during this time. I directed more of my attention to areas of organizational consulting as well as to interpersonal and small group conflict resolution.

The second development occurred when a group of PNCC-related faculty secured a major grant in 1985 from the William and Flora Hewlett Foundation to develop a Theory and Practice Center for Conflict Resolution in the Maxwell School of Syracuse University. The establishment of the Program on the Analysis and Resolution of Conflict (PARC) served as an intellectual and supportive home for faculty and graduate students doing work in this field. I served for thirteen years as associate director of PARC, and was mainly responsible for directing PNCC and heading several of PARC's applied endeavors, such as the Campus Mediation Center, the Conflict Resolution Consulting Group, and the Summer Annual Institute on Creative Conflict Resolution.

The third development occurred when I began to work extensively with the Maxwell School's Executive Education Program. In addition to offering an executive master of public administration degree, the school's program developed and delivered leadership and conflict resolution trainings for public sector supervisors, managers, and union officials in local, state and federal government. In my role as director of training and organizational development, I gained valuable experience and delivered well over two hundred workshops for many prestigious agencies, such as the Social Security Administration, the Patent and Trademark office, the Department of the Interior, the Census Bureau, and the New York State Departments of Education, Health, and Labor.

The last major transition recently took place when I accepted the role of chairperson and professor of the Graduate Department of Conflict Analysis and Resolution at Nova Southeastern University in Ft. Lauderdale, Florida, a prestigious robust program with ten faculty members and over four hundred masters' and doctoral students pursuing residential or online education. This shift into heavy administrative work has been very challenging for me; I sincerely hope that my long experience in the field will help me be successful in this new role.

THE ROLE OF MENTORS

When I reflect on this intellectual, academic and practice journey, I am acutely aware that I have greatly benefited from several key "influencers." Throughout my career, I have been very fortunate to have the writings, guidance, and support of some wonderful mentors who generously nurtured my burgeoning interest in peace and conflict studies. My first real excitement about working in the area of modern peace history was developed through influential books by Charles Chatfield and Lawrence Wittner. A professor at Wittenberg University in Ohio, Chatfield had just published a book entitled

For Peace and Justice: Pacifism in America 1914–1941, and Wittner, a professor at SUNY Albany, had come out with the sequel, *Rebels Against War: The American Peace Movement, 1941–1960*. After corresponding with Chatfield on several occasions, he graciously agreed to guide and mentor me in my dissertation research and served as the de facto head of my dissertation committee.

As luck would have it, another mentor, James Laue at Washington University in St. Louis was leading a workshop along with his colleague Gerry Cormick the week before my first semester began at Syracuse. Laue's work on conflict intervention roles and ethics was instrumental in my early academic career; it introduced me to examining the nexus of nonviolent activism and negotiation skills in fostering social change—in other words, how the effort in "getting to the table" needs to be coupled with effective negotiation skills "at the table."

Within a year after assuming the position of director of the Nonviolence Studies Program at Syracuse University, I had the good fortune to discover Gene Sharp's groundbreaking and monumental work on *The Politics of Nonviolent Action*, which essentially covered such questions as the following: What is nonviolent action? What are the variables and dynamics of how it works? What are the various forms it can take? How has it been used successfully throughout history? I soon developed a highly beneficial mentor relationship with Gene Sharp and worked with him to create several courses in nonviolent action history, philosophy, strategy, methods, and ethics, which eventually became the basis for an undergraduate major and minor within the College of Arts and Sciences.

During these early years of my academic life at Syracuse, I was also very fortunate to work under the tutelage of Professor Louis Kriesberg, a renowned sociologist and noted scholar of social conflict. Professor Kriesberg took me under his wing, shared his knowledge and advice, co-taught with me my first semester, and worked closely with me for many years as he served as the first director of PARC and I served under him as associate director.

John W. (Jack) Lawyer was a full time communication and conflict resolution consultant when I met him in the mid-1970s. Immediately, I was impressed with his presence, materials and skills, which he continually demonstrated in his workshops with business, ministry and educational clients. I soon became his apprentice, then junior associate, and then his partner in leading workshops and co-authoring several books. Jack, along with one of his associates, Kevin McNulty, helped me tremendously in expanding my knowledge and skills in organizational consulting and training; I am forever indebted to them for nurturing my competence and confidence in the consulting arena.

In my later years at Syracuse University, I benefited greatly by my friendship and professional relationship with Catherine Gerard, first in her role as associate director of the Maxwell School's Executive Education Program and then later in her role as co-director and director of PARC. Catherine's abilities to work successfully with leaders in the public sector both in the United States and abroad is evidenced by repeated requests from numerous prestigious clients that she work with them. She willingly shared with me her expertise on a whole range of critical theory and practice models in leadership and change management, and I have benefited greatly by observing and then modeling much of her workshop teaching style and pedagogy. Importantly, Catherine and Education Executive Director William Sullivan's contacts in New York state government and in the federal sector led to numerous training opportunities with high level executives and managers with numerous agencies throughout New York and the United States, including leadership training with over 8,000 managers at the Social Security Administration, and negotiation/facilitation work with their over 40 labor-management councils, including the National Partnership Council.

ROLE OF ORGANIZATIONS AND NETWORKS

The role of professional organizations, and the education and networking possibilities they have facilitated, have significantly enhanced my professional development. When I was working on my dissertation on a radical pacifist organization (CNVA), I joined the Conference on Peace Research in History (CPRH), a group of peace historians affiliated with the American Historical Association. CPRH served as a wonderful support, networking, and mentoring group; the CPRH journal *Peace and Change* published three of my early articles. I also served for several years on that journal's editorial board.

Another organization, the Conference on Peace Research, Education and Development (COPRED), served as an important umbrella organization for faculty, students, and activists who were working to promote peace studies in higher education. COPRED membership was critical for me and my fellow students in helping us to understand what was developing in peace and nonviolent studies throughout higher education in the United States. I benefited greatly from the support and advice of fellow directors of peace studies programs. For several years I served on COPRED's executive committee and then as its vice-president during the 1980s.

Two other organizations greatly aided my professional development. As conflict resolution became more popular in higher education and among the general populace, a new organization was formed to appeal more to educators and practitioners working in the conflict resolution field. Under the leadership of James Laue and Margaret Hermann of the University of Georgia, the National Conference on Peacemaking and Conflict Resolution organized yearly conferences with training workshop and academic panel presentations, starting in 1983. NCPCR served as an important bridge-building organization between academics and practitioners and certainly advanced both knowledge and skills in conflict resolution.

Significantly, the William and Flora Hewlett Foundation's huge commitment to advancing theory building and practice in conflict resolution afforded me the opportunity to work closely with some of the leading scholars in the United States. The Hewlett Foundation has financially supported over a dozen university centers, institutes, or programs as well as several training and practice groups. At Syracuse University, PARC is one of the first university organizations to have benefited from the Hewlett Foundation's generosity for more than a decade. While I served as associate director of PARC, I benefited greatly from the knowledge and assistance of scholars from other Hewlett Centers as I traveled to Hewlett sponsored conferences, visited other Hewlett Centers, or invited Hewlett-affiliated scholars to participate in events at Syracuse University.

ROLE OF CONTINUING EDUCATION

It would be difficult to overestimate the influence of continuing education workshops on my intellectual journey and my professional career. I consider myself a lifetime learner and "workshop groupie," and have attended many different workshops and training events over the years, including multi-day workshops on mediation, facilitation, workplace mediation, negotiation, gestalt therapy, neuro-linguistic programming, leadership, power and spirit, covert processes in group life, strategic planning, and future search. Among the most influential of these workshops were several workshops on interest-based negotiations hosted by the Program on Negotiation at Harvard University and Northwestern University, the workshop on Leadership, Power and Spirit with Robert Marx, and the workshop on Future Search with Marvin Weisbord and Sandra Jainoff. Both workshops held at the Albert Einstein Institute for Organizational Development in Cape Cod, and several workshops on the Psychodynamics of Group Development and Group Life were modeled after the Tavistock approach and held at Yale University, Toronto, and London. Together these workshops added significantly to my knowledge and skills for more effective teaching, consulting, scholarship, and leadership, especially in my role now as chair of a large graduate school degree granting department in conflict analysis and resolution.

THE INFLUENCE OF SCHOLARSHIP

In my long career in academia and consulting, I have gained much wisdom from scholars in the field. While many books, articles, and presentations have had a profound effect on my research, teaching, and practice, for this chapter I will comment only on works that have had a decided effect on my conflict consulting practice, to which I have devoted considerable attention in the last decade. Moreover, the selected works have altered the way I look at the world, the meaning I assign to people and events, and my own thinking about conflict analysis and resolution that inform my strategy and actions. The six works I will comment on are *Reframing Organizations: Artistry, Choice, and Leadership* by Lee Bolman and Terrance Deal[1]; *The Wisdom of Solomon at Work: Ancient Virtues for Living and Leading Today* by Charles Manz and others[2]; *The Reflective Practitioner: How Professionals Think in Action* by Donald Schön[3]; *Process Consultation II* by Edgar Schein[4]; *Influencing with Integrity: Management Skills for Communication and Negotiation* by Genie Laborde[5]; and *Conflict Resolved? A Critical Assessment of Conflict Resolution* by Alan Tidwell.[6] Several of these books are primarily situated in organizational life and focused on consulting and/or leadership, yet I believe they have significant relevance to our work as conflict practitioners and scholars. Indeed, all of my conflict intervention work has been heavily influenced by my awareness and integration of this material. I will comment on each of these books with the order and length of the comments indicative as to their utility to my current work, which is heavily engaged in conflict resolution intervention.

Reframing Organizations: Artistry, Choice, and Leadership

This work by Lee Bolman and Terrance Deal[7] illuminates four frames which serve as windows to look out on the world and lenses which bring the world into perspective and sharper focus. These frames function as a cognitive map which affects what to look for, what it means and what to do. Therefore the frames serve both as a diagnostic tool and as a model for planning strategy and taking action. The frames help us to make sense of our experience, allow for sophisticated judgment, and enable us to engage in multifaceted and effective action. Furthermore, knowledge and use of multiple frames facilitates a more holistic and penetrating perspective on people and events, helps to avoid individual bias and psychic blindness, and expands choices and effectiveness.

Let me now explicate the four frames before speculating on how they might add value to the theory and practice of conflict analysis and resolution. Through their research on effective organizational leaders, Bolman and Deal identify four frames or perspectives that leaders can use to make sense of complex situations and to guide their strategy and actions. The four frames or lenses are the structural frame, the human resource frame, the political frame and the symbolic frame.

STRUCTURAL FRAME

Structural leaders see their primary task as addressing confusion and chaos by clarifying goals, roles, and expectations. The main activities of a structural leader are to establish, maintain and reaffirm procedures and policies, focus on tasks, facts, and logic (as opposed to personalities and emotion), and to design and implement structure to fit circumstances and align with the environment. It is important for the leader to make sure the structure is clear to everyone and appropriate for what needs to be accomplished, so that people can perform well and achieve goals. Meetings are formal occasions to transmit facts and information, conduct objective analysis, and make rational decisions. The metaphor for understanding the structural frame is the "well-oiled machine" or "factory," with the leader serving as the *architect* or *analyst.*

HUMAN RESOURCE FRAME

The human resource leader addresses anxiety and uncertainty by primarily focusing on identifying human needs and desires, and building positive relationships. The leader's main task is to keep people involved and participative, and to maintain open communication so that participants share information and feelings. By being responsive to the needs of individuals and supportive of their goals, leaders can count on their dedication and loyalty. Leaders demonstrate their responsiveness by communicating warmth and concern, hearing and respecting the aspirations of others, and giving people the resources, autonomy, and opportunity to succeed and do their job. Decision-making is an open, empowering, consensus-based process to ensure understanding and commitment. The metaphor for understanding the human resource frame is the "extended family," with the leader serving as the *facilitator* or *servant.*

POLITICAL FRAME

The political leader addresses conflicts and feelings of disempowerment by creating forums where issues can be negotiated and alliances redrawn. A good leader is an advocate and astute negotiator who understands politics and is comfortable with conflict, recognizing that conflict is often about scarce resources and the distribution of resources (who gets what). The main agenda of the political leader is to manage conflict as productively as possible by creating a power base and exercising influence carefully, particularly with key players. Recognizing that individuals and groups will not get everything they want and that there will always be enduring differences in values, beliefs, information, perceptions, and interests, the leader creates arenas where people can jockey for influence, negotiate their differences, and come up with reasonable compromises. The political leader understands that meetings and decision-making forums are mainly an opportunity to air conflicts, exercise or gain power, and win concessions. The metaphor for this frame is the "jungle," with the leader acting as the *advocate* or *negotiator* who assists the parties with survival.

SYMBOLIC FRAME

The symbolic leader deals with the formidable barriers of loss of direction and hope, by providing vision, meaning, and inspiration. Symbolic leaders believe their most important job is to give people something that they can believe in. They realize that events have multiple meanings, so what is important about events is not what actually happened, but what it means to people. The focus of symbolic leaders is on creating meaning, belief, and faith; they do this by the use of metaphors, ceremonies, rituals, myths, stories, and artifacts. The symbolic leader communicates passion, is visible, and inspires. Meetings and conflict resolution procedures are used to develop shared values and negotiate meaning, and maintain an environment of co-cooperativeness, responsibility, and accountability, while participants act out in various roles and share symbolic gestures in a dramatic ritual. Indeed, the metaphor for this frame is the "theatre" or "temple," with the leader serving as *playwright, poet*, or *prophet.*

USING FRAMES

Let's examine how the intentional use of these multiple frames can enhance our conflict intervention practice. I believe this knowledge can affect our practice on several levels: the ability to understand the dynamics of the dispute, the ability to build rapport with the disputants, the ability to understand our role in a holistic way, and our ability to formulate and deliver more effective interventions. For instance, familiarity with the *structural frame* facilitates empathy and understanding for disputants who see much of their existence in terms of rules, policies, and procedures, and believe strongly in rationality and logic. Consultants will create safety and comfort for disputants with a high structural valency (disposition) by emphasizing clear goals and defined process to their interventions, and by enforcing adherence to ground rules and procedures that are established.

The structural frame also has implications for how consultants perceive their role and how they determine success and outcome of their intervention. Consultants who view themselves as *analysts* or *architect*s are mainly concerned with building and establishing a conducive environment in which rational disputants can exchange facts and information. The intervention itself is seen as a formal occasion for making decisions based on new information, with the outcome being the ability to feel at peace about the rationality of the decision and to return to a life of some more predictability and order. Satisfaction will be primarily measured on the settlement of the conflict along rational lines: Were the issues at least partially resolved and an agreement reached? Was the decision the "best" that could have happened given the facts and logic of the situation, including the personalities and idiosyncrasies of the disputants and the possible penalties of no settlement? Did the intervention allow the parties to claim *authorship* of any agreements by having developed it, shaped it, and agreed to it?

From the vantage point of the human resource frame, the role and work of the consultant will be quite different. The leadership role is *servant* or *catalyst* of the "extended family," and the work of the consultant is to demonstrate caring for family members, serving human needs, and tending to the human interactions and the relationship among members. Fulfillment and satisfaction of the intervention will be measured by the extent to which feelings were expressed and understood, fundamental human needs were acknowledged and accepted, and communication was open and honest. The sessions will be viewed as somewhat informal occasions for sharing feelings and for involvement in issue exploration and joint problem solving to engender commitment. The consultant will view himself/herself as an understanding, empathetic parent figure whose main job is to support and empower the disputants, communicate warmth and concern, listen/respect their aspirations, and extend opportunity to the disputants to discuss their different perceptions and problem solve. In this frame, the ultimate goal will be the repairing of the relationship made possible by the increased understanding and empathy from the human dialogue that takes place and the transformation of the human heart.

Consultants operating from the political frame will view their role and the intervention process quite differently. Their role will be that of the *negotiator* or *overseer of the jungle* who will keep the inhabitants safe by being an advocate for the parties and the process, and will assist the parties in the hard, trade-off bargaining that would allow each of them to survive. The job of the consultant will be to provide an arena for negotiation and compromise and, if appropriate, rally the disputants against an even more formidable outside enemy (perhaps legal institutions and procedures, or people who would covertly or overtly benefit from the continuation of hostility). The consultant will look for common interests and use persuasive techniques to influence key stakeholders to bargain and settle. Most importantly, consultants will recognize that enduring differences in values, beliefs, information, interests, and perceptions of reality are laws of the jungle, and the goals of a conflict intervention are to assist the parties to recognize both their power and the limitations of their power and to bargain in a trade-off environment. Satisfaction will emerge from the fact that power was acknowledged and exercised, that losses were minimized and some gains were realized, some form of justice was achieved, and survival was assured.

Consultants who operate out of the symbolic frame exercise considerable influence through the definition of their role and their behavior. Given the consultant's assumption that much of life is ambiguous and uncertain, the consultant's self-perceived chief job is to create meaning for the participants. The consultant as *prophet* or *poet* or *playwright* isn't concerned so much with facts, logic, and rational analysis, as with creating hope, faith, meaning, and direction, through the use of symbols supported by rituals, ceremonies, stories, and metaphors. The intervention itself is viewed as a dramatic event for "actors" to acknowledge and share responsibility, produce symbols (such as an apology or some other form of an "olive branch"), negotiate meaning of certain actions and events, confirm values, and provide opportunities for bonding, even among those who were (or are) in conflict. Some of the main tools for the consultant are to interpret the conflict story by teasing out meaning and positive purpose, to articulate a persuasive and inspiring vision of a less conflictual reality, to demonstrate to the actors their key roles as contributors to a more compelling and meaningful story, and to use dramatic and visible symbols (stories, rituals, and artifacts) to involve and inspire people. Success of the intervention will be measured not so much in terms of settlement of outstanding issues, or repairing of the relationship, but rather in assigning new meaning to the whole experience of the conflict and the intervention, the restoration of faith in the continuing mystery of life, and the feeling among the disputants and the consultants of living a life that has significance.

APPLICATIONS TO CONSULTING

Now that we have explored how the consultant might operate within each of the frames, which ones might be the most important for consultants seeking to enhance their capability to effectively engage? Bolman and Deal's research supports the contention that many of us rely most heavily on one or two frames to support our analysis, diagnosis and interventions. Traditionally, managers (and I suspect consultants) tend to rely on logic and structure, good communication, and rapport building skills to control the situation and gain trust and co-operation from stakeholders. This observed tendency suggests that the political and symbolic frames are the most underutilized frames; their use, therefore, might be the most potentially beneficial. I believe this could apply to consultants and their practice. With regard to the political frame, the ethics of justice, as well as the acknowledgement of the primary role and need for disputants to engage power and exert influence over decisions, are central to the success of the intervention and disputant satisfaction. Even within a context of limited resources and jungle-like rivalries, the consultant's abilities to create an effective arena, and to engage and direct the parties in interest-based negotiations, are an ongoing and considerable part of the consulting challenge.

Expanded and intentional use of the symbolic frame might have the most potential to expand our understanding of the magic of conflict intervention and enhance our consulting practice. Consultants might more consciously use the tools of the symbolic frame, such as story telling or myths, to shape meaning, create inspiration and hope for the parties, and redirect their efforts. Let me share a personal experience in which my conscious use of the symbolic frame seemed to have a significant positive impact on the parties. I was working as a facilitator with a national labor-management partnership council in a large federal social service agency. The respective labor and management teams were not making progress on any agreements, and there was much bickering and contentious behavior between the teams and even among the teams. The negotiators seemed entrenched in their positions and blamed each other for the lack of movement. I knew I needed to do something, but was not sure what to do. Fortunately, I remembered a story that former President Jimmy Carter told about the 1978 Camp David negotiations between the Egyptians and the Israelis. Carter spoke about a key moment in the negotiations that he thought was pivotal in reaching an agreement between President Anwar Sadat of Egypt and Prime Minister Menachem Begin of Israel. After several weeks and many attempts to forge an agreement, it looked like all was lost and the parties were packing their bags to go home. Carter visited the Israeli delegation to say farewell to Begin and his associates. It so happened that Begin had requested pictures of President Carter for his numerous grandchildren. Following the suggestion of one of his young staff members, Carter had signed the pictures and placed the name of one of Begin's grandchildren on each of the pictures. As Begin accepted the pictures from Carter, the Prime Minister gazed at each one and slowly spoke the name of each grandchild. As he did this, Begin's eyes filled with tears. Moments later Begin ordered his entourage to unpack their bags and redouble their efforts to reach an agreement. According to President Carter, the overall interest of negotiating an agreement that might create a better life for children and grandchildren then became the overriding concern in the minds of both men. While undoubtedly this was always an interest that motivated the negotiators to come to Camp David, it might have been lost or left backstage as powerful heads of state engaged in tough, positional bargaining to win victories and satisfy egos. The picture incident instead placed the interest of a more peaceful future for children and grandchildren solidly at center stage, refocusing the parties on their ultimate goals. Days later, an agreement was reached establishing peace between the Israelis and the Egyptians that has lasted for over 30 years.

What does this have to do with the symbolic frame and the way in which I conduct my interventions? At the height of tension between my federal government labor-management teams, I told them the story I had heard about Camp David. After the story, I pulled a picture of one of my daughters out of my wallet, asked them to look at it, and then told them how this daughter had been in the throes of a serious illness, but was now making progress, at least in part because of the emotional support and financial help provided by the agency they represented. I also told them how this assistance had allowed our family to hire very good medical care for our daughter, which seemed to make a difference in her recovery. I told them how grateful my family and I were to the agency that made that high quality care possible and available to her, and how much more we would have suffered had they not been there for us in a time of critical need. I made clear that the humane and compassionate assistance from folks in their agency had made a significant impact.

The story had the intended effect. As at Camp David, the intervention seemed to refocus the parties on why they were negotiating (their ultimate interest of serving the public at a time of critical need), who would benefit by their possible co-operation, and who would lose from their in-fighting. Just as at Camp David, the parties did not discuss the story, but immediately vowed to redouble their efforts to work together and "get it done." The parties then labored well into the night to come up with "yesable proposals" that culminated in a more fruitful dialogue and important agreements the next day.

"SPIRIT" IN CONSULTING: *THE WISDOM OF SOLOMON AT WORK*

The second book that I mentioned, *The Wisdom of Solomon at Work: Ancient Virtues for Living and Leading Today* (2001) has also had a significant impact on my consulting practice. It therefore may add to our understanding of the role and exemplary characteristics of conflict consultancy. In *The Wisdom of Solomon*, Charles Manz, Robert Marx, and their colleagues consider the notion of "spirit" in writing about virtues that have endured the passage of time, virtues reflected in and reinforced by different religious traditions over the centuries. Each of the virtues is introduced through a biblical character and demonstrated through stories from the Old Testament: the Faith of Job, the Courage of David, the Compassion of Ruth, the Integrity and Justice of Moses, and the Wisdom of Solomon. Although the authors primarily give examples of these virtues being exercised and modeled in professional business practice, the understanding of and modeling of these virtues might very well be important in uncovering the heart and soul of effective consultants. Let me suggest some ways in which these virtues might relate to the essence of both conflict resolution interventions and consulting practice.

Compassion, courage, and faith in any consultant will be tested early on and throughout the intervention. Compassion, often characterized as having empathy for the struggle and suffering of others, is defined in *The Wisdom of Solomon* as "how deeply we choose to see beyond ourselves and how deeply we choose to respond to what we see."[8] This trait will be a major determinant of the consultant's ability to create and maintain rapport with the disputants, and the willingness of the parties to transform their understanding of the dispute and broaden their options on ways to address the dispute. Consultants' courage, defined as staying present to life's most difficult challenges, to work with them, and to learn from them, will be tested when consultants attempt to enforce ground rules and introduce various interventions to assist the parties. Most of all, faith, to consistently do the right thing and strongly believe in the ethos and benefits of the chosen conflict intervention, is essential, as the consultant faces many challenges to his/her assumptions, values and beliefs.

It is the acting out of faith, courage, and compassion that enhances the potential for integrity and justice. The authors view integrity as the virtue that leaders display by acting responsibly and empowering others to be responsible for and address their own inner struggles.[9] Conflict consultants display integrity throughout the process by allowing the parties to define issues, explore options, and voluntarily commit to action plans if they so desire.

Consultants pursue justice when they emphasize fairness and model impartiality, equality, and respect for the disputants and their rights throughout the intervention.

All these virtues are in support of the most fundamental virtue, the wisdom of Solomon, which is characterized by a wise and discerning mind that allows one to display superior judgment and a sound course of action. At best, consultants are able even to access transcendent wisdom, a deeper form of knowing that flows from reflection upon experience and is sensitive to human encounters with life.

INTEGRATING REFLECTION AND PRACTICE: *THE REFLECTIVE PRACTITIONER*

A third book that I continually revisit and which has had a considerable influence on my consulting work is *The Reflective Practitioner: How Professionals Think in Action* (1990) by Donald Schön. This work has allowed me to think about what I do, assume a more professional and confident persona, and talk about what I do and what I am in a professional context. Schön postulates that successful practitioners do much more than the common notion of some that we "fly by the seat of our pants" or engage in an impulsive "hit-or-miss" mentality and behavior. In his study of professional practitioners in various fields, Schön discovered that the successful practitioner was indeed reflecting-in-action and, in fact, becoming a researcher and testing theory in the practice context. Like good jazz musicians, successful professionals get a "feel for" the material they are working with, and make on-the-spot minor adjustments to phenomena they encounter. When professional practitioners are "in the groove" (in the consulting context, "in the groove" might be when numerous interventions yield the desired result), the actions become more repetitive and routine and the intuitive, spontaneous performance yields intended results. But when intuitive performance leads to surprises, be they pleasing, promising, or unwanted, expert practitioners then need to respond by reflection-in-action. In doing this, the professional reflects on the understandings that have been implicit in his/her actions, understandings that he/she surfaces, criticizes, restructures and embodies in further action. As the professional surfaces and critiques his/her initial understanding of the phenomenon, constructs a new description of it, and tests the new description by an on-the-spot experiment, a new theory in action emerges. The experiment thus serves to generate a new understanding of the phenomenon and a change in the situation brought about by the new action.

Why might this perspective offered by Schön be important to consultants and the field of conflict resolution theory and practice? I suspect it might be useful in several ways. One way is how we think about ourselves and present ourselves to the public. At best, we are practitioners who perform in professional situations much like lawyers, doctors, accountants, teachers or other professionals. By logging time in our profession, we also "practice" our craft so we are prepared and ready to encounter somewhat similar situations again and again. Therefore, our professional practice becomes more repetitive and routine, and our knowing-in-practice becomes tacit and spontaneous. Our reputation among our peers and the public as "successful professionals" is enhanced, and our confidence and competence grows.

However, Schön warns that this upside of professional practice also has a potential downside. As we become more respected and comfortable in our practice, and our analysis and actions become more predictable and repetitive, we might be susceptible to over-learning, and prone to miss important opportunities to think about what we are doing. The way to overcome this vulnerability is to continue to operate as a reflective practitioner throughout our careers, so we can display principled flexibility, continue to learn and respond to both familiar and unfamiliar phenomena, enhance our effectiveness with our clients, and strengthen the public's perception of what we do and our status as a profession.

Process Consultation

Edgar Schein's work on process consulting is contained in several books and various articles. For this paper, I will limit my comments to one of his more recent works. Schein defines process consulting as, "a set of activities or interventions on the part of the consultant which helps the client perceive, understand and then act on the events which occur in their environment in order to improve the situation as defined by the client."[10] Implicit in this definition and approach is the necessity of keeping the client as the main focus and driver of the intervention, and the consultant in a facilitator role whose main purpose is to enlarge the awareness of key actors of the organization so that they can make informed decisions based on more accurate data. Schein further elaborates on this facilitator role by distinguishing process consulting from two other familiar and popular forms of consulting: the doctor-patient model and the pair of hands model. The doctor-patient model treats the symptoms of organizational distress as a pathology that needs to be cured by the doctor in the guise of the consultant. The doctor/consultant is the obvious expert and the patient/client is asked to follow the prescription, creating a heavy dependency of the client on the consultant in a "rescue-me" relationship. This model relies heavily on expert diagnosis, the issuance of recommendations to follow, and the administration of "treatment."

The "pair of hands" model is more of a "serve-me" model, with the consultant being heavily dependent on clients who prescribe what they want done and expect the consultant to deliver the results. The client defines the problem and the scope of work and the client essentially attacks the problem through the consultant's expertise. To distinguish it from the previous two models of consulting, Schein presents the process model as more of a "let's work together" model, in which the consultant is an objective researcher and commentator on what is, and what could be, happening in the environment (often called the "present state" and the "desired state"). The consultant collects and organizes valid data, presents that data back to the client system, and engages the client in problem solving and action planning through facilitation—all with the intent of increasing awareness and expanding choice. Schein presents this model as more of a partnership alliance, as opposed to a dependency model, and a "learn to learn" approach.

Each of these works has been instrumental in enriching both the understanding and the effectiveness of my consulting practice. The flexible cognitive disposition advocated by Bolman and Deal enhanced my thinking of diagnostic concepts and tools available to expert conflict consultants. The ability and willingness to use all four described frames has enlarged my comprehension of the many nuances of disputes, as well as expanded my intervention options and my ability to gain and maintain rapport with disputants. The *Wisdom of Solomon* material reminds me continually of the core values or virtues underlying the theory and practice of conflict consulting. Donald Schön's work on *The Reflective Practitioner* reinforces my view of conflict consulting as a professional practice, and helps my understanding of what I am doing and how I explain what I do to my critics and admirers. Edgar Schein's work on process consulting guides me to effective strategies for collaboration when working with groups and organizations.

Influencing with Integrity and *Conflict Resolved*?

These two books are wonderful resources for conflict consultants, although space and time here limit my comments to some of the ideas and concepts that have proved most germane to my work. *Influencing with Integrity* (1984) continually reminds me of the importance of establishing outcomes with clients, the absolute necessity of rapport (and noticing when you lose it!), the advantages of sensory acuity, the need for flexibility and a resourceful state, and the power of knowledge of one's hierarchy of values. Of particular value has been the author's meeting procedure formula referred to as PEGASUS, consisting of the following steps: *P*resent Outcomes, *E*xplain Evidence (criteria for success), *G*ain agreement on outcomes, *A*ctivate Sensory Acuity, *S*ummarize each major decision, *U*se relevancy challenge, and *S*ummarize next steps.

Conflict Resolved? (1998) by Australian Professor Alan Tidwell is a provocative and very critical assessment of the field, containing numerous helpful insights. Two that were most helpful to me were the distinctions between conflict settlement, which has as an outcome a decision and an allocation of blame and responsibility; conflict management, which results in more acceptable levels of intensity and costs of the conflict; and conflict resolution, which calls for much more intellectually rigorous and deeper analysis of the context and situation, making real resolution very difficult to achieve.

Of more importance to me was Tidwell's insistence on a three-pronged requirement of absolute conditions for conflicts to possibly result in resolution. The three requirements are opportunity, capacity, and will (or volition). Opportunity includes items such as sufficient time, access to the parties and decision-makers, and the absence of social and societal impediments to resolution. Capacity includes skills and other critical resources to communicate, negotiate, and settle long-standing and profound grievances. Will or volition includes a conscious desire to engage in resolution and end the conflict, emerging from a humanitarian perspective, an enhanced understanding of the dynamics of the dispute, or a realization about the cost of continuing the conflict, including simple fatigue. Tidwell's stress on these absolute pillars that must be in place for conflict resolution efforts to have a chance for success helps me understand more profoundly some of the factors that influenced the dynamics of the conflicts for which my interventions did not come close to achieving the success I had envisioned.

FRAMEWORKS AND CONCEPTS

In addition to the six books mentioned above, my conflict teaching, research and consulting practice is certainly influenced by other scholars and practitioners in the field who have assisted me immensely with their insights and guidance. Among the authors are Chris Argyris, Joseph Luft and Harry Ingham, Peter Senge, and Daniel Goleman.

Much of Chris Argyris's work on communication, barriers to learning, and consulting have been useful to me in my work. For this article, I want to focus on one message of his to which he continually refers—what Argyris calls his Core Values that inform all of his work. According to Argyris, one's consulting work should always be guided by three inter-related guideposts: (1) the need for valid data; (2) the necessity of free and informed choice; and (3) the importance of internal commitment to the choice. The consultant can help the client acquire valid information through process consultation and other even more rigorous data gathering procedures which prove credible to the client and counter client's defensiveness and denial tendencies. Then, based on high quality data about current behavior and its consequences, the client now can make a free and informed choice about whether or not to undergo a change effort. The valid information and the free and informed choice all help to ensure greater internal commitment to the implementation of the elected action. These core values are important anchors for my consulting work, particularly when I engage in process consulting and facilitation efforts with groups.

Joseph Luft and Harry Ingham are the co-authors of the well-known Johari Window framework. I constantly remind myself that my role as a consultant needs to be guided by the goal of expanding awareness to the client and, essentially serve as an "agent of opening." One effective way of doing this is to provide a context and strategy for the client system to engage in self-disclosure to minimize the hidden area, and to allow feedback from the consultant and others to minimize the blind area. By diminishing the "hidden" and "blind" areas, consultants are assisting clients in expanding the "open area" and providing the key to learning and choice.

Peter Senge's work on mental models has proved enormously helpful to me. Senge reminds us that we carry unwritten, and often unspoken, models or images in our head that unwittingly shape what we see or hear, pay attention to, guide the meaning we assign to behavior and events, and, ultimately, guide our thoughts and actions. These models or "scripts" are particularly powerful since they operate mostly at the covert or unconscious level. Our tendency is to seek out evidence to corroborate and deepen our mental models, as opposed to giving credence to contradictory evidence. The result thus is to develop "psychic blindness" and limit chances for learning.

In addition to Senge's caution about the powerful effects of unexamined mental models, he also supports the idea that human beings have the ability to create more helpful mental models that will facilitate the work and outcomes they desire. In other words, we should engage in the challenging work of confronting our individual mental models that are not congruent with the outcomes we seek for our work, and create ones that will facilitate success in our work. For instance, in my consulting practice, I try to adopt these mental models and look for evidence that will corroborate and deepen them into both my conscious and unconscious mind:

- People in organizations face great challenges in accomplishing good work and building positive relationships;

- People are doing the best they can at any time given their circumstances;
- People represent their world as they experience it and as they remember it;
- People are motivated by desire for a good night's sleep;
- People have a significant capacity for self-examination, creativity and good will.

I recently have been greatly influenced by the work of Daniel Goleman and his associates in the area of emotional intelligence. Goleman essentially defines emotional intelligence as the ability to understand self, work with others, and be effective in leading change. The five components he has identified are self-awareness, self-management, motivation (drive to achieve goals), empathy (awareness of others' needs) and social skills (managing relationships).

Goleman's research paints a compelling picture to support the value and importance of emotional intelligence (E-I). His research examined capabilities that drove outstanding performance of leaders in public and private organizations. He divided capabilities into three categories: (1) technical skills like planning and budgeting; (2) cognitive competency, as in the ability to do high level analytical and conceptual thinking; and (3) emotional intelligence as defined above. His research found that more than half the difference that distinguished "star" performers from "average" performers could be attributed to E-I (90 percent of the difference could be attributed at the CEO level). His research concludes that technical and cognitive capabilities are "threshold capabilities" which help you land a job and stay above water in the workplace. However, the factor that separated the "outstanding performers" over their career was mainly due to emotional intelligence. What is the implication of Goleman's findings to the life of a consultant? I believe it gives us a powerful context in which to place our skills and approaches, and gives us additional justification for the power and importance of the work we promote through our training and other interventions. Additionally, it gives us a model of behavior to emulate and a benchmark of exceptional performance and attributes to strive for.

In conclusion, let me summarize some of the insights I have gathered throughout my career based on the discussion above.

1. Academic work is vitally important. It gives you exposure to brilliant minds, reflective practitioners, powerful models and frameworks, and research that can greatly assist your credibility, growth and performance as both a scholar and a consultant.
2. It is important to have "anchors" that provide guidance and grounding for your work. These can be mentors, books, articles, model practitioners,

concepts, frameworks, or other insights, whose presence provides direction and a code of conduct to follow. Your anchors and your guiding principles will also help in maintaining consistency of behavior, as well as provide intellectual and philosophical support for your efforts.

3. Along with your cognitive and ethical anchors, it is essential to be an eclectic conflict resource person who can competently assess situations, and consider a variety of strategies and tools to attempt to influence conflict variables and dynamics. Your diagnostic abilities to make sense out of what is going on in the conflict, and your ability to select an appropriate intervention approach, will be critical to your teaching and consulting success.
4. Select your role models and mentors carefully. Allow yourself to work in the shadows of "seasoned professionals" that model the skills, approaches, and ethics that you want to strive for and emulate. Your willingness to serve time in an apprentice situation will pay dividends for many years. Find mentors that bring a variety of experiences, knowledge and intervention choices to their work; discuss with them how and why they make the choices they do as they go about their work. I am lucky that I have been blessed with the many generous and talented mentors mentioned previously in this chapter.
5. Acknowledge the reality of an uneven playing field. In my organizational interventions, I would like to assume that "people leave their titles at the door." However, I know now that unless leaders of an organization spearhead and champion behavioral and structural change, our consulting efforts will not produce the intended results. High quality contracting with clients, and ongoing support and communication with leaders, are vitally important.
6. Humility is a much needed asset for conflict consultants. More and more I am convinced of all that I don't know and how much I still have to learn. My anchors help me make accurate diagnoses and facilitate helpful interventions much of the time, but human behavior is always more complex and unpredictable than our models and theories. Humility will help temper our personal claim for success, and help us cope with the inevitable disappointment resulting from interventions that don't work out as we desired. Remember, we are only one factor in a very complex and intricate system that has most likely evolved over many years. Although we wield considerable influence, we do not control the minds or behaviors of anyone but ourselves.
7. Curiosity and compassion for people is a must. For the most part I believe my primary responsibility is to be an impartial observer and commentator on human behavior, in particular regarding how humans handle

differences and disputes in very challenging and stressful interpersonal, group and organizational settings. Hopefully, my data gathering, data organizing, feedback, and facilitating/coaching skills lead clients to expand their awareness of what is occurring in their environment, and to then voluntarily choose attitudes and behaviors that "ease the pain," leading to mutually satisfying substantive and relationship outcomes.

8. Knowledge of yourself is one of your greatest assets. As a conflict intervener, you are a critical variable in the conflict situation. Your decisions and behavior will alter the context and influence the parties. Self-knowledge gained from your own observations and analysis, and through feedback from others through conversation or style instruments, is critical in helping you continually learn and develop in a way that you can productively assist others.
9. In this profession, life and professional experience can be a blessing. Interestingly, the research on emotional intelligence supports the finding that emotional intelligence tends to increase with age and maturity. I believe the same is true about consulting expertise and effectiveness. Being able to access a rich mixture and accumulation of lifetime experiences and hard-earned lessons from facing life's challenges often makes us more understanding, compassionate, and tolerant of differences, and allows us to be more patient and caring for our clients, the dilemmas they face, and their efforts to change.
10. Appreciate the opportunity to do work in this field while marveling at its challenges. Conflict analysis and resolution work is ultimately a laboratory to learn about the wonderful mystery of human behavior temporarily caught in a puzzling and frightening web of social conflict. Our efforts to provide insight through analysis and reflection, our ability to serve as a communication conduit, and our facilitation of efforts to consider alternative approaches to better the situation for people and groups are all gifts to be nurtured and appreciated. And once in a while, it is even okay to appreciate ourselves for choosing to work in a profession that potentially has such a significant positive impact on people, organizations, and society.

BIBLIOGRAPHY

Argyris, Chris. *Overcoming Organizational Defenses: Facilitating Organizational Learning*. Wellesley, MA: Allyn and Bacon, 1990.

Bolman, Lee G., and Terrance E. Deal. *Reframing Organizations: Artistry, Choice and Leadership*. San Francisco: Jossey-Bass, 2003.

Chatfield, Charles. *For Peace and Justice: Pacifism in America 1914–1941.* Knoxville: University of Tennessee Press, 1971.

Goleman, Daniel. *Working with Emotional Intelligence.* New York: Bantam, 1998.

Laborde, Genie. *Influencing with Integrity: Management Skills for Communication and Negotiation.* Palo Alto, CA: Syntony, 1987.

Luft, Joseph. *Group Processes: An Introduction to Group Dynamics.* Houston: Mayfield, 1984.

Manz, Charles C., et al. *The Wisdom of Solomon at Work: Ancient Virtues for Living and Leading Today.* San Francisco: Berrett-Koehler, 2001.

Schein, Edgar H. *Process Consultation Revisited.* Reading, MA: Addison-Wesley, 1999.

Schön, Donald A. *The Reflective Practitioner: How Professionals Think in Action.* New York: Basic Books, Inc., 1990.

Senge, Peter M. *The Fifth Discipline: The Art and Practice of the Learning Organization.* New York: Knopf Doubleday, 1990.

Tidwell, Alan C. *Conflict Resolved? A Critical Assessment of Conflict Resolution.* London: Pinter Publishers, 1998.

Wittner, Lawrence S. *Rebels Against War: The American Peace Movement, 1941–1960.* New York: Columbia University Press, 1969.

NOTES

1. Lee G. Bolman and Terrance E. Deal, *Reframing Organizations: Artistry, Choice, and Leadership* (San Francisco: Jossey-Bass, 2003).
2. Charles C. Manz, et al., *The Wisdom of Solomon at Work: Ancient Virtues for Leaving and Leading Today* (San Francisco: Berrett-Koehler Publishers, Inc., 2001).
3. Donald A. Schön, *The Reflective Practioner: How Professionals Think in Action* (New York: Basic Books, Inc., 1990).
4. Edgar H. Schein, *Process Consultation II* (Reading, MA: Addison-Wesley, 1998).
5. Genie Laborde, *Influencing with Integrity: Management Skills for Communication and Negotiation* (Palo Alto, CA: Syntony, 1987).
6. Alan C. Tidwell, *Conflict Resolved? A Critical Assessment of Conflict Resolution* (London: Pinter Publishers, 1998).
7. Bolman and Deal, *Reframing*.
8. Manz, *Wisdom*, 84.
9. Manz, *Wisdom*, 84.
10. Schein, *Process*, 34.

Conclusions

Chapter 20

Where Do We Go From Here?

Jessica Senehi and Sean Byrne

Johan Galtung argues, "If the road to peace passes through conflict resolution then a transnational, transdisciplinary conflictology is a must for peace studies."[1] Peace and conflict studies (PACS) is in need of "bi-, multi-, and transdisciplinary integration."[2] The rapid changes in local, national, and global societies in a post-state world necessitates that PACS devise new cutting-edge and inclusive analytical and praxis tools that are creative, critical, and serve the need of local people. The material covered in this book points us in this direction. The empowerment of other voices in the grassroots and bottom-up peacebuilding activities challenges the "liberal peace" paradigm to go further. In fact, Roger Mac Ginty, Andrew Williams, and colleagues at the School of International Relations at St. Andrew's University suggest the creation of a hybrid PACS model that takes into account local contexts and knowledge, grassroots peacebuilding approaches, and new structures and analytical lenses, as well as intermeshing the best of old and new approaches and structures.[3]

In addition, Mac Ginty (2008) believes that a new PACS hybrid model would rethink and reshape many of the theoretical assumptions and practices that underlie the field. He suggests that a new hybrid PACS infrastructure would include peacebuilding review, transforming relationship and trust-building mechanisms, co-creating an authentic reconciliation process, imagining peace as holistic process, protecting local economies, balancing and integrating traditional and indigenous conceptions and methods of peacemaking, promoting local ownership of peace to prevent peace freezing, external third parties acting as servants rather than masters of peace, and antagonists having the right to reject a poor peace.[4] Adopting such a critical approach to

PACS can ensure an inclusive, holistic, and sustainable peace process that goes beyond negative peace or the absence of war to the realization of positive peace addressing direct, indirect, cultural, and structural violence to forge a just and sustainable peace for all.[5]

The breadth, complexity and depth of the PACS field necessitate a recurrent internal critical dialogue of appropriate theoretical lens, epistemologies, and practices that meet local needs.[6] The nexus between theory and practice must take note of the multiple, interlocking tensions and concerns in the PACS field that require recrafting, rejuvenation, and rethinking. In the following pages we explore ten of these issues.

INDIGENOUS KNOWLEDGE AND METHODS OF PEACEMAKING

In a multicultural world there are many ways of seeing, caring, and doing. There is no standard approach to peacemaking and peacebuilding. Yet external Western liberal peace models centered on problem-solving and democracy predominate within the global South and, indeed, the global North, with its diversity of cultural groups.[7]

Indigenous peacemaking systems are embedded within cultural contexts and practices. For example, indigenous reconciliation ceremonies such as the Palaver in Liberia, *umbuntu* in South Africa and Keoee among the Oromo of Ethiopia maintain and deepen intercultural relationships that are necessary to sustain peace.[8] It is critical to include indigenous people as equal partners in any peace process.

EMPOWERMENT OF YOUTH'S ENERGY

Young people's voices and stories remain marginal within the topsy-turvy milieu of everyday life. Children and young people are particularly vulnerable and, at the same time, resilient to the impact of war, and direct and indirect violence.[9] Young men are forced to join militias while girls tend to the orphans, elderly, and the homeless. Young people's voices need to be included in the peacebuilding process. As the future leaders of the community, they will shape and recreate the political process. Creating a civic forum where young people can actively participate as an equal partner harnesses the energy and vitality of the younger generation. Alternatively, discarding the passion and ideas of the youth by treating them as disposable and unimportant seriously damages and undermines the future of that society.[10]

BRING WOMEN INTO LEADERSHIP POSITIONS

Women's knowledge and ways of doing are frequently marginalized by the militarized patriarchal structures.[11] Women are active in grassroots peacebuilding initiatives reflecting diverse background and skills, yet their voices are often relegated to the margins of political, cultural, and socio-economic processes. Women are the lifeblood of the community and they build capacity within society. It is important that women are inbuilt as equal partners with men into peacemaking and peacebuilding systems. Transformational conflict resolution includes rebuilding and restoring relationships between men and women to work together toward peaceful outcomes.

CREATIVITY AND IMAGINATION

The creativity of the arts and humanities fires the social imagination and creates endless possibilities to change and remold structures and relationships creating community consensus around shared values and ideas to forge a plan of collective actions.[12] Local communities formulate and reproduce shared cultural knowledge about conflict and peacebuilding through various art forms such as storytelling, drama, photography and street theatre. These art forms include people in a creative process creating many dialogues, meanings and relationships that are both transcultural and intergenerational.[13]

REFLEXIVE PRAXIS SYNERGY

A "social cubism" analytical model that combines and integrates historical, economic, political, religious, demographic and psychocultural multidimensional lenses can understand the complexity of social conflicts.[14] A multi-track interdependent peacebuilding system makes multi-level and multi-model connections between the various multitude of actors and components of the peace process.[15] While good theory building necessitates good analytical and praxis skills and vice versa, it is important for good PACS practitioners, scholars and policy-makers to "walk the talk."[16] Howard Zehr comments that for the PACS field to survive, teachers and students must behave as true peacemakers. Thus, it is important for leaders in our field to model appropriate behavior for the many students that we mentor. In addition, operationalizing key theoretical concepts such as transformation or capacity building in terms of both theory and practice may mean different things to different people.[17]

ECOLOGICAL AND HUMAN SECURITY

The interconnected wholeness of the life cycle connects all forms of life, including humans, spiritually and biologically to the earth.[18] Ecological security includes the cultural, economic, political, psychological, and social dimensions that include all species and the biodiversity of the earth to live in harmony with and satisfy their basic human needs. The use of green technology and recycling preserve natural resources, such as the rainforests and Irish bogs, and seek to sustain our ecosystems. Peacebuilding and conflict transformation approaches need to include the ecological dimension, as human activities don't occur in a vacuum. Human security, with its focus on the rights of the individual over the interests of the state, illustrates the complexity and intractability of social conflict that needs to be included in a model of peacebuilding.

HUMAN RIGHTS AND JUSTPEACE FOR ALL

Human rights are embedded within the framework of international organizations, covenants and treaties and are certainly an integral component of the liberal, democratic peace agenda. When human rights are violated in intractable protracted conflicts, violent behavior follows suit.[19] The Justpeace or social justice dimension of PACS is built on a foundation of accountability, compassion, forgiveness, healing, and reconciliation. People need to heal from past atrocities to prevent the "transgenerational transmission of trauma" that sow the seeds of future violent conflict.[20]

SOCIAL MOVEMENTS AND THOSE ON THE MARGINS

Indirect violence occurs when the environment, civil rights, and women's issues (among others) aren't addressed directly by central government. Social movements, such as the disability rights movement, actively campaign and advocate nonviolently and directly for those individuals and groups that lie on the margins of society.[21] Social movements highlight and move issues that lie hidden and embedded in technocratic jargon to bring groups in from the cold. Social movements work to promote social change and build a culture of peace to transform society nonviolently.

INCLUSIVE OWNERSHIP OF PEACE

Diverse segments of the population often have different perceptions of the peace dividend and relationships change as trust is built and circumstances change on the ground.[22] However, a stalled or frozen peace may result from antagonists holding "the peace process in suspended animation rather than return to violent conflict."[23] Spoilers or dissidents, such as the Continuity and Real Irish Republican Armies, and the Orange Volunteer Force in Northern Ireland, can step into the political vacuum as the conflict escalates into violence and the initial public optimism evaporates. The grassroots need to be broadly included in peacemaking, peacebuilding, and cross-community development activities through economic and political incentives so that they buy into and support a sustainable peace process. For example, the International Fund for Ireland (IFI) and the European Union (EU) Peace and Reconciliation Funds have supported cross-community projects that promote contact and prosperity for all. This process is also tied into the 1998 Belfast Agreement, which includes a wide range of new political power-sharing institutions. [24]

RECALIBRATION, REJUVENATION, AND REORIENTATION OF PACS THEORETICAL ASSUMPTIONS AND PRACTICES

The underlying deep roots of conflict must be addressed and peacemaking and peacebuilding interventions must be designed with the local cultural context in mind.[25] All levels of society must be included and involved in envisioning, imagining, and dreaming of what the peace should look like in conjunction with external third party interveners. The "social cubism" analytical model and multi-track peacebuilding system are important in building a sustainable and positive peace.[26]

CONCLUSION

It is important to conclude this book by underlining the importance of a healthy and critical approach to the PACS field. This study highlights the necessity of building people, their cultural context, and diverse opinion and groups into a broad peacebuiding approach. We close this book by calling on the PACS community to make a commitment to sit down and seriously evaluate the field to determine where we are and where we are going in terms of reflexive praxis and how we, as individuals and groups, conduct ourselves in terms of our behavior and actions. We need to develop a new ethic of behavior as we need to create a new ethic of PACS.

Rather than concentrate on the Euro-ethnocentric liberal peacebuilding model, we should focus on local indigenous knowledge, voices, and peacemaking approaches that are central in shaping a peacebuilding methodology.[27] Such an "emancipatory peacebuilding" process encourages local peacemaking actors, networks, and practices to forge a social peace at "the everyday level," empowering the agency, aspirations, dignity, needs, opportunities, and stories of local people to co-create authentic relationships and partnerships at the grassroots level.[28]

BIBLIOGRAPHY

Byrne, Sean. *Economic Assistance and the Northern Ireland Conflict: Building the Peace Dividend.* Cranbury, NJ: Associated University Presses, 2009.

Byrne, Sean, and Jessica Senehi. "Revisiting the CAR Field," in *Handbook of Conflict Analysis and Resolution*, Dennis Sandole, Sean Byrne, Ingrid Sandole-Staroste, and Jessica Senehi, eds. London: Routledge, 2009.

Galtung, Johan. "Towards a Conflictology: A Quest for Trans-Disciplinarity," in *Handbook of Conflict Analysis and Resolution*, Dennis Sandole, Sean Byrne, Ingrid Sandole-Staroste, and Jessica Senehi, eds. London: Routledge, 2009.

———. *Peace by Peaceful Means: Peace and Conflict, Development and Civilization.* Thousand Oaks, CA: Sage, 2009.

Lederach, John Paul. *Preparing for Peace: Conflict Transformation Across Cultures.* Syracuse, NY: Syracuse University Press, 1995.

Mac Ginty, Roger. *No War, No Peace: The Rejuvenation of Stalled Peace Processes and Peace Accords.* New York: Palgrave Macmillan, 2008.

Mac Ginty, Roger, and Andrew Williams. *Conflict and Development.* London: Routledge, 2009.

Richmond, Oliver. "A Genealogy of Peace and Conflict Theory," in *Palgrave Advances in Peacebuilding: Critical Developments and Approaches*, Oliver Richmond, ed. New York: Palgrave Macmillian, 2010.

Volkan, Vamik. *From Ethnic Pride to Ethnic Terrorism.* Boulder, CO: Lynne Rienner, 1998.

NOTES

1. Johan Galtung, "Towards a Conflictology: A Quest for Trans-Disciplinarity," in *Handbook of Conflict Analysis and Resolution*, Dennis Sandole, Sean Byrne, Ingrid Sandole-Staroste, and Jessica Senehi, eds. (London: Routledge, 2009), 511.
2. Galtung, "Towards a Conflictology," 516.
3. Roger Mac Ginty and Andrew Williams, *Conflict and Development* (London: Routledge, 2009), 175–181.
4. Roger Mac Ginty, *No War, No Peace: The Rejuvenation of Stalled Peace Processes and Peace Accords* (New York: Palgrave Macmillan, 2008), 180–190.
5. Johan Galtung, *Peace by Peaceful Means: Peace and Conflict, Development and Civilization* (Thousand Oaks, CA: Sage, 1996).
6. Sean Byrne and Jessica Senehi, "Revisiting the CAR Field," in *Handbook of Conflict Analysis and Resolution*, Dennis Sandole, Sean Byrne, Ingrid Sandole-Staroste, and Jessica Senehi, eds. (London: Routledge, 2009), 525–530.
7. See Rice, Ch. 11.
8. See Tuso, Ch. 13.
9. See McEvoy-Levy, Ch. 9.
10. See McEvoy-Levy, Ch 9.
11. See Snyder, Ch. 10.
12. See Cormier, Karari, Kumar, Neustaeter, Read, and Senehi, Ch. 14.
13. See Cormier, Karari, Kumar, Neustaeter, Read, and Senehi, Ch. 14.
14. See Byrne and Nadan, Ch. 4.
15. See Boudreau, Ch. 2.
16. See Stimec, Poitras, and Campbell, Ch. 8.
17. See Katz, Ch. 19.
18. See Levy and Vaillancourt, Ch. 12.
19. See Maytók, Ch. 15.
20. Vamik Volkan, *Bloodlines: From Ethnic Pride to Ethnic Terrorism* (Boulder, CO: Lynne Rienner, 1998).
21. See Bâ and LeFrançois, Ch. 5; Hill and Hansen, Ch. 6; Funk and Woolner, Ch. 18.
22. See Hayes, Ch. 17.
23. Mac Ginty, *No War, No Peace*, 183.
24. Sean Byrne, *Economic Assistance and the Northern Ireland Conflict: Building the Peace Dividend* (Cranbury, NJ: Associated University Presses, 2009).
25. See Rice, Ch. 11; Tuso, Ch. 13.
26. See Byrne and Nadan, Ch. 4; Kellett, Ch. 16.
27. John Paul Lederach, *Preparing for Peace: Conflict Transformation Across Cultures* (Syracuse, NY: Syracuse University Press, 1995).
28. Oliver Richmond, "A Genealogy of Peace and Conflict Theory," in *Palgrave Advances in Peacebuilding: Critical Developments and Approaches*, Oliver Richmond, ed. (New York: Palgrave Macmillan, 2010), 14–40.

Index